THE ROUGH GUID

D0520914

Chick Flicks

**ROUGH
GUIDES**

www.roughguides.com

Credits

The Rough Guide to Chick Flicks

Editor: Katie Stephens
Layout: Sachin Tanwar
Picture research: Michele Farham
Proofreading: Orla Duane
Production: Aimee Hampson and Katherine Owers

Rough Guides Reference

Series editor: Mark Ellingham
Editors: Peter Buckley, Duncan Clark,
Matthew Milton, Ruth Tidball, Tracy Hopkins
Joe Staines, Sean Mahoney
Director: Andrew Lockett

Publishing Information

This first edition published September 2006 by
Rough Guides Ltd, 80 Strand, London WC2R 0RL
345 Hudson St, 4th Floor, New York 10014, USA
Email: mail@roughguides.com

Distributed by the Penguin Group:
Penguin Books Ltd, 80 Strand, London WC2R 0RL
Penguin Putnam, Inc., 375 Hudson Street, NY 10014, USA
Penguin Group (Australia), 250 Camberwell Road, Camberwell,
Victoria 3124, Australia
Penguin Books Canada Ltd, 90 Eglinton Avenue East, Toronto,
Ontario, Canada M4P 2YE
Penguin Group (New Zealand), 67 Apollo Drive, Mairongi Bay,
Auckland 1310, New Zealand

Printed in Italy by LegoPrint S.p.A

Typeset in Bembo and Helvetica Neue to an original design by
Henry Iles

A catalogue record for this book is available from the British
Library

ISBN 13: 978-184353-710-6
ISBN 10: 1-84353-710-9

1 3 5 7 9 8 6 4 2

THE ROUGH GUIDE TO

Chick Flicks

by
Samantha Cook

Contents

The Icons:

Women's Books And Women's Movies:

Women Of The World:

The Information:

Introduction

The chick flick. Most of us recognize one when we see one, but as a genre it is difficult to define. Regarded more as a guilty pleasure than as an art form, it's a breed of movie that's given little attention in comparison to other, more recognized genres. Mention chick flicks and people tend to come over all condescending, bandying words around like light, frothy, formulaic. This book doesn't knock froth. In fact, it delights in it. What, after all, would a cappuccino be without froth, or a bubble bath? But it also broadens the scope, using "chick flick" as an umbrella term for the rich body of movies out there that have particular appeal to women.

While we adore melodramas, flock to weepies in droves, and are absolute suckers for rom-coms, an action movie can also be a chick flick if told from a female point of view, as can a horror movie. Witness the huge popularity of *Terminator 2* with female audiences, or the appeal of Agent Clarice Starling in *The Silence Of The Lambs*. As will be revealed throughout this book, the chick flick comes in many guises. There are, of course, constants. Be it a fairy-tale fantasy or a terminal illness movie, a musical or a costume drama, a chick flick will include, in some combination, the following ingredients: female bonding, friendship, and family crises; mothers and daughters; strong women and suffering women; sacrifice, sickness, love and loss. Above all, a chick flick will bring emotion – feelings – to the fore.

The Rough Guide To Chick Flicks is a heartfelt valentine to the movies that women love to watch, and offers a glittering grab bag of good-ies, whatever your viewing mood. It may well be the first book ever to gather together, with the same delight, reflections on *Dirty Dancing* and on new Iranian cinema, flappers and feminism, the gaudy excess of Gainsborough studio's costume dramas and the dry irony of Jane Austen. Hugh Grant sits cheek by jowl with Cary Grant; scriptwriter Frances Marion cosies up with Julia Roberts. When it heads off around the world it gives as much space to silent Chinese melodrama as to *Amélie*, and, in discussions of the chick flick/chick lit crossover, is as excited by the work of Jacqueline Susann as by Virginia Woolf. It's a book that adores any movie in which women – clowns and femmes fatales, wicked ladies and working girls, fast-talking broads and silent icons – occupy centre stage, and that thinks the ranks of remarkable women (and men) behind the scenes should take a long-overdue bow.

The **History** charts an enthusiastic course from the vamps and virgins of early cinema to the post-feminist ironists and kooky comediennes of the new millennium, taking in along the way the stars and the filmmakers, the screenwriters and the costume designers who made an impact. Arranged by decade, it includes dozens of movie reviews to point you in specific directions. The **Canon**, meanwhile, gets focused, whittling down a century's worth of fabulous movies to just fifty must-sees. Undoubtedly it will generate some lively debate, for while some of these are your archetypal chick flick – *Steel Magnolias* and *Beaches, Ghost* and *Pretty Woman* to name just a few – others may raise a few eyebrows. You'll find blockbusters and indie gems, classics and box office flops, all arranged in alphabetical order. There's also a **top ten countdown**, where I admit my own passions and not-so-guilty pleasures. Every film reviewed is strongly recommended, and not an inch is wasted trashing the chick flick turkeys – with the exception of one quick rant about the world's **most overrated chick flick** on p.63. (The **most underrated** is given loving strokes on p.112.) Diversions come in the form of **side features** on interesting and quirky themes. If you've enjoyed *Black Narcissus* and want to dig out some more classic nun films, or if you become intrigued after watching *Camille* by the role of courtesans in the movies, you'll pick up some good recommendations here. Some tough decisions had to be made when compiling the Canon, and of course there are omissions. Hopefully, any personal favourite that you don't find there will be covered in another chapter, perhaps as one of the capsule reviews included at the end of every section in the book. Each essay about the major **Icons**, for example, is followed by a handful of reviews about that person's most popular or significant films.

Those of us who love movies usually love books, too. Women's literature and women's films have always had an intimate relationship – just think *Bridget Jones's Diary*, *Gone With The Wind*, or any of Jane Austen's novels. What's more, the lives of many female authors are fascinating in themselves, making more than worthy subjects for a juicy biopic. The **Women's books and women's movies** chapter focuses on some of the more fascinating female authors in history, and, naturally, reviews the best films based on their work.

When we move away from Hollywood, the chick flick becomes even more mercurial. It was fascinating to sift through neorealism and New Australian cinema, French comedies and post-Tiananmen melodramas, plucking out films that are of particular interest to female audiences. And it was gratifying to find so very many – so many, indeed, that the **Women of the world** chapter could have been twice the length that space constraints allowed.

The final chapter, the **Information**, rounds up the best books and websites relating to anything and everything on planet chick flick. And as this is as much a book to dip into as to read from start to finish, there's a full **index** to point you to particular films, names and themes. Whether you're planning to start at page one and read through till the end, to browse at leisure, or to use the book as a reference source, why not get going with the **chick flick playlist** (see p. ix.), a very personal compilation of some splendid singalong songs. Quirky and classic, dancey, dreamy and dramatic, with a few laughs and more than a few tears for good measure, it's a fitting soundtrack for this book, and a great place to start reading. Welcome to the world of the chick flick – vast, surprising, and brimful of gems.

Samantha Cook, 2006

Acknowledgements

Heartfelt thanks to Greg Ward, for his unbounded love and unwavering support, not least in sharing way beyond the call of duty endless evenings watching weepies, costume dramas and rom-coms; Pam Cook, for a lifetime of generous help and wise advice, and for bringing me up to love chick flicks in all their many forms; Jim Cook, for his enthusiastic support, his encyclopedic memory for great quotes, and for directing me towards some unexpected gems; Ulrike Sieglohr, for advice on the Middle East; Julian Ward, for China tips and checking; and The Girls, for an idyllic afternoon under the mulberry tree shouting out favourite film titles. At Rough Guides, a very big thank-you to Katie Stephens, my unflappable and eagle-eyed editor, and to the equally unflappable Andrew Lockett at HQ.

The alternative chick flicks playlist

...because there's more to chick flick soundtracks than "I Will Always Love You" and "Wind Beneath My Wings".

1 Do Your Thing
Basement Jaxx *Bend It Like Beckham*
An impossibly infectious dance tune – with the immortal refrain "And a boom boom boom and a bang bang bang (boom, bang, boom, bang bang)" – from Brixton's finest house music outfit.

2 Moon River
Danny Williams *Breakfast At Tiffany's*
Henry Mancini's small, sweet and perfectly formed song won an Oscar – and though no one knows for sure what it is, a "huckleberry friend" sounds like a delightful thing to have.

3 All By Myself
Jamie O'Neal *Bridget Jones's Diary*
Who hasn't bellowed along to this one, eyes screwed shut, in a frenzy of self-pity after a glass too many?

4 Respect
Aretha Franklin *Bridget Jones's Diary*
And who hasn't snapped out of it with a feisty rendition of this? (As also seen in *Thelma & Louise*.)

5 Just Blew In From The Windy City
Doris Day *Calamity Jane*
While it was the film's yearning "Secret Love" that won the Oscar, the rambunctious "Windy City" has Doris giving it more oomph, at her gutsy thigh-slapping best with every throaty "no, sir-eee!".

6 As Time Goes By
Dooley Wilson *Casablanca*
"You must remember this…" – who could ever forget?

7 Kids In America
The Muffs *Clueless*
Kim Wilde's lo-fi mid-1980s original revisited a decade later by this Californian garage-punk outfit.

8 These Arms Of Mine
Otis Redding *Dirty Dancing*
Nobody sings about love like the Love Man himself. Wrap yourself up in his magnificent voice and swoon.

9 You Don't Own Me
The Blow Monkeys *Dirty Dancing*
This campy version of Lesley Gore's powerful pre-Girl Power proclamation – also immortalized by Goldie Hawn, Diane Keaton and Bette Midler in *The First Wives Club* – sneaks onto this list as a shameless excuse to plug the 1960s original. Defiance has never been sexier or more stylish.

10 Everyday Is A Winding Road
Sheryl Crow *Erin Brockovich*
A drive time favourite for moody mornings.

11 Unchained Melody
The Righteous Brothers *Ghost*
Grand melodrama meets blue-eyed soul. Just try and hit that high note while choking back the lump in your throat.

12 Angkor Wat Theme II
Michael Galasso *In The Mood For Love*
A heartbreakingly delicate string arrangement that weeps with remorse and regret.

(continued overleaf)

13 I Say A Little Prayer
The cast *My Best Friend's Wedding*

Penned by Burt Bacharach, this is probably the best singalong love song ever recorded. Root out Aretha Franklin's definitive version, grab your favourite karaoke hairbrush, and enjoy.

14 The Ballad Of Lucy Jordan
Marianne Faithfull *Thelma & Louise*

For any woman who, at the age of 37, realized she would never drive – to Paris – in a sports car – with the warm wind in her hay-ayr…

15 Playground Love
Air *The Virgin Suicides*

Chick flicks come over all woozy with help from the psychedelic Gallic electronica twosome. (Try saying that with a mouthful of popcorn.)

16 The Way We Were
Barbra Streisand *The Way We Were*

Babs is at her divaesque best with this bittersweet torch song to nostalgia and loss.

The History: from melodrama to chick flicks

Seduced by the American Dream: Greta
Garbo in *Ninotchka* (1939)

The History:
from melodrama to
chick flicks

The early years

Other than comedy, the staple genre in the earliest cinema was **melodrama**. Deriving from the words *melo* (music) and *drama*, the theatrical form, which placed more emphasis on stirring music and visual iconography than on dialogue, was hugely popular in the late nineteenth century, and well suited to the silent movies. Melodramatic plots involved highly wrought situations or crises, doomed love, dysfunctional families, tragedy, illness and hardship. Their heroines faced terrible emotional or physical danger with resolve, bravery and untold sacrifice. Drawing on influences from Greek tragedy to sentimental Victorian novels and paintings, melodramas told stories of good versus evil by using iconic, readily understood images, familiar motifs and archetypes ("The Girl", "The Boy"), dramatic music and non-naturalistic, highly gestural acting styles. Realism wasn't the issue or the aim in the earliest melodramas, which were far more concerned with emotional impact and the teaching of worthy moral lessons.

However, as the movie industry developed, so did the form. Rather than simply presenting stagey tableaux, young filmmakers like **D.W. Griffith** and Frank Borzage began to use their cameras, editing for continuity and often cross-cutting between scenes of depravity (a moustache-twiddling villain, a voracious vamp) and purity (an angelic, usually poor young woman, or perhaps an innocent child) for maximum effect. Location settings added a sense of realism. Griffith, who in this period produced classic melodramas like *Hearts Of The World* (1918), *True Heart Susie* (1919) and the astonishing *Broken Blossoms* (1919), also used the genre to increase psychological intensity in his epics *The Birth Of A Nation* (1915) and *Intolerance* (1916), two of the most influential films ever made. It was a form that was to have a huge influence on the women's movies that were to follow.

In the very earliest days, film actors were uncredited, partly due to the simplicity of the form, and partly because the studios feared that credited actors would demand higher salaries. In 1910, however, producer Carl Laemmle, seeking to stoke up publicity for his pictures, took **Florence Lawrence**, one of the prettiest actors from his Vitagraph studio, and made her the centre of a sustained publicity campaign. Calling her the "Vitagraph Girl", spreading rumours she had been killed in an accident, he then organized public appearances in theatres around the country. Florence was a big hit – fellow actress Norma Talmadge gushed, "I would rather have touched the hem of her skirt than … shaken hands with St Peter" – and thus the first "star" was born. Cheap fan maga-

zines, directed mainly at a female readership, reproduced images, gossip and news about the "stars", and audiences for the movies themselves grew and grew.

Most beloved of all Hollywood's stars was the demure-looking, mischievous **Mary Pickford**, known as "America's Sweetheart". A major force in the industry, in 1912 she introduced the director D.W. Griffith to two of her friends, **Lillian** and **Dorothy Gish**. Both sisters were fine actresses, but Lillian, with her serious intensity, became Griffith's favourite. After playing leading

roles in *The Birth Of A Nation* and *Intolerance*, she went on to become one of the major stars of the 1920s, turning out moving performances in the greatest melodramas, while Dorothy excelled in perky comedy roles. **Pearl White**, meanwhile, was playing plucky Pauline in the *Perils Of Pauline* series (from 1914), getting entangled in a number of cliffhanging scrapes that involved, among other things, pirates, Indians, gypsies and, more than once, being tied to the railway tracks. A talented stuntwoman, White began by doing all her own stunts, until her massive popularity led the studios to use doubles instead. At the other end of the spectrum came **Theda Bara**, whose name, an anagram of Arab Death, suggested untold wickedness. Bara, who played an evil seductress ("Kiss me, my fool!") simply called

The lady is a vamp: Theda Bara in *Cleopatra* (1917)

Mary Pickford: "America's Sweetheart"

Mary Pickford (1893–1979), "Little Mary", was the most popular movie star of her day. A child stage actress who started her film career aged 12, she had a natural, tomboyish energy in front of the camera, and soon developed a canny business acumen that belied her fragile Victorian beauty. Demanding respect for her considerable acting and comedic skills – director George Cukor once called her the first Method actress – she set her own salary when she first met director D.W. Griffith at the age of 16, and throughout her career insisted that her earnings be on a par with her male contemporaries. After cornering the market in plucky, resourceful girl-next-door roles in films like *The New York Hat* (1912) and *Tess Of The Storm Country* (1914), she soon began writing and producing, and in 1916 left top producer Adolph Zukor, who would not let her approve her scripts, to move to First National, where she was offered $675,000 a year and fifty percent of the studio's profits. She turned next to directing (usually uncredited), and in 1919, along with Charlie Chaplin, D.W. Griffith and the swashbuckling movie heart-throb Douglas Fairbanks Sr., formed the hugely powerful independent film company United Artists. Though she was in reality one of the most influential women in Hollywood, Pickford quickly learned that her fans didn't like it when she played "grown-up" roles (the dual leads in 1918's *Stella Maris*, say), and so continued to play well below her age while exerting ever greater, and often uncredited, control behind the scenes.

In March 1920 Mary Pickford and Fairbanks Sr. scandalously extricated themselves from their marriages and married each other, much to the delight of their fans. Their 22-room mansion, Pickfair, built in the then-rural area of Beverly Hills, started a trend for movie folk to move to the Hollywood suburbs; the couple became Hollywood royalty, and Pickfair the industry's social hub. Though Pickford's acting career took a downturn in the late 1920s, when she had finally become too old to play adolescents, she remained a major Hollywood player, and in 1929 was even nominated for an Oscar for her first talking role in the melodrama *Coquette*. Ever the shrewd businesswoman, she unabashedly invited the Academy Award judges to tea at Pickfair – and won the award. Pickford made her last film, *Secrets* (1933), at the age of 41, having notched up an extraordinary 250 movies. "The little girl made me. I wasn't waiting for the little girl to kill me," she later said. She continued to work in radio and film production, winning a Lifetime Achievement Oscar in 1975, four years before her death.

"The Vampire" in the melodrama *A Fool There Was* (1915), was the original "vamp", a word that entered the language to describe a sexy, predatory temptress. Photographed in exotic, scanty garb, glaring at the lens with huge kohl-lined eyes, Theda, it was claimed, was the daughter of an Arabian concubine, born in the shadow of the Sphinx, and boasted mysterious spiritual powers – not bad going for a woman who started life as Theodosia Goodman, a nice Jewish girl from Cincinnati.

It was not only as stars that women shone in the burgeoning movie industry. The novelty of the medium, and the intense speed with which films were churned out, created a febrile atmosphere in which anyone with talent and enthusiasm was able to multitask. Women writers very quickly came to the fore, among them the prolific screenwriter **Frances Marion** (see Icons), who wrote her first film, Mary Pickford's *The Foundling*, in 1915, and her last in 1940. Indeed, although writers were rarely credited in the earliest movies, it has since been estimated that more than half of all the Hollywood films produced before 1925 were penned by women.

🎬 The New York Hat
dir D.W. Griffith, 1912, US, 16m, b/w

An entertaining, quintessential Mary Pickford short, directed with verve by a young Griffith. "Little Mary" shines as the poor girl who, living with her cruel, miserly father, is delighted when the local pastor buys her a smart new hat. Local gossips, however, threaten to spoil the kindness of the gesture.

🎬 A Fool There Was
dir Frank Powell, 1915, US, 67m, b/w

Bad to the bone, the delicious Theda Bara sets the bar high for femmes fatales in this dark melodrama about an amoral vamp who lures a respectable married man to his doom.

🎬 Broken Blossoms
dir D.W. Griffith, 1919, US, 90m, b/w

Victorian-style melodrama done as only Griffith knew how. Lillian Gish tugs at the heartstrings as the wide-eyed Cockney sparrow who, having fled her violent, drunken father (Donald Crisp), falls for a young Chinese poet (Richard Barthelmess). Happiness in this poignant inter-racial love affair can only be fleeting, however, when the brutal father comes back on the scene...

The 1920s: the Jazz Age

In the 1920s the movies became a major art form. By now US film production was concentrated on the west coast, in Los Angeles and its suburb, Hollywood, where the climate was good and land was cheap. Conceived and realized at a phenomenal rate, melodramas held their own with Westerns, epics and comedies, while fabulous new movie theatres sprang up to house ever-increasing audiences. Major melodramas of the period include D.W. Griffith's *Way Down East* (1920) and *Orphans Of The Storm* (1921), as well as **Frank Lloyd's** classic tale of fallen virtue, *Madame X* (1920), **Erich von Stroheim's** *Greed* (1924), and **King Vidor's** *The Big Parade* (1925), set in World War I. Artistic and technological innovations, including the development of the close-up, permitted actors to develop a more naturalistic style than their counterparts in the earliest movies and on the Victorian stage, while the influence of expressionism, imported from Germany, created an emotional visual palette. Expressionist director **F.W. Murnau's** first Hollywood film, the exquisite *Sunrise* (1927), was a little dark for popular tastes, but won three Oscars – for Best Cinematography, Actress (Janet Gaynor) and "Unique and Artistic Picture" – at the first ever Academy Awards ceremony in 1929.

While the idea of directing particular genres to particular audiences had not yet taken hold, the **star system**, which by now was going full tilt, saw certain individuals appealing to women more than men. Italian-born **Rudolph Valentino** (see Icons), a male vamp, won hundreds of thousands of swooning female fans (and no few young gentlemen admirers) with his soulful eyes, hypnotic stare and graceful body – which his movies invariably revealed at its exotic best. Rarely has a star been surrounded by so much hysteria. His awesomely erotic tango in *The Four Horsemen Of The Apocalypse* (1921) started a nationwide tango craze, while all over the US men began slicking down their hair and powdering their faces to emulate his look – much to the disgust of various newspaper journalists, who accused Valentino of "feminizing" the American male.

The Jazz Age was also the era of "It girl" **Clara Bow**, a flame-haired New Yorker who charlestoned her way through flirty flapper movies like *The Plastic Age* (1925), *Mantrap* (1926) and *It* (1927). A staple of the fan magazines, she represented the epitome of modern female sex appeal, her cupid's bow lips copied faithfully by a generation of fashionable young moviegoers. In 1928 "the hottest jazz baby in films" was the highest-paid movie star in the world, earning $35,000 a week, but, like so many silent stars (and partly due to her broad Brooklyn accent), she didn't cross over into talkies. By the mid-1930s she had declined seriously, plagued by alcoholism, gambling and mental breakdown. The independent-minded **Louise Brooks,** with her sleek black bob, flashing eyes and charismatic screen presence, looked set to give Bow a run for her money, until, contemptuous of the shallow Hollywood scene, in 1928 she left Hollywood in disgust. She went on to work in Germany with director G.W. Pabst, putting in an extraordinary performance as the

intoxicating Lulu in his dark masterpiece *Pandora's Box* (1929), and the same year playing the charismatic Thymiane in his stylized *Diary Of A Lost Girl*. Though Brooks later attempted a comeback in the US, like Bow she disappeared from movies in the 1930s, turning to dance teaching, writing and painting.

Other jazzy flappers included a young **Joan Crawford** (see Icons), whose early appearances in movies like *Our Dancing Daughters* (1928) entailed a lot of feverish dancing and swigging of champagne; Crawford, however, was determined to be a star, and unlike many of her contemporaries, was here to stay. The **Gish sisters** also continued to thrive throughout the 1920s; Lillian even directed Dorothy in the gently

The death of a legend

On August 23, 1926, upon the announcement that **Rudolph Valentino**, the world's most famous lover, had died – of an infection caused by peritonitis – two of the hundreds of distraught fans outside his hospital in New York attempted to kill themselves on the spot. Stories flooded in of fans all around the world – men and women – committing suicide, many of them ritualistically surrounding themselves with his photographs. Popular crooner Rudy Vallee immediately recorded a tribute to the icon, "There's A New Star In Heaven Tonight", which became an instant hit, while Valentino's ex-wife Jean wrote another called "We Will Meet At The End Of The Trail".

Such was the distress surrounding the demise of this icon that two funerals were held. In New York, the crowd of 100,000 hysterical mourners stormed the funeral home, where, in a publicity stunt, four actors had been hired to impersonate fascistic bodyguards. Rumours spread that the Valentino family, wanting to protect him from possible harm, had replaced the star's body, displayed in the open casket, with a waxwork replica. At the service, the exotic film star Pola Negri, dressed in ostentatious widow's black, claimed that she and Valentino had been due to be married and threw herself, wailing, onto the coffin.

Rudolph Valentino was then transported to Hollywood by train, which was watched by thousands of fans along its route. At the second funeral, rose petals were scattered from an aeroplane over the cortege as yet more hysteria ensued. This time Negri sobbed in an enormous bed of scarlet roses with her name spelled out in white at the centre, while many of Hollywood's major players also wept throughout the service. Though Negri eventually recovered and married a prince, for many years, on the anniversary of Valentino's death, a mysterious woman, dressed in black and hidden by a long veil, would lay flowers at his crypt in the Hollywood Forever Cemetery; today's fans, dressed as sheiks or in widows' weeds, make the same pilgrimage. Valentino would probably have loved it – in death, as in life, surrounded by mystery, romance and sheer, spectacular theatre.

mocking *Remodeling Her Husband* (1920), about a husband who accuses his wife of being a frump, which became the second-biggest earner of all Dorothy's comedies.

Way Down East
dir D.W. Griffith, 1920, US, 123m, b/w

Lillian Gish is incandescent as the wronged country girl in this classic melodrama. Abandoned after the tragic death of her baby, she flees to a kindly farming family hoping to start anew. When her secret comes out, however, the hapless girl is cast out into the snow, where she stumbles onto a giant ice floe that carries her towards a waterfall... This is said to be the first film to use a close-up – moving in on Lillian's anguished face – to heighten emotional effect.

The Four Horsemen Of The Apocalypse
dir Rex Ingram, 1921, US, 134m, b/w

The movie that brought the ravishing Rudolph Valentino to a panting female audience. Set in World War I, the smouldering one plays French/Argentinian artist Julio, who lives only for pleasure, dancing sexy tangos and dallying with married women. The dramatic arrival of the four horsemen – War, Famine, Pestilence and Death – changes everything, however, as Julio finally learns the meaning of duty and sacrifice.

Orphans Of The Storm
dir D.W. Griffith, 1921, US, 143m, b/w

Starring the Gish sisters at the peak of their powers, this is a spectacular historical melodrama, set during the French Revolution. Dorothy proves her mettle as a serious actress playing Louise, the abandoned daughter of an aristocrat who is adopted by a kindly, poor family – after she's blinded by the plague, her new sister, Henriette (Lillian), takes her to Paris for an operation, where the two run into dire danger.

Sunrise
dir F.W. Murnau, 1927, US, 95m, b/w

Murnau's innovative direction, employing split screens, moving cameras and wonderful special effects, elevates a simple tale – a farmer (George O'Brien) is tempted by an evil vamp from the city (Margaret Livingston) into drowning his beloved wife (Janet Gaynor) – into a lyrical, highly emotional masterpiece.

The Wind
dir Victor Sjöström, 1928, US, 95m, b/w

A tour de force from Lillian Gish in her last silent film. Letty (Gish) looks after her cousin's children on a windblown Texas ranch, but, thrown out by the jealous lady of the house (Dorothy Cumming) and with nowhere to go, she marries a rough cowboy (Lars Hanson). After killing a rapist (Montagu Love) in self-defence during a terrible storm, she tries desperately to bury his body, while the dreadful wind threatens to drive her insane.

The 1930s: classical Hollywood cinema

The 1930s was Hollywood's golden era. Sound arrived, colour arrived, the star system was firmly entrenched, and a huge creative outpouring ensued in every area of filmmaking. Though the Depression cast its shadow over the movies, both in their subject matter and in the decreasing number of ticket sales, cinema was still by far the most popular art form, and there were more than enough lush melodramas and weepies to satisfy female audiences. Many of the most successful women's movies were based on popular novels. In the maternal melodrama *Stella Dallas* (1937; see Canon), for example, **Olive Higgins Prouty** gave us a strong, complex and conflicted woman battling to make her way in the world, while **Fannie Hurst**'s stories of struggling working women formed the basis for weepies like Michael Curtiz's *Four Daughters* (1938), in which a young woman sacrifices her happiness for her sister, and *Imitation Of Life* (1934), a mixed-race melodrama that was remade by Douglas Sirk in the 1950s. The decade's major women's movie – indeed, the most popular movie of all time – *Gone With The Wind* (1939; see Canon), was based on the blockbuster novel by Southern writer **Margaret Mitchell**. The big studios also hired major women writers to bring a female point of view to movies that were intended to win female audiences. MGM alone employed leading literary lights Zoe Akins, Lenore Coffee, Lillian Hellman, Anita Loos, Frances Marion, Dorothy Parker and Adela Rogers St Johns, among others, as screenwriters. For more on the female authors behind some of the greatest women's movies, see "Women's books and women's movies" (see p. 207).

Due partly to the coming of sound, and the corresponding need for well written scripts, this was also the era of the **screwball comedy**, which pepped up the athletic slapstick of the silents with sophisticated wordplay. Screwball spawned a new breed of heroine – sparky, smart and subversive – the like of which hasn't been seen since. Madcap heiresses, runaway brides and razor-sharp career girls; these brainy and beautiful women invariably outshone their male co-stars, who, whether urbane or hapless, generally took a back seat. Queen of the screwball heroines was the ravishing **Carole Lombard** (see Icons), who cornered the market in irrepressible blonde kooks, and whose career was tragically cut short after a plane crash in 1942. Others included the merry, more homely Irene Dunne, who teamed up with **Cary Grant** (see Icons) to hilarious effect in the sparkling battle-of-the-sexes screwball *The Awful*

Carole Lombard: screwball queen in a satin gown

Truth (1937). Grant was a brilliant comic foil, turning up again opposite fast-talking Rosalind Russell in *His Girl Friday* (1939; see Canon) and a splendidly crazed **Katharine Hepburn** (see Icons) in *Bringing Up Baby* (1938). Claudette

Every ruffle tells a story: the great 1930s costumiers

Adrian

Adrian Adolph Greenburg (1903–59), known simply as Adrian, was the 1930s Hollywood costumier par excellence. After training in New York and Paris, and giving Rudolph Valentino a dashing Russian officer look for *The Eagle* (1925), he joined director Cecil B. DeMille at Pathe Studios, and in 1928 followed him to MGM. It was at this opulent studio that he made his name, designing glamorous gowns for all the major female stars. He was particularly associated with MGM queen Norma Shearer, whom he described as every American woman's ideal, but he also dressed the sexy platinum blonde Jean Harlow, swathing her in white on white to represent modern decadence (in *Red Dust*, 1932; *Bombshell*, 1933; and *Dinner At Eight*, 1933, among others); Joan Crawford, whom he weaned from flighty flapper to sophisticated working woman in movies like *Dance, Fools, Dance* (1931), *Grand Hotel* (1932) and *The Bride Wore Red* (1937); and, his personal favourite, Greta Garbo. Declaring, "Never put anything fake on Garbo!", Adrian emphasized the Swedish actress's ethereal beauty in all her MGM movies, creating strikingly effective looks in *Anna Christie* (1930), *Mata Hari* (1932), *Grand Hotel*, *Queen Christina* (1933), *Anna Karenina* (1935), *Camille* (1936) and *Ninotchka* (1939). In *The Women* (1939), the designer

The era of glamour: designer Adrian with the iconic Joan Crawford

was able to dress practically all MGM's top female stars – among them Norma Shearer, Joan Crawford, Rosalind Russell, Paulette Goddard and Joan Fontaine – in one fell swoop; he went to town, kitting each woman out in individual designs, and even creating a stunning ten-minute Technicolor fashion show in an otherwise black-and-white movie.

Adrian understood that movie costumes worked as metaphors, expressing character, feelings and coded messages; he also made sure each design suited each star's personality and their figure. "It is much more important for a woman to dress her personality than her body," he told *Ladies Home Journal* in 1932. "So many women feel like they would adore to look like Garbo, but are really more like Shearer. They should consider their inner as well as their exterior selves and dress the combination." His clothes had a huge influence on other movie costumiers, and were also copied by ready-to-wear designers throughout the US; it's Adrian we have to thank for halter necks, as well as the monochrome palette, huge shoulder pads and voluminous sleeves that dominated the look of the 1930s and 40s. In 1942, when the studios were cutting their huge costume budgets, he established his own fashion house, providing designs for the major studios and creating off-the-peg outfits for the thousands of women who longed to look like their favourite movie stars.

Travis Banton

Known for his luxurious, sensual fabrics and the unfussy silhouettes of his designs, Travis Banton (1894–1958) trained in Paris before becoming head designer at Paramount. Banton created sexy on-screen looks for stars as different as Carole Lombard (sleek, feline) and Mae West (ripe, opulent), designing many of their personal outfits as well. He also perfected Marlene Dietrich's androgynous style, dressing her in mannish suits and hats, and complementing director Josef von Sternberg's dramatic lighting techniques by using reflective, sensual fabrics (see *Dishonored*, 1931; *Shanghai Express*, 1932; *Blonde Venus*, 1932; *The Devil Is A Woman*, 1935, among others). Along with their fluid lines, Banton's designs often included veils, hats and trains, which added to the impression of movement and energy.

Orry-Kelly

Bette Davis's favourite, the Australian-born Orry-Kelly (1897–1964), who came to New York as an actor, was introduced by Cary Grant to the head of Warner Bros' wardrobe department in the early 1930s. He specialized in unfussy lines, quality fabrics and subtle colouring, enlivened with fine textural detail and embroidery. Though his main work was in the 1950s (he was responsible for Marilyn Monroe's outrageous, practically see-through dress in *Some Like It Hot*, 1959, for example), he was also behind the saucy, sassy costumes in the Busby Berkeley musicals of the 1930s. With a major actress like Bette Davis, he understood that costumes should help her inhabit her character, creating designs that shaped both her body and her persona in classics like *Jezebel* (1938), *Dark Victory* (1939), *The Old Maid* (1939), *The Little Foxes* (1941) and *Now, Voyager* (1942).

Walter Plunkett

Walter Plunkett (1902–82) started out as an actor but soon turned to costume design, specializing in period costumes. Although he worked on movies as varied as *King Kong* and *Little Women* (both 1933), he is best known for *Gone With The Wind* (1939), to which he applied incredible attention to detail and a flamboyant eye for colour. Katharine Hepburn, herself a fastidious researcher, would often rehearse in Plunkett's costumes, which, because they looked and felt exactly as they would have done in the period they represented, helped her inhabit her character. As well as *Little Women*, Plunkett designed for Hepburn in *Christopher Strong* (1933), *Alice Adams* (1935) and *Sylvia Scarlett* (1935), among others. Just as popular with stars like Irene Dunne and Judy Garland, he was also responsible for Fred Astaire and Ginger Rogers' look, creating comfortable, fluid and glamorous garments that showed their dancing to the best advantage. Plunkett was nominated for the Best Costume Design Oscar ten times, but won only once, sharing the award with Orry-Kelly and Irene Sharaff for the elegant musical *An American In Paris* (1951).

Colbert, who was also an accomplished dramatic actress, pulled off, with a roguish Clark Gable, one of the most popular screwballs ever with the classic *It Happened One Night* (1934).

Heritage movies and prestige dramas like *The Barretts Of Wimpole Street* (1934) pulled in the female audiences, too, as did **musicals**. Moviegoers adored the easy grace of Fred Astaire and Ginger Rogers, who after first taking to the dance floor in *Flying Down To Rio* (1933), made at least one film together per year until the end of the decade. Operettas, especially those starring the squeaky clean Nelson Eddy and Jeanette MacDonald, were also popular, along with the audacious trompe l'oeil chorus line extravagan-zas – *42nd Street* (1933), *Dames* (1934), the *Gold Diggers* series (1933–38) – from master choreog-rapher Busby Berkeley.

By now Hollywood had become synony-mous with **glamour**. Fabulous Art Deco sets, sparkling jewels, reflective satin evening gowns and luminous, beautifully lit faces shimmered off the screen, enchanting Depression-era audiences hungry for beauty. Though the Oscars didn't include Costume as a category until 1948, the 1930s movie costumiers – and in many cases the costumes themselves – became stars in their own right. Showing the actors to their best advan-tage, costumes could tell, enhance and subvert a film's story, and they influenced the fashions of a decade.

Director **George Cukor** (see Icons) emerged on the scene with the melodrama *Tarnished Lady* (1931) – featuring the silent star and stage actress Tallulah Bankhead as a fallen woman – and rap-idly became one of the most significant directors of the decade. He was known as a great "wom-an's director", not only for making the kinds of films that appealed to female audiences, but also for his affinity with the finest movie actresses of the day. He brought the strong-willed **Katharine Hepburn** to the world in the family drama *A Bill Of Divorcement* (1932), going on to work with her throughout the 1930s (and way beyond) in movies like *Little Women* (1933), *Sylvia Scarlett* (1935) and *Holiday* (1938). Hepburn won her first Best Actress Oscar for her close-to-life performance as the ambitious actress in *Morning Glory* (1933); a classy but spiky woman, she had yet, however, to fully win audiences' hearts, and by the end of the decade was being derided by some as "box office poison".

The lady that everyone loved to love, on the other hand, was **Norma Shearer**, a style icon who personified both old-fashioned graciousness and modern sophistication. Dressed impeccably, often by top designer Adrian, Shearer was an ambitious woman, an unconventional beauty who brought intelligence and humour to her performances. Married to MGM studio head Irving Thalberg, she had considerable control over the films she chose – slick comedies like *The Divorcee* (1930), for example, for which she won an Oscar as the wife who plays her philandering husband at his own game – and as the 1930s progressed she moved into classy prestige dramas. Shearer won three more Oscar nominations, for *The Barretts Of Wimpole Street* (1934), *Marie Antoinette* (1938), and, slightly less convincingly (she was by now in her 30s) *Romeo And Juliet* (1936), before return-ing to the modern day in George Cukor's *The Women* (1939). The movie, however, was a kind of swansong, for as the 1940s ushered in a new style of heroine – the tough career woman – her heyday was behind her.

Shearer's reign at MGM proved tricky for her stablemate **Joan Crawford**, who, hav-ing started out in feisty flapper roles in the silents, had matured as a star by the mid-1930s. Specializing in spunky young working girls looking for love *and* financial security, modelling a number of amazing Adrian-designed ensembles along the way, she had yet to reach the iconic status she was to achieve during the war years. If women loved Norma and admired Joan, they were simply crazy about **Bette Davis** (see Icons), who by the end of the decade was making waves at Warner Bros, fearlessly campaigning for better contracts and more respect from her studio. Putting in distinctive, uncompromising

The power of the hat: Greta Garbo gets seduced by capitalism in *Ninotchka* (1939)

performances in classic women's pictures like *Jezebel* (1938), *The Old Maid* (1939) and *Dark Victory* (1939), Davis is now recognized as one of Hollywood's all-time great actresses. Like Joan Crawford, **Barbara Stanwyck** (see Icons) excelled at playing plucky working-class women with a sparkle of intelligence and a bittersweet vulnerability, and like Davis she was respected for her forthrightness and strength. Unlike her contemporaries, however, Stanwyck's light touch and mischievous air made her ideal for comedy, too, and she shone in dizzy screwballs like *The Mad Miss Manton* (1938), in which she plays a sparky socialite sleuth.

The 1930s was also the decade of **Greta Garbo**, "the Swedish Sphinx", who with her fragile beauty and enormous eyes suggested untold depths of old European wisdom and pain. An iconic silent star, she made a hugely successful transition to talkies, lit like a goddess and playing women with shady pasts in movies like *Anna Christie* (1930), *Mata Hari* (1931), *Anna Karenina* (1935) and *Camille* (1936; see Canon). Shrouded in mystery, Garbo also had enough wit and intelligence to turn her hand to a little self-parody in *Ninotchka* (1939), in which she plays a dour Russian agent seduced both by America's decadent ways and a rather fabulous hat. In 1930 the charismatic Austrian-born director Josef von Sternberg brought another glamorous European, **Marlene Dietrich**, to the world in *The Blue Angel*. The sultry star got her big Hollywood break later the same year playing opposite Gary Cooper in *Morocco*, and was soon being promoted by her studio, Paramount, as a rival to MGM's Garbo. The archetypal world-weary cabaret singer, Dietrich reprised that role with von Sternberg again and again in passionate, slightly skewed movies like *Dishonored* (1931), *Shanghai Express* (1932), *Blonde Venus* (1932) and

The Devil Is A Woman (1935). After a slump in her career in the second half of the decade, she showed, like Garbo, a lighter, self-mocking side as the saloon keeper in the Western romp *Destry Rides Again* (1939).

Other stars included the saucy **Mae West**, who, trussed up like some Edwardian floozy, drawling sly innuendos and double entendres, camped it up outrageously in bawdy comedies like *I'm No Angel* and *She Done Him Wrong* (both 1933), many of which she wrote herself. Even sexier was the teenage **Jean Harlow**, the platinum blonde bombshell who exploded onto the world as the double-crossing femme fatale in Howard Hughes' aerial drama *Hell's Angels* (1930), uttering the infamous (and usually misquoted) line, "Would you be shocked if I changed into something more comfortable?" Peroxide sales in the US hit the roof, while salacious rumours abounded about this confident sex symbol who, it was said, never wore underwear, always slept in the nude and trimmed her pubic hair into the shape of a love heart. A natural comedienne, Harlow went on to carve out a sassy, brassy comedy niche with *Bombshell* (1933), a satire on the movie business in which she plays the "If girl", and *Dinner At Eight* (1933), a classic ensemble piece. She was often paired with rugged Clark Gable, in movies like *The Secret Six* (1931), *Red Dust* (1932) and *Wife Vs Secretary* (1936); tragically, she died of kidney failure aged just 26 while they were making their sixth film, *Saratoga* (1937). A double was used to finish the movie, which became the highest-grossing film of the year, setting all-time house records.

One unique and often overlooked figure in 1930s Hollywood was the trailblazing director **Dorothy Arzner** (see Icons), who, firmly entrenched in the mainstream, brought a female point of view to her movies. All of them featured strong, interesting characters, and equally force-ful stars: *Christopher Strong* (1933), for example, gave Katharine Hepburn one of her finest hours, while comic genius Rosalind Russell was able to extend her range into high drama as the brittle *Craig's Wife* (1936). Although *The Bride Wore Red* (1937) was a flop for Joan Crawford, it did feature the drop-dead gorgeous dress of the title, designed by Adrian and worn by the star in the movie's climactic scene.

Queen Christina
dir Rouben Mamoulian, 1933, US, 100m, b/w

Garbo is at her most alluring as the seventeenth-century Swedish queen who flees an arranged marriage by dressing as a boy. After falling for the dashing Spanish ambassador (John Gilbert), she abdicates for love, and, in the iconic final scene, sails off on the prow of a ship, resembling for all the world an exquisite figurehead.

The Barretts Of Wimpole Street
dir Sidney Franklin, 1934, US, 110m, b/w

Typical of MGM's elaborately staged prestige dramas, this hugely popular movie was based on the lives of the poet Robert Browning (Fredric March) and the invalid Elizabeth Barrett (Norma Shearer). Shearer is charming, if mannered, languishing on a chaise longue while battling her possessive father (Charles Laughton, marvellous) to let the course of true love run smooth.

Of Human Bondage
dir John Cromwell, 1934, US, 83m, b/w

The movie that made Bette Davis a star. Playing a vulgar, promiscuous waitress, the actress spits out her cockney-accented vitriol with a relish that borders on the psychotic. A compelling, if curious performance, and certainly a camp delight.

It Happened One Night
dir Frank Capra, 1934, US, 105m, b/w

This screwball classic was the first movie to sweep the boards at the Oscars, winning Best Picture, Director, Actor, Actress and Adapted Screenplay. Claudette Colbert is superb as spoiled heiress Ellie, on the run from her father (Walter Connolly), who won't approve of her recent marriage. Sniffing a story, the hard-bitten, out-of-work newshound Peter (Clark Gable) tails the stubborn firebrand, setting off a chalk-and-cheese road trip that sizzles with sexual chemistry.

My Man Godfrey
dir Gregory La Cava, 1936, US, 96m, b/w

Another daft and very wonderful screwball, with all the essential ingredients – a dizzy heiress (Carole Lombard), an eccentric family, a hapless hero with hidden depths (William Powell) – and a heart-warming Depression-era message to boot.

The Awful Truth
dir Leo McCarey, 1937, US, 91m, b/w

Cary Grant and Irene Dunne are a match made in heaven as the volatile divorcing couple who put all their energies into ruining each other's chances to find new love. Witty, fast and irrepressible, with the two leads at their seductive, mischievous best.

The Women
dir George Cukor, 1939, US, 132m, b/w & col

Based on Clare Boothe Luce's play, directed by "women's director" Cukor, with glorious gowns by Adrian and an all-female cast, this is an outrageously bitchy cult classic. Three of the most fabulous stars of the day (Joan Crawford, Rosalind Russell and Norma Shearer) crackle and fizz as glamorous divorcees cat-fighting and backstabbing their way through other women's husbands.

The 1940s: the war years and the women's picture

Hollywood was still at its peak well into the 1940s. Technological advances in the use of sound, lighting, colour and cinematography

Career girl Wendy Hiller finally falls for romance in *I Know Where I'm Going!* (1945)

meant that movies became more polished, taking on the shape and form that they have kept right up to the present. Because of the war in Europe, women made up by far the majority of the movie audience, and while many male stars were called up, or enlisted, a large cache of female stars was left to take centre stage. Like the melodramas of the 1930s, these 1940s **"women's pictures"**, made with the female audience in mind, featured strong women battling the odds in order to survive. Frequently set against a background of war, where the fellas risked all on the battlefield, very often these movies concerned themselves with everyday acts of heroism performed by women on the domestic front.

Screwball continued to sparkle early in the decade, with Barbara Stanwyck on lusty form as the con woman in Preston Sturge's *The Lady Eve* (1941), and as Sugarpuss O'Shea, the wisecracking stripper in Howard Hawks's *Ball Of Fire* (1941). Carole Lombard was as funny as ever in *Mr & Mrs Smith* (1941), and in the frenetic *To Be Or Not To Be* (1942); after her death in a plane crash following a patriotic war bond rally, however, the genre lost some life. There were

Wicked ladies and swaggering blades: Gainsborough melodramas

Between 1942 and 1946, London's **Gainsborough Pictures** produced a string of hugely popular costume melodramas based on bodice-ripping novels by female authors. Visually opulent, these were rumbustious, rude and hugely enjoyable romps, brimming with wanton gypsies, rebellious women, jewel thieves, highwaymen and brutal, moustache-twiddling aristocrats. While critics tut-tutted at their visual excess and cheeky flamboyance, movies like *The Man In Grey* (1943), *Madonna Of The Seven Moons* (1944) and *The Wicked Lady* (1945; see Canon) offered thrilling adventures that appealed hugely to deprived female audiences going through the major cultural, social and economic disruptions of World War II. Gainsborough created a stable of British stars who were every bit as glamorous as those in the US – actresses like Phyllis Calvert, Patricia Roc, Jean Kent and, especially, bad girl **Margaret Lockwood,** and their sexy, often sadistic suitors Stewart Granger and **James Mason** – all adored by a generation of women. Costume designer **Elizabeth Haffenden** created flamboyant and deliciously sexy outfits, with tasselled, midriff-baring gypsy dresses or cleavage-heaving bodices for the women; skin-tight pants, mysterious semi-fetishistic masks and dramatic swirling capes for the men.

Gainsborough also produced contemporary melodramas; of these, the tragic *Love Story* (1944) and *They Were Sisters* (1945), which both featured all the heightened emotion of the costume dramas, were favourites. After the war, the Spanish-set *Caravan* (1946), with its emphasis on fights, derring-do and male rivalry, was aimed as much towards the men returned home from war as at their women, who were more than happy to feast their eyes on Stewart Granger in tight flamenco garb.

In 1946, due to disagreements with Gainsborough's notoriously puritanical distributor, J. Arthur Rank, who disapproved of the melodramas, studio head Maurice Ostrer stood down. Sydney Box took over, producing *Jassy* (1947), a Technicolor extravaganza about a gypsy girl (Margaret Lockwood) who has second sight; like Rank, however, he was more interested in making contemporary "social issue" films. Box's sister, **Betty Box**, Britain's first major female producer, oversaw a couple of popular comedies, including the mermaid fantasy *Miranda* (1948), while his wife, **Muriel Box**, the studio's head screenwriter, wrote some fascinating scripts foregrounding women's struggles for recognition and independence (*The Years Between*, 1946; *The Brothers*, 1947; *Good-Time Girl*, 1948). Overall, however, the movies lacked the mischief and the sparkle of the costume melodramas, the audiences stayed away, and in 1950 Gainsborough's doors were finally closed.

echoes of screwball in *The More The Merrier* (1943), an impish comedy which, dealing with the sad lack of eligible bachelors during the war, touched a nerve with the female audience. Overall, however, **patriotism** took over where the frothy fantasies of the 1930s left off. Some movies managed to combine fierce romantic passion with stoicism – the multi-Oscar-winning *Casablanca* (1942; see Canon) for example – while others, including *Since You Went Away* (1944), starring Claudette Colbert and Jennifer Jones, upped the quiet courage quotient. Enter English-born redhead **Greer Garson**, who celebrated the heroism of ordinary people in the rousing *Mrs Miniver* (1942). Garson also shone in 1940's *Pride And Prejudice*, playing a spirited Elizabeth opposite Laurence Olivier's sulky Mr Darcy, the weepie amnesia melodrama *Random Harvest* (1942) and *Madame Curie* (1943), in which, of course, she discovers radium.

A more ambiguous figure was **Bette Davis**, who came into her own in the 1940s after battling with her studio, Warner Bros, for more control over her work. In 1941 she became the first female president of the Academy of Motion Picture Arts and Sciences, while her mighty performances as bitchy hellcats or suffering heroines dominated melodramas like *The Letter* (1940), *The Little Foxes* (1941), *Now, Voyager* (1942), *Old Acquaintance* (1943) and *A Stolen Life* (1946).

The 1940s was also the decade of the dark, low-budget movies that became known as **film noir**. Often featuring a smouldering femme fatale, who with a sashay of her satin-clad hips or a cool exhale of cigarette smoke could drive a man to his death, these hard-boiled films weren't directed towards women, but certainly hold a lot of illicit pleasure for female audiences. Even if they were punished in the end, **femmes fatales** like Jane Greer (*Out Of The Past*, 1947; *The Big*

Steal, 1949), Gene Tierney (*Laura*, 1944; *Leave Her To Heaven*, 1945), Lana Turner (*The Postman Always Rings Twice*, 1946), Ava Gardner (*The Killers*, 1946) and Rita Hayworth (*Gilda*, 1946; *The Lady From Shanghai*, 1947) had a lot of nasty fun along the way. **Joan Crawford** resuscitated her faltering career with the shadowy maternal melodrama-cum-*noir* *Mildred Pierce* (1945; see Canon), for which she won an Oscar, and threw herself with relish into twisted psychological thrillers like *Humoresque* (1946) and *Possessed* (1947); **Barbara Stanwyck**, too, while continuing to shine in rollicking comedies (*Lady Of Burlesque*, 1943; *Christmas In Connecticut*, 1945), took her tough working-class heroines to a dark place with *Double Indemnity* (1944) and *The Strange Love Of Martha Ivers* (1946).

At the other end of the spectrum, **musicals**, particularly the lavish productions put out by major studio MGM, went from strength to strength, with full-colour Judy Garland extravaganzas like *Meet Me In St Louis* (1944) and *Easter Parade* (1948) bringing optimism, hope and happy endings to harrowed wartime audiences.

In **Britain**, the elegiac restraint and stiff upper lip offered in the delicate weepie *Brief Encounter* (1945; see Canon), a quality production based on a Noel Coward play, was countered by the cheerful excess of **Gainsborough studios**, whose outrageous costume dramas were attracting domestic female audiences in droves. Rather more elevated, but equally vigorous, **Michael Powell** and **Emeric Pressburger**'s studio, The Archers (see p.121), also offered a feast of pleasures for women who had been starved of colour and fantasy in the grim war years, from the wryly uplifting tale of modern womanhood *I Know Where I'm Going!* (1945) to the brilliant hues and unrestrained passion of *Black Narcissus* (1946), *The Red Shoes* (1948) and *Gone To Earth* (1950).

Kitty Foyle

dir Sam Wood, 1940, US, 108m, b/w

Glamorous hoofer Ginger Rogers – who was also a very fine comedienne – proved in this classic women's movie that she was more than capable of carrying a dramatic role. She won an Oscar for her spirited performance as a good-hearted, working-class girl torn between her wealthy ex-love (Dennis Morgan) and a penniless doctor (James Craig).

Waterloo Bridge
dir Mervyn LeRoy, 1940, US, 108m, b/w

Vivien Leigh followed *Gone With The Wind* with this superb weepie, which she claimed was her personal favourite. She plays a down-on-her-luck ex-ballerina, who, brokenhearted by the death of her lover, Roy (Robert Taylor), in World War I, resorts to prostitution to survive. Discovering that Roy is alive, and trying to keep her profession secret from him, creates a torment that's difficult to bear…

Dance, Girl, Dance
dir Dorothy Arzner, 1940, US, 90m, b/w

An enjoyable dance movie, elegantly directed by one of the only female directors working in classical Hollywood. Both Maureen O'Hara, who stars as Judy, an aspiring ballerina, and Lucille Ball, as her brash burlesque dancer friend Bubbles, are terrific, and the famous scene when Judy turns on the male audience at the burlesque club is as moving as it is startling.

Gainsborough glamour: Margaret Lockwood and James Mason in *The Wicked Lady* (1945)

The Letter
dir William Wyler, 1940, US, 95m, b/w

Singapore provides the steamy setting for this simmering melodrama-cum-early *film noir,* in which the very wicked Bette Davis convinces all around her she is innocent of murder – until an incriminating letter threatens her safety. The fine character actress Gale Sondergaard offers typically sinister support.

The Lady Eve
dir Preston Sturges, 1941, US, 97m, b/w

The combination of Preston Sturges, Barbara Stanwyck and Henry Fonda is a happy one: Stanwyck, in particular, is on top form as the fast-talking con-artiste who sets her sights on innocent herpetologist Charles "Hopsy" Pike (Fonda). In cahoots with her dad (the brilliant Charles Coburn), she takes him at cards, falls in love, and remains, as ever, feisty and independent till the end.

Mrs Miniver
dir William Wyler, 1942, US, 134m, b/w

Filmed to encourage America to enter World War II, this simple tale of an ordinary English family's experience of the war – including a rousing chorus of "Onward, Christian Soldiers" in a bombed church – was said by Winston Churchill to have done more for the war effort than "a flotilla of destroyers". Greer Garson won an Oscar for her role as the noble matriarch of the title.

Since You Went Away
dir John Cromwell, 1944, US, 172m, b/w

A domestic front tearjerker in the same spirit as *Mrs Miniver*, this time setting the action in the American Midwest, where the stoical Claudette Colbert struggles to raise her two daughters (Jennifer Jones and a teenage Shirley Temple) after father is lost in action.

I Know Where I'm Going!
dir Michael Powell and Emeric Pressburger, 1945, UK, 92m, b/w

Consummate filmmakers Powell and Pressburger, known for the saturated colour of their later movies, here concoct an enchanting romance in stunning black and white. Wendy Hiller is superb as the brisk career girl whose trip to a Scottish island to marry a rich industrialist is thwarted by eccentric locals, passionate storms and the call of true love.

Possessed
dir Curtis Bernhardt, 1947, US, 108m, b/w

Not to be confused with her 1931 movie of the same name, this nightmarish women's picture has Joan Crawford in fine *film noir* fettle as a disturbed woman who recounts to a psychiatrist her murderous tale of obsessive love.

The Heiress
dir William Wyler, 1949, US, 115m, b/w

Wyler adapts Henry James's novella *Washington Square* with a melodramatic flourish while remaining true to its dark, devastating heart. Olivia de Havilland won the second Oscar of her career playing the dowdy young woman wronged by both her disdainful father (Ralph Richardson) and her suitor (Montgomery Clift) in this bleakest of costume dramas.

The 1950s: invasion of the blonde bombshells

The 1950s saw the rise of rock'n'roll, and, in the cinema, the rise of troubled teenage stars. Young, moody Method actors like James Dean and Marlon Brando achieved immediate iconic status, sulking and muttering their way through a new generation of gritty movies; their female co-stars, meanwhile, tended to play supporting roles. There were exceptions: Vivien Leigh put in an Oscar-winning performance as the damaged Blanche DuBois opposite Brando in *A Streetcar Named Desire* (1951), for example, while ex-child star Elizabeth Taylor grew up to play high-maintenance firebrands in overblown movies like *Giant* (1956), *Raintree County* (1957),

Cat On A Hot Tin Roof (1958) and *Suddenly, Last Summer* (1959) – but none of these could claim to be women's movies. As the great women stars of the 1930s and 40s reached middle age, the young actresses that rose to replace them were, in many cases, less easy for female audiences to relate to.

This was the era of the blonde bombshell. **Marilyn Monroe**, for example, who came to typify the physical feminine ideal of the 1950s, burst onto the world with a small part as a dumb blonde in the smart movie *All About Eve* (1950), making a striking contrast with her co-star, the articulate, cynical and middle-aged Bette Davis. Monroe, who generally emitted an unsettling aura of vulnerability – exceptions include the glorious *Gentlemen Prefer Blondes* (1953; see Canon) – longed to be taken seriously as an actress; her contemporary, **Jayne Mansfield**, however, seemed happy to use her extraordinary hourglass figure to great comic effect in glossy satires like *The Girl Can't Help It* (1956) and *Will Success Spoil Rock Hunter?* (1957).

While Mansfield's bubblegum burlesque was enjoyable, Britain's blonde bombshell, the down-to-earth **Diana Dors**, was easier to identify with. With an end-of-the-pier sauciness – in

one notorious incident she cheerfully stripped off down to a mink bikini while riding a gondola in Venice – Dors could also turn her hand to serious drama, as seen in the gritty *Yield To The Night* (1956), in which, as Ruth Ellis, the last woman to be hanged for murder in the UK, she gives a powerhouse performance, stripped of make-up and dressed in a shapeless prison gown.

Meanwhile, a pouting, tousle-haired wild child named **Brigitte Bardot** was shaking up staid postwar France with her sexually potent performance in Roger Vadim's *Et Dieu… créa*

Smart blonde Judy Holliday in *Born Yesterday* (1950)

la femme (*And Woman… Was Created*, 1956). The original sex kitten, uninhibited and unapologetic, her liberated persona had a huge influence on the sexual revolution of the 1960s, not only in her home country, but also around the world.

For flat-chested brunettes, salvation came in the form of the young **Audrey Hepburn**

Brigitte Bardot: the original sex kitten

(see Icons), who blew audiences away with her gamine performance as a princess slumming it with Gregory Peck in the delightful *Roman Holiday* (1953). With her short, rat-nibbled fringe and easy elegance, she represented a different kind of 1950s woman: youthful, independent and brainy, a free spirit before her time. Another tomboy, **Doris Day** (see Icons), began the decade with a typically athletic and comically perfect turn in *Calamity Jane* (1953), and ended it – after a range of intriguing roles in movies as different as the searing biopic *Love Me Or Leave Me* (1955) and Hitchcock's *The Man Who Knew Too Much* (1956) – battling with **Rock Hudson** in *Pillow Talk* (1959; see Canon), the first of their funny, sophisticated "sex comedies".

Older women were not entirely written out of the picture, either, particularly in the work of director **Douglas Sirk** (see Icons). Tapping into postwar American angst with his edgy, colour-saturated melodramas, Sirk used swelling music, stylized sets and exciting camera work to mine profound depths of despair and loss. **Jane Wyman**, in her early 40s, fell hard for a younger Rock Hudson in Sirk's *Magnificent Obsession* (1954) and *All That Heaven Allows* (1955), while the heartbreaking maternal melodrama *Imitation Of Life* (1959; see Canon), which boldly brought the painful "race issue" to a pre-civil rights audience, saw a powerhouse performance from **Lana Turner** as a flawed single parent. Turner, a sexy starlet of the 1940s who was now pushing 40, also played a troubled single mother with a teenage daughter in the far inferior *Peyton Place* (1957), based on

Not so dumb after all: the triumph of Judy Holliday

"You have to be smart to play a dumb blonde over and over and keep the audience's attention." – Judy Holliday

Having won acclaim as a successful comic actress on Broadway, and following a scene-stealing turn in the Katharine Hepburn-Spencer Tracy comedy *Adam's Rib* (1949), **Judy Holliday** proved herself to be the funniest, smartest dumb blonde of them all. With her virtuoso performance as the gangster's moll Billie Dawn in George Cukor's *Born Yesterday* (1950) – all kooky vocal styling and clownish physical presence – the Jewish New Yorker with a genius-rated IQ shook up Hollywood by winning the Best Actress Oscar over favourites Bette Davis (*All About Eve*) and Gloria Swanson (*Sunset Blvd.*). After another nuanced comedy performance in Cukor's *The Marrying Kind* (1952), at the height of America's anti-Communist hysteria, Holliday was interrogated, like many film people, by the House Un-American Activities Committee. Her intentionally baffling responses to questioning about her affiliations were typical examples of just how smart playing dumb could be.

Senator: Have you ever on any other occasion sent a telegram protesting or asking for protection for certain groups?

Holliday: I once sent a telegram to Washington about something, I think probably to our senator, but I don't know just what.

Senator: Which senator?

Holliday: Whoever it was, or maybe it was the President. I do remember it was something about protesting something by telegram to Washington.

Senator: About what? What were you protesting about?

Holliday: I don't know.

Senator: What was the subject of the telegram?

Holliday: I don't know.

Holliday was eventually cleared of any connection with Communist organizations. The stigma stuck, however, and though she continued to do fine work in the theatre, her movie career faltered. Returning to movies sporadically in *It Should Happen To You* (1954), *The Solid Gold Cadillac* (1956) and *Bells Are Ringing* (1960), she lit up the screen each time. Judy Holliday died of cancer in 1965, aged just 43.

Grace Metalious's salacious blockbusting novel. Meanwhile, at the age of 51, Rosalind Russell, who throughout the 1930s and 40s had bustled around in business suits playing acerbic career girls, barnstormed her way through the vivacious *Auntie Mame* (1958), one of her best-known roles, while the hugely successful *All About Eve* – nominated for fourteen Oscars and winning six – had Bette Davis at her peak as a 40-year-old Broadway star with a fondness for whiskey.

In 1950 British-born actress **Ida Lupino**, who had specialized in playing brittle, down-on-their-luck broads in hard-boiled Warner Bros movies like *They Drive By Night* (1940), *High Sierra* (1941) and *The Man I Love* (1947), formed her own production company and set to directing. Spare, dark, almost *film noir*, her low-budget movies dealt with sensitive subjects including rape (*Outrage*, 1950), bigamy (*The Bigamist*, 1953, in which she also co-stars) and serial killers (*The Hitch-hiker*, 1953), and offered no easy solutions. As a female movie director, sitting in a director's chair that read "Mother of Us All", Lupino was a ground-breaker and an inspiration to the generations that followed.

All About Eve
dir Joseph L. Mankiewicz, 1950, US, 138m, b/w

A sharp, eminently quotable black comedy about female friendship, competitiveness and ageing. Bette Davis was born to play the jaded Broadway star Margo Channing, who, despite her barbed cynicism ("Fasten your seat belts. It's going to be a bumpy night!"), is won over by sweet, innocent fan Eve Harrington (Anne Baxter). Deliciously nasty, with Davis and her co-stars at their peak.

Born Yesterday
dir George Cukor, 1950, US, 103m, b/w

Cukor showcases the talents of the marvellous Judy Holliday, who won an Oscar for her portrayal of Billie Dawn, the not-as-dumb-as-she-looks blonde who takes umbrage when her millionaire boyfriend (Broderick Crawford) arranges for her to be lady-fied.

High Society
dir Charles Walters, 1956, US, 107m

A delightful musical remake of *The Philadelphia Story* (1940). Glacial 1950s blonde Grace Kelly plays Tracy, who, set to marry dull George (John Lund), must first fend off her suave ex-husband, the songwriter C.K. Dexter-Haven (Bing Crosby), as well as New York gossip reporter Mike (Frank Sinatra), who arrives with wisecracking photographer Liz (Celeste Holm) to cover the society wedding of the year. Sharp comedy, desirable sets, fabulous songs and gorgeous gowns – pure joy.

Yield To The Night
dir Lee Thompson, 1956, UK, 99m, b/w

Fictionalizing the real-life case of Ruth Ellis, the last woman to be hanged in the UK, this is a gritty, genuinely harrowing account of her last days in prison. Diana Dors, stripped of all glamour, is a revelation in this difficult role, appearing at once coolly unrepentant and awkwardly vulnerable while waiting for her death sentence.

Funny Face
dir Stanley Donen, 1957, US, 103m

One of the chicest musicals ever, with gorgeous Audrey Hepburn utterly enchanting as a bookish beatnik who is made over as a couture model by fashion photographer Dick Avery (Fred Astaire). Exquisite Givenchy frocks, smart Gershwin songs and smooth-as-butter choreography – it's all just too, too divine.

The Pajama Game
dir George Abbott and Stanley Donen, 1957, US, 101m

Based on the joyous Broadway musical with a left-wing message, *The Pajama Game* has Doris Day at the peak of her powers, giving a typically gutsy performance as a singing, dancing union rep who falls in love with her boss.

The Three Faces Of Eve
dir Nunnally Johnson, 1957, US, 91m, b/w

Schizophrenia Hollywood-style: a melodrama given a portentous edge by being based on a true story. Though the medical angle looks rather hokey nowadays, the young – and then relatively unknown – Joanne Woodward is just astonishing as the woman battling with three personalities.

Auntie Mame
dir Morton Da Costa, 1958, US, 143m

Rosalind Russell sparkles her way through this glossy, nicely written comedy as the effervescent flapper raising her orphaned nephew – a role she had already made her own on Broadway. Colourful, kinetic and heart-warming, with some stupendous gowns designed by top costumier Orry-Kelly.

The 1960s: kitchen sinks and go-go boots

The so-called Swinging Sixties, the decade that brought us hippies, civil rights, feminism, free love and gay rights, came up with very few films made with women in mind, and even fewer that women loved. Hollywood was in a crisis: as many in the film business had feared, TV, which had snuck its way onto the scene in the 1950s, had polished up its act and was draining away movie audiences. Filmmakers made an effort to define cinema as high art (in contrast to "vulgar," "commercial" television), producing historical **prestige movies** like *Doctor Zhivago* (1965) – which, adapted from Boris Pasternak's Nobel prize-winning novel, was panned by the critics and loved by the public – and the phenomenally expensive, and phenomenally long, *Cleopatra* (1963), which got as much publicity for the fiery off-screen love affair between Elizabeth Taylor and Richard Burton as for its high-camp, epic storytelling. These movies were popular, but hardly reflected the exciting times. In Britain, meanwhile, the gritty **kitchen sink dramas** that had revolutionized the nation's middle-class theatre world found their way to the big screen. Populated by "angry young men" busting to break free from their social restraints, they may have ripped apart the complacent attitudes of a class-bound society, but held little delight for female audiences. The put-upon Ingrid (June Ritchie) in *A Kind Of Loving* (1962), who complained, "It's *rotten* being a girl sometimes," just about summed it up. At least the *film noirs* of the 1940s, which also revolved around the plight of damaged and frustrated male protagonists, had their fascinating femmes fatales – films like *Saturday Night And Sunday Morning* (1960) and *Billy Liar* (1963), on the other hand, had a misogynist streak, portraying women as downtrodden, avaricious and disposable.

The epic romance of *Doctor Zhivago* (1965)

Exceptions included the ground-breaking *Cathy Come Home* (Tony Garnett and Ken Loach, 1966), a film which started life as a BBC TV play and which, using documentary vox pops, improvisation and inexperienced actors, dealt with the issue of homelessness in Britain. Resulting in the founding of the housing charity Shelter, it also worked as a heart-rending maternal melodrama, with an outstanding performance from Carol White as the tragic young mother.

At the other end of the spectrum, *Dr No* (1962) introduced movie audiences to the suave international spy James Bond, and – with Ursula Andress emerging from the sea as Honey Ryder, wearing only a bikini and a strap-on dagger – to the **Bond girl**. Sexy and sexually liberated, these girls could have their cake and eat it too: they were adored, if slightly feared, by men, while female audiences could find all sorts of appeal in this parade of witty villainesses and adventuresses. From Tatiana Romanova (Daniela Bianchi), the Soviet spy in *From Russia With Love* (1963), to Pussy Galore (Honor Blackman), the husky-voiced pilot in *Goldfinger* (1964), all the best 1960s Bond girls were self-assured and independent, instrumental in helping Mr Bond save the day. The decade even had its own female Bond with the offbeat, very Swinging Sixties *Modesty Blaise* (1966). Roger Vadim's sci-fi fantasy *Barbarella* (1968), meanwhile, was just as camp and even saucier, relying on a lot of sex-kittenish pouting from a young, catsuit-clad **Jane Fonda** (see Icons).

The camp cavalcade continued with *Whatever Happened To Baby Jane?* (1962), which brought the two cat-fighting Hollywood divas **Bette Davis** and **Joan Crawford** together to poke nasty fun at their own star images. In general, however, older women got short shrift in this youth-obsessed decade. Even Mrs Robinson

(Anne Bancroft) in *The Graduate* (1967), while undoubtedly foxy, is ultimately sad and manipulative, representing all that is rotten in the older generation. **Audrey Hepburn**, however, grew up gracefully in *Breakfast At Tiffany's* (1961; see Canon) and *Charade* (1963), before going on to play the inimitable Eliza Doolittle in *My Fair Lady* (1964). Marilyn Monroe, too, gave her most mature, and moving, performance as divorcee Roslyn in *The Misfits* (1961). It was to be her last; she died of an overdose a year later.

That Touch Of Mink
dir Delbert Mann, 1962, US, 99m

A classic Sixties sex comedy in which the inimitable Doris Day battles with Cary Grant's roguish, and greying, lothario after his Rolls Royce splatters her with mud. Fizzy fun, with both stars showing no sign of losing their touch.

Whatever Happened To Baby Jane?
dir Robert Aldrich, 1962, US, 133m, b/w

Bette Davis and Joan Crawford go head-to-head in this melodramatic horror movie about two fading starlet sisters living a torturous life together in their creepy Gothic mansion. Full of iconic moments (the rat on the tray, for example), it stays just this side of pantomime due to the grand performances of its stars and the fascinating use of real footage from their early movies.

Doctor Zhivago
dir David Lean, 1965, US, 193m

Omar Sharif became an instant heart-throb with his portrayal of the soulful Yuri Zhivago, torn between his mistress Lara (Julie Christie) and his wife (Geraldine Chaplin), in this colossal, and very snowy, romantic epic set against the Russian Civil War. Audiences adored it.

Modesty Blaise
dir Joseph Losey, 1966, UK, 119m

Fab op-art spy thriller inspired by a British comic strip. Played by the sultry Italian actress Monica Vitti – the darling of Italian neorealist director Michelangelo Antonioni – super-spy Blaise had not only some of the grooviest outfits, and hairstyles, of the decade, but also her own sexy sidekick, the beautiful 1960s icon Terence Stamp.

Funny Girl
dir William Wyler, 1968, US, 151m

Although Omar Sharif co-stars, Barbra Streisand, who had played the role on Broadway, dominates this biopic about the ugly duckling vaudeville comedienne Fanny Brice. Her first film role, it's a gutsy, Oscar-winning performance (she tied with Katharine Hepburn for *The Lion In Winter*), which made Babs an instant star.

The 1970s: feminism enters the fray

The 1970s was an exciting time in Hollywood. The collapse of the old studio system and the relaxation of censorship laws, along with a feeling of angry disillusionment in the light of the Vietnam War and a string of political scandals, led to a huge **creative renaissance**. In came the new wave of young, mostly male, film-school-educated directors – Francis Ford Coppola, Steven Spielberg, William Friedkin, George Lucas, Alan J. Pakula, Martin Scorsese – who, using naturalistic acting, hand-held cameras, nervy editing and pop music scores, engaged, directly or subtly, with political issues. The influence of **feminism** was pervasive. While ex-sex symbol **Jane Fonda** discovered Women's Lib, faced the press with Black Power salutes and hung out with the Vietcong, the boy wonder

Feminist firebrand Jane Fonda in *Klute* (1971)

New World films

New World Pictures (1971–83), masterminded by B-movie director Roger Corman, launched the careers of household-name directors like Jonathan Demme, John Sayles and Joe Dante. The company was also notable for involving women at every level, including writer-directors like Stephanie Rothman and Barbara Peeters, who made their movies with female audiences in mind and, unlike their male colleagues, never achieved real success in the mainstream. New World unashamedly produced "exploitation" pictures – low-budget, subversive movies that used parody, sly humour, sex, violence and cheap sci-fi to titillate, poke fun and get across anti-establishment ideals – and when directed by women, they had a definite feminist slant. Nurses in skimpy uniforms, bad girls on the run, female vampires, convicts, bikers – all of them had audacity, verve and guts. These women were powerful, frightening, and more than able to play the guys at their own game.

Stephanie Rothman brought her feminist sensibility to New World's commercially successful and parodic *The Student Nurses* (1970) and the cult hit *The Velvet Vampire* (1971), a lesbian vampire movie, before forming her own production company, Dimension Pictures, with her husband. She then directed and co-wrote *Terminal Island* (1973), in which a group of abused women in a fictional penal colony turn the tables and create a utopian community. By the mid-1970s, however, Rothman had disappeared from the movies. **Barbara Peeters** directed, amongst others, the New World revenge movie *Bury Me An Angel* (1972), in which tough biker girl Dag (Dixie Peabody), surrounded by fawning male sidekicks, seeks out the man who killed her brother. In the 80s she turned to TV directing, but like Rothman, has since disappeared from the scene.

directors were also addressing gender issues in their own, at times clumsy, ways. Pakula made the feminist-tinged *noir Klute* (1971), starring Fonda in a tough new incarnation, while Peter Bogdanovich gave screwball a modern twist with Barbra Streisand in *What's Up Doc?* (1972), Scorsese created a gritty fairy tale with *Alice Doesn't Live Here Anymore* (1974; see Canon), and liberal filmmaker Martin Ritt brought his left-wing consciousness to *Norma Rae* (1979), the movie that catapulted feisty **Sally Field** into the limelight. Among women filmmakers making interesting work on the fringes, film star/stage actress **Barbara Loden** wrote, directed and starred in the challenging, in her words "anti-movie", *Wanda* (1971).

Spielberg's *Jaws* (1975) and Lucas's *Star Wars* (1977) marked the arrival of the "blockbusters", huge-event films filled with special effects and boosted by massive publicity campaigns; at the other end of the spectrum, small independent movies, often doing the rounds of independent festivals, brought women directors centre stage. In the cheapo Z-movie "exploitation" genre, for example, a breed of huge, scary females – often taking violent revenge on the men who had mistreated them – titillated and terrified the hell out of men and gave women a delighted laugh.

Mainstream successes like *Love Story* (1970), *The Way We Were* (1973; see Canon), *The Turning Point* (1977) and *An Unmarried Woman* (1978), which engaged with modern women's dilemmas while using traditional weepie/romantic comedy forms, were early examples of the chick flick genre as we now know it; meanwhile, the backlash started, with popular movies like *Kramer Vs Kramer* (1979) – which gave Meryl

Streep her first major role – showing women being punished for wanting more than their lot.

Love Story
dir Arthur Hiller, 1970, US, 99m

The grandmother of the modern terminal illness weepie, starring Ryan O'Neal as the WASP and Ali MacGraw as the stroppy girl from the wrong side of the tracks. You'll love it or hate it – either way it's hard, nowadays, to take the infamous "Love means never having to say you're sorry" line seriously.

Wanda
dir Barbara Loden, 1971, US, 102m

A bleak, low-budget movie in which the glamorous Barbara Loden (who also directed and wrote) plays against type as white-trash wife and mother Wanda, who abandons her family and takes to the road, hooking up with a sleazy bank robber and joining him in his drifter's life. The film's pared down, realist style has something of the European art cinema about it, and it certainly raised questions about the plight of poor, uneducated women in America.

What's Up, Doc?
dir Peter Bogdanovich, 1972, US, 94m

Screwball Seventies-style. Barbra Streisand is fabulous, funny and sexy as the off-the-wall kook hounding a hapless, bespectacled musicologist (Ryan O'Neal), and causing havoc in her wake.

The Turning Point
dir Herbert Ross, 1977, US, 119m

Ballet, friendship, motherhood, ambition, regrets – *The Turning Point* has all the ingredients of a prime chick flick, plus Mikhail Baryshnikov as the soulful love interest. Shirley MacLaine and Anne Bancroft are great as the old rivals reflecting on their past.

An Unmarried Woman
dir Paul Mazursky, 1978, US, 130m

This is typical of the male-directed, feminist-inspired dramas of the era, with Jill Clayburgh as a new divorcee

struggling to find herself. The palatable face of Women's Lib, it plays out a bit like a Woody Allen movie.

Norma Rae
dir Martin Ritt, 1979, US, 110m

Before *Silkwood, Erin Brockovich* or *North Country,* came this terrific drama, based on the struggles of real-life textile worker Crystal Lee Sutton to get her Alabama cotton mill unionized. Sally Field, who won an Oscar for her performance, pulls out all the stops as the working-class woman who has the guts to put her neck on the line while struggling to break free from the constraints of being a wife and mother.

The 1980s: working girls

While Rocky, Rambo and Arnie, along with some super-tough female heroines (Sarah Connor in *The Terminator*, 1984; Lieutenant Ripley in *Aliens*, 1986) were upping the testosterone level a notch in Hollywood, the 1980s was also the decade in which the **chick flick** as we currently know it – including smart rom-coms, post-feminist screwballs and tear-drenched melodramas – took shape. Hollywood saw a boom time for women behind the scenes, writing, directing and producing. In 1980 **Sherry Lansing** became Hollywood's first female president of an existing major studio (20th Century-Fox) – and resigned two years later to go independent. She went on to produce two of the biggest movies of the decade, both of them complex and women-centred: *Fatal Attraction* (1987), in which Glenn Close plays, with psychopathic relish, a woman scorned, and *The Accused* (1988), which won **Jodie Foster** (see Icons) an Oscar for her uncompromising performance as the working-class rape victim who dares to fight back. Meanwhile, New

Diane Keaton has it all in *Baby Boom* (1987)

World Pictures graduate (see p.28) **Gale Anne Hurd** also formed her own production company, bringing us the decade's defining sci-fi fantasies, *The Terminator* – which she also wrote – and *Aliens*, with their iconic action heroines. Another chick flick in disguise, the feminist chiller *Blue Steel* (1990; see Canon), was offered by director **Kathryn Bigelow**, who had already ventured into dangerous territory with her sexy vampire movie *Near Dark* (1987).

Other new women directors making fresh, interesting work included Penelope Spheeris (1981's indie-punk documentary *The Decline Of Western Civilization*) and Amy Heckerling (1982's cult teen movie *Fast Times At Ridgemont High* and the likeable baby comedy *Look Who's Talking*, 1989). Joyce Chopra's *Smooth Talk* (1985) took an unsettling look at an adolescent girl's sexual awakening and launched the quirky Laura Dern on her way towards indie stardom, while

Donna Deitch produced a touching, if slow-moving, lesbian love affair, complete with Patsy Cline soundtrack, in *Desert Hearts* (1985). **Patricia Rozema**, who went on to direct the punchy Jane Austen adaptation *Mansfield Park* in 1999, offered a stunning debut with the original, ethereal *I've Heard The Mermaids Singing* (1987), but it was **Susan Seidelman** (see Icons), with her smash-hit female fantasy *Desperately Seeking Susan* (1985; see Canon), who seemed most set for long-term success. By the end of the decade, however, after a handful of halfhearted semi-flops, her career had lost energy, and the chick flick genre had lost a great talent. **Barbra Streisand** (see Icons), too, had something of a struggle on her hands when, fulfilling a long-held ambition, she donned her director's hat (and producer's, co-writer's, star's and composer's hats) to make *Yentl* (1983). A worthy musical about a young Jewish girl who disguises herself as a boy in order to study the Talmud, the film won some accolades, but Babs herself was mocked, her ambition lambasted as egotism. New York novelist **Nora Ephron** (see Icons) did better, penning *Silkwood* (1983), *Heartburn* (1986) — based on her auto-biographical novel — and the less successful *Cookie* (1989, for Susan Seidelman), before hitting pay dirt with *When Harry Met Sally...* (1989; see Canon), the rom-com of the decade, and one that has left its mark on practically every romantic comedy since.

While movies like *An Officer And A Gentleman* (1982) and *The Witches Of Eastwick* (1987) presented us with hackneyed male fantasies dressed up as chick flicks, the "Greed is Good" decade did spawn its very own genuine chick flick sub-genre: the **working girl comedy**. Reminiscent of the sparky movies of the 1940s, in which quick-witted career women in colossal shoulder pads hunted for love or sparred with cads, the new-style comedies showed women – like their forebears still cutting a dash in dapper shoulder

Return of the weepies, blockbuster-style: Steven Spielberg's *The Color Purple* (1985)

pads – grappling with ambition, glass ceilings, male chauvinist pigs (sometimes, as in 1988's *Working Girl*, in female form) and, in a new twist, unexpected broodiness. For this is also the decade when **babies** got big, with comedies like *Three Men And A Baby* (1987), *Look Who's Talking* (1989) and, the chickiest flick of the brood, *Baby Boom* (1987), in which a driven career woman (a sprightly performance from **Diane Keaton**; see Icons) realizes that she can, indeed, Have It All.

In addition, the 1980s gave us a fine crop of enduring three-hankie **weepies**, including *Sophie's Choice* (1982), *Terms Of Endearment* (1983; see Canon), *The Color Purple* (1985) and *Beaches* (1988; see Canon) brought the director-producer team **Merchant Ivory** centre stage with their lush adaptation of E.M. Forster's *A Room With A View* (1985); and had a generation of girls singing into their hairbrushes with musical **dance movies** *Fame* (1980), *Flashdance* (1983) and, best of all, *Dirty Dancing* (1987; see Canon).

Nine To Five
dir Colin Higgins, 1980, US, 110m

Seminal "You go girl!" 1980s comedy, with three frustrated secretaries (Jane Fonda, Lily Tomlin and Dolly Parton, effervescent in her first movie role) uniting to turn the tables on their chauvinist boss. With its chirpy theme song (courtesy of Dolly), whacky fantasy sequences and three-cheers ending, this is classic Eighties stuff.

A Room With A View
dir James Ivory, 1985, UK, 117m

Merchant Ivory's sumptuous adaptation of E.M. Forster's novel launched the ongoing craze for period dramas based on literary works – some of which ended up being better than others. This is a delight, with the perfectly Edwardian-looking Helena Bonham Carter, aroused by the glorious Tuscan countryside, having to choose between the attentions of bohemian George (Julian Sands) and her uptight fiancé (Daniel Day-Lewis). Poor thing.

I've Heard The Mermaids Singing
dir Patricia Rozema, 1987, Can, 83m

A dreamy and sweet-natured indie movie about a scatty fantasist who falls in love with her glamorous female boss and inadvertently gets involved in art fraud. Quirky and original, with an endearing central figure in Polly (Sheila McCarthy).

Moonstruck
dir Norman Jewison, 1987, US, 102m

This nicely crafted, old-fashioned romance won heaps of audience affection and three Oscars, including one for Cher, splendid as a late-30s widow who falls, despite herself, for her dull fiancé's impulsive younger brother (Nicolas Cage). It's all set in a highly romanticized Italian-American Brooklyn, so expect lots of checked tablecloths, bowls of steaming spaghetti, and, of course, a big, fat moon.

Working Girl
dir Mike Nichols, 1988, US, 113m

Though the main preoccupation – how to get ahead in a man's world while still staying "feminine" – is dated, there's still much to like about this witty, office-based comedy, a manifesto for undervalued secretaries the world over. Melanie Griffith gives one of her best performances as ambitious secretary Tess, who has to deal not only with her sexist male colleagues, but also her evil female boss (Sigourney Weaver, marvelously camp). Harrison Ford provides love interest.

The 1990s: chick flick power

By the early Nineties everyone knew what a chick flick was, and everyone knew that they made good money. This was a fruitful and productive time for women working in the movies, both in the independent sector and in the mainstream. From Australian director **Jane**

Campion's triumphant, poetic *The Piano* (1993; see Canon) to Amy Heckerling's super-smart teen movie *Clueless* (1995; see Canon), chick flicks helmed by women made strong inroads into any genre you care to imagine. Martha Coolidge turned clichés upside down in her unsettling saga of burgeoning sexuality, *Rambling Rose* (1991), Maggie Greenwald reappraised the Western from a female point of view in *The Ballad Of Little Jo* (1993), Nicole Holofcener came up with a sharply witty New York comedy of manners in *Walking And Talking* (1996), and Sofia Coppola made a stunning debut with the otherwordly chiller *The Virgin Suicides* (1999). Literary works provided rich pickings: British direc-

Awash with emotion: *Titanic* (1997)

tor Sally Potter gave us a strange and beautiful Virginia Woolf adaptation with *Orlando* (1992), starring arthouse darling Tilda Swinton; Gillian Armstrong took Louisa May Alcott to the multiplexes with her star-studded *Little Women* (1994); and Patricia Rozema grappled successfully with Jane Austen's complex novel *Mansfield Park* (1999)– for more on these, see "Women's books and women's movies", p.207.

Black and Asian women also came to the fore. In the US Julie Dash gave us the mythic *Daughters Of The Dust* (1991) and Mira Nair the inter-racial love story *Mississippi Masala* (1991), while in the UK, *Bhaji On The Beach* (1993) was the first of young Asian Londoner **Gurinder Chadha**'s (see Icons) exuberant takes on culture,

age, race and gender clashes in Anglo-Indian communities. Back in Hollywood, screenwriter Nora Ephron, following her massive success with *When Harry Met Sally...*, turned to directing with *Sleepless In Seattle* (1993) and *You've Got Mail* (1998). Both sat comfortably in the *When Harry...* mould, offering a smart, modern twist on classic romances (1957's *An Affair To Remember* and the sweet comedy *The Shop Around The Corner,* 1940, respectively). With their lovable, ditzy *Sally* clones, they also backed angelic-faced actress **Meg Ryan** (see Icons) into a corner – which, with Jane Campion's help, she was to dramatically reject in the next decade.

Though the sweeping romance *The English Patient* (1996) seemed set to dominate the 1990s, it was quickly trumped by James Cameron's monumental *Titanic* (1997; see Canon), which used a passionate love affair to underpin the story of the doomed ship and became the biggest box office hit ever. The decade also gave us the seminal chick flick *Pretty Woman* (1990) – which shot a gawky, toothy girl from Smyrna, Georgia to superstardom – the surprise hit *Ghost* (1990), and the ultimate gal buddy movie, *Thelma & Louise* (1991). After the baby boom of the 1980s, suddenly **nuptials** were in the air, starting with Richard Curtis's phenomenal success *Four Weddings And A Funeral* (1993), a wry display of modern English mores which was credited with saving the British film industry – and certainly provided a shot in the arm for British actor **Hugh Grant** (see Icons). Australian director P.J. Hogan presented us with two more ambivalent, and more interesting, views of matrimony with the drily humorous *Muriel's Wedding* (1994) and *My Best Friend's Wedding* (1997), one of **Julia Roberts**'s best, most self-deprecating roles. Roberts (see Icons) turned up again, gently poking fun at herself and her own "intimacy issues", in *Runaway Bride* (1999), which reunited the *Pretty Woman* dream team of Roberts, Richard Gere and Hector Elizondo. Meanwhile, as usual, some chick flicks came in heavy disguise – *The Silence Of The Lambs* (1990; see Canon), for example, which was perhaps Jodie Foster's finest hour, or even *Jackie Brown* (1997), in which maverick director Quentin Tarantino used funky 1970s blaxploitation icon Pam Grier to reintroduce us to the delights of a tough girl with a gun. Gal–pal movies *Fried Green Tomatoes At The Whistle Stop Café* (1991), *Boys On The Side* (1995) and *The Truth About Cats & Dogs* (1996) were on more familiar territory.

With Merchant Ivory still at the top of their game with *Howards End* (1991) and *The Remains*

Of The Day (1993), the decade also went crazy for adaptations of **classic literature**: in addition to Armstrong's *Little Women*, Rozema's *Mansfield Park* and Potter's *Orlando*, we had Ang Lee's *Sense And Sensibility* (1995), scripted by British comedienne/actress Emma Thompson, Franco Zeffirelli's spare, naturalistic *Jane Eyre* (1995), and Gwyneth Paltrow showing off her impeccable English accent in the gauzy, sunny *Emma* (1996) and *Shakespeare In Love* (1998). For more on literary adaptations, see 'Women's books and women's movies', p.000.

Daughters Of The Dust
dir Julie Dash, 1991, US, 112m

Set in 1902, this lyrical drama follows the fortunes of a black Gullah family, living on a barrier island off the coast of South Carolina, who are planning to move to the mainland. Ambitious and arty, using Gullah dialect and mysterious symbolism, it never made the mainstream, but has its own haunting charm.

Fried Green Tomatoes At The Whistle Stop Café
dir Jon Avnet, 1991, US, 130m

Forming, with *Steel Magnolias* (1989; see Canon) and *Divine Secrets Of The Ya-Ya Sisterhood* (2002), a neat little trio of Deep South-set ensemble pieces, this bittersweet comedy drama benefits from four sterling actresses – Jessica Tandy, Kathy Bates, Mary Stuart Masterson and Mary-Louise Parker – whose intelligent performances prevent it from collapsing into pure slush.

The Ballad Of Little Jo
dir Maggie Greenwald, 1993, US, 121m

Forget Clint Eastwood's *Unforgiven* (1992) – this is a far more interesting reappraisal of the Western, scrutinizing the genre from a woman's point of view. In the mid-nineteenth century Josephine (Suzy Amis), rejected by her family after giving birth to an illegitimate baby, escapes West. Realizing she won't survive long as a single woman, she slashes her face, disguises herself as a man and renames herself Little Jo. Based on a true story, it's tough, compelling and moving stuff.

Bhaji On The Beach
dir Gurinder Chadha, 1993, UK, 101m

Chadha's breezy comedy-drama follows a mixed group of Indian women from Birmingham as they take a day out together in sunny Blackpool. This is essentially old-fashioned and warmhearted stuff, in which, despite all their differences, everyone comes to understand each other, and themselves, much better in the end.

Boys On The Side
dir Herbert Ross, 1995, US, 117m

The first in Drew Barrymore's long, and continuing, run in above-par chick flicks; this is a sub-*Thelma & Louise* gal-pal/road movie in which she takes to the road with Whoopi Goldberg and Mary-Louise Parker. Naturally they're all running from something, but can't run from themselves… It sounds corny, but there's a gritty, witty edge, and heartfelt performances from all the female leads.

The Truth About Cats & Dogs
dir Michael Lehmann, 1996, US, 97m

The wonderful comic actress Janeane Garofalo stars as a funny, self-deprecating and just slightly overweight radio host, who, when the gorgeous Ben Chaplin shows signs of interest in meeting her for real, persuades her beautiful friend Noelle (Uma Thurman) to take her place. A kind of female version of *Cyrano de Bergerac*, with a heart-warming "love yourself as you are" message.

Shakespeare In Love
dir John Madden, 1998, US, 123m

With a waggish script from Tom Stoppard, this combines bawdy comedy, literary adaptation and period drama in one fell, very original, swoop, turning the British passion for classic adaptations on its head. It's also a touching love story – Gwyneth Paltrow (as the cross-dressing Viola) and Joseph Fiennes (as the Bard) make an appealing couple.

The Virgin Suicides
dir Sofia Coppola, 1999, US, 97m

Coppola's haunting debut, about five gorgeous and slightly strange teenage sisters who arouse dangerous passions in their small Midwestern town. Set in the mid-1970s, it's a ravishing movie, and the performances, particularly from Kirsten Dunst as the sexually awakened Lux, linger in the memory.

Where next? 2000 and beyond

Although in Hollywood the genre was striding ahead with glossy comedies like *Miss Congeniality* (2000) – a klutzy FBI agent goes undercover as a beauty queen – and *Legally Blonde* (2001) – dumb blonde proves to be not so dumb after all – and gaining Academy Award kudos with the searing Julia Roberts vehicle *Erin Brockovich* (2000; see Canon) and Baz Luhrmann's eye-popping *Moulin Rouge!* (2001; see Canon), some of the most talked about chick flicks were small indeed. *You Can Count On Me* (2000; see Canon) caused a gentle storm at the independent festivals, while *My Big Fat Greek Wedding* (2001), put together on a shoestring by Greek-American stand-up comedienne Nia Vardalos, and *Bend It Like Beckham* (2002; see Canon), a small British movie about an Asian girl's love of football, were surprise smashes. Rave reviews around the world went to *Rabbit-Proof Fence* (2002) and *Whale Rider* (2002), both Antipodean girls' adventure stories with a heart. **Small films** often allowed big stars to play against type: Jennifer Aniston got frumpy in *The Good Girl* (2001), while goody-two-shoes Katie Holmes was a revelation as the stroppy punk in the delightful *Pieces Of April* (2003). Most dramatic of all was Meg Ryan's transformation from 1990s angel to mousy neurotic in Jane Campion's arresting *In The Cut* (2003; see Canon), a brave and beautiful film, which, though it won none of the accolades of

One of Katie Holmes's lesser-known outfits: *Pieces Of April* (2003)

The Piano, proved without doubt that Campion is still a force to contend with. With its delicate reworking of 1950s melodrama, the triumphant *Far From Heaven* (2002; see Canon) brought indie director Todd Haynes into the limelight, along with its star, Julianne Moore. The same year, Moore played another frustrated 1950s house-wife in *The Hours* (2002), which also starred Meryl Streep, and Nicole Kidman as a depressive Virginia Woolf. Even the presence of these great actresses couldn't save this dismal film, though it has to be appreciated for presenting us with not one but three woman-centred stories.

In **Britain**, *Four Weddings And A Funeral* and *Notting Hill* (1999) were followed by one of the highest-grossing chick flicks ever, *Bridget Jones's Diary* (2001; see Canon). The old "if it ain't broke don't fix it" formula applied to Richard Curtis's *Love Actually* (2003), a patchy romantic ensemble piece studded with stars, including Emma Thompson, Hugh Grant and Laura Linney; *Calendar Girls* (2003), which attempted to do for Women's Institute widows what *The Full Monty* did for male strippers; and *Pride & Prejudice* (2005), with golden girl Keira Knightley as Lizzie and Matthew Macfadyen doing a good job of living up to his predecessor Colin Firth as the sexy, brooding Mr Darcy. Director Gurinder Chadha followed *Bend It Like Beckham* with another take on Austen's novel, *Bride & Prejudice* (2004), which took the star-crossed lovers to Bollywood and back – it didn't have the originality of her previous film, however, nor of Mira Nair's rich *Monsoon Wedding* (2001), which it resembled.

Meanwhile, a growing love affair with all films **Far Eastern** brought us some fine chick flicks. The swordplay movie *Crouching Tiger, Hidden Dragon* (2000), with its inspiring action heroines and poignant love stories, was a massive crossover success, while Wong Kar-Wai's lusciously bittersweet *In The Mood For Love* (2000; see Canon) took romance to its extreme. 2005's *Memoirs Of A Geisha*, based on Arthur Golden's bestselling novel, is undeniably gorgeous, with a raft of fine Chinese stars including Gong Li and Zhang Ziyi (a controversial move, given that the book was set in Japan), but ultimately a little cold.

My Big Fat Greek Wedding
dir Joel Zwick, 2001, US/ Can, 95m

Comedienne Nia Vardalos's warmhearted, low-budget look at Greek-American culture is a makeover movie and a wedding movie rolled into one – a winning combination that made it the most profitable film of all time.

The Good Girl
dir Miguel Arteta, 2001, US/Ger/Neth, 93m

Low-key and a bit low-energy, but Jennifer Aniston's performance as Justine, a frumpy wife who gets swept away by high-maintenance Jake Gyllenhaal, is a revelation, and refreshingly the movie never goes for any easy answers.

Lovely & Amazing
dir Nicole Holofcener, 2001, US, 91m

Holofcener is one of the rising stars of the indie scene, producing smart contemporary comedies with a perceptive feminine slant. Here Jane (Brenda Blethyn), her two grown

Kick flicks, chick flick style: *Crouching Tiger, Hidden Dragon* (2000)

daughters (Emily Mortimer and Catherine Keener) and adopted 8-year-old Annie (Raven Goodwin) fret and bitch their way through a sharply observed, unsentimental and ultimately very moving account of family life, female insecurity and unexpected glimpses of love.

Monsoon Wedding
dir Mira Nair, 2001, US/It/Ger/Fr, 113m

Director Nair gives us an ebullient, visually stunning family melodrama revolving around a lavish Punjabi wedding. Shot in just thirty days, its riot of colour, music and passion appealed as much to Western audiences as Indian ones, and it set the bar high for an evolving sub-genre of ethnic wedding movies.

My Life Without Me (Mi vida sin mí)
dir Isabel Coixet, 2002, Sp/Can, 106m

A sweet, indie cancer movie, in which young mum Ann (the marvellous Sarah Polley) creates an urgent "To Do" list before she dies – which includes having an affair with an enigmatic stranger, played by Mark Ruffalo with his usual aplomb. Debbie Harry puts in a brilliantly grumpy turn as Ann's movie-loving mother.

Calendar Girls
dir Nigel Cole, 2003, UK/US, 108m

Featuring a raft of the nation's finest actresses – Helen Mirren, Julie Walters, Annette Crosbie, Celia Imrie, among others – this British comedy deals with ageing, friendship and sexism in the decidedly unseamy underbelly of the Women's Institute. Based on a true story, it could be a little braver, but three cheers anyway for making a funny feature film that pushes older women to the forefront, rather than shoving them to the back.

Pieces Of April
dir Peter Hedges, 2003, US, 80m

Katie Holmes, in the short period between playing drippy Joey in teen TV soap *Dawson's Creek* and slobbering over Tom Cruise, puts in a fantastic performance in this sharp, touching indie comedy. She shines as punky April, who invites her estranged family – including her difficult, dying mother (Patricia Clarkson) – to Thanksgiving dinner in her grimy New York apartment, and faces an increasingly frantic race against time when her oven packs in.

Miss Congeniality 2: Armed And Fabulous
dir John Pasquin, 2005, US, 115m

Sandra Bullock reprises her role as Gracie Hart, the tomboyish FBI agent turned beauty queen, this time tasting the high life in Vegas as she strives to save her beauty queen pal (Heather Burns) and promoter Stan Fields (William Shatner). The fun, as in the first film, is in the knowing post-feminist premise and Bullock's openhearted clowning – and here, her chemistry with her brutish female bodyguard, Sam (Regina King), offers another twist.

Opposite: *Thelma and Louise* (1991): an outlaw movie, buddy film and top chick flick. Susan Sarandon (left) and Geena Davis star.

The Canon: 50 essential chick flicks

The Top Ten

1 Thelma & Louise (1991)
At last. An outlaw movie where it's the girls who get to don the stetsons, sling the guns and drive around in a convertible looking cool. Beautiful to look at, with fabulous performances (and a super-sexy cameo from a young Brad Pitt), it's a heartachingly sweet buddy film to boot. (See p.131)

2 Brief Encounter (1945)
Melancholia is at its most elegant in this elegiac British classic. You might think you're going to laugh, but you'll actually end up crying. Buckets. (See p.64)

3 The Way We Were (1973)
Barbra Streisand and Robert Redford share their finest hour in this poignant tale of politics, passion and paradise lost. (See p.135)

4 Gone With The Wind (1939)
Scarlett O'Hara and Rhett Butler. That unforgettable theme tune. Sumptuous costumes. Glorious sets. Quite simply, three hours of pure, unadulterated joy.(See p.86)

5 Imitation Of Life (1959)
The most emotionally affecting of Douglas Sirk's mighty Technicolor melodramas: a delicious maelstrom of racial tension, doomed love, cold ambition and shocking betrayal. (See p.91)

6 The Piano (1993)
Ravishing and strange, Jane Campion's poetic movie about a woman's struggle to exist on her own terms is one of a kind. (See p.109)

7 Stella Dallas (1937)
This heartbreaking story of maternal sacrifice, based on a weepie bestselling novel, is a 1930s classic. The mighty Barbara Stanwyck is just phenomenal. (See p.127)

8 Breakfast At Tiffany's (1961)
Based on an original story by Truman Capote, this iconic movie is off the scale in terms of super-cool Sixties style, with Audrey Hepburn in Givenchy gowns, a love-lorn George Peppard, and a classic theme tune from Henry Mancini. (See p.57)

9 Now, Voyager (1942)
Bette Davis is at her most divine in this makeover story with a tear-jerking twist. It's a classic women's picture, boasting iconic visual motifs and one of the most memorable closing lines ever. (See p.106)

10 Bridget Jones's Diary (2001)
Gratifyingly true to the satirical spirit of the original novel, with brilliant performances and laugh-out-loud set pieces, this is perfectly pitched fun for kooky singletons and smug marrieds alike. (See p.61)

The Canon:
50 essential
chick flicks

It's a difficult endeavour, choosing the fifty top chick flicks. Not simply because of the wealth of wonderful movies out there, but also due to the fact that definitions can get tricky. The phenomenally popular *Four Weddings And A Funeral,* for example, with its focus on nuptials, friendships and true love, might seem upon first glance to be a chick flick worthy of inclusion. Closer inspection, however, reveals *Four Weddings* to be a rom-com, a comedy that's directed just as much towards men as it is to women. You might say the same of *When Harry Met Sally…,* which *is* included here – but while *Four Weddings* is basically all about Hugh, *Harry* gives us the delectable Meg in the rounded, credible, funny character that is Sally. That's the difference. All the movies chosen for inclusion – whether they're soft and fluffy, sharp and sassy, or even dark and bloody – abound in complex, brave, brilliant and funny women, from Bette Davis and Doris Day to Barbra Streisand and Jodie Foster. And they are, with the odd honourable exception (*Silence Of The Lambs,* perhaps?), all films directed primarily towards women. Which is not to say that the men in your life are going to tear their eyes out rather than watch them with you (though you might have a hard time dragging them along to see *Dirty Dancing*). *Thelma & Louise,* for example, is a favourite among many male moviegoers, while films like *Gone With The Wind* and *Brief Encounter* are out-and-out classics. There's even a Martin Scorsese movie in there!

Adam's Rib

dir George Cukor, 1949, US, 101m, b/w
cast Katharine Hepburn, Spencer Tracy, Judy Holliday,
Tom Ewell, David Wayne, Jean Hagen *cin* George Folsey
m Miklós Rózsa

Adam's Rib is the battle-of-the-sexes comedy par excellence, a sophisticated gem sparkling with smart repartee and sexual chemistry. The sixth of **Katharine Hepburn** (see Icons) and **Spencer Tracy**'s nine films together, it shows these real-life lovers at their peak: entirely at ease with their chalk-and-cheese attraction – her angular, WASPish beauty and his rumpled bar-room masculinity – relaxed, sexually compatible and very much in love. Written by their good friends **Ruth Gordon** and **Garson Kanin**, themselves a husband-and-wife writing team, the sparky, Oscar-nominated script is intimate and very real; at times, as the stars slip into tender, improvised banter, it feels almost as though we are eavesdropping on their true-life love affair.

Adam (Tracy) and Amanda (Hepburn) Bonner are lawyers working on opposite sides of the same case. Amanda, defending Doris (**Judy Holliday**), a wronged wife who shot and injured her husband (**Tom Ewell**) while he dallied with his floozy (**Jean Hagen**), uses all her wit and ingenuity to argue that men and women are equal, that marriage should be a partnership, and that the double standards governing male-female relationships should be ripped apart. Adam, meanwhile, defending the injured husband, becomes increasingly exasperated at her clever courtroom tactics. Their relationship is played out in equal part between the courtroom and the bedroom, and in each they flirt, canoodle, sulk, yell, bicker and weep their way towards imminent divorce.

George Cukor (see Icons), the great "women's director", was at his peak when working with the screen goddesses of classical Hollywood, and was particularly fond of Hepburn. The actress, in her early 40s when this film was made, never looked better, slinking around the courtroom displaying not only her razor-sharp intellect, but also her clotheshorse figure in stunning outfits by her favourite costume designer, **Walter Plunkett**. Hepburn, so often spiky, is as sexy and soft here as she is smart, displaying a warm physicality sometimes lacking in her other movies. The moment when Amanda, while screening a home movie for their dinner party guests, crawls across the floor and nuzzles her head on her sulky husband's lap before quietly returning to her place is deliciously natural and unguarded. Cukor, who was openly, if discreetly, homosexual, must also have had a lot of fun with Kip (**David Wayne**), a bitchy client of Amanda's who, despite professing to be in love with her, is patently gay (and, as a songwriter, probably modelled on Cole Porter). And the scene in which Amanda urges the jury to imagine Holliday and Hagan as men, before the two women morph into drag – complete with wide ties and handlebar moustaches – adds another quirky Cukorian note.

Look out for the young Judy Holliday, who, with her clownish physical presence and bruised toughness brings sweetness and real depth to the role of Doris, the gun-happy wife. As yet little noticed in Hollywood, the rising stage actress was nonetheless adored by Cukor, Tracy and Hepburn, who backed her vigorously, insisting her part be beefed up. As a result, and with Hepburn's influence, she won the lead in Cukor's *Born Yesterday* (1950), a career-defining and Oscar-winning role for this most brilliant of dumb blondes.

An Affair To Remember

dir Leo McCarey, 1957, US, 115m
cast Cary Grant, Deborah Kerr, Cathleen Nesbitt, Richard Denning, Neva Patterson, Robert Q. Lewis *cin* Milton Krasner *m* Hugo Friedhofer

"Men never get this movie!", wails Rosie O'Donnell to Meg Ryan in an intertextual chick flick moment during *Sleepless In Seattle* (1993). The movie in question is *An Affair To Remember*, an engaging hybrid of sophisticated comedy and unabashed weepie. Nickie Ferrante, suave millionaire playboy (the kind of role **Cary Grant** was born for), and coolheaded Terry (**Deborah Kerr**) meet on an ocean liner, and, although she is at first immune to his charms, they start a gentle affair. Unfortunately, in the real world

Cary Grant and Deborah Kerr find the nearest thing to Heaven

neither of them is single, and neither leads lives that they are particularly proud of. Once they hit shore, and their charmed affair has to end, they vow to sort themselves out and, if they still feel the same about each other, to meet in six months' time at the top of the Empire State Building ("the nearest thing we have to heaven in New York"). Tragically, however, an accident befalls Terry on the way to their assignation, meaning she misses their date and, worse, is left paralysed... And so the tear-jerking starts, leading to a corker of a denouement that's milked for all it's worth – if not (whisper it) a little more than it's worth. Fortunately, by then you've been well and truly drawn in, and the film could get away with just about anything.

Even the most hardened cynic couldn't fail to be charmed by *Affair's* first half, which positively crackles with feisty, flirty sparring between the two leads. Kerr plays it sassy and confident, a perfect foil for Grant's easy charm. A sugary interlude where Nickie introduces Terry to his saintly grandmother, who lives in a kind of Arcadia on the French Riviera – cue granny expertly banging out the movie's emotional refrain on the piano, Terry singing along, dewy-eyed – sets off their affair in earnest, while also reminding them, as they leave granny's little slice of heaven to climb back aboard ship, that nothing precious and beautiful can last forever...

Back on the boat, the dialogue zips up a notch and feels delightfully real. By the time Nickie gulps, "I want to be worthy of asking you to marry me", and Terry counters in jumbled confusion, "That's just about the nicest thing anyone's ever said to me! Your voice cracked! Let me tell you in the morning! Marriage is a very serious step for a girl like me! … Do you like children?", you are rooting for the pair of them, these two imperfect people who have found each other and created their own little dream world.

Once Terry fails to make their date, the movie unashamedly shifts into schmaltz mode. Sacrilegious to say, but the wonderful Cary Grant is vaguely ridiculous as a struggling artist, moodily turning out heartbroken masterpieces in his garret, while Kerr, conducting bands of cutesy kiddy choirs from her wheelchair, seems to have lost some of her edge. But even so… Nickie waiting till midnight at the top of the Empire State Building, his hope fading with each new strike of the clock; Terry tossing and turning in fever, longing for her lost love – not to mention that humdinger of a finale – all add up to make this classic love story absolutely irresistible. Perhaps *Sleepless In Seattle*'s Tom Hanks has the last word when, aghast after hearing a tearful rundown of the plot, he declares: "That's a *chick's* movie!"

Alice Doesn't Live Here Anymore

dir **Martin Scorsese, 1974, US, 112m**
cast **Ellen Burstyn, Kris Kristofferson, Billy "Green" Bush, Diane Ladd, Alfred Lutter, Jodie Foster, Harvey Keitel** *cin* **Kent Wakeford**

Alice Doesn't Live Here Anymore tends to be usually ignored in discussions of **Martin Scorsese**'s work. Uneasily sandwiched between *Mean Streets* (1973) and *Taxi Driver* (1976), two of the director's most searing accounts of tortured masculinity, this sweetly affecting movie is, however, up there among his best. With its exhilarating camerawork and edgy dialogue, its classy soundtrack – Dolly Parton, T-Rex, George Gershwin among others – and flashes of dark humour, it is an energetic, spirited film that has a lot to say about dreams lost, longed for and refound.

Dreams lost and found for Ellen Burstyn as Alice

The audacious opening scene – young Alice at home in Monterey (a lurid orange dreamscape reminiscent of *The Wizard Of Oz*), with Alice Faye singing "You'll Never Know" on the soundtrack – sets the tone. "I can sing better than Alice Faye, I swear to Christ I can!", the girl vows, before starting to warble in a wavery, unremarkable voice. "You get in here before I beat the living daylights out of you!", bellows her mother. "And if they don't like it," Alice whispers, "they can blow it out their ass!" Suddenly the screen shrinks to a pinpoint and we are in Socorro (the Spanish for "help," interestingly), New Mexico, 25 years later. Mott the Hoople blasts onto the soundtrack, and Scorsese's feverish camera swoops into grown-up Alice's home. Battling an aggressive slob of a husband, Don (**Billy "Green" Bush**), and sparring affectionately with Tommy (**Alfred Lutter**), her smart-ass 11-year-old son, Alice's journey begins.

Alice (**Ellen Burstyn**) may be treated badly, but she is no victim. She refuses to submit to Don's abuse, confiding in her best friend that she could easily live without a man. And, very soon, she is left to discover if that is true. A hilarious road trip with Tommy ensues as Alice vows to get to Monterey to fulfil her long-held ambition to be a singer. She flees Phoenix, and a job singing in a bar, after her young lover, Ben (**Harvey Keitel**), turns out to be seriously bad news; in Tucson, she wearily settles for a waitressing job before hooking up with nature-loving rancher David (**Kris Kristofferson**), a big bear of a new man who, as Tommy chirrups gleefully, "makes his own ice cream!" So what now? Will Alice follow her dreams to Monterey, or let herself be waylaid by romance?

Burstyn won an Oscar for her remarkable performance, a breathy, vulnerable delivery interspersed with dry humour, petulance and gritty resolve. "Can't I have everything?", she retorts when David demands to know what she wants. A loving mother, Alice struggles with mothering, and, as much as she can be uptight, she can also be funny and free-spirited. She is also a woman's woman. The farewell scene with her best friend in Socorro, as they fantasize about how things might be if they could just drive off together (the trip that Thelma and Louise managed eighteen years later – but then, look how *they* ended up), is both moving and funny. She even comes to love Flo (**Diane Ladd**), the gum-snapping waitress with big hair and dirty mouth who gives her the advice that lies at the heart of the film – "Figure out what it is you want, and just jump in there with both feet."

Once Alice does figure out what she wants, we're delivered a finale so satisfying that it's hard not to join the diners in the café in their corny spontaneous applause. Not quite the fairy tale ending young Alice dreamed of, perhaps – but, even better, one rich in real-life possibilities.

Jodie Foster: rising star

Though **Jodie Foster** is generally remembered as having burst upon the movie world with her astonishing performance as Iris, the child prostitute in Martin Scorsese's *Taxi Driver*, she had actually worked with the director two years earlier, playing a key part in *Alice Doesn't Live Here Any More*. Wisecracking Audrey, Tommy's friend, who plays truant, drinks liquor and pronounces Tucson to be "weird capital of the world", was one of the young Foster's characteristically-mature-beyond-her-years tomboy roles, played with typical assurance by this talented child star.

As Good As It Gets

dir James L. Brooks, 1997, US, 138m
cast Jack Nicholson, Helen Hunt, Greg Kinnear, Cuba
Gooding Jr., Skeet Ulrich, Shirley Knight *cin* John Bailey
m Hans Zimmer

As Good As It Gets is true to its name: a pragmatic, hopeful and ultimately rather special movie, it convinces us that things can improve, people can change, and that each of us, with our foibles and flaws, can find love. Melvin (**Jack Nicholson**) is a romantic novelist, an abusive obsessive-compulsive who, when his neighbour, Simon (**Greg Kinnear**), is beaten up by burglars, is forced, to his disgust, to look after Simon's scruffy little dog. **Helen Hunt** plays Carol, the Brooklyn waitress who serves Melvin lunch each day. When she has to leave work to look after her sick son, Melvin so desperately needs her to serve his food as usual that he pays for full-time care and medical treatment for the boy. Thus begins a clumsy, faltering and deliciously real love-hate romance, through which, despite himself, Melvin stumbles his way to forming adult relationships.

Although it is often described as Nicholson's movie, what brings *As Good As It Gets* to the chick flick canon is Helen Hunt, who, previously best known for her award-winning role in the popular TV sitcom *Mad About You*, is terrific as lonely single mother Carol. Her level gaze, dry delivery and comic timing convey a straightness that scythes through Melvin's appalling, uncontrolled behaviour, and she's just as convincing whether angry, tender, confused or sad. A woman who shows empathy and compassion from the outset, Carol faces a more subtle, but no less profound, shift than Melvin: away from a focus on her son and towards a focus on herself, with all the pain that might entail. The third player in the love triangle (though it's perhaps more of a love square if you include Verdell, the dog) is Melvin's beleaguered gay neighbour, played by former TV chat show host Kinnear.

The actors are helped, of course, by **James L. Brooks**'s witty, intelligent script and confident direction. This was the third directorial/screenwriting movie outing for the TV comedy producer/writer (and deviser of *The Simpsons*), who had previously worked with Nicholson on 1983's five-hankie weepie *Terms Of Endearment* (see p.129) and created a comic gem with *Broadcast News* (1987). Melvin was a role just made for Nicholson, who gets to spit out venomous lines like: "People who talk in metaphors ought to shampoo my crotch." Hunt's range, meanwhile, can take her deftly from ultra-boundaried – "I am not going to sleep with you; I will never sleep with you ever. Ever. Not ever. I'm not kidding" – to the more hesitant, "You bother me. You're not ready, and you're too old to not be ready … But there were extraordinary kindnesses that did take place…".

What makes this film such a great chick flick is the simple truth that Carol, however lonely, is never going to settle for Melvin at his worst. When, however, we see him at his best, finally able to pay her "a compliment", as he puts it, and speaking some of the most gently romantic dialogue ever heard on screen, this sweet-hearted movie really couldn't get any better.

Beaches

dir Garry Marshall, 1988, US, 123m
cast Bette Midler, Barbara Hershey, John Heard, Spalding Gray, Grace Johnston, Mayim Bialik, Marcie Leeds *cin* Dante Spinotti *m* Georges Delerue

Chick flick maestro **Garry Marshall**, who also has *Pretty Woman* (1990), *Frankie and Johnny* (1991) and *Runaway Bride* (1999) to his name, consistently manages to stay on the right side of schmaltz, no matter how soppy his material. That said, he had his work cut out for him with *Beaches*, which tops its triple whammy of female friendship, mother love and terminal illness with an unabashedly weepie theme tune ("Wind Beneath My Wings") that has since become a karaoke favourite.

The movie follows the friendship between flamboyant Jewish entertainer CC (**Bette Midler**) and restrained WASP Hillary (**Barbara Hershey**), who first meet as young girls on the beach in Atlantic City. Young Hillary (**Marcie Leeds**), dressed in a pretty white frock, is snivelling because she's lost; CC (an uncannily

Midleresque **Mayim Bialik**) is smoking under the boardwalk, dolled up like some pint-sized showgirl. Within minutes the poor little rich girl is wowed by watching CC audition for a Hollywood scout – though, just a bit too loud, and a bit too pushy, she loses the gig to a pretty but vacuous "hand-walking queer" – and the two vow to remain friends. After years of keeping in touch only by letter, Hillary, now a top Stanford-educated lawyer, packs up and comes to New York, moving in with CC, who is still struggling to make it big. As the women's lives change over the years, so their relationship develops, weathering jealousy, long separations and bitter fights – until one day Hillary, now a single mother, starts to feel very, very tired…

To really enjoy *Beaches* you need to enjoy Bette Midler, who must take a lot of the credit for reducing the movie's schmaltz factor. She puts in a powerhouse performance as the demanding, driven and egotistical CC, belting out enough full-length numbers to fill a bona fide musical, and showing her range in everything from avant-garde rep theatre to Broadway and the Hollywood Bowl. She also gets all the great comic lines, of which there are many. Hershey, appropriately enough, pales somewhat in comparison – and it's hard not to be distracted by the size of her lips, which were pumped with collagen in an attempt to make her look younger (she was 40). But as a foil for the vibrant Midler, she does a good job, achieving just the right balance between repression and repressed anger. Always struggling with her image as the "good girl" – rebelling by sleeping with the man CC loves, or punishing her by refusing to answer her letters – even in her illness Hillary is no angel. "You're not dead yet, so stop living as if you are!", CC yells, after Hillary has spent yet another day in her pyjamas gazing moodily out of the window, jealous, once again, of CC – this time for being alive.

Beaches' iconic deathbed scene – a quiet demise on yes, you guessed it, a beach – is remarkably restrained, notwithstanding Midler's soaring "Did you ever know that you're my hero?" refrain. It is a subtle and genuinely affecting moment, only undermined by the overlong epilogue, which involves yet another Midler show-stopper and lots of bonding with Hillary's bossy young daughter Victoria (**Grace Johnston**).

Bend It Like Beckham

dir **Gurinder Chadha, 2002, UK/Ger, 112m**
cast **Parminder Nagra, Keira Knightley, Jonathan Rhys Meyers, Anupam Kher, Juliet Stevenson** *cin* **Jong Lin**
m **Craig Pruess**

British director **Gurinder Chadha**'s lively movies, from 1993's *Bhaji On The Beach* (which spawned a whole genre of affectionate British-Indian comedies, including *East Is East*, 1999, and *Anita And Me*, 2002) to her Jane-Austen-goes-to-Bollywood *Bride & Prejudice* (2004), always have fun with the collisions between tradition and modernity, family and community, cultural clashes and diversity. In 2002 Chadha (see Icons) was catapulted to worldwide fame with the feel-good feminist fairy tale *Bend It Like Beckham*, a low-budget sleeper hit that went on to become one of the most popular British films ever made. This huge success was partly due, in the States at least, to the presence of hot new star **Keira Knightley**, whose appearance the same year in the number-one hit *Pirates Of The Caribbean* kept *Bend It* on US cinema screens far longer than expected. However, this gently subversive girl film has far more going for it than Knightley – who, if truth be told, isn't great, with both her Mockney accent and her timing all over the place. Far better is **Parminder Nagra**, the film's star, who packs a powerful punch as Jess/Jesminder, an earnest Indian girl who is besotted with David Beckham, and whose dream of playing professional women's football goes against everything her Sikh family believe in. Spotted kicking a ball around by fellow football-player Jules (Knightley), Jess joins a local women's team coached by the handsome Joe (**Jonathan Rhys Meyers**). Attempting to keep her sporting activities a secret from her family is, however, harder than it at first seems. With no professional women's team in the UK, the arrival of a scout for an American team raises the stakes, and Jess finds herself having to make some painful choices.

In addition to Knightley's patchy performance, the script can, at times, get clunky – "I hope I get my two As and a B for uni," says Jess to her friend, in case we hadn't picked up on the fact that she's a bit of a brain – but the movie's raw energy makes up for any minor flaws. The bouncy soundtrack mixes upbeat tunes from bhangra to Basement Jaxx and, mischievously, Victoria Beckham, while the football scenes, even for viewers who have no interest in the sport, are genuinely exciting. Chadha knows how to direct ensembles, and the montage that intercuts the crucial final match with Jess's sister's long-awaited wedding makes for a stirring climax. The enthusiastic young actors are joined by veteran Bollywood star **Anupam Kher** as Jess's quiet dad, and **Juliet Stevenson**, who gives

Girl sports

Bend It Like Beckham is that rare thing – a sports movie made in Britain. By far the vast majority of films about sport come from the US, where the drive to win – to be "the best" – is something to celebrate rather than be ashamed of. Even so, within the genre, female sports movies are few, and recommendable titles are even fewer. Which is a shame, given that a good sports film can show girls struggling against the odds, testing their limits, striving for respect and facing the twin challenges of losing *or* winning – in effect, experiencing all the things that classic heroes do. Perhaps it's significant that sportswomen in the movies are invariably tough cookies, usually putting their chosen activity above everything else, even – gasp! – romance.

Champion sports movies include *Pat And Mike* (1952), in which Katharine Hepburn reveals both her athletic prowess and comic genius while wrangling with Spencer Tracy; *Heart Like A Wheel* (1983), a biopic about a hardhead-

ed female hot rod racer; *A League Of Their Own* (1992), a nostalgic slush-fest about an all-girl baseball team (starring Madonna, Geena Davis and Rosie O'Donnell); the visceral *Girlfight* (1999), featuring a fabulous performance from Michelle Rodriguez as the tough contender from the wrong side of the tracks; and *Million Dollar Baby* (2004), another boxing film, which offers a complex, nuanced figure in Maggie (Hilary Swank). The formulaic *Bring It On* (2000), starring Kirsten Dunst, gets a runner-up prize for winning the underrated activity of cheerleading a little respect; her dreary *Wimbledon* (2004), on the other hand, should be disqualified.

Hilary Swank slugs it out in *Million Dollar Baby* (2004)

a virtuoso comedy turn as Jules's anxious mother, convinced her sporty daughter is turning into a lesbian.

Along with Knightley, many people involved in this ebullient film have since gone on to greater things. Nagra went straight off to Hollywood, where she took a leading role in the mega-hit TV series *ER*, while Rhys Meyers picked up parts in Woody Allen's *Match Point* (2005) and *Mission: Impossible III* (2006). Chadha, meanwhile, is also working in Hollywood, and in 2005 announced plans for a sequel to *Bend It*. It will be interesting to see, should Nagra, Rhys Meyers and, in particular, Knightley return, just how such a film might differ from this low-key treat.

Black Narcissus

dir **Michael Powell and Emeric Pressburger, 1946, UK, 100m**
cast **Deborah Kerr, Sabu, David Farrar, Flora Robson, Kathleen Byron, Jean Simmons, Jenny Laird** *cin* **Jack Cardiff** *m* **Brian Easdale**

Black Narcissus is a ravishing movie. It's also about nuns, which guarantees a ripping yarn – and this one, a passionate tale of female lust and internal torment, is a cracker. Adapted from the novel by **Rumer Godden**, the story is simple: **Deborah Kerr** plays the headstrong Sister Clodagh, who is sent with four other nuns to set up a school and dispensary in an abandoned maharajah's palace in a remote Himalayan village. All five, particularly the mysteriously "problematic" Sister Ruth (a fabulously demented **Kathleen Byron**), find themselves disturbed by this strange, pagan place, and slowly faith, holy vows and even sanity begin to unravel.

Sensual to the point of eroticism, and deliciously over the top without being ridiculous, the movie uses lighting and colour unlike any other. Its palette of ripe reds, blues and greens contrasts with the nuns' oatmeal-coloured robes and unadorned faces in the same way that Powell and Pressburger's restrained script, which leaves so many things unsaid and half said, works with the stunning art direction to intensify the overwrought atmosphere. Unbelievably, too, not one scene was shot on location: the looming snowcapped mountain that haunts Sister Clodagh was a painted backdrop at Pinewood Studios; the exterior views of the lofty cliff-top palace are shots of a model.

From the moment we see inside the palace, which was once inhabited by the maharajah's concubines, it's plain that the nuns are in trouble. Filigree latticework casts long shadows and sends warm breezes through every room; erotic murals line the walls while exotic birds, free of their swinging cages, flutter overhead; the ghostly songs of the previous female occupants ring through the night… And then there is the rajah's agent, Mr Dean (**David Farrar**), a brusque fellow who has gone native (which includes, it is implied, sleeping with the local girls), and who makes it clear that the Sisters are not welcome. With his unruly mop of hair and flashing violet eyes, his bare legs

Nun so brave

Everyone loves a movie nun. And even if countless films, from Ken Russell's histrionic *The Devils* (1971) to the lame *Nuns On The Run* (1990), play on the skewed notion that beneath every wimple lie lacy scanties and barely suppressed rampant nymphomania, the best nun movies are chick flicks par excellence. The Mother Superior of them all has to be *The Song Of Bernadette* (1943), a feast of heavenly choirs and holy apparitions in which the young Jennifer Jones spends nearly three hours either smiling beatifically or weeping nobly. Though Bernadette certainly suffers, María Luisa Bemberg's intense *I, The Worst Of All* (1990) is even more harrowing, telling the true story of an idealistic seventeenth-century Mexican poet (Assumpta Serna) who enters the convent in order to write, becomes embroiled in terrible politicking, and doesn't even get a sainthood as compensation. It takes a special man to rival Jesus in a Sister's affection, and when movie nuns face temptation we get some wonderfully compelling moral grapplings. In the delightful WWII-set *Heaven Knows, Mr Allison* (1957), for example, the lovely Deborah Kerr forms a sweet friendship with a marine (Robert Mitchum, as lazily sexy as ever) when they wash up on a desert island and have to hide from the dastardly Japanese. Brutish Peter Finch bothers an uncharacteristically dressed-down Audrey Hepburn in *The Nun's Story* (1959), which sees the gamine give a mature performance as the wavering Sister Luke. (Hepburn took to the habit again in 1976 with the bittersweet *Robin And Marian*, another great nun's tale.) And in *Change Of Habit* (1969), Elvis's final film – a curiosity that deals with rape, Black Power, and rage reduction therapy among other gritty social issues – it's the King of Rock'n'Roll himself who awakens all sorts of unholy impulses; this time in Mary Tyler Moore, who, after coming to work with the handsome doctor (guess who) in a rough area of New York, sheds her habit, dons a mini-dress and has to make some tough choices.

When it comes to neurotic nuns, *Black Narcissus* (see p.53) must surely take the cake. *Agnes Of God* (1985) is more earnest, starring Meg Tilly as the young sister who, after being discovered in her cell with a murdered newborn baby, is investigated by tough-talking psychologist Jane Fonda. Spanish director Pedro Almodóvar, meanwhile, pushes things to the edge with the blasphemous *Dark Habits* (1983), in which the depraved Sister Rat (Chus Lampreave) and Sister Sin (Carmen Maura) are certainly doing it for themselves.

and very short shorts, he certainly cuts a disarming figure. His verbal volleys with Sister Clodagh drip with sexual tension – "*You* do not believe in solitude," she snaps as he puffs his pipe and gazes upon an erotic painting – while jittery Sister Ruth can't take her darting eyes off him. Add to this heady mix the mute "beggar maid" (for which read prostitute), Kanchi (a young **Jean Simmons**, blacked up), all jangling ankle bracelets and lascivious pouts, and the vain young general (**Sabu**), who is quite the dandy in his embroidered frock coats and jewelled turbans – it is his perfume, bought from London's Army and Navy stores, that gives the film its title – and it's clear that no amount of hard work, prayer or self-flagellation is going to save these hapless Sisters.

Before long the nuns begin remembering things they want to forget. Sister Phillippa (**Flora Robson**) replaces her sustenance crops with gardens of flowers, and Sister Honey (**Jenny Laird**) convinces herself she has killed a baby. When Sister Ruth dons a blood-red dress and aggressively applies scarlet lipstick in front of Clodagh, rushing down into the valley (a particularly delirious sequence, her dress stunning against the virulent green of the bamboo forest) to be rejected by her love object, Dean, the movie hurtles into horror territory. Byron's teeth-baring feral smile and red-rimmed eyes may well be the most unforgettable image in a film brimming with them.

Blue Steel

dir Kathryn Bigelow, 1990, US, 102m
cast Jamie Lee Curtis, Ron Silver, Clancy Brown, Elizabeth Pena, Louise Fletcher, Philip Bosco *cin* Amir Mokri *m* Brad Fiedel

Blue Steel, **Kathryn Bigelow**'s *film noir* follow-up to her cultish vampire movie *Near Dark* (1987), displays the earlier work's same sexy, smart style, but replaces a landscape of sulphurous yellow with a cool blue, very 1980s, urban palette. After shooting a man six times on her first day on the job, over-enthusiastic rookie cop Megan Turner (**Jamie Lee Curtis**) is put on desk duty, until a string

Rookie cop Jamie Lee Curtis – playing the guys at their own game

of murders around town are linked to bullets inscribed with her name. Slowly she comes to realize that her new lover, suave commodities broker Eugene (**Ron Silver**), is the murderer. Getting her male colleagues – not to mention Eugene's bullish lawyer – to believe her, however, is almost impossible. Accusing her of irrationality, and demanding aggressively that she come up with hard proof, they also judge her, and dismiss her, for having slept with him. Meanwhile, both Megan and those she loves are in increasing danger.

Curtis, with a memorable body of work as the plucky scream queen in a string of 1970s horror movies behind her, makes a compelling heroine. With her tomboy resilience and rakish grin, Megan is a woman both brave and flawed, a woman whose mistakes lead to devastating consequences. Her implied attraction to guns, and perhaps even to violence – an early scene in which she dresses herself up in her new uniform is as fetishistic a sequence as you're likely to see – offers an elegant twist on the old cops-and-crooks-are-two-sides-of-the-same-coin theme, and is also reflected in her poor choice of lover. The movie hints at the things that have driven Megan to make the choices she does – growing up with an abusive father and a weak mother, for example – but never bludgeons the point home. Uneasy implications are left to our imagination, which, especially given how much we are rooting for Megan, makes for an unsettling experience. Megan is asked three times how she came to be a cop. To her partner she jokingly answers, with a straight face, "Ever since I was a kid I wanted to shoot people." To a potential suitor she replies, "I like to slam people's heads up against walls," and watches coolly as he backs off. And the third time she is asked, she simply replies, "Him." Her meaning is tantalisingly ambiguous: on the one hand she might be saying that it was wanting to rid the streets of murderers like Eugene that inspired her to join the force; or is she referring to Eugene as being the same as the "him" inside her, the psycho who gets a thrill out of guns?

Ron Silver puts in a deliciously creepy performance as the maniac who will never die – witness his tormented schizo soliloquys, or the disturbing sex scene where Megan first discovers quite how misguided she has been. He is a monster as nightmarish as any of those Curtis had to battle in *Halloween* (1978) or *Terror Train* (1980); the fact that he wines and dines her, and takes her for romantic helicopter rides over Manhattan, simply makes him all the more terrifying. Kudos must go to Bigelow for making a terrific thriller that dares to tell the story, without judgement or condemnation, of a woman who plays dangerous games with men – and ultimately wins.

Breakfast At Tiffany's

dir Blake Edwards, 1961, US, 115m
cast Audrey Hepburn, George Peppard, Patricia Neal, Buddy Ebsen, Mickey Rooney *cin* Franz Planer *m* Henry Mancini

Breakfast At Tiffany's is a stylish, sophisticated and bittersweet treat. It's also the quintessential **Audrey Hepburn** movie – and for generations of girls who've longed to emulate Audrey's style, this is the mother lode. As good-time girl Holly Golightly, Hepburn (see Icons) looks fabulous in every scene, whether dressed in a succession of little black *Givenchy*-designed frocks and witty hats, waving around an extra-long cigarette holder, or waking up tousle-haired and gingerly removing her gold-tasselled earplugs. The iconic

Her tune: Holly Golightly dresses down for "Moon River"

opening sequence sets the tone: Holly emerges from a New York cab in the early morning, impeccable in a black evening gown, pearls, tiara and dark shades. Meanwhile, the plaintive "Moon River" theme wafts by as she gazes in the window of Tiffany the jewellers, daintily nibbling on a breakfast pastry.

Holly is a party girl who lives on her wits and on the favours of rich, older men. Having fled a shady past, she has recreated herself as a Manhattan sophisticate, dressed herself up like a couture model, and remains determined not to attach herself to anyone or anything. When Paul (**George Peppard**), a struggling writer, moves into her apartment block, they start a faltering friendship that forces Holly to both face her past and open her eyes to her future.

Truman Capote, who wrote the controversial novella on which the movie is based, originally conceived Holly as an out-and-out prostitute. He actually wanted Marilyn Monroe for the role (how different a film that would have been), but the star was unavailable. And although the notoriously demure Hepburn turned down initial approaches from director **Blake Edwards** – and, in fact, was never entirely convinced about the wisdom of the casting – she was eventually persuaded on board by his assurances that Holly would be portrayed as charming rather than crude. Hepburn, who at the age of 31 had just three months earlier given birth to her first, longed-for baby, ended up making the part of Holly her own. No longer the gamine of *Roman Holiday* (1953), *Sabrina* (1954) or *Funny Face* (1957), the actress was moving on, maintaining her mischievous persona while also playing a knowing, world-weary woman. In Peppard she also had, for the first time, a leading man who was roughly her own age, rather than an older mentor figure.

As Edwards promised, the Holly of the movie is eminently lovable. Although undeniably self-absorbed and irresponsible, a disingenuous tease, she is also vulnerable – a "lovely, very frightened" woman, as Paul puts it – who is fleeing her demons and the "mean reds", those moments when "you're afraid and don't know what you're afraid of". Hepburn's sprightly performance, her charisma and charm, all conspire to have us fall in love with her – along with her halting rendition of Henry Mancini's enchanting "Moon River", of course, which shows us, lest we be in any doubt, that Holly is an innocent, more of a lost soul than a con artist.

And after all, Holly is not the only one who sells herself. Paul, though he looks like the all-American boy, blonde and square-jawed, is dependent on an older, married patroness (the wonderfully predatory and purring **Patricia Neal**), who keeps him in suits and rent. Only when he has found his muse in Holly can he free himself, start writing again, and fight for true love. The film's sweetly romantic finale diverges wildly from the cynicism of Capote's book. And, holding as it does a tender promise of love in a brittle, heartless world, it works just fine.

The Bridges Of Madison County

dir Clint Eastwood, 1995, US, 135m

cast Meryl Streep, Clint Eastwood, Annie Corley, Victor Slezak, Jim Haynie *cin* Jack N. Green *m* Lennie Niehaus

"The old dreams were good dreams," photographer Robert Kincaid (**Clint Eastwood**) tells sad-eyed housewife Francesca (**Meryl Streep**). "They didn't work out, but I'm glad I had 'em." Delicate and deeply romantic, *The Bridges Of Madison County* is an old-fashioned film all about dreams: dreams lost, found, abandoned and clung onto, dreams that last a lifetime and beyond.

While sorting out their dead mother's affairs, a middle-aged brother (Victor Slezak) and sister (Annie Corley) are shocked to discover that she has asked to be cremated and that her ashes be scattered from a local covered bridge. Envelopes containing mysterious 30-year-old photographs of their mother looking relaxed and happy also contain a small key, which opens a chest holding a camera, a letter and three secret journals. To their horror, the letter, written shortly before her death, tells them about the intense four-day affair she had some thirty years ago – the pure, once-in-a-lifetime love that she gave up for her family.

"His name was Robert Kincaid", begins her first journal, as we are taken back to 1965. With her husband (**Jim Haynie**) and two teenagers away at the state fair, Francesca is looking forward to having her farmhouse to herself for four days. When a tousled stranger drives up in a dusty pickup truck, looking for a local covered bridge to photograph for *National Geographic* magazine, she impulsively offers to take him there herself; she then asks him in for iced tea, and

Middle-aged romance

If we're to believe the movies, there's nothing quite as melancholy as **middle age**. Divorced, widowed or simply left on the shelf, middle-aged romancers tend to have given up on love, which makes its appearance in a lonely life all the more poignant. This is the stuff of the finest melodramas: Douglas Sirk's *All That Heaven Allows* (1955), for example, in which Jane Wyman's yearning widow is sorely tempted by her handsome young gardener (Rock Hudson); and Todd Haynes's homage to Sirk, *Far From Heaven* (2002, see p.81). *The Best Years Of Our Lives* (1946) takes a slightly different approach with its touchingly unsentimental portrayal of Myrna Loy and Fredric March's hesitant attempts to love each other again after he returns from World War II.

Some stars have made a virtue of their increasing age – witness the fiercely independent Katharine Hepburn, who played feisty spinsters finding fleeting love in *The African Queen* (1951), with Humphrey Bogart; *Summertime* (1955), with Rossano Brazzi; and *Rooster Cogburn* (1975), with John Wayne. Another Hepburn, Audrey, is both wise and courageous as an ageing Maid Marian who encounters her old love, Robin Hood (Sean Connery), in the elegiac *Robin And Marian* (1976). More recently, as the baby boomers reach their prime, things are getting more upbeat. Robert Redford, who continues to play romantic leads as he approaches his 70s, melts hearts in weepies like *The Horse Whisperer* (1998), with Kristin Scott Thomas, while in the 50-something fantasy *Something's Gotta Give* (2003), Diane Keaton (approaching 60 and looking stupendous) juggles the attentions of both Jack Nicholson and Keanu Reeves. Incidentally, any chick flick featuring Jack is a dead-cert for middle-aged romance, from *Terms Of Endearment* (1983; see p.129), where he meets his match in a cranky Shirley MacLaine, to *As Good As It Gets* (1997; see p.48), in which he woos the lovely Helen Hunt.

Beyond Hollywood, the French have a fine filmic tradition of appreciating late-blossoming love, including Eric Rohmer's sweetly witty *Conte d'automne* (*An Autumn Tale*, 1998), while the German *Fear Eats The Soul* (1973) offers a heart-rending update of Sirk's *All That Heaven Allows*. *Bread And Tulips* (2000), from Italy, is touching and funny in its portrayal of a bored housewife who finds herself a richer life.

finally to join her for dinner. This is small-town Iowa, where for a married woman even to be seen with a strange man counts as front-page news, but Italian-born Francesca, whose youthful dreams have long since withered away, is ripe and ready to take such a risk.

Though the subplot, which revolves around the effect of Francesca's confession on her children, works to structure and pace this finely wrought tale, the two-handers between Eastwood and Streep, two colossal Hollywood icons, pack the most powerful punch. Gracefully directed and beautifully performed, these are subtle, satisfying scenes, gently exploring what has led each of these people to this point in their lives, and achieving an intense intimacy that goes way beyond their once-in-a-lifetime sexual passion. Eastwood, at 65, may have been a little old to play Robert, but his distinctively relaxed style is as attractive as ever, and if anyone can embody a wandering free spirit Eastwood can. Streep (see Icons), meanwhile, dark-haired and a little heavier than usual, gives one of her more mannered performances, all accent and nervous gestures. Reserved, and with an air of haunted unhappiness, she is convincing as a woman who has lost herself in the demands of her husband and children, and whose heart cracks open with the inexorable pull towards something she knows she will have to give up.

Francesca's decision to stay with her family comes from experience, age and no little pain. But although she abandons her dreams, she never forgets them, and, in the end, her dying request is heartbreakingly simple. For this woman who has chosen to live her life for others, it is only after death that her own dreams can come true.

Bridget Jones's Diary

dir **Sharon Maguire, 2001, UK/Fr, 97m**
cast **Renée Zellweger, Colin Firth, Hugh Grant, Jim Broadbent, Gemma Jones, Sally Phillips** *cin* **Stuart Dryburgh** *m* **Patrick Doyle**

Mention the words chick flick and most people think immediately of *Bridget Jones's Diary*. Adapted from the blockbusting satirical novel

The Darcy Effect

Playing Mr Darcy certainly does something for a man. **Colin Firth** became a heart-throb overnight with the 1995 BBC TV adaptation of *Pride And Prejudice*. Previously known for his stage work and a few minor film roles, suddenly Firth was a Byronic sex god, and the vision of him emerging in a dripping wet shirt after a dip in a pond has become an iconic erotic image. Similarly, in 2005 women started noticing something rather appealing about the hitherto so-so TV actor **Matthew Macfadyen** after he appeared, opposite Keira Knightley, as the tormented Darcy in Working Title's *Pride & Prejudice*. Other Mr Darcys include the devastatingly handsome **Laurence Olivier**, who was already an established sex symbol and one of the nation's most celebrated actors by the time he filmed the 1940 screen version, and Kiwi actor **Martin Henderson**, who edged onto the A-list after taking the role in Gurinder Chadha's Bollywood-influenced *Bride & Prejudice* (2004).

by **Helen Fielding**, which itself was taken from the author's sardonic plight-of-a-single-girl newspaper column, this funny, intelligent film was a much-anticipated event, and has since become the archetypal girls' night out – or in – movie.

Bridget the book, which to date has sold roughly ten million copies worldwide, spearheaded the chick lit phenomenon of the 1990s. All earnest discussions at the time about whether its portrayal of a neurotic single woman, obsessed with her weight and her love life, set feminism back by decades missed the point somewhat, ignoring Fielding's irony and her knowingness – ingredients that the film delights in. Parallels with Jane Austen's *Pride And Prejudice* are, if anything, more explicit on screen than in the book – choosing **Colin Firth** (whose Mr Darcy in the 1995 BBC TV adaptation had become a worldwide sex symbol) to play the upper-class lawyer Mark Darcy was a masterstroke – and, partly by losing the original diary's daily rundown of calorie, alcohol and cigarette intake, there is less emphasis on anxiety and relentless (hilarious) failure. The film clearly shows us Bridget relishing all the things she knows are bad for her – and even when she drunkenly wails along to the sobfest "All By Myself," wearing her slobby pyjamas and using a rolled-up mag for a mike, we can't help but feel she is enjoying the drama of her self-pity as much as we are.

Renée Zellweger all by herself – for this scene at least

Taking Bridget herself from the page to the screen was always going to be a challenge. Part of the book's sly humour is that we can't really know whether Bridget is overweight or not, because we are only told what she, a guileless and rather unreliable narrator, thinks of herself. In the end, the filmmakers plumped for plump,

Most overrated chick flick: *Notting Hill*

Five years after the phenomenal success of *Four Weddings And A Funeral* (1994), Working Title came up with this cynical return to formula. Scripted by Richard Curtis, who knows a thing or two about people-pleasing, **Notting Hill** should, by rights, be far funnier, fresher and more romantic than it is. Hugh Grant, who proved in *Bridget Jones's Diary* (2001) and *About A Boy* (2002) – both of which also came from the Working Title stable – that he could do so much better, bumbles and bores as William, a book shop owner. The usually effervescent Julia Roberts, meanwhile, here all lank straightened hair and jutting jaw, gracelessly plays "the most famous film star in the world" as if she's having a really, really bad day. And as for her big line, the one that is supposedly set to get us all weeping – "I'm just a girl, standing in front of a boy, asking him to love her" – words simply fail. Girl? Boy? The two of them have as much chemistry as a couple of dead fish. Bella (Gina McKee), the token wheelchair-user – who is also infertile (the revelation of which is passed over and forgotten in seconds) – and Honey (Emma Chambers), Will's "kooky" sister, are woefully underwritten, while Rhys Ifans provides unbelievably annoying support as Spike, Will's supposedly hilarious friend. All in all, *Notting Hill* is a sad waste of talent, money and time.

only, in a surprise twist, to cast skinny American actress **Renée Zellweger** (see Icons) as the hapless heroine. It was a brilliant move. With her considerable comic skills firing on all cylinders, Zellweger creates a lovable movie klutz in the mould of Lucille Ball or Judy Holliday. Her pitch-perfect performance won her an Oscar nomination – and sparked off an international obsession with her fluctuating weight that continues to this day. **Hugh Grant** (see Icons) is also a revelation as the two-timing Daniel Cleaver. Grant has always maintained that he's much more like Cleaver than the bumbling English fops that became his trademark after *Four Weddings And A Funeral* (1994) – a claim that the Divine Brown fiasco of 1995, when the actor was caught in a compromising position with the LA prostitute while dating the model/actress Liz Hurley, would seem to confirm.

In the film's sequel, *Bridget Jones: The Edge Of Reason* (2004), Bridget becomes more slapstick – Zellweger seems to have developed a comedy waddle for the role – and displays more low self-esteem (it's hard to imagine the Bridget of the first film, who tells Cleaver, "If staying here means working within ten yards of you, frankly I'd rather have a job wiping Saddam Hussein's arse," having anxieties about being good enough for Mark). Like the book it was based on, it was less successful than *Bridget Jones's Diary*, and many thought that everyone's favourite singleton might finally bow out. Not so the irrepressible Bridget, however, who returned to

The Independent newspaper in 2005, ten years after her first appearance, and, perhaps predictably, almost immediately found herself pregnant.

Brief Encounter

dir **David Lean, 1945, UK, 86m, b/w**
cast **Celia Johnson, Trevor Howard, Stanley Holloway, Joyce Carey, Cyril Raymond, Valentine Dyall** *cin* **Robert Krasker** *m* **Sergei Rachmaninov**

Brief Encounter, adapted from a play by **Noel Coward**, has become a byword for stiff-upper-lip Britishness. It's often described fondly as an anachronism, with **Celia Johnson** and **Trevor Howard**'s clipped tones sounding like something from another world; in fact, this deeply romantic film was from another world even when it was released. Set in the 1930s, it was already an elegy for a lost era, showing deprived postwar audiences a world of cosy country railway stations and trundling steam trains, a world where milk chocolate and sugar, fur coats and brandy were freely available – and where even forbidden love seemed possible. But, as Howard so sadly puts it, "not yet … not quite yet".

Johnson plays Laura, a housewife who, during one of her weekly trips into town, encounters married doctor Alec (Howard) in the railway refreshment room. He removes a piece of grit from her eye, they meet the next week by accident, and so begins a tentative, unconsummated affair. Contemporary critics hailed the film as a masterpiece; British audiences, however, living through the major social and cultural disruptions of the war, didn't identify with the couple's restraint, and flocked instead to see the saucier Gainsborough melodramas (see p.17) being produced in Britain at the time.

Today, however, it's clear that *Brief Encounter*, far from being repressed, faces the pain of desire and loss full on. A tear-jerking classic and a gay favourite, it's an intensely emotional film, and one in which ordinary things are imbued with extraordinary significance. The railway station, for example, is an expressionistic work of art, its shadowy tunnels and steamy platforms contrasting with the bright, bustling refreshment room. And the performances are wonderful. Johnson, Oscar-nominated, is especially fine, portraying glee, recklessness, longing and despair with just a flash of her huge, wistful eyes or impish grin. Beautifully lit, and elegantly dressed in

Brief encounters and snatched goodbyes: a world where nothing lasts...

1940s fashions – which, as it is set a decade earlier, only adds to the film's sense of disorientating dreaminess – she is utterly compelling. Ultimately, this is Laura's story, told through her memories and her voice-over, which is addressed, in her imagination, to her dull but kind husband Fred (**Cyril Raymond**), telling him all the things she longs to say but knows she must not.

Indeed, what is actually said out loud in *Brief Encounter* is relatively unimportant. In the opening scene, when Alec and Laura are parting forever, the chatter of Dolly (**Everley Gregg**), the gossipy acquaintance who has joined them, and the banter between the guard and the waitress flow unheard through the depth of the lovers' silence. And when Alec leaves, softly touching Laura's shoulder, Dolly's jabbering is lost beneath the scream of the trains. Later, as Dolly continues to talk, Laura smiles politely while thinking, "I wish you'd stop talking – I wish you were dead!", the savagery and forbidden desire of her interior world deeply buried beneath the surface. In so many heightened moments the lovers' expressions, their eyes, the scream of the trains and the swell of the soundtrack – **Rachmaninov**'s passionate *Piano Concerto No. 2* – tell their story far more effectively than words ever could. "I wish I could think of something to say," Alec despairs during their last moments together. "It doesn't matter – not saying anything I mean," Laura replies. Talking isn't important; what is going on inside is. Faced with such violent feelings, there is no option but to repress them, and for Laura, who lies easily but cannot maintain the deception, who yearns for sexual fulfilment but settles for Fred, there is nothing more to say.

Camille

dir George Cukor, 1936, US, 108m, b/w
cast Greta Garbo, Robert Taylor, Lionel Barrymore, Elizabeth Allan, Henry Daniell *cin* William H. Daniels
m Herbert Stothart

Alexandre Dumas's novel *La Dame aux Camélias* (1848) has become one of the most popular romantic tragedies of all time, its story adapted into a play, an opera – Verdi's *La Traviata* – and countless films.

This, however, is the definitive *Camille*, and **Greta Garbo** is the definitive Marguerite Gautier, the doomed "Lady of the Camellias". One of the classics of Hollywood's golden era, the movie boasts brilliant performances all round, a finely honed script and all the grandeur of MGM's lavish sets – an extravaganza of ruffles, velvet drapes and enormous, sparkling chandeliers, designed by genius art director **Cedric Gibbons** – as well as confident direction from **George Cukor**, who is known as the ultimate "women's director" for his great work with Hollywood's finest actresses. The costumes, too, by MGM costumier **Adrian**, are dazzling, a feast of frothy, swishing tulle, sparkling sequins and flashing jewels – one standout being the crinoline studded with a flock of 3D birds and a bird's nest filled with eggs.

In the end, though, this is Garbo's movie. One of the few silent stars to successfully cross over into talkies, Garbo is the archetypal screen goddess, her ethereal beauty and husky voice perfect for the tragic courtesan Marguerite. Displaying acres of sleek back and shoulders in very low décolletage, her sexiness is cool rather than overt, and she brings a kind of knowingness to the role, playing it, as

Doom, grandeur and Garbo

The oldest profession

In the world of art, the courtesan, or kept woman, has a different standing from the **prostitute**. Movie prostitutes are often rebellious, revealing the hypocrisy of society at large; **courtesans**, the mistresses of important or wealthy men, occupy a more privileged position, and yet, like caged songbirds, also represent the hopelessness of the human condition. That's not to say they don't express hope – quite the reverse. Dreams of a better, freer life, one filled with love, are something that movie prostitutes and movie courtesans share. Both yearn for redemption, but while the prostitutes at least have the possibility of a fairy tale ending (think *Pretty Woman*), courtesans rarely do.

Perhaps the most devastating movie image of a courtesan is in Max Ophüls's *Lola Montès* (1955), in which Lola is kept in a gold cage, displayed to a circus audience, as her life unfolds in flashback. Baz Luhrmann may well be invoking Ophüls when he introduces us to Nicole Kidman as Satine, the exquisite courtesan in *Moulin Rouge!* (2001; see p.100), who swoops into the cabaret on a flying trapeze. In the musical *Gigi* (1958) courtesanship gets chirpy, with the help of Vincente Minnelli's colourful direction and Cecil Beaton's flamboyant production and costume design, while 2005's sumptuous *Memoirs Of A Geisha* lays out in minute detail what it takes to become a human "work of art". Chinese cinema features its fair share of courtesans – including Gong Li in *Farewell My Concubine* (1993) and Zhang Ziyi in *House Of Flying Daggers* (2004) – and, especially in the 1930s, had a whole sub-genre about sad-eyed streetwalkers, including Ruan Lingyu in the heart-rending silent melodrama *The Goddess* (1934) and Zhao Huishen in *Street Angel* (1937). Chinese audiences also adored the classic women's movie *Waterloo Bridge* (1940), in which Vivien Leigh gives one of her finest performances as a woman whose streetwalking past comes back to haunt her.

More than a few stars owe their iconic status to playing a prostitute. Marlene Dietrich will be forever associated with a string of fallen "nightclub singers" in movies like *The Blue Angel* (1930), *Morocco* (1930), *Blonde Venus* (1932) and *Shanghai Express* (1932), which also features the wonderful Chinese-American star Anna Mae Wong as a courtesan. Louise Brooks embodies the dark beauty of a sexually liberated woman in both *Pandora's Box* (1929) and *Diary Of A Lost Girl* (1929), an image that is explicitly echoed by Melanie Griffith's black-wigged Lulu in Jonathan Demme's quirky *Something Wild* (1986). In *Breakfast At Tiffany's* (1961; see p.57) the charming Audrey Hepburn transforms kept woman Holly Golightly into something of a sweetheart, while Jane Fonda makes Bree a feminist hero in *Klute* (1971). Shirley MacLaine's kooky toughness creates memorable hookers in *Irma La Douce* (1963) and *Sweet Charity* (1968), the latter a remake of Federico Fellini's *Nights Of Cabiria* (1956), which features a remarkable performance by Giulietta Masina as the archetypal tough tart with a soft heart.

Cukor commented, "as if she were the author of her own misery". One of the demimonde of nineteenth-century Paris – a world in which, in this film, gaudily attired ladies drink too much and wantonly kick their legs into the air – Marguerite smiles on the outside, but suffers within. A kept woman who surrounds herself with her beloved camellias, she dislikes sad thoughts –"although they come sometimes" – and once she starts coughing delicately into her lacy handkerchief, we know her fate is sealed. Meanwhile, the puppyish Armand (a young, handsome **Robert Taylor**), as wide-eyed as Marguerite is jaded, longs, unlike the other men, to love her and take care of her – and soon, even while still beholden to the sadistic Baron de Varville (**Henry Daniell**), Marguerite allows herself to love the romantic Armand back. Together, dreaming of a simple world in which they can be happy, they take off for a blissful spell in the country. When Armand's father (**Lionel Barrymore**) arrives, however, and persuades her to do the right thing, the heartbroken Marguerite makes the ultimate sacrifice, and thus, in a moment, their bucolic idyll is shattered.

Although "Garbo laughs!", the publicity campaign for the 1939 comedy *Ninotchka*, implied that the actress had never laughed in a movie before, she does laugh often in *Camille*, sometimes with a throaty glee, but more often with a brittle desperation. The scene in which the cruel Baron pounds out a tune on the piano while he and Marguerite throw back their heads and laugh hysterically at what is unspoken – that rather than love between them there are only lies – is as painful a sequence as you'll see on screen.

Camille's death scene, meanwhile, is one of the all-time greats. Marguerite's fragility and Armand's desperation, their poignant fantasy that they might return to the countryside, rediscover what is irretrievably lost, and the courtesan's dark referral to her very existence as being a "stain on our love", all culminate in a final moment that devastates with its impossible beauty, in the way that only Garbo's face can.

Casablanca

dir **Michael Curtiz, 1942, US, 102m, b/w**
cast **Humphrey Bogart, Ingrid Bergman, Claude Rains, Paul Henreid, Sydney Greenstreet** *cin* **Arthur Edeson**
m **Max Steiner**

You may never have seen *Casablanca*, but you know all about it – the endlessly quotable (and misquoted) dialogue, the unforgettable "As Time Goes By" refrain, the iconic image of Bogie in his white tux, hunched over a bourbon bottle. At once a suspenseful wartime drama, dry comedy, romantic melodrama and exotic location movie, it's one of the most popular films ever made, and still today it hits all

Play it again, Sam

Although it is well documented that Rick never actually says "Play it again, Sam" in *Casablanca* most people, perhaps instinctively sensing that it simply sounds better, still defiantly misquote the line. It is Ilsa who first insists, "Play it, Sam. Play 'As Time Goes By' ... Sing it Sam." Rick actually says, "You played it for her, you can play it for me. If she can stand it, I can! Play it!" The line "Play it again, Sam" does, however, appear in the Marx Brothers' spoof *A Night In Casablanca* (1946), and, of course, in Woody Allen's *Play It Again, Sam* (1972), in which the hopeless Allan Felix (Allen) misguidedly aspires to be as cool as his hero, Humphrey Bogart.

Torn between two lovers: high adventure for Ingrid Bergman

the right notes. Though it crackles with wry humour, *Casablanca* is also dream-like and seductive, infused with melancholy and loss. Much like the British *Brief Encounter* (1945; see p.64), it longs for an earlier, by implication prewar, world where things seemed simpler and forbidden love could flourish; unlike *Brief Encounter*, however, *Casablanca* was made during the war, not after it, and thus its patriotic agenda drives the romance.

Casablanca, a major port for refugees fleeing Nazi Europe, is shown (entirely on studio sets) as an exotic, chaotic place of limbo, populated by fleet-footed pickpockets, poker-backed Nazis, anxious refugees and cool opportunists. Foremost among the last are the hard-bitten Rick (**Humphrey Bogart**), who owns a popular gin joint, and the pragmatic police chief Louis Renault (a superbly sharp performance from **Claude Rains**). Louis continually insists that beneath his tough shell Rick is a sentimentalist; and, when one day the heroic Resistance fighter Victor Laszlo (**Paul Henreid**) walks into the bar with his companion Ilsa (**Ingrid Bergman**), it seems that the policeman may well be right. As Rick drowns his sorrows, the nostalgic strains of "As Time Goes By" tinkling in the background, the screen blurs into flashback – to a time in pre-Occupation Paris when he and Ilsa enjoyed a passionate, happy love affair; an affair which ended the day the Nazis invaded and she disappeared without a trace. When it is revealed that Ilsa is married to Victor, and that she was so even during their time in Paris (though she claims that she believed that he'd died in a concentration camp), Rick's bitterness threatens to put all three of them at risk.

Though much of the dialogue is so familiar, the fact that it remains fresh is partly due to phenomenal performances all round. Rains and Henreid in particular portray their characters as complex and multilayered, while even the actors with smaller roles deliver their often witty lines with brio. Lit like an angel, her eyes perpetually gleaming with tears, Bergman is tremendous as the woman torn between the two men she loves and her desire to do her patriotic duty. None of the actors knew which two of the love triangle would end up together until the final scene was shot, which may have helped their affecting performances. This was Bergman and Bogart's only movie together, which is something of a surprise given the sultry chemistry between them – a chemistry that was all the more extraordinary considering that Bogart, a few inches shorter than his Nordic co-star, often had to wear stacked heels or stand on boxes, or be filmed sitting while she stood.

Despite these physical constraints, Bogart was never better than as the tortured, love-bruised cynic who comes to believe in something greater than himself. Rick effectively symbolizes the US in December 1941, the very point at which the nation shifted from a policy of isolationism to enter the war against the Nazis. And it is Rick, rather than Ilsa, who makes the ultimate sacrifice. That the love story of two people is shown to be of little importance in a world under the dark shadow of war may well be the most romantic element of this deeply romantic movie.

Clueless

dir **Amy Heckerling, 1995, US, 98m**
cast **Alicia Silverstone, Stacey Dash, Brittany Murphy, Paul Rudd, Donald Faison, Elisa Donovan, Justin Walker**
cin **Bill Pope** *m* **David Kitay**

Clueless is that rare thing: a chick flick and teen movie that received not only critical acclaim, but also huge audiences. Director **Amy Heckerling**, who made a splash with 1982's *Fast Times At Ridgemont High* before going on to direct John Travolta in the *Look Who's Talking* movies, returned to high school for this super-smart girl film, which takes **Jane Austen**'s *Emma* and brings it bang up-to-date in Beverly Hills. **Alicia Silverstone** is Cher, a rich, blonde hottie who "wants to use her popularity for good" by matchmaking the clueless, less fortunate souls she sees around her. Austen's Harriet Smith is transformed into Tai (**Brittany Murphy**), the grungy new girl who starts out as Cher's latest project and ultimately overtakes her in the popularity stakes; love object Frank Churchill becomes Christian (**Justin Walker**), a James Dean looka-like; and Mr Knightley turns up as Josh (**Paul Rudd**), Cher's older, Nietzsche-reading ex-stepbrother. While sorting out everybody else's love life, Cher neglects her own, fails to see what's under her nose, and ultimately has to reassess her priorities so that true love can prevail.

It's a classic story, of course, and *Clueless* handles it brilliantly. The film is extremely funny, with its fair share of visual jokes – high school girls, their post-surgery noses bound in plaster cast, are shown perpetually pinned to their mobile phones (and this a good few years before that became a common sight) – but mostly through its audacious use of language. Heckerling spent time hang-ing out with high school kids, taking their catchphrases and add-ing some of her own. Some of the best exist only in the world of this movie – for example, calling pretty girls Bettys and ugly boys Barneys (after Betty and Barney Rubble of *The Flintstones*), and hot guys Baldwins (after the good-looking movie actor brothers of the 1990s). Others, such as "Hel*lo*!", "As *if*!" and "What*ever*", are all too familiar.

What Cher says, in voice-over and on screen, is never less than compelling, whether she's expressing profound ideas in vacuous lan-guage ("After all," she reasons while debating the rights of the poor, "it does not say RSVP on the Statue of Liberty"), talking nonsense with total conviction ("Isn't my house classic! The columns date all the way back to 1972!"), or coming up with outrageous deadpan gems ("I was surfing the crimson wave – I had to haul ass to the ladies"). Despite her way with words, Cher's innocent voice-over soon reveals that she's somewhat misguided. So, while it's clear to us that Christian is not going to make a pass at her any time soon – his interest in fashion and Tony Curtis movies is something of a giveaway – she doesn't pick up the clues. However, Cher too is not entirely what she seems. She may be clueless, but she's certainly not un-self-aware – giving makeovers, she explains, offers "a sense of control in a world of chaos" – and, though we may start the movie scorning her as a spoiled airhead, it doesn't take long before we're entirely won over.

Much of this is down to Silverstone, who, aged 17, gives a nuanced performance that allows us to like Cher as much as we laugh at her. Though the actress was expected to go on to great things, in a suitably ironic twist it was ugly duckling Brittany Murphy who actually became Hollywood's darling, turning in credible performances in hip movies like *8 Mile* (2002) and *Sin City* (2005), while also doing hugely popular semi-clad photo shoots for *Maxim* magazine. Totally bug*gin'*, as Cher might say.

Desperately Seeking Susan

dir Susan Seidelman, 1985, US, 103m
cast Rosanna Arquette, Madonna, Aidan Quinn, Mark Blum, Robert Joy, Will Patton, Steven Wright *cin* Edward Lachman *m* Thomas Newman

At first glance, the plot of *Desperately Seeking Susan* – bored suburban housewife Roberta (**Rosanna Arquette**), intrigued by a personal ad, tracks down its free-spirited author Susan (**Madonna**), gets knocked unconscious, suffers amnesia and believes she *is* Susan – could be read as just another mistaken-identity comedy caper. **Susan Seidelman's** film is, however, much more than this. Written, produced and directed by women, and with two great female leads, this was the kind of film that gave female audiences in the 1980s hope for a new style of cinema – one that showed feminism could be fun – and it still stands up today as an inspiration to the many great chick flicks that followed it.

Although it started out as an arthouse feature, *Susan* became a huge commercial success, partly on the back of its star, Madonna, who was little known when first cast, but a superstar by the time the film was released. Her street-smart, sassy image spawned a generation of Madonnabes, all kitted out in midriff-exposing clothes, droopy boots, tangled hair and junk-store jewellery – the kind of ragbag glamour modelled by Susan herself in the movie. Sexily itinerant and supremely in control, Susan was a heroine for the pre-Spice Girls generation, and, though her look is now overly familiar, the powerful appeal of her persona lives on. Although many Madonna-bashers dismiss her performance, huffily sniffing that she's simply "playing herself", it would be mean-spirited to deny that her energy and charisma play a big part in making this quickfire comedy as charming as it is.

While *Susan* almost fits into the 1980s "yuppie in peril" minigenre – as seen in films like Martin Scorsese's *After Hours* (1985) and Jonathan Demme's *Something Wild* (1986), where crazed women (Arquette in another finely judged performance, Melanie Griffith in a Louise Brooks wig respectively) pose a real threat to buttoned-up, repressed men – there are also echoes of earlier, classic screwball movies (1938's *Bringing Up Baby*, say, or 1952's *Monkey Business*), whose heroines (Katharine Hepburn and Ginger Rogers) are as liberating as they are neurotic, delightful as they are dark.

This is a girl's world: Rosanna Arquette (left) with Madonna

And there's something, too, of a *Girl's Own* element to this cracking adventure story, in which the plucky heroines take risks and follow clues, vanquishing the villains and saving the day with very little help from their easy-on-the-eye guys. Seidelman's real masterstroke is in setting a girl's story in a girl's world – a world of beauty parlours, vintage clothes stores and dressing rooms, where fashion and fairy tales, masquerade and romance allow Roberta, and us, the delicious fantasy that we can, if even for a short while, become the object of our dreams. And which of us doesn't empathize with the simple longing to dress up that lies at the heart of the movie – the need to don the perfect outfit, be it (as in this case) a pair of sparkling boots or an oversized leather jacket, and to be transformed? It's enough to make Madonna wannabes of all of us.

Dirty Dancing

dir Emile Ardolino, 1987, US, 100m

cast Jennifer Grey, Patrick Swayze, Jerry Orbach, Cynthia Rhodes, Jack Weston, Jane Bruckner *cin* Jeff Jur *m* John Morris

Although the massive sleeper hit *Dirty Dancing* has become something of a joke – "No one puts Baby in the corner!" – it is a fond joke, and the movie holds such a treasured place in so many women's hearts that it has earned itself the proud status of not only blockbuster, but also cult classic.

It's the summer of 1963, and, just as they have done for years, a host of middle-class Jewish families are descending on a Catskills holiday camp. **Jennifer Grey** plays Baby, a 17-year-old Plain Jane who adores her daddy, gets good grades and thinks only of joining the Peace Corps. That is until she meets Johnny (**Patrick Swayze**), the camp's bad-boy dance teacher, and, under his close instruction, learns a few of his moves. Clad in a tight T-shirt, Cuban heels and shades, and with the acting ability of a plank, Swayze could be faintly ridiculous were it not for his graceful, dynamic and yes, dirty, dancing. Snake-hipped and broad-shouldered, he has an undeniably commanding physical presence, and after ninety minutes lingering

Teacher–pupil romance, 1980s-style

upon his rippling torso you really do start to understand what Baby sees in him.

However, when she first catches sight of him, grinding with his glamorous partner (Cynthia Rhodes) on the dance floor, Baby is as excited by their abandon as she is by Johnny himself. Although they have to put a lid on their natural instincts when entertaining the holidaymakers, the wrong-side-of-the-tracks entertainment staff really let rip back at the staff quarters (which, although they are out of bounds, Baby manages to wander around freely), black and white bumping and grinding in ways the nice Jewish girl has barely dreamed of. Before she knows it, the truculent Johnny has defiantly swept her onto the dance floor and, though clumsy at first, she soon warms up, finishing the number knock-kneed and triumphant. Within moments, it seems, she finds herself with just a few days to rehearse in order to take the place of Johnny's partner at an important show.

If Swayze knows how to dance, **Emile Ardolino**, who died in 1993, certainly knew how to direct dance scenes. Even Baby and Johnny's "dancing on a log" sequence (when, drenched in water, they practise a particularly tricky balancing-above-the-head move), daft as it is, works. Each dance cranks up the sexual tension to such a pitch that when they do eventually sleep together the release is palpable. The music, too, is exceptional. While the movie's theme song – "I've Had The Time Of My Life" – has long since passed its sell-by date, the rest of the soundtrack is extremely classy, studded with steamy soul numbers from the likes of Otis Redding and Solomon Burke.

Transformed from nice girl into hotpants-clad sex kitten, Baby is a great heroine. Fearless and unashamed, off the dance floor she is in control – partly through her money and class, but also through sheer feistiness. Because of her, Johnny can finally find the courage to demand the creative control he longs for, and can even stop acting as a gigolo for the older female guests. But can their forbidden love ever be?

The finale, when Johnny, who has previously walked out, storms back into the camp during its last night show, hisses the immortal, "No one puts Baby in the corner!", and whisks her onto the stage, is as corny as you like. The metaphor for a nation on the brink of change, about to be blown apart by the youth revolution and civil rights movement, may be heavy-handed, but as a joyously sexy coming of age story *Dirty Dancing* can't be beat.

Dancing queens

The dance floor – be it school gymnasium, disco or ballet stage – offers a ready-made arena for anything from heartfelt dreams and gritty resolve to physical virtuosity and steamy love scenes. It's hardly surprising, then, that dance movies (as distinct from musicals, which have their own delightful niche, or even Fred and Ginger's movies, which are in a league of their own) make such splendid chick flicks.

At their best, dance movies use their performances to echo the narrative and achieve emotional depth: Powell and Pressburger's *The Red Shoes* (1948; see p.119), for example, in which the ballet literally overtakes the story. Others, like the feminist-tinged *The Turning Point* (1977), an affecting account of female friendship, ambition and ageing, work instead as elegant vehicles in which to showcase some glorious choreography. In the aerobics-, ambition- and MTV-crazed 1980s, a certain type of dance movie – frenetic, hip and teen-focused – really took off. Alan Parker's stage school soap *Fame* (1980) set the ball rolling, followed by *Flashdance* (1983), with its iconic audition scene – and its iconic slashed sweatshirts – *Footloose* (1984), directed by *The Turning Point*'s Herbert Ross, and, of course, *Dirty Dancing* (1987; see p.75), with its exuberant chutzpah. More recent copycats, like *Center Stage* (2000), which takes *Fame*'s backstage drama to ballet school, or Robert Altman's ponderous *The Company* (2003), seemed dated even upon release.

In the 1990s the Latin and ballroom dancing craze took dance movies to a new place. With tongue firmly in cheek, Baz Luhrmann's heart-warming *Strictly Ballroom* (1992) celebrates the savagery and sassy creativity of the competition circuit, while the charming Japanese rom-com *Shall We Dance?* (1995) sees a buttoned-up businessman transformed by the cha-cha-cha. The 2004 Hollywood remake, with Richard Gere, Jennifer Lopez and Susan Sarandon, is just as gently appealing.

Hip-hop took the genre to the streets: *Save The Last Dance* (2001) has white ballerina Julia Stiles getting funky with the help of her black friends, while *Honey* (2003) offers an inspiring fairy tale for the streets. And in *Take The Lead* (2006), a classic "maverick teacher turns around tough students" story, the unfeasibly handsome Antonio Banderas combines urban style with ballroom dancing to create something brand new.

Erin Brockovich

dir Steven Soderbergh, 2000, US, 133m
cast Julia Roberts, Albert Finney, Aaron Eckhart, Marg
Helgenberger, Cherry Jones, Peter Coyote *cin* Ed
Lachman *m* Thomas Newman

The true story of a single mother who took on a monster corporation and went on to make American legal history, *Erin Brockovich* is a stylish political detective story and a brilliantly pitched women's picture. Spiky, gutsy and struggling to feed her kids, Erin (**Julia Roberts**) just wants to be "a good mom, nice person, decent citizen". Having forced her way, through dogged persistence, into a filing job at a law firm owned by Ed Masry (**Albert Finney**), she is startled to find blood-test records in real estate files. Thus begins a tireless quest that threatens her relationships with her children and her gentle boyfriend George (**Aaron Eckhart**), reveals a shocking cover-up by a major utilities company and sets in place the biggest direct-action lawsuit in US history.

The movie looks great. **Steven Soderbergh**'s cool style and the dreamy musical score underpin the creeping realization of just what Erin has stumbled upon, while the naturally lit landscape, which turns from burnished gold through poisonous yellow to mercurial silver, lends an unsettling sense of doom. Roberts (see Icons) won an Oscar for her career-best performance, and suddenly the most bankable female star in Hollywood was being taken seriously as an actress. Although widely described as a departure from her usual doe-eyed tomboys, Erin isn't actually such a leap from the sassy girl-from-the-wrong-side-of-the-tracks/Cinderella roles that Roberts already excelled in. Much was made of her "trashy" look, and especially her heaving cleavage, but, while she does appear in her first scene in unfamiliar frosted eye shadow and huge, brassy hair, as the film goes on the hair gets surreptitiously smaller and the make-up less garish until pretty soon Erin has morphed back in the Julia we know and love.

Fiercely intelligent and unabashedly feminine, Erin has no qualms about using her sexual attributes to gain access to official information. She employs her compassion to get suffering people

Good mom, nice person, decent citizen: Julia Roberts brings a corporation to its knees

to trust her, operating on an instinctive, human level that's in stark contrast to the constrained, rigid lawyers around her. She's also tough and guarded, and when George first seduces her warns him not to be too nice: "It makes me nervous." No such worries with Masry, in whom she finds a father figure and a mentor. Kind, combative and challenging, he listens to her and has faith

Office politics

While working women form the heart of many a fine chick flick, for the richest crop of triumphant office-based movies we should turn to the comedies of the 1980s, when a generation of women were grappling with ambition, post-feminism and unfeasibly large shoulder pads. The decade set off with *Nine To Five* (1980), in which put-upon secretaries Jane Fonda, Dolly Parton and Lily Tomlin kidnap their slimy boss and run the company without him. In *Baby Boom* (1987) Diane Keaton manages to Have It All (that is, a super-successful working life, a gorgeous man – in this case, Sam Shepard – *and* a cute baby), while in *Working Girl* (1988) the (not so) dumb blonde Tess (Melanie Griffith) battles her way to the top, toppling super-bitch boss Sigourney Weaver along the way. Blonde ambition and office-based comedies faded out in the 1990s, only to re-emerge sexier, and a little more skewed, in *Secretary* (2002), in which Maggie Gyllenhaal and her sadistic boss James Spader offer a whole new twist on harassment in the workplace.

These movies have more than a sniff of screwball about them, recalling the fast-paced and anarchic Hollywood comedies of the 1930s and 1940s, in which independent women – career girls or madcap heiresses – cause a huge amount of havoc. Rosalind Russell, one of the smartest and funniest screwball heroines of them all (and a woman just born to wear shoulder pads), not only runs rampage through Cary Grant's newsroom in the uproarious *His Girl Friday* (1939; see p.88), but elsewhere occupies office chairs on both sides of the desk: as a savvy secretary who uses her wiles to snare her boss in *Hired Wife* (1940), and as the ambitious ad exec in *Take A Letter, Darling* (1942), who hires the hapless Fred MacMurray as her secretary and escort.

in her, and their sparky, loving bond provides both the movie's key relationship and its light relief. Erin's affair with George, by bringing romance into the mix, is more complex. When he walks out, tired of coming second to her work, she appeals not by talking about the case, but about its effect on her self-esteem: "For the first time in my life I've got people respecting me. I've never had that before, *ever*. Don't ask me to give it up…". By asking him to stay, she is challenging the very basis of traditional gender roles – she is asking him to stand behind her and support her, to put himself second. And when she takes him to see the people she has been working for, her simple, "I want to show you what you helped to do," quietly celebrates not only George, but also all those countless unseen and unrecognized carers and homemakers who form the backbone of the big stories – and whose work is as crucial to any story as what goes on in the foreground. In this way the movie is profoundly feminist, and as an examination of the struggle involved in balancing work and personal life it can't be bettered.

Far From Heaven

dir Todd Haynes, 2002, US/Fr, 107m
cast Julianne Moore, Dennis Quaid, Dennis Haysbert, Patricia Clarkson, Viola Davis, James Rebhorn, Celia Weston *cin* Edward Lachman *m* Elmer Bernstein

A film of delicate, haunting beauty, *Far From Heaven* is a 1950s-style melodrama that draws on the Douglas Sirk classics *All That Heaven Allows* (1955) and *Imitation Of Life* (1959; see p.91), yet never descends to parody or camp. Nor is it merely a homage: this wistful movie, based on the impossibility of forbidden desire, is as relevant today as it would have been in the postwar, repressive, small-town America that it portrays.

Hartford, Connecticut, 1957. The Whitakers, Cathy (**Julianne Moore**) and Frank (**Dennis Quaid**), are the couple with everything – a fine home, two lovely children, a loyal black maid. Frank is a high-flying executive, while Cathy throws perfect dinner parties and does good works. But, despite appearances, all is not well. Frank is secretly gay, and no amount of counselling or self-flagellation is going to rid him of his forbidden feelings. Cathy, trying to understand what to her is unthinkable, turns to kindly gardener Raymond (**Dennis Haysbert**) for solace. However, not only is Raymond a gardener and a single parent, but also he is black, and thus their tender, halting love can never be.

Every performance in this movie is pitch perfect, every character believable. These are people who struggle, do the wrong thing, and ultimately suffer. Moore is heartbreaking as the well-meaning homemaker who naively believes in a fairer, more equal world, yet who still undermines her black maid, Sybil (**Viola Davis**), lies to protect her husband's secret, and, finally, sacrifices what is most precious to her. Pregnant and heavier than usual during filming, Moore absolutely looks the 1950s part, while her fragile beauty only emphasizes Cathy's vulnerability. Quaid, too, is outstanding in a comeback role that replaces his trademark cheeky grin with a performance of restrained frustration and desperation, while Haysbert's gentle gardener, with his strong physical presence, melting smile and tartan shirts, bears an uncanny resemblance

Julianne Moore and Dennis Haysbert: forbidden love

to Rock Hudson in *All That Heaven Allows*. Unlike Rock, however, Raymond's desire for a bigger life – for himself and his daughter – is doomed simply because of the colour of his skin.

As in Sirk's movies, *Far From Heaven* allows huge wellings of emotion that cannot be directly expressed – profound love, loss and sorrow – to spill over into what we see on the screen. Unlike Sirk, however, director **Todd Haynes** creates an effect that is less disturbing than seductive, recalling the sheer gorgeousness and glamour of an earlier era. You could almost drown in the film's luscious colours, which come either from art (unusually, in a business where computer graphics are the norm, the dazzling opening credits were hand painted) or nature – the blaze of orange and red trees was filmed during a genuine New Jersey autumn. **Sandy Powell**'s costumes pulse with colour too, and, along with the spot-on set design, define the characters and highlight their emotional world. Haynes' classy direction and nuanced screenplay, **Edward Lachman**'s fine cinematography, and **Elmer Bernstein**'s poignant score enrich this feast of a movie even further.

This is a film pervaded by loss, one in which the lovers endlessly say goodbye. There's no happy ending here, not even a tacked-on Sirkian one. A few spring blossoms, the first in a movie painted with the rich reds of autumn, are the only sign of hope in a finale that leaves us in touch with an exquisite sadness so often, and so desperately, pushed beneath the surface.

Gentlemen Prefer Blondes

dir **Howard Hawks, 1953, US, 91m**
cast Jane Russell, Marilyn Monroe, Charles Coburn,
Tommy Noonan, Elliott Reid, Taylor Holmes, George
Winslow *cin* Harry J. Wild *m* Jule Styne, Hoagy
Carmichael

Adapted from **Anita Loos**'s bestselling Jazz Age novel, stage play and musical, *Gentlemen Prefer Blondes* is a delicious 1950s Technicolor treat that belongs to its stars, **Jane Russell** and **Marilyn Monroe**. From the opening musical number, "Two Little Girls From Little Rock", these fabulous icons dazzle like firecrackers, fizzing and sizzling through one of the funniest celebrations of female friendship ever seen on screen.

Monroe is superb as gold-digging showgirl Lorelei, a breathy blonde bombshell who knows how to use her body to get what she wants – diamonds, mostly. With none of the damaged vulnerability that she displays in so many of her movies, the actress is at her comic peak, delivering a ream of hilarious dumb blonde lines – "Is this the way to Europe, France?", she asks as she approaches the boat dock for a transatlantic trip – and wonderfully skewed logic – "I want you to find happiness and stop having fun," she tells Russell, who refuses to date men for their money – with shimmering genius. She has a perfect comedy partner in Russell, who plays Lorelei's wisecracking, feisty (and brunette) friend Dorothy, who, unlike Lorelei, doesn't care about diamonds, and prefers "a man who can run faster than I can".

Gentlemen is a fantastic musical, its energetic numbers including not only the iconic "Diamonds Are A Girl's Best Friend" – aped thirty years later by Madonna in her "Material Girl" video – and Russell's irrepressibly catchy "Bye Bye Baby", but also the gloriously camp "Anyone Here For Love?", in which a frustrated Russell pouts longingly while the oblivious, and ridiculously hunky, all-male Olympic team (dressed only in flesh-coloured trunks) gyrate and flex around her. The plot, a brilliantly crafted farce, delivers too. Lorelei wants to marry dull but wealthy Gus Esmond (**Tommy Noonan**) ("daddy", as she calls him), but is thwarted by his controlling father. Undeterred, she persuades her love-struck beau to pay for her and Dorothy to take the boat to France, planning to meet him there. Also on the boat is Malone (**Elliott Reid**), a spy sent by Mr Esmond Sr. (**Taylor Holmes**), and Piggy (**Charles Coburn**), a

bumbling (and married) lothario who owns a diamond mine – when introduced, Lorelei hallucinates a diamond the size of his head, and, with her eye on his wife's huge diamond tiara, can't resist flirting with him. Add into the mix the muscly Olympic team and Henry Spofford III (**George Winslow**), a gruff 11-year-old millionaire, and you've got a fast-paced comedy treat.

When the girls discover that Malone, with whom Dorothy has fallen in love, has photos of Lorelei and Piggy in a compromising position, they employ all sorts of dastardly female wiles to retrieve them ("If we can't empty his pockets between us," says Dorothy, "we're not worthy of the name woman"). However, the diamond-fixated Lorelei then uses the pictures to blackmail Piggy into giving her the tiara, only to be thwarted when they arrive in France by Malone, Piggy's wife and the police. Penniless once more, and working at a local club, Lorelei performs the movie's most famous musical number, "Diamonds Are A Girl's Best Friend", an extravaganza of red and pink in which she advises a bevy of lovelies to opt for rocks over romance. A melee of arrests, double crosses and mistaken identities ensues – including Russell's genius impersonation of Lorelei in court, pouting and shimmying in a platinum wig – before, in a triumphant

Girls are a girl's best friend: Monroe and Russell

finale, the dumb blonde is revealed to be not so dumb after all. The cheeky final shot provides the perfect end to this gem of a movie, proving that girls, not diamonds, are undoubtedly a girl's best friend.

Ghost

dir **Jerry Zucker, 1990, US, 127m**
cast **Patrick Swayze, Demi Moore, Tony Goldwyn, Whoopi Goldberg, Vincent Schiavelli, Rick Aviles**
cin **Adam Greenberg** *m* **Maurice Jarre**

Despite everything, and certainly against our better judgement, *Ghost* works. It's a weepie that will be forever associated with one scene: that much-parodied and giggle-inducing performance at the potter's wheel. It's a romantic comedy directed by **Jerry Zucker** (best known for zany classics *Airplane!*, 1980, and *Top Secret!*, 1984). And what's more, it's a supernatural thriller that depends in large part on the chemistry between beefcake **Patrick Swayze** and **Whoopi Goldberg**. On paper, at least, it all seems a bit unlikely.

The story, too, is a load of hokum. Stockbroker Sam (Swayze) and potter Molly (**Demi Moore**) are young and in love, yet Sam is unable to tell Molly he loves her, only ever responding to her proclamations with "ditto". After a botched mugging leads to his murder, Sam returns as a ghost, hooking up with tetchy psychic Oda Mae (Goldberg) to contact Molly, save her from the bad guys, and avenge his death.

So how did *Ghost* end up being such a great movie? The script and the direction are assured, and Moore is hard not to like as Molly, the dewy-eyed gamine who struggles to live without the love of her life. Apparently Moore can cry out of one eye at a time on demand, and her grief in this film is touchingly convincing. Patrick Swayze, however, was a surprising choice. Fresh from his hip-grinding debut in the rather wonderful *Dirty Dancing* (1987; see p.75), the Hollywood hunk had yet to gain much respect from his peers, and he fought hard to be considered for a role that a whole host of leading men had turned down. His audition, however, reduced Zucker and writer **Bruce Joel Rubin** to tears, and nailed the part immediately. Gargoyle-faced, and with a dramatic range that extends to various degrees of nostril flaring, Swayze is actually rather good in what is not an easy role – less convincing, maybe, as a wheeler-dealer stock-broker, but more than believable as the frustrated, lovelorn ghost. There are enough glimpses of his toned pecs and spray-on jeans to satisfy our baser urges, and he and Whoopi make a likeable, sparky comic duo. Goldberg is in her element as the medium who discovers, with Sam's help, that she's not the charlatan she believed herself to be, and won a Best Supporting Actress Oscar for her performance.

Ghost's special effects – Sam walking through doors, for example – appear charmingly old-fashioned now, though the shadowy dark spirits that whisk off evildoers when they die are still creepy, their weird moans created from a slowed down tape of babies wailing. The murder mystery element, though nicely paced, is little more than a backdrop, but the comedy is spot on, providing just the right amount of light relief. Ultimately, however, the film is about an all-consuming love. Although impossible to take entirely seriously, even the notorious potter's wheel antics develop, after all the clay-squelching stuff, into a genuinely tender and erotic scene. The use of the swelling "Unchained Melody" to accompany their lovemaking is sheer genius; sexy and unabashedly emotional, it's also reprised to weepy effect during the heart-wrenching finale.

Sam and Molly's bittersweet reunion fires on all cylinders. (Unsurprisingly, the movie cops out of showing Moore and Goldberg kissing, though Oda Mae is the vessel through which the lovers connect.) Gloriously cheesy, it's also a beautiful piece of film-making, touching the part of us that longs for love, and life, not to end – but knows at heart that they must.

Gone With The Wind

dir Victor Fleming, 1939, US, 222m
cast Vivien Leigh, Clark Gable, Olivia de Havilland, Hattie McDaniel, Leslie Howard, Butterfly McQueen *cin* Ernest Haller *m* Max Steiner

The most popular film of all time, *Gone With The Wind* was, right from the start, a phenomenon, and the saga of its production history

– not to mention its reception – is now legendary. The script was adapted from the romantic Civil War novel by first-time (and one-off) author **Margaret Mitchell**; published in 1936 to little fanfare, by the time the film was released the book had sold a record-breaking 1.5 million copies. In the three years it took to take the movie from script to screen, producer **David O. Selznick** engineered an extraordinary publicity frenzy, most famously with the nationwide "Who will play Scarlett?" talent search – held despite, some say, Selznick having (secretly) decided on **Vivien Leigh** as early as 1937. The production itself was vexed, running way over budget and dispensing with at least three directors (including famed "women's director" George Cukor, who gave up after one month, unhappy with the script) – even **Victor Fleming** himself quit for a month, claiming a nervous breakdown. The movie finally debuted on December 15, 1939 with a glittering gala performance in Atlanta – a gala that the film's black stars, as this was the segregated South, could not attend – and the following year it received (more record-breaking statistics) thirteen Oscar nominations. It won eight (Best Picture, Director, Actress, Screenplay, Color Cinematography, Art Decoration, Editing and Supporting Actress), along with special awards for the "use of color for the enhancement of dramatic mood" and "pioneering use of coordinated equipment".

Visually stunning, shot in vibrant Technicolor, the movie entertains on every level: as an epic saga, a lush melodrama and a passionate love story. Costing the then unheard-of sum of $4 million to make, everything about it is marvellously overblown, from the sets, the cinematography, the gorgeously hued costumes and the iconic soundtrack, right down to its playing time, which, including a musical interlude, runs to nearly four hours. Scarlett O'Hara may well be cinema's greatest ever heroine: an independent-minded Southern belle, she grows from a selfish teenager into a fierce, courageous woman who, having lost nearly everything in the Civil War, will defend her beloved family plantation, Tara, to the death. More than a decade of dramatic historical events provides a vivid backdrop to her complicated love life, and, in particular, her sexy relationship with the dashing, charismatic Rhett Butler (**Clark Gable** – but of course you knew that).

While it did touch on controversial subjects like rape and adultery, the movie had to be more careful around issues of race than the book. The word "nigger" was dropped early on

"Frankly my dear ... who cares if it's true?"

There are enough anecdotal – and maybe apocryphal – snippets about *Gone With The Wind* to fill a book. Here's a favourite: in 1939, when Hollywood movies were still answerable to the rigorous censorship of the Production Code, Rhett's now infamous last words were seen as too risqué. Apparently, with pale alternatives like "Frankly my dear ... I just don't care", "...it makes my gorge rise", "...my indifference is boundless" and "...nothing could interest me less", producer David O. Selznick chose in the end to go with the gutsy "Frankly my dear ... I don't give a damn" and pay a $5000 fine. In the book, incidentally, the line reads simply, "My dear, I don't give a damn," which just doesn't sound the same.

Rhett and Scarlett: he's no gentleman, and she's certainly no lady

from the script, as were any references to the Ku Klux Klan. Though the film has since been criticized as racist – modern audiences find it hard to stomach the simple-minded and squawking Prissy (**Butterfly McQueen**), for example – watching them today, it is striking how significant the film's black characters are. **Hattie McDaniel**, in particular, puts in a funny, strong and scene-stealing turn as Mammy, making her the first African-American actor to be nominated for – and to win – an Oscar (for Best Supporting Actress, which she won over her co-star **Olivia de Havilland**). Indeed, part of the huge impact of *Gone With The Wind* is that it is an elegy for, rather than a celebration of, the doomed Old South, with all its contradictions and its many flaws. "Look for it only in books," the prologue says, "for it is no more than a dream remembered, a civilization gone with the wind…". That modern audiences still experience such a huge wave of emotion while watching this colossus of a movie is testament to its enduring power.

His Girl Friday

dir **Howard Hawks, 1939, US, 92m, b/w**

cast **Rosalind Russell, Cary Grant, Ralph Bellamy, Gene Lockhart, Porter Hall, Helen Mack** *cin* **Joseph Walker** *m* **Morris W. Stoloff**

The frantic tip-tap of the Remington typewriter, the rat-a-tat of battle-of-the-sexes spats, wailing police sirens, ricocheting gunshots and endless, nerve-jangling telephone bells – *His Girl Friday* is one noisy movie. It's also a fast-moving crime story and a sparky romance to boot, boasting the smartest, scrappiest heroine ever to wield a reporter's notebook. Based on *The Front Page,* **Ben Hecht** and **Charles MacArthur**'s play about two newspapermen, the film adds a mischievous twist by replacing one of the leads with a woman, flinging a healthy slug of sexual chemistry into the mix to create a hugely enjoyable screwball classic.

Guided with a sure hand by comedy director **Howard Hawks**, the movie sets its thoroughly modern romance against a grainy urban backdrop of smoky newsrooms and shadowy jailhouses. Ace reporter Hildy Johnson (**Rosalind Russell**), who used to work for – and was married to – the unscrupulous newspaper editor Walter Burns (**Cary Grant**), turns up in his office to tell him she is going to re-marry. Sick of the press, yearning to be respectable and live a halfway normal life, she introduces her new fiancé, Bruce (**Ralph Bellamy**), a well-meaning but painfully slow insurance agent from the sticks. Walter, however, wants what he can't have, and knowing that newshound Hildy won't be able to resist chasing the latest big story – involving a corrupt mayor, a wrongfully accused man on death row, and an innocent woman browbeaten by the press – he sets his trap and waits. And with just hours to go before she embarks on her new life, Hildy gets caught up, despite herself, in the thrill of the scoop and her old, wisecracking relationship with her ex.

Russell is fabulous as the sassy Hildy, confidently striding through the newsroom in gorgeous pinstriped outfits and an impudent zigzaggy hat. Graceful, clever and funny, she's cool in a crisis and can swagger with the best of the guys – and with just one arch of her elegant eyebrow it's clear she has Walter's number. She's the kind of fast-talking movie dame they just don't make any more, and a very particular kind of screwball heroine. No kooky blonde or madcap heiress, Hildy is tough and human, a career girl trying to escape her man rather than ensnare him. Grant, meanwhile, handsome and witty, towering above his co-stars, manages to be at once suave and shockingly rude, leaving Hildy, like one of the guys, to carry her own bags and pay for her own lunch: "You're a newspaper man!", he bellows. Though his ungentlemanly ways may have been outrageous in 1940, his sly humour and simmering sexuality have a delicious appeal for post-feminist audiences not too concerned about having doors opened and restaurant bills paid.

His Girl Friday is a strong ensemble piece – the newspapermen, in particular, in cocked hats and shirt sleeves, playing cards and puffing on cigarettes, are like some lugubrious, hard-bitten chorus – but the screen really lights up with Hildy and Walter's two-handers. Theirs is an exhilarating love story, one that's based on talking – fast-talking, sweet-talking, sparring, sniping and flirting – and that entails a meeting of equal minds. Through their words the sexual chemistry simply crackles, providing a breathless,

Office romance, screwball-style

turbo-charged foreplay that eventually seduces Hildy back into the newspaper game.

Imitation Of Life

dir Douglas Sirk, 1959, US, 125m
cast Lana Turner, John Gavin, Sandra Dee, Juanita Moore, Susan Kohner, Daniel O'Herlihy *cin* Russell Metty *m* Frank Skinner

Imitation Of Life was the last film made by **Douglas Sirk** (see Icons), the director responsible for some of the finest melodramas in 1950s Hollywood. Based on the bestselling novel (1933) by **Fannie Hurst**, it is a heart-wrenching mother-daughter story played out against the terrible backdrop of America's racial divide. Despite its sensitive subject matter, it became Universal Studio's most financially success-ful movie to date, and, with Sirk's confident use of music, lighting and production design – not to mention sterling performances from the four female leads – its emotional impact is as resonant today as it was fifty years ago.

The story revolves around two single-mother families who meet at Coney Island. The white family, Lora (**Lana Turner**) and her daughter Susie (**Sandra Dee**), take in the homeless black woman Annie and her fiery daughter Sarah Jane (**Juanita Moore** and **Susan Kohner** respectively, each Oscar-nominated for Best Supporting Actress), and eventually Lora hires Annie as her house-keeper. As the women grow together over the years, each yearns for things she cannot have. Lora is determined to be an actress, and, when she succeeds, to be taken seriously. Susie craves her mother's attention, and later her boyfriend, Steve (**John Gavin**). Troubled Sarah Jane strives to pass as white, while Annie, who craves her daughter's love, also dreams of the day she will have a huge, dignified funeral. And, despite their love for one another, each is flawed. Lora steamrollers over those who care about her, from Steve, who is willing to abandon his own dreams in order to support her, to Annie, whom she sees only in terms of her own household – expressing shock when she discovers that the black woman has friends of her own – and even her lonely daughter. The daughters aren't much better: Sarah Jane is unbearably cruel to Annie, while Susie's interest in Steve appears to be an outright attempt to get at her mother. Even the saintly Annie is not perfect, her love for Sarah Jane threatening to smother her. In Lora's big, perfect American home, complete with leather-bound books, stone-clad walls and white sofas, each woman is, tragically, trapped by what she longs for.

There are moments of shocking violence. The scene in which Sarah Jane is beaten up in an alley by her white boyfriend, who is horrified when he discovers that she is black, is difficult to watch, and, with its crazed jazz soundtrack reaching fever pitch, to listen to. An earlier sequence, in which Sarah Jane defiantly serves Lora and her friends with a vitriolic forelock-tugging outburst, is just as shocking, explicitly stating the unspeakable – that well-meaning Lora is part of the system that keeps Annie and Sarah Jane trapped. And there are moments of terrible sorrow, too. When Annie finally says goodbye to Sarah Jane, pretending to Sarah Jane's friend that she is her daughter's childhood maid so as not to reveal her secret, the loss is almost unbearable. "Sooo, honey chile, you had you a mammy," teases the friend later. "Yes – all my life," whispers Sarah Jane, who has finally got what she wanted.

Imitation Of Life's lingering finale, which can only be seen through a blur of tears, acts as some kind of catharsis, unleashing a huge wave of loneliness, longing and soaring love. The tacked-on happy ending that follows, as Sirk knows full well, means little in the face of such relentless and impossible sorrow.

In The Cut

dir Jane Campion, 2003, US, 119m
cast Meg Ryan, Mark Ruffalo, Jennifer Jason Leigh, Kevin Bacon, Nick Damici, Sharrieff Pugh *cin* Dion Beebe *m* Hilmar Órn Hilmarsson

As with her earlier triumph *The Piano* (1993; see p.109), **Jane Campion** created a poetic and visually stunning work of art with

In The Cut. Unlike the earlier film, however, this one failed to achieve the accolades, being a far trickier, more explicit and at times shockingly violent piece. Based on the bestselling crime novel by **Susanna Moore** (who also co-wrote the screenplay), the movie is both a thriller and a love story, albeit one that looks at love with a suspicious eye. Frannie (**Meg Ryan**) is a vaguely unhappy creative writing teacher who, along with her half sister Pauline (a typically sexy performance from **Jennifer Jason Leigh**), masks her romantic heart under a street-savvy New York veneer. Pauline feeds her hunger for romance by falling for unsuitable men, while Frannie loses herself in her love of words – in the subway carriage poems that she feels are speaking directly to her, and in sepia-toned nostalgic fantasies handed down from her mother. After stumbling across a mysterious, shadowy couple engaging in fellatio in a back room of a bar, and catching sight of a tattoo on the man's wrist, Frannie is sexually hooked, unable to forget what she has seen. When she meets blue-collar policeman Malloy (**Mark Ruffalo**), who is investigating a particularly nasty serial killer, and spots the same tattoo upon his wrist, she is caught up in an erotic journey that threatens to annihilate every certainty she lives by and, eventually, to annihilate her.

In The Cut's *noir*ish vision of New York is stunning, saturated with colour – all blood-red Chinese lanterns and moody green neon – and replete with visual symbols. Disorientating and dreamy, it is a world in which, from the opening moments – when Pauline dances in a shower of blossom accompanied by a haunting version of "Que Sera, Sera,", and Frannie, waking up, mistakes the blossom for snow – no one should count on what they believe to be true. Romance and passion, especially, are shown to be capricious. The sex scenes between Malloy and Frannie, though agressively explicit, have their own tender and highly intimate quality, while even the serial killer woos his prey with an engagement ring before slashing them to pieces. Pauline and Frannie, on the other hand, their relationship unencumbered by sexual passion, enjoy an innocent physicality reminiscent of tumbling puppies.

All three leads put in subtle, slightly mysterious performances totally in keeping with the movie's tone. The role of Frannie – ordinary-looking, serious, flawed – was a dramatic departure for Ryan (see Icons), a world apart from the tousle-haired cutie she'd trademarked in movies like *When Harry Met Sally...* (1989; see

Meg Ryan (left) gets sexy

p.138) and *Sleepless In Seattle* (1993). Doing the rounds promoting *In The Cut*, she was lambasted as being difficult and unfriendly, and, having compromised her career by choosing integrity and creative risk-taking over box office success, has yet to win the press back. Ruffalo (see Icons), who had made a small splash in movies like *You Can Count On Me* (2000; see p.143), had only recently recovered from a brain tumour before filming *In The Cut*; a little vulnerable and a little damaged, he makes an intriguingly ambivalent romantic hero.

Frannie's journey, which in its final stages becomes a shocking nightmare of violence and grief, is to a place where she can kill off her romantic fantasies and let in something more real. Seen in these terms, though the movie's ending differs somewhat from the dark finale of the book, its impact, if anything, is even greater.

In The Mood For Love (Huayang nianhua)

dir Wong Kar-Wai, 2000, HK/Fr, 97m

cast Maggie Cheung, Tony Leung, Rebecca Pan, Lai Chin, Siu Ping-Lam, Chin Tsi-Ang *cin* Christopher Doyle, Mark Li Ping-Bing *m* Michael Galasso

"He remembers those vanished years. As though looking through a dusty window pane, the past is something he could see but not touch. And everything he sees is blurred and indistinct." So the subtitles tell us as this ravishing film ends and Chow (**Tony Leung**), desperate to unburden himself, whispers a long-held secret into the ancient walls of the mysterious Cambodian temple Angkor Wat. *In The Mood For Love*, a visually stunning meditation on the nature of yearning and loss, is also a treatise on how memory seduces and deceives us. In the bustling, turbocharged Hong Kong of 1962, journalist Chow moves into his new rented apartment on the same day that Mrs Chan (**Maggie Cheung**) arrives next door. Though both are married, both are alone. Chow's wife is working, while Mr Chan is, as so often, away on business. Eventually, the two lonely people discover that their spouses are having an affair – with each other. Hurt and puzzled, they begin spending time together, enacting scenes in which they confront their partners, and eventually working closely on a martial arts series that Chow is producing for a newspaper. A kind of halting, mournful love develops between them, while all around, in the relentlessly modern setting of 1960s Hong Kong, things are changing fast.

As its title suggests, this is both a sumptuous mood piece and a heartbreaking romance. Reminiscent of classic Chinese melodramas in its foregrounding of self-sacrifice over consummated passion, the film also evokes memories of the archetypically British love story *Brief Encounter* (1945; see p.64), and was a direct influence on Sofia Coppola's super-cool *Lost In Translation* (2003). Though set in the 1960s, *In The Mood For Love*, magpie-like, pilfers from iconography – music, fashion, pop culture – from the 1940s onwards. The effect is dreamlike, as though we have been invited to rummage through an attic of half-forgotten mementoes.

Wong Kar-Wai, the darling of new Hong Kong cinema, is a notoriously rigorous taskmaster, refusing to work with scripts and instead allowing his movies to organically evolve. His regular collaborators Cheung and Leung, models of cool restraint, put in extraordinary performances richly nuanced with unexpressed longing. Meanwhile, the gorgeous art direction and cinematography, along with the exquisite costumes and haunting score, create an overwhelmingly emotional experience. The lovers' claustrophobic urban world, saturated with passionate colour and satiny light, is rendered full of possibility, while the music, a combination of popular Chinese songs, silky Nat King Cole standards and lilting instrumental themes, is melancholy in the extreme. The recurring image of clocks and the endless repetition of Mrs Chan and Mr Chow's daily domestic routines show time's relentless march forward, while the slow motion, stop-motion and crackly old gramophone records create the effect of time slowing down – if only in the protagonists' wishful dreams. Chronology is irrelevant in this poetic love story, but if you want to keep track of the literal order of events, you could do worse than follow the progression of Mrs Chan's glorious cheongsams (those tight, decorative and high-collared Chinese dresses). Shimmering like exotic flowers, the satin cheongsams tell much of the story of *In The Mood For Love* – and rarely has a story been so beautifully told.

Like Water For Chocolate (Como agua para chocolate)

dir Alfonso Arau, 1991, Mex, 114m
cast Lumi Cavazos, Marco Leonardi, Regina Torné,
Ada Carrasco, Yareli Arizmendi, Claudette Maillé, Pilar
Aranda, Mario Iván Martínez *cin* Emmanuel Lubezki
m Leo Brower

The hugely successful Mexican movie *Like Water For Chocolate*, based on the bestselling novel by **Laura Esquivel** (who, incidentally, was married to the director at the time), has all the ingredients of a great melodrama. With its array of beautifully drawn female characters, it's an accomplished ensemble piece suffused with Mexican culture – food, history, music – a culture in which the struggle between duty, tradition, family and passion looms large. Tita (**Lumi Cavazos**), who runs a ranch in early twentieth-century Mexico with her mother, older sisters and female housekeepers, is passionately in love with the handsome Pedro (**Marco Leonardi**). They long to marry, but family tradition demands that the youngest daughter stay at home and take care of her mother for life. Tita's hardhearted mother (**Regina**

Foodie chick flicks

Whether arousing hunger or revulsion, memories or dreams, food has the power to unleash deeply held passions. In chick flicks, food preparation can give women (and some men – see Ang Lee's sprightly *Eat Drink Man Woman*, 1994) a welcome form of personal expression, while the meals they cook are invariably far more than simply something to eat. Foodie chick flicks equate food with female sensuality and subversive power (*Babette's Feast*, 1987; *Like Water For Chocolate*, 1991; the preposterous Sarah Michelle Gellar vehicle *Simply Irresistible*, 1999; *Chocolat*, 2000), and/or make the dinner table an arena for explosive family melodrama (*Soul Food*, 1997; *What's Cooking?*, 2000; *Pieces Of April*, 2003). Note, too, that movie men who can cook generally turn out to be the good guys, though there are exceptions (Hannibal Lecter comes to mind).

Torné) offers Pedro Rosaura (**Yareli Arizmendi**), one of her other daughters instead, and he accepts in order to be close to the one he really loves. Heartbroken, forced by her mother to hide her tears and to prepare the wedding feast, Tita weeps silently into the wedding cake mixture, and, as they eat it, the wedding guests are overcome with a strange sadness and uncontrollable nausea. What follows is a twenty-year-long family saga – taking in revolution, family secrets, erotic obsession, curses and ghosts – in which the intensely emotional power of food, and the magic that can occur in the kitchen, is always to the fore.

Cavazos is terrific as Tita, struggling to do what is right for herself and those she loves, and who, almost despite herself, pours her repressed passion into her cooking. Her difficult choices, her quiet power and her very many sacrifices put her right up there with the great tragic heroines of classic Hollywood melodramas, and Cavazos, a young actress, carries it off beautifully. She is surrounded by strong performances, especially from **Claudette Maillé** as Gertrudis, the quietly rebellious sister, who, erotically overcome after eating Tita's seductive meal of quail in rose petals, runs away to join the revolution, and Arizmendi as Rosaura, who, having threatened to keep her own daughter unmarried, is ultimately consumed by Tita's unconscious, and highly unpleasant, curse. Torné is evil incarnate as the wicked witch mother, though even her harshness is revealed to mask a sad secret. Add to the pot the ranch staff – mischievous Chencha (**Pilar Aranda**) and the wise old Nacha (**Ada Carrasco**) – and you have a richly satisfying mix of women. This is not just Tita's story; each woman has her own narrative, for which Tita, and her food, are the catalyst.

The book upon which the film was based is a classic of magical realism, the Latin American literary genre that became wildly popular in the 1980s. The movie, wisely, carries its magical elements lightly and always for maximum impact – the shawl Tita knits during her long, lonely nights stretching out behind her for miles as she rides off on a carriage, for example, or the firework sparks that crackle when her erotic urges are ignited. By focusing on magic as poetry rather than sheer whimsy, *Like Water For Chocolate* raises itself above other, more recent fantasy-infused movies like *Amélie* (2001) or *Eternal Sunshine Of The Spotless Mind* (2004), and is dated only by a somewhat intrusive and clunky soundtrack.

Mildred Pierce

dir Michael Curtiz, 1945, US, 113m, b/w
cast Joan Crawford, Jack Carson, Zachary Scott, Eve
Arden, Ann Blyth, Bruce Bennett *cin* Ernest Haller *m* Max
Steiner

Based on the pulp novel by **James M. Cain** (whose work also formed the basis for the classics *Double Indemnity* and *The Postman Always Rings Twice*), *Mildred Pierce* is a *film noir* with a difference. Though it shares many of the trademarks of that hard-boiled B-movie genre – from its dramatic shadows-and-light cinematography and expressionistic sets to its unreliable voice-over and cynical sensibility – this is also one of the classic Hollywood "women's movies" of the 1940s, a melodrama aimed at a mainly female audience and told from a woman's point of view. It also, of course, stars the fabulous **Joan Crawford** (see Icons). Master cinematographer **Ernest Haller** had a special empathy for lighting and framing Crawford's enormous eyes and mighty cheekbones, and in this film her mannish face becomes nothing short of iconic. Whether bustling around in a frilly apron or stumbling through the dead of night swathed in mink, Crawford gives a tour de force performance, for which she won the only Oscar of her career. **Eve Arden**, a breath of fresh air as Ida, Mildred's wisecracking friend, and **Ann Blyth** as the unredeemable Veda, were also Oscar-nominated.

Shots ring out in a beach house; a man gasps, "Mildred", and falls dead; a car drives off into the rain-soaked night. Having been sent packing by a patrolling officer when it appears she is about to throw herself off a pier, Mildred (Crawford) seduces her old friend, Wally (**Jack Carson**), back to the beach house, locks him in with the corpse and flees. Upon arriving home, Mildred is told by the police that her husband has been shot, and, despite the cries of her distressed daughter Veda, is taken to the station for questioning. Here she discovers to her horror that her first husband, Bert (**Bruce Bennett**), has been arrested, and, in an attempt to clear his name, begins her flashback narration. Suddenly we are in the sunny suburbs, and presented with the incongruous sight of Joan Crawford baking pies. "I was always in the kitchen," Mildred says bitterly. "I felt as though I'd been born in a kitchen and lived there all my life – except for the few hours it took to get married." Very quickly Mildred and Bert decide to split, and her life as a single mother begins. Tough and resourceful, Mildred, desperate for her two daughters "to amount to something" takes a job waitressing; her Achilles' heel, however, is the monstrously selfish Veda, played with chilling relish by the usually angelic Blyth. As she gives in to everything Veda wants at the expense of her own happiness, Mildred is soon lured into an increasingly deadly *noir* nightmare.

A bleak depiction of masculinity – all the men in Mildred's life are sleazy, weak or bullying – *Mildred Pierce* also offers a hellish vision of mother-daughter love, given a snidey twist by the nasty, perhaps apocryphal, stories that have since emerged about Crawford's real-life mothering. While Mildred is not beneath lying, marrying for money and who knows what else, it is clear that Veda, her china-doll face flashing pure hatred as she spits out vitriol – "You'll never be anything but a common frump!" – and psychological abuse – "It's your fault I'm the way I am. Help me!" – is this movie's true femme fatale.

Moulin Rouge!

dir Baz Luhrmann, 2001, US, 128m

cast Nicole Kidman, Ewan McGregor, Jim Broadbent, Richard Roxburgh, John Leguizamo *cin* Donald M. McAlpine *m* Craig Armstrong

Spectacular and breathtakingly ambitious, *Moulin Rouge!* is a musical whirlwind that either leaves you cold or seduces you utterly. The third (after *Romeo + Juliet* and *Strictly Ballroom*) in **Baz Luhrmann**'s so-called Red Curtain Trilogy, it's a theatrical love story that freely swipes from opera, classic Hollywood, pop music, Bollywood, farce, Greek myth and burlesque – as well as taking great care with authentic historical detail – to create a sensational and utterly original experience.

Ewan McGregor is splendid as Christian, the innocent poet caught up in the world of the Bohemians in fin de siècle Paris, while the fragile **Nicole Kidman**, with her luminous blue-white skin and scarlet lips, encapsulates old Hollywood glamour as Satine, the consumptive courtesan. Their love story, set against the decadent world of the Moulin Rouge cabaret, shifts deftly from high tragedy to the broadest comedy, and features a rich ensemble of characters: die-hard romantic Toulouse-Lautrec (**John Leguizamo**); Zidler (**Jim Broadbent**), the Moulin's devilish owner, who also owns Satine; the lustful Duke (**Richard Roxburgh**), to whom Satine must surrender; a narcoleptic Argentinian tango dancer (**Jacek Koman**); and Le Chocolat (**Deobia Oparei**), the African cabaret artiste.

For all its chutzpah, this is a profoundly emotional film. Opening – after an evocative credit sequence – with a heartbroken Christian in his garret tapping out the story on a battered typewriter, the movie tells us immediately that Satine is doomed, and reminds us of this often, in moments of still, intense beauty. And after the kinetic comedy of the first thirty minutes (in which much play is made of double entendres, misunderstandings and mistaken identity – and in which Kidman proves herself to be a very talented comedienne), we are offered quiet, even naturalistic moments. When the lovers spend time in Christian's garret, for example, the glamorous Satine dressed simply in a faded kimono, all the artifice and travesty of the cabaret is stripped away. Though these scenes help to make *Moulin Rouge!* a satisfying emotional experience, it is the film's sumptuous, utterly unnaturalistic visual language that lingers in the memory. **Catherine Martin** (Luhrmann's wife and genius collaborator) and her team won Best Art Direction/Set Decoration and Best Costume Design Oscars for their magical, fantastic world of absinthe-green

Spectacular, spectacular!: the Moulin Rouge elephant

Joseph Oller and Charles Zidler's legendary music hall, the Moulin Rouge, opened in Montmartre in 1889. Extravagantly decorated, this was the wildest show in town, attracting royalty, poets, prostitutes and politicians. Famed for its aggressively sexy cancan girls, the Moulin Rouge also staged displays of brand-new inventions, harebrained or otherwise, and featured sideshow freaks, ribald stand-up comedians, flatulators – who farted to music – wild monkeys, and bare-legged girls cavorting on donkeys. In the garden, a giant elephant (bought from a Parisian theme park after the Great Exhibition of 1889) housed an Arabian-themed nightclub. Gentlemen entered via the elephant's leg, and climbed a spiral staircase to smoke opium and watch private belly dancing shows. Views of Paris, from within the elephant's belly or from the opulent howdah on top of its back, were incomparable – particularly, no doubt, after a slug or two of absinthe.

Tinkerbell fairies and tantric cancans, where lovers dance on giant jewel-encrusted elephants and magical sitars save the day.

What is extraordinary about *Moulin Rouge!* is the way in which it combines these stunning visuals with barnstorming musical numbers to create something as touching as it is camp, as heart-felt as it is heightened. Satine and Christian's courtship scene, for example, a jaw-dropping starlit set piece atop the Moulin's giant elephant, is genuinely moving, not least because of the purity of the actors' untrained singing voices. While each lover spars with their own beautifully reprised theme (the sunny, optimistic "Your Song" for Christian, the plaintive "One Day I'll Fly Away" for Satine), Christian eventually woos the courtesan with a medley of pop songs from U2 to The Beatles that, against all the odds, wins her, and us, over. Later, the "Roxanne" montage, a tour de force that rapidly cuts between a sexy, growling Argentinian tango, an anguished harmony sung by Christian and the silent rape of Satine by the Duke, is as powerful a piece of movie making as you'll see. However, it is the film's one original composition, Christian and Satine's blindingly romantic "Come What May", that forms the musical heart of this movie – a movie that lives and breathes the Bohemian ideals of Truth, Beauty, Freedom and, above all, Love.

Muriel's Wedding

dir **P.J. Hogan, 1994, Aus/Fr, 106m**
cast **Toni Collette, Rachel Griffiths, Sophie Lee, Bill Hunter, Jeanie Drynan, Gennie Nevinson** *cin* **Martin McGrath** *m* **Peter Best**

With its poppy Abba soundtrack and bright, jarring palette, *Muriel's Wedding* is often described as a quirky Cinderella story, both feel-good and kitsch, the chick flick par excellence. All that is true, but scratch the surface and you also find a seam of depression and despair far darker than anything seen in similarly skewed visions of suburban Australia, such as *Strictly Ballroom* (1992) or *Priscilla Queen Of The Desert* (1994). If this is a fairy tale, it is a savage one, streaked as it is with foul language, deceit, violence, mental illness, cancer and suicide.

Muriel, vulnerable but not very likeable, is the archetypal ugly duckling. Trapped in the suffocating confines of seaside town Porpoise Spit, her only escape from her doltish family, depressed mother, abusive father and vicious friends is to retire to her room

Wedding belles

As rites of passage go, a wedding is a big one. Everything, from drunken uncles and battling in-laws to lovelorn bridesmaids and jittery brides, is ripe with dramatic potential – not to mention the emotional impact of a heartfelt public expression of faith, hope and love.

If you're feeling slushy, you can pick from an almost unlimited choice of happy-ending wedding movies. Rare was a classic Hollywood romantic comedy that didn't end in a walk down the aisle, but the sophisticated *The Philadelphia Story* (1940), with Katharine Hepburn and Cary Grant, goes further by basing its whole story around a society wedding – as does its glorious musical remake, *High Society* (1956), with Frank Sinatra, Bing Crosby and Grace Kelly. More recent choices include the warmhearted *Betsy's Wedding* (1990), the 1980s spoof *The Wedding Singer* (1998), low-budget runaway success *My Big Fat Greek Wedding* (2001), and *Bride & Prejudice* (2004), Gurinder Chadha's Bollywood take on Jane Austen. Many movie weddings extend into days-long feasts, thereby increasing the scope for drama: *The Wedding Banquet* (1993), a US-Taiwanese romantic tangle, for example, or *Monsoon Wedding* (2001), set in India, or even the WASPy *The Wedding Date* (2005), starring Debra Messing and Dermot Mulroney (a wedding movie stalwart). For frock fantasies, look no further than the delectable soft-focus sequence in *Funny Face* (1956), which has Audrey Hepburn twirling through the churchyard in a divine Givenchy gown. The girls in *Gentlemen Prefer Blondes* (1953; see p.83) look pretty spectacular, too.

Anyone feeling a little more ambivalent can root for a fine fleet of runaway brides, among them feisty heiress Claudette Colbert in the screwball *It Happened One Night* (1934); Ginger Rogers, who flees four weddings in *It Had To Be You* (1947); Julia Roberts, whose addictive jilting makes headlines in *Runaway Bride* (1999); and Reese Witherspoon, who sees sense at the last minute in *Sweet Home Alabama* (2002). And if you want to give matrimony a miss altogether, see *Four Weddings And A Funeral* (1993), *Muriel's Wedding* (1994), *My Best Friend's Wedding* (1997; see p.105) and the wicked British mockumentary *Confetti* (2006).

That Julia Roberts – she just can't commit (*Runaway Bride*, 1999)

and listen to Abba, fantasizing about the big fairy tale wedding that would show them, once and for all, that she amounts to something. Life changes when she meets the free-spirited Rhonda, who escaped Porpoise Spit long ago and who, extraordinarily, seems to like Muriel for who she is. Their talent show turn, lip-synching Abba's "Waterloo" in front of a cheering crowd that includes her sour-faced (ex-) friends, is an unalloyed joy; Muriel even gets to be Agnetha, "the sexy one", her white satin bell-bottoms stretched taut across thighs that are as broad as her grin. It's an irresistible scene that's partly responsible for the movie's feel-good reputation, and the delicious revenge of that moment, when the underdogs finally show the bullies where they can stuff it, would in many films be the triumphant finale. But this is no ending for Muriel. She has more scores to settle. Her scars go very deep indeed.

Muriel's Wedding is a film about deeply unhappy people that is both laugh-out-loud funny and gut-wrenchingly painful. Its ability to usher us deftly from comedy into tragedy, and back again, is partly due to strong performances from the two leads, both of whom light up the screen in early film roles. Muriel is no virtuous victim – she obsesses, steals and lies, breaks promises and abandons those who love her. There's a terrible savagery about her self-loathing, and that we care for her so deeply is largely down to **Toni Collette**, who plays lumpen and liberated, victimized and rebellious with equal aplomb. **Rachel Griffiths** is also brilliant as the vivacious Rhonda, who, struck down in the most terrible way, has to face her deepest fears – and who, along with Muriel's bitchy friends, has the funniest, and filthiest, dialogue in the movie.

After a fair amount of heartache, Muriel does get the big wedding she has dreamed of. She gets her fairy tale dress and handsome groom, and the thrill of triumph as her old friends beg to be her bridesmaids. She barely seems to notice, however, that she is now effectively alone, and it takes a devastating family tragedy to show her what she needs to do in order to thrive. A Cinderella story ripped down to its barest bones, revealing raw wounds as it goes, ultimately *Muriel's Wedding* gives us a fairy tale ending that's not about finding a prince, but about finding oneself; a happy-ever-after that means leaving old damage, and old dreams, behind.

My Best Friend's Wedding

dir **P.J. Hogan, 1997, US, 105m**

cast Julia Roberts, Rupert Everett, Cameron Diaz, Dermot Mulroney, Philip Bosco *cin* Laszlo Kovacs *m* James Newton Howard

Three years after *Muriel's Wedding*, director **P.J. Hogan** – no relation to Paul "Crocodile Dundee" Hogan – once again turned his idiosyncratic eye to love and marriage with *My Best Friend's Wedding*. **Julia Roberts** plays Jules, a chain-smoking commitment-phobe who has been best friends for nine years, often at long distance, with sports writer Mike (**Dermot Mulroney**). When Mike and Jules split up after "one hot month together" at college, they agreed that if neither was married by the grand old age of 28, they'd marry each other. Consumed with jealousy when she discovers, three weeks before her 28th birthday, that Mike is about to get hitched, Jules heads to Chicago with just four days to wreck the wedding and win the groom for herself. She hasn't reckoned, however, on the "irritatingly perfect" Kimmy (**Cameron Diaz**), who is 20 years old, blonde, beautiful and rich, and also knows – *really* knows – about true love. Jules, ignoring the counsel of the urbane George (**Rupert Everett**), her gay editor, employs increasingly devious tactics to get Mike back, and meanwhile, for us at least, the "best friend" of the title becomes a little ambiguous. Is Mike, whom she rarely sees, really Jules's best friend any more? What about George? And where does the chirpy Kimmy, who is determined to make Jules her own best friend – and maid of honour – fit in?

This is an intelligent, funny and touching movie, combining Hogan's own brand of subversive humour with the best of classic screwball comedy. Jules joins the ranks of amoral, scheming madcaps like Katharine Hepburn and Carole Lombard who will do anything to win their man, however dull he may be (Mulroney to a tee). Roberts, in a career slump after her phenomenal success in *Pretty Woman* (1990; see p.115), is back on fine form here.

Switching easily from knockabout comedy – falling off chairs and the like – to fast-talking craziness, she turns up the charisma full blast to make dog-in-the-manger Jules someone we actually care about. Diaz, too, with a toothy beam to rival her co-star's, puts in a fine performance as Kimmy, the dizzy blonde with the power to disarm, as ingenuous and demonstrative as Jules is sneaky and heartless. And the wonderful Everett, who has more than a touch of Cary Grant's urbane mischievousness, steals every scene he's in.

The opening credits sequence, a camp but strangely haunting performance of "Wishin' And Hopin'", has echoes of *Muriel's Wedding*, and although music is less foreground here, it is just as crucial. From "You Don't Know Me", when Jules and Mike meet at the airport, to "Annie's Song", warbled out by the best man and his teenage friends after snorting helium balloons at the wedding brunch, music always comments on and undercuts the action. The standout musical number – in fact, the movie's standout scene – is "I Say A Little Prayer", a barnstorming ensemble piece led by George in an attempt to embarrass Jules that is pure laugh-out-loud genius.

In the end, of course, the right guy gets the right girl. Test audiences wisely rejected an alternative ending that had Jules meeting up with a handsome stranger at the wedding reception. Far more satisfying is Hogan's delightful vision of a world where heterosexual romance and fairy tale weddings aren't the be-all and end-all. As George so aptly puts it: "Maybe there won't be marriage, maybe there won't be sex – but by God, there'll be dancing."

Now, Voyager

dir **Irving Rapper, 1942, US, 117m, b/w**
cast **Bette Davis, Paul Henreid, Claude Rains, Gladys Cooper, John Loder, Bonita Granville, Janis Wilson**
cin **Sol Polito** *m* **Max Steiner**

There are many makeover movies in the chick flick canon, but *Now, Voyager*, based on the 1941 book by the popular novelist **Olive**

Higgins Prouty (who also wrote *Stella Dallas*; see p.127), shows what happens *after* the ugly duckling is turned into a swan. With its evocative title – taken from American poet Walt Whitman's "Now, Voyager/Sail Thou Forth to Seek and Find" – this is a classic, classy weepie, the story of one woman's long and unconventional journey to fulfilment, of sorts. Replete with affecting visual refrains – ocean liners, moonlight glinting on water, curls of cigarette smoke, camellias – and an emotional Oscar-winning score from **Max Steiner** (of *Gone With The Wind* fame), *Now, Voyager* never hits a false note.

Bette Davis, all nerves and nicotine, with Paul Henreid

The original idea was to have two actresses take on the role of Charlotte Vale, the repressed frump who transforms, with the kindly assistance of psychiatrist Dr Jaquith (**Claude Rains**), into a butterfly. **Bette Davis** (see Icons), however, proving her mettle as one of Hollywood's all-time greats, puts in a stunning, Oscar-nominated performance as Charlotte both before *and* after. Horribly oppressed by her sadistic mother (**Gladys Cooper**), and locked away in her bedroom reliving memories of a torrid shipboard affair she had long ago, the fat, bushy-browed Charlotte is on the verge of a nervous breakdown when a concerned sister-in-law (**Bonita Granville**) brings in the doctor. Jaquith whisks her off to Cascades, his rehabilitation centre, where, with the help of weaving and lots of therapy, she loses weight and slowly gains confidence. He then sends her on a long sea voyage, in place of a never-seen woman called Renee Beauchamps; Charlotte, now elegant and poised, and with a raft of stunning outfits borrowed from Renee's wardrobe, tells no one her real identity until she meets fellow traveller Jerry (**Paul Henreid**). Jerry renames Charlotte/Renee yet again, calling her Camille – a play not only on Alexandre Dumas's doomed "Lady of the Camellias" (portrayed with tragic intensity by Greta Garbo six years earlier; see p.66), but also on the word chameleon, which, as yet still feeling her way to her true identity, Charlotte remains. Although they fall in love, Jerry is married – to a punishing woman not unlike Charlotte's mother – with two daughters, and they agree, painfully, to split. Their passion is not so easy to contain, however – cue the film's much-copied, intimate moment in which Henreid places two cigarettes in his mouth, lights them both, and hands one to Davis. Much sexually anguished smoke puffing ensues as Steiner's score (which, apparently, Davis disliked for being too intrusive) swells behind them.

Back home, away from the enchanted world of the ocean liner, it is clear that Charlotte's journey has only just begun. The road to self-expression and a fully lived life is not easy, and the still-fragile Charlotte, who wears the camellias Jerry has sent her long after they have withered and died, has a lifetime of yearning, despair and obsessive guilt to overcome. While romance may seem tragically just out of reach, her final bid for happiness is a monumentally courageous gambit, allowing her the possibility of giving and receiving love in a way she has never before been able to. In this light, her heroic, and now iconic, entreaty, "Oh Jerry, don't let's ask for the moon. We have the stars!", gives us cause to both celebrate and to mourn.

The Piano

dir Jane Campion, 1993, Aus, 121m
cast Holly Hunter, Harvey Keitel, Sam Neill, Anna Paquin,
Kerry Walker, Tungia Baker *cin* Stuart Dryburgh
m Michael Nyman

This lyrical, affecting movie, set against the brutal beauty of New Zealand in the mid-nineteenth century, centres on Ada (**Holly Hunter**), who has been mute, by choice, since the age of 6. With her illegitimate young daughter, Flora (**Anna Paquin**), always by her side, she is a defiant woman who, as her father tells her, has a "dark talent" for wilfulness, and whose silence exerts a strange power over those around her. Ada's otherworldly voice-over – "The voice you hear is not my speaking voice, but my mind's voice" – opens and closes the movie, but otherwise she speaks only in secret sign language, translated to the rest of the world by her spirited daughter. At a deeper level, however, it is through her extraordinarily expressive eyes and precise body movements, as well as her passionate, untamed piano playing, that Ada communicates. Hunter is phenomenal in the role, conveying pride, fury and longing through looks and gestures alone.

Packed off by her father from Scotland to New Zealand, where she is to marry Stewart (**Sam Neill**), a white settler, Ada is heartbroken when her future husband insists she leave her beloved piano behind on the beach where she and her daughter have arrived. Pining, Ada insists that George Baines (**Harvey Keitel**), another settler – who, unlike Stewart, has gone native, speaking Maori and decorated with Maori tattoos – lead her and Flora back to the beach. Here, lit up by a rare and blissful smile, she spends the day playing her piano in the spray of the crashing waves, before heading back home at dusk through the tangled rainforest. Thus begins a Gothic love story, in which Baines holds the piano hostage, luring Ada to his cabin so that he can watch her play and, eventually, "do things" in exchange for returning the piano to her key by key. As Ada slowly becomes drawn to Baines, both Flora and Stewart become less and less able to control their jealousy, ultimately leading to a devastating explosion of betrayal and violence.

The Piano is a beautifully composed work. **Michael Nyman**'s lilting musical theme swells and ebbs like the relentless Pacific tide on the lonely beach, accompanying images of delicate and poetic beauty. There is an overriding feeling of dreaminess: the local Maori, tattooed, top-hatted and chattering unintelligibly, are a mischievous, mysterious presence; and just as off-kilter are the white settlers, whose gory staging of the Bluebeard story creates one of the film's most unsettling scenes. At the heart of the movie, the hesitant and poignant physicality between Ada and Baines – he tracing a hole in her woollen stocking with his finger, or kissing her face through a scarf – is just as mysterious, revealing the tenderness of a love that goes beyond words.

This is also a story about the fierce passion between mother and daughter – their faces are often shown together in close-up, echoing each other – and the pain of their inevitable separation. Paquin, as the possessive and ultimately treacherous daughter, puts in a complex and heartbreakingly true performance; both she and Hunter won Oscars, as did **Jane Campion** (see Icons) for her screenplay.

Ada ultimately chooses the messiness of the real world over the safety of silence – a choice that surprises even her. But, as her voice-over, the voice of her mind, tells us, she will never quite let go of her "weird lullaby", just as we will never quite forget the haunting image of Ada and her piano floating in "a silence where hath been no sound … a silence where no sound may be".

Pillow Talk

dir **Michael Gordon, 1959, US, 105m**
cast **Doris Day, Rock Hudson, Tony Randall, Thelma Ritter, Nick Adams, Marcel Dalio** *cin* **Arthur E. Arling**
m **Frank De Vol**

The sparkling *Pillow Talk* – the first and finest of **Doris Day**'s bedroom comedies – marked a sea change for both its stars. Day (see Icons), whom audiences were most used to seeing in high collars, dirndl skirts (or in the case of *Calamity Jane*, in mud-splattered buckskins), emerged here as sexy and sophisticated, her curvaceous frame swathed in stunning gowns designed by top movie couturier Jean Louis (the designer responsible for creating Rita Hayworth's iconic satin *Gilda* dress). While Day was revealing a new, more overt sexuality, she had nothing to prove as a comedienne. Her dashing co-star **Rock Hudson** (see Icons), however, shows himself for the first time to be a brilliant comic actor, underplaying with a kind of wry Cary Grant cool, and throwing in heaps of self-parody. With a palpable on-screen chemistry emanating partly from their physical compatibility – both so glossy and sleek, she platinum blonde, he dashingly dark – and partly from their strong off-screen friendship, they made a perfect comedy duo. And they were ably backed by reliable character

Doris and Rock: comedy duo extraordinaire

actors **Tony Randall** and **Thelma Ritter**, who did here what they always did best – he playing the analyst-dependent neurotic, she the hard-bitten, hard-drinking maid.

Pillow Talk opens with a slow pan up Day's long, bare, sexy leg as it introduces us to Jan Morrow, Manhattan-based interior designer and archetypal Modern Woman. With a fab career and a dream apartment, the only thing spoiling her life is Brad Allen (Hudson), the womanizing songwriter who hogs their shared phone line while crooning to a succession of unsuspecting love-lies. In a sequence of saucy split-screen scenes Jan and Brad, who haven't actually met, battle over the phone – she accuses him of being a selfish slimeball, he pronounces her to have "bedroom troubles".

Most underrated chick flick:
Pillow Talk

Doris Day has been seriously maligned. This super-talented comedienne is far too often derided as the eternal virgin, a wholesome sap, and the so-called "sex comedies" she made with **Rock Hudson** in the late 1950s and early 60s are glibly accused of setting feminism back twenty years. One wonders – have any of these people actually *seen* a Doris/Rock movie? *Pillow Talk*, the first and the best of the three they made together, would be a good place to start. An effervescent battle-of-the-sexes comedy, it looks just wonderful, with a sophisticated champagne-fizz sheen and palpable chemistry between its two gorgeous stars. Audiences at the time got how great it was – the film won an Oscar for its crackling, very funny screenplay (Day and co-star Thelma Ritter were also nominated), and went on to become the second-largest-grossing film of the decade – and it is only since the sexual revolution of the 1970s that it has been so betrayed.

Such was this movie's success that Doris and Rock went on to replay their roles as feisty fashion plate and predatory rogue in *Lover Come Back* (1961), and again as a married couple in *Send Me No Flowers* (1964), but *Pillow Talk* remains the funniest and the freshest of the lot. And as for Doris – a wholesome sap? *Pillow Talk* has her as an independent New York career girl who is more than a match for her man. Throughout, we see her in a succession of delicious outfits, designed by top couturier Jean Louis, and spouting endless perfect put-downs. She's got a voice like honey and she gets to kiss Rock Hudson. What could possibly be the problem?

Having heard about her from their mutual friend, Jonathan (Randall), Brad first sees Jan at a nightclub and is blown away by her sexy bare back and swaying backside (frankly, you'd have to be dead not to be – she's wearing an incredibly gorgeous open-backed white sheath dress that caused something of a stir at the time). In order to win her into bed, Brad pretends to be shy Texas boy Rex Stetson, complete with Southern drawl and old-fashioned good manners. A game of cat and mouse ensues, with lots of humour arising from the film's famous split-screen scenes, in which Jan and Brad appear to be canoodling or playing footsie from their sudsy baths. There's also plenty of play at the expense of Rock's homosexuality, which was one of Hollywood's best-kept open secrets. At one point Brad, during one of his phone spats with Jan, insinuates that Rex must be gay not to have made a pass at her. When they next meet, Rex expresses an inordinate interest in recipes and cocks his little finger while drinking – much to Jan's consternation.

The movie was a major box office success, spawning two more Doris/Rock movies, and a few more in the same vein that matched Day with debonair actors James Garner, Rod Taylor and Cary Grant. By 1968, however, the formula was wearing thin, and the sophisticated sex comedy had had its day. For audiences nowadays, however, its knowing, fizzy humour, glossy 1950s palette and sheer sassy energy should carve it out a place as a modern classic, not nearly as old-fashioned as those Doris Day detractors would have us believe.

Postcards From The Edge

dir **Mike Nichols, 1990, US, 101m**
cast **Meryl Streep, Shirley MacLaine, Gene Hackman, Dennis Quaid, Richard Dreyfuss** *cin* **Michael Ballhaus**
m **Carly Simon**

Postcards From The Edge, the semi-autobiographical novel by Hollywood screenwriter/actress **Carrie Fisher**, is a darkly comic tale of drug dependency and detox. For the screenplay, director **Mike Nichols** asked the writer to beef up the book's allusions to Fisher's vexed relationship with her mother, and the movie hit pay dirt. **Meryl Streep** (see Icons) plays Suzanne Vale, a tough-on-the-outside but oh-so-fragile movie actress whose career is floundering due to her addiction to various illegal substances. After an accidental overdose sends her into detox, she's offered a shot at redemption with a role in a cheesy B-movie – on condition that she stays off the drugs, and stays with her mother, for the duration of the shoot. Living with her mother, however – the glamorous, vain and demanding Doris (**Shirley MacLaine**), who has something of a taste for the spotlight herself – is the one thing guaranteed to send Suzanne running straight back to her old habits.

Fisher, daughter of movie stars Debbie Reynolds and Eddie Fisher (who left the marriage for Elizabeth Taylor), is ambivalent about the movie, having since spent a decade and a half insisting that Doris is not, actually, Debbie, and that this is not, actually, a true story. Although many snippets of dialogue are taken from real life, the big confrontation and reconciliation scenes are fiction, added to make a coherent story out of something rather messier. Despite Fisher's reservations, however, and in no small part due to her super-sharp writing, *Postcards* is a brilliant sketch of an ambivalent, intense relationship, in which both women are difficult but neither is a demon. When Doris throws a welcome home party for Suzanne and steals the show with a barnstorming cabaret performance, we can sympathize with Suzanne's muddle of fury and grudging pride, while Doris's challenges to her super-smart daughter – "You always felt you were my intellectual superior, ever since you were 14 years old" – are as insecure as they are angry. With Suzanne secretly snaffling prescription pills from the bathroom cabinet and Doris sneaking a slug or three of vodka into her smoothie, it's clear that each is as bad as the other, and perhaps neither is as bad as all that – simply designed, as Suzanne puts it, "more for public than private".

Streep and MacLaine have a lot of fun with Fisher's snappy script. Having branched out into comedy a year earlier with Susan Seidelman's *She-Devil*, Streep finds her pace here. Pale-faced and jittery, she delivers her wise guy one-liners with the same weary black humour and half-masked vulnerability that Fisher herself exudes, and is convincing as an old soul who has yet to grow up. MacLaine, meanwhile, having won an Oscar for playing another impossible mother, Aurora, in *Terms Of Endearment* (1983; see p.129), gives, if anything, an even more complex performance here. Coiffed, painted and swathed in fur coats, Doris is an innocent narcissist who, it transpires, understands more than it seems. A woman who gave her 9-year-old daughter sleeping pills, Doris accepts that damage is part of her legacy, something passed down from generation to generation – or rather, from mother to mother, as fathers in this world are all notably absent or comically silent. It is Suzanne's gruff director, Lowell (**Gene Hackman**), who ultimately takes on the role of idealized daddy, insisting that she get over her mother, and herself. Only then can she, as Doris has urged her to, at long last "enjoy her turn".

Pretty Woman

dir Garry Marshall, 1990, US, 119m
cast Julia Roberts, Richard Gere, Ralph Bellamy, Jason Alexander, Hector Elizondo, Laura San Giacomo
cin Charles Minsky *m* James Newton Howard

Drawing on classic fairy tales from Cinderella to Pygmalion, *Pretty Woman* was a fable for the "Greed is Good" 1980s, and was also the movie that made a megastar of **Julia Roberts**. She gives a terrific, Oscar-nominated performance as the smart, vulnerable girl from the wrong side of the tracks, with a freshness that recalls a young Audrey Hepburn – another great Cinderella story stalwart. Her directness and vivacity are the perfect foil for **Richard Gere**'s icy cool, and their coupling has genuine chemistry – so much so that **Garry Marshall** went on to pair the two again in 1999's *Runaway Bride*, a superior rom-com that nonetheless didn't go on to achieve the phenomenal status of this chick flick classic.

A Cinderella story for the 1990s

Roberts plays Vivian, a hooker who works Hollywood Blvd, the famed boulevard of dreams, with her street-smart friend Kit (**Laura San Giacomo**). Kit, acclimatized to life on the streets, spends their rent money on drugs; Vivian, however, is turning tricks in order to survive. One night she encounters rich workaholic Edward (Gere), who refuses to get emotionally involved with anybody; the nearest thing he has to a friend is his avaricious lawyer Stuckey (**Jason Alexander**). Vivian intrigues him, however, and very quickly he is paying her to be his escort for the week. It soon transpires that Edward and Vivian are not as different as they first appear. His silence when she says, "Your parents must be proud of you," signals a wounded core as vulnerable as Vivian's own, and it's easy to surmise that his drive to succeed comes from a simple need to be loved by his father. When she tells him that, like most hookers, she never kisses on the

Makeover movies

Pretty Woman is a classic makeover movie, an update on the old Cinderella story that promises us everything will be all right if we can just get a new wardrobe and a glossy hairdo. Roberts cornered the market in Cinderella roles for a while, from Vivian, who trades in her miniskirts and thigh-high boots for shoulder pads and straw hats, to Kiki in *America's Sweethearts* (2001), whose transformation from fat frump to feisty clotheshorse wins her a prince in the form of John Cusack. Even in *Erin Brockovich* (2000; see p.78) the poverty-stricken single mom transforms into some kind of latter-day superhero while losing the bad make-up and big hairdos along the way.

The queen of makeover movies, however, has to be the delectable **Audrey Hepburn**, whose roles in *Roman Holiday, Sabrina, Funny Face* and *My Fair Lady* all involve a butterfly-like transformation from gamine to sophisticate (or, in *Roman Holiday*, the reverse). Intriguingly, Hepburn's signature movie, *Breakfast At Tiffany's* (1961; see p.57), shows what happens *after* the makeover, when Cinderella has turned into a princess – and suggests that perhaps it's not all it's cracked up to be. Similarly, **Bette Davis**, the transformed Charlotte Vale in *Now, Voyager* (1942; see p.106), discovers that glamorous frocks, though certainly not to be sniffed at, are not all that's needed for a happy ending. Another cynical take on Cinderella comes with *Muriel's Wedding* (1994; see p.102), where the fairy tale is revealed as a nightmare, and the Prince as an absolute pig. *Miss Congeniality* (2000) gives the whole thing a light-hearted post-feminist twist as **Sandra Bullock**, the klutzy tomboy agent, changed back to her former self after a spell as a beauty queen, finds herself missing her high heels and the wonders they did for her posture.

mouth, and he responds that neither does he, it is clear that she's not the only one used to sex without love. Edward's gruff, "We both screw people for money," finally hammers the point home.

Ultimately, however, though the film does expose some of the cynicism of a society where being rich gets you respect and being poor leaves you powerless, any dark sensibility is dusted away pretty fast. This is a movie in which not only the tart, but practically everyone, has a heart of gold. **Hector Elizondo** is a quiet scene-stealer as Barney, the hotel manager. His love-hate bond with Vivian, like the squabbly, affectionate friendship she has with Kit, is in stark contrast to Edward's money-obsessed relationship with the slimy Stuckey. If Vivian is Eliza Doolittle then Barney, as much as Edward, is her

Henry Higgins, procuring her first glamorous frock, for example, and teaching her which knife and fork to use.

The film is at pains to show us that Vivian is vulnerable – witness the scene where those snooty shop assistants on Rodeo Drive throw her out of the store, or her sad comment that "people put you down enough – you start to believe it." More satisfying, however, are the sequences that reveal her toughness: during a fight with Kit she rejects the idea of getting a pimp, wanting to maintain control; in another with Edward she insists upon her right to get a fairy tale ending. Which, of course, she does – though in this fairy tale, rescued by her handsome prince, the princess "rescues him right back". That's why, though it certainly looks a little dated now (especially those designer outfits Vivian picks up on Rodeo Drive, all padded shoulders and oversized buttons), *Pretty Woman* still holds its own as a lightweight, undemanding chick flick favourite.

Rebecca

dir **Alfred Hitchcock, 1940, US, 130m, b/w**
cast **Joan Fontaine, Laurence Olivier, Judith Anderson, George Sanders, Nigel Bruce, Gladys Cooper** *cin* **George Barnes** *m* **Franz Waxman**

Rebecca, adapted from the hugely popular Gothic romance novel by **Daphne du Maurier**, was rich material for **Alfred Hitchcock**. This was his first Hollywood film, and although battles with the notoriously controlling producer **David O. Selznick** left the director unjustly dissatisfied with the finished product, his later work was to recall many of the motifs that appear here. With dark secrets and psychological twists, an anxious, preyed-upon young woman, and a leading character who appears only in the distressed minds of those around her, *Rebecca* is a profoundly unsettling study of obsession, eroticism and paranoia.

Joan Fontaine plays a shy, ordinary young girl who, while working as a ladies' companion in Monte Carlo, meets the suave Maxim de Winter (**Laurence Olivier**). Having recently lost his wife, Rebecca, in a tragic boating accident, Maxim is taciturn, moody and proud; he is also, perhaps surprisingly, drawn to this plain young woman, and they begin an affair. After an impulsive wedding, Maxim takes the second Mrs de Winter home to Manderley, his enormous mansion in Cornwall, where the ghost of the glamorous Rebecca looms large. Beginning, as does the novel, with the iconic line "Last night I dreamed I went to Manderley again", the film is told as an extended flashback from the point of view of the second Mrs de Winter, its dreamy opening sequence returning her to the site of so much of her pain and anxiety. Maxim's second wife is never named, which only adds to our sense of her invisibility and instability; the dead Rebecca, meanwhile, is never seen, which gives her all the more power. Once home, Maxim is cold and distant towards his second wife, appearing unable to get Rebecca out of his mind; matters are not helped by Manderley's sinister housekeeper, Mrs Danvers (**Judith Anderson**), who, through a series of subtle psychological bullyings, makes it clear that the second Mrs de Winter is not welcome. Tight-lipped, black-clad and gliding silently through the house like a malevolent spirit, Mrs Danvers is one of cinema's great villainesses, terrorizing the second Mrs de Winter with cold insinuation and, it transpires, murderous intent. The scene where she comes upon the hapless young woman nosing around the west wing, which has been jealously guarded and preserved exactly as it was when Rebecca lived there, is delicious in its chilling perversity. Fingering the dead woman's beautiful things and wildly flinging open the window while hissing, "listen to the sea … listen to the sea … listen to the sea …", the dreadful Mrs Danvers is as twisted as any Hitchcock villain you care to name.

Fontaine's nervy performance, although irritating, is undeniably effective, her stooped, rabbit-in-the-headlights quality embodying the part of the drab, downtrodden girl with low self-esteem. Apparently Olivier, who thought Fontaine wasn't up to the part, was never very friendly with his co-star during filming, and the story goes – though you can never be too sure with a publicity-conscious, myth-making duo like Hitchcock and Selznick at the helm – that the director played on this by informing the actress that none of the cast liked her. Whatever happened, it worked, and Fontaine, along with Anderson and Olivier, all received Academy Award nominations. The film ended up with eleven nominations in total – including one for Hitchcock (who famously ended his illustrious career having never won an Oscar) – and won two, for Best Picture and Best Cinematography.

The Red Shoes

dir **Michael Powell and Emeric Pressburger,
1948, UK, 133m**
cast **Moira Shearer, Anton Walbrook, Marius Goring,
Léonide Massine, Ludmilla Tcherina** *cin* **Jack Cardiff**
m **Brian Easdale**

Based on the nightmarish fairy tale by **Hans Christian Andersen,**
The Red Shoes is the definitive ballet movie – exquisite, otherworldly
and darkly tragic. It tells the story of Vicky Page (**Moira Shearer**),
a young, ambitious dancer who, pulled between her equally ambitious composer lover Julian (**Marius Goring**) and her Svengali, the
icily brilliant Lermontov (**Anton Walbrook**), is forced, with hor-
rible consequences, to choose between love and her art. Produced
by the genius team of **Michael Powell** and **Emeric Pressburger**,
the film is achingly beautiful, a lushly coloured and elegantly composed feast that has influenced a host of filmmakers including Gene
Kelly, Martin Scorsese and Baz Luhrmann. Upon release, however,
The Red Shoes was hushed up by Rank, its production company,
who thought it was a disaster and refused to premiere it in the UK.
Nonetheless, after becoming an arthouse hit in the US, it went on
to win Oscars for its ravishing production design, by artist **Hein
Heckroth**, and its score, before eventually becoming one of the
biggest British films ever made.

The stunning flame-haired Shearer, who was second dancer to
Margot Fonteyn at Sadler's Wells, procrastinated for months about
taking the role, worried that going into movies might take her
away from ballet, her true love. To some extent she was right, and
although she became a popular film star, appearing in two more
Powell and Pressburger productions – the musical extravaganza
The Tales Of Hoffmann (1951) and the twisted *Peeping Tom* (1960)
– she had little positive to say about *The Red Shoes*, grumbling
instead about Powell's direction and finding the story a little
absurd.

At the heart of the film is the seventeen-minute "Ballet of The
Red Shoes", the increasingly painful tale of a dancer whose dazzling

Dying for her art: Moira Shearer

ruby-red ballet slippers dance her to a bloody death. Rather than film-ing it straight on, as if watching it in a theatre, Powell and Pressburger create a passionate, visceral experience, drawing us right into the dance and immersing us in its magic. The staging and choreography, by **Robert Helpmann** and famous Russian dancer **Léonide Massine**, are extraordinary, and regular Powell and Pressburger collaborator **Jack Cardiff** uses stunning effects – dancers appearing to hover in the air at the pinnacle of their jumps, scraps of newspaper transforming into real-life dancers – to bring the fairy tale to life. Using a corps of 53 dancers, the ballet took six weeks to shoot. The dancers, many of whom were the most accomplished in their field, sustained countless injuries as they worked in this new medium, unused to performing take after take for the camera, dancing on concrete floors, or being hitched up in harnesses for hours.

Though its grim ending may not be quite as savage as Andersen's original tale, in which the doomed ballerina has her feet hacked off by a woodsman, *The Red Shoes* was truly radical, like some virulent scarlet gash across monochrome postwar

Fairy tales and faraway places: the films of Powell and Pressburger

Michael Powell (1905–90) and **Emeric Pressburger** (1902–88), the mavericks of postwar British cinema, produced extraordinary movies the like of which had never been seen, nor would be again. Powell, a young English director, and Pressburger, an émigré screenwriter from Hungary, met in the late 1930s while working for Alexander Korda's studio, London Films. After collaborating on a handful of patriotic war movies, they went on to form their own production company, The Archers. Their first film, *The Life And Death Of Colonel Blimp* (1943), was a humanistic and vivid reflection on love, memory and duty, which, because of its sympathetic portrayal of a German character, Winston Churchill tried to have banned.

Working as independents allowed Powell and Pressburger considerable freedom. Based on artistic collaboration and a constancy of vision, and influenced as much by European art movies as Hollywood, their films felt – and certainly looked – very different from other British movies of the time. Not in the slightest concerned with realism, they made quixotic films saturated with visual delight. Influenced by painting, theatre, music and myth, these were gloriously composed works of art, made to appeal to a popular (mainly British) audience.

While not explicitly geared towards female audiences, many of Powell and Pressburger's films make marvellous women's movies, foregrounding strong, complex heroines at the centre of passionate conflicts – the delightful romantic comedy *I Know Where I'm Going!* (1945), for example, which features one of their few modern heroines, Joan Webster (Wendy Hiller). Brisk and chic in smart Utility suits, Joan is an ambitious career girl who faces a struggle with the conflicting attractions of the modern world and the magical lure of Scotland's mythic past. Filmed in shimmering black-and-white, it's as visually glorious as any of their movies, using light and shade, fog and silvery moonlight to tell its dreamy tale. A dream state also pervades *Black Narcissus* (1946; see p.53), in which a mysterious Himalayan nunnery becomes the arena for explosive erotic passion and tragedy; *The Red Shoes* (1948; see p.119), a retelling of Hans Christian Andersen's gruesome fairy tale; and *Gone To Earth* (1950), based on Mary Webb's 1917 bodice-ripper about an untamed gypsy girl (Jennifer Jones).

Unabashedly revelling in the world of magic and romance (in all its forms), Powell and Pressburger's movies pack a huge emotional impact. They are simply wonderful, and not to be missed.

Britain. During the war, audiences had become used to seeing people dying for duty, or for the greater good – suddenly, in the age of rationing and making do, they were being presented with a woman who would die for her art. Nowadays, for female audiences, the effect is just as powerful, for there is real pain at the heart of this enchanting film. The lingering image, long after those wicked red shoes have finally faded to black, is of a woman who, desperate to live up to her creative potential, can only dream of having real choices – and unable to have what she dreams of, can in fact have nothing at all.

Romy And Michele's High School Reunion

dir David Mirkin, 1997, US, 91m

cast Mira Sorvino, Lisa Kudrow, Alan Cumming, Janeane Garofalo, Julia Campbell, Vincent Ventresca *cin* Reynaldo Villalobos *m* Steve Bartek

Romy And Michele's High School Reunion is a delightful, kooky tale, one of the best in a rash of dumb-blondes-that-aren't-so-dumb movies that raked it in at the box office in the wake of 1995's *Clueless* (see p.71). With a lower profile than *Clueless* and the *Legally Blonde* duo (2001 and 2003), *Romy* is slightly more skewed and a little more surreal, with a spot-on 1980s soundtrack that wisely veers away from cheese in favour of songs which will awaken a jolt of recognition in anyone who grew up in that decade.

Romy and Michele (**Mira Sorvino** and **Lisa Kudrow** respectively, both superb), friends since high school in Tucson, Arizona, share an apartment in LA. With their arch vocal stylings and mannered patter, it could be easy to dismiss them as archetypal airheads, but they win us over almost immediately. Early in the film we see them at a disco, all dressed up in their self-designed, over-the-top outfits, convinced they look cute but unable to pull, and bemoaning their lack of boyfriends. "Swear to God, sometimes I wish I was a lesbian," Romy sighs. "Do you want to try to have sex some time, just to see if we are?", Michele suggests. Romy, horrified at first, considers for a moment before pronouncing that if neither of them are married by the age of 30 then she should come back and ask again. Satisfied with this solution, they do their own little dance, oblivious to the cooler-than-thou dancers around them.

An invitation to their ten-year high school reunion throws the girls into crisis as they evaluate their lives and realize how little they have achieved since being bullied by the obligatory trio of high school bitches. Romy hits upon the idea of going dressed as businesswomen, and when, on their road trip to the reunion, it dawns on them that to pull the ruse off they need to actually think of a *business*, they decide to say they invented Post-It Notes. A rare quarrel ensues over who is the brainiest and prettiest of the pair, and on reaching the reunion they huffily go their separate ways, only to suffer trauma, confusion and a number of crazed fantasy sequences before being reunited again. When Michele finally admits that she'd never actually noticed their lives weren't up to much, and that she'd loved high school simply because she'd had such a great time with Romy, there isn't a dry eye in the house. Later, in a surreal tour de force, Sandy Frink (**Alan Cumming**), the school geek who made millions developing a super-rubber for training shoes, shyly invites Michele, whom he has loved from afar for years, to dance. "Only if Romy can dance with us," she replies, and the three of them proceed to perform a downright hilarious ensemble piece to Cyndi Lauper's "Time After Time".

A subplot featuring the always-superb **Janeane Garofalo** as the archetypal school rebel, all black eyeliner and roll-ups (another inventor, *she* develops a quick-burning paper that lets you get through a cigarette in one drag), a hapless fat girl and a mysterious Stetsonned stranger, adds even more body to this deceptively lightweight film; one which ultimately reminds us that, though high school – and indeed, adulthood – may sometimes be hell, they have glimpses of heaven too.

The Silence Of The Lambs

dir Jonathan Demme, 1990, US, 118m

cast Jodie Foster, Anthony Hopkins, Scott Glenn, Ted Levine, Brooke Smith *cin* Tak Fujimoto *m* Howard Shore

Part Gothic horror, part detective story, *The Silence Of The Lambs* is also a profoundly feminist film. Of the many factors that contribute to its brilliance – taut direction, superb performances, a razor-sharp script – it is, for female audiences at least, FBI agent Clarice Starling who gives it its edge. A nuanced performance from **Jodie Foster** (see Icons) as Starling won her the Best Actress Oscar, and the film, which enjoyed huge box office success, also picked up Academy Awards for Best Picture, Director, Actor and Screenplay – a sweep of five that hadn't been seen since *One Flew Over The Cuckoo's Nest* in 1975.

Although otherwise faithful to **Thomas Harris**'s bestselling thriller, the film foregrounds Starling, the driven FBI rookie, honing her character to make her more independent, more isolated and more complicated than the Clarice of the book. Brainy and ambitious, she is sent by her father-figure boss (**Scott Glenn**) to a high-security asylum in order to glean information from the brilliant psychopath Hannibal Lecter (**Anthony Hopkins**) on how to find the serial killer known as Buffalo Bill (**Ted Levine**). Bill flays his female victims before stuffing Death's Head Moth cocoons down their throats; Lecter, meanwhile, is a psychiatrist turned cannibal who, in return for feeding her small clues, insists on delving into Clarice's psyche.

Because the murderer is transsexual, the film has been accused by gay groups of being homophobic; in fact, as Lecter himself says, Bill's ambiguous sexuality is less important than his psychotic desire to transform himself. He desires the women he kills not for their bodies, but for their skins; while wanting to annihilate them, he also wants to join them. Similarly, Clarice's relationship with Lecter is not sexual in the conventional sense – although undeniably predatory, he is more interested in her mind than her body. Another asylum inmate shouts that he can "smell her cunt"; far more disturbing is that Lecter can smell her Evian skin cream, and knows that she sometimes wears L'Air du Temps perfume – "but not", he purrs, "today".

At heart, *The Silence Of The Lambs* is an icy psychological thriller. Though there are moments of unforgettable visceral horror, these are few. From Lecter's hooded, unblinking eyes to the killer's strange, strangulated voice and **Howard Shore**'s atmospheric score, the film terrifies in deeper, subtler ways – not least in the extraordinarily tense scene in which Starling the hunter, trapped in Bill's pitch-black cellar, becomes, for the first time, the hunted. It is dreadful to watch her, frightened and exposed, through the killer's eyes, the sickening green light as seen through his infrared goggles giving her vulnerability an even scarier edge. The quiet scenes between Lecter and Starling are equally intense, shot in huge close-up, with Clarice struggling under her reserved surface to avoid being consumed by the doctor's questions. Vulnerable but never a victim, Clarice is courageous enough not only to stand head on with the most appalling serial killers, but also to trawl her own memories and her darkest fears. To save Bill's latest victim, Catherine (**Brooke Smith**), she has to let Lecter in, and as he digs around to discover what drives her – what is at the heart of her need to save the world – she is taking the biggest risk of all.

Steel Magnolias

dir Herbert Ross, 1989, US, 117m
cast Shirley MacLaine, Sally Field, Olympia Dukakis, Julia Roberts, Dolly Parton, Daryl Hannah, Tom Skerritt, Sam Shepard *cin* John A. Alonzo *m* Georges Delerue

You'd be hard pushed to find many men who'd admit to having seen, let alone liked, *Steel Magnolias*, one of the crop of 1980s chick flicks that dealt with female friendship, stormy mother–daughter relationships and/or fatal diseases. The film follows the fortunes of six Southern women over a sequence of years, opening in a pretty small town in Louisiana, where everyone is in a frenzy preparing for the wedding of Shelby Eatenton (**Julia Roberts**). After battling over every small detail, Shelby and her harassed mother, M'Lynn (**Sally**

Field), head to the local beauty parlour, run by the effervescent Truvy (**Dolly Parton**) and Annelle (**Daryl Hannah**), her dorky new assistant. There, as their hair is coiffed and teased into Southern-style bouffants, they are joined by recent widow Clairee (**Olympia Dukakis**) and the foul-tempered Ouiser (**Shirley MacLaine**). As the women bicker, gossip and laugh, wisecracks flying, the movie startlingly shifts gear as Shelby has a violent diabetic seizure. So begins a saga that reveals the deep striations of pain and fortitude running beneath the sugar-coated Southern belle exterior.

These are all tough women, in their own way, and *Steel Magnolias* is a nicely executed ensemble piece starring some of Hollywood's finest character actresses. Roberts was the youngest and least experienced of the cast – considered to be too unattractive for the role of Shelby, she only barely won the part over Winona Ryder, who was ultimately rejected for being too young. Snagging an Oscar nomination for her performance, within a year Roberts was the biggest superstar of them all. Country singer Dolly Parton, who had had some success with her feisty performances in *Nine To Five* (1980) and *The Best Little Whorehouse In Texas* (1982), struggles a little to keep up with her elevated co-stars, but coasts along on her natural charm. Hannah, meanwhile, who until then had been best known for her great beauty, stretches her wings in a Plain Jane role that has her shifting from gawky through trashy to seriously flaky. The true stars, however, are Olympia Dukakis, Shirley MacLaine and Sally Field. Dukakis is terrific as the drily witty Clairee, delivering her lines with a kind of slinky Mae West drawl, while MacLaine does her thing as the noisy, foulmouthed and outrageous bitch with a heart. Together they make an appealing comic duo, an odd couple to rival Walter Matthau and Jack Lemmon. The restrained Field, who spends much of the movie struggling to contain huge waves of emotion, has a lot to carry; the scene where she finally breaks, wailing with graveside fury and despair, packs a searingly painful punch that is softened only by superb comic timing from Dukakis and MacLaine.

Robert Harling's screenplay, based on his own play (set entirely in the beauty parlour), abounds in aphorisms, making it one of the most quotable chick flicks of the 1980s. Many of the best lines go to grouchy Ouiser – ranging from, "Oh he's a real gentleman – I bet he takes the dishes out of the sink before he pees in it," to "I'm not crazy, I've just been in a very bad mood for forty years!" – but other sly gems include Truvy's, "You know I'd rather walk on my lips than criticize anybody…", and Clairee's unabashed, "If you don't have anything nice to say about anybody, come sit by me!"

Stella Dallas

dir **King Vidor, 1937, US, 105m, b/w**
cast **Barbara Stanwyck, John Boles, Anne Shirley, Alan Hale, Barbara O'Neil, Tim Holt** *cin* **Rudolph Maté** *m* **Alfred Newman**

Based on the bestselling novel by **Olive Higgins Prouty**, *Stella Dallas* is a three-hankie movie, a heart-rending tale of mother-daughter love that will leave you ragged. The story begins in 1919, when Stella (a tour de force performance from **Barbara Stanwyck**; see Icons), a fun-loving, ambitious mill-hand's daughter, wins the heart, and very quickly the hand, of businessman Stephen Dallas (**John Boles**). Soon frustrated in her marriage to a man who turns out to be dull and controlling, Stella also feels trapped, initially, by the birth of her daughter, Laurel (**Anne Shirley**). However, as Stephen spends more time away working in New York, Stella gradually loses interest in partying, grows to love Laurel with a passion, and puts all her considerable energy into raising her daughter single handed. Meanwhile, Stephen meets his ex-girlfriend, Helen (**Barbara O'Neil**), now a rich widow, who can offer Laurel a life that Stella simply can't. It soon becomes clear that Stella must make a terrible decision.

Quite apart from being a story of a mother's sacrifice, *Stella* is a searing tale of one woman's struggle simply to be. Telling Stephen soon after they meet, "I want to be like all the people you've been around, educated and speaking nice – I don't want to be like me! But oh, not like the people here, but like all the people in the movies. I've wanted to be different ever since I met you!", Stella can never quite find her niche in the world. Much of her out-of-placeness is portrayed through her clothes, which speak volumes. Adorned in feathery hats and strung with cheap beads, her garish self-made dresses laden with ruffles and bows, she patently doesn't fit in with Stephen, Helen and their tasteful WASP lifestyle. Early in their marriage, the stuffy Stephen appeals to her not to wear "those earrings, that cheap imitation necklace", to which she responds, "You can tell me how to talk and act, but not how to dress! After all, I've always had stacks of style." That Stella takes so long to see how out of place she really is only adds to the terrible poignancy.

There is huge sadness, too, in the beautifully drawn mother-daughter relationship. Laurel loves her mother as much as Stella

adores her, giving rise to some of the most painful scenes ever seen in any women's movie: when it slowly transpires that none of Laurel's posh friends are going to turn up to her thirteenth birthday party, for example, and the two walk bravely arm in arm into the dining room to enjoy the lovingly prepared dinner alone; or when, some years later, the two of them overhear from their train sleeper Laurel's friends talking about how vulgar Stella is, and each pretends she doesn't hear. The image of Laurel quietly creeping into her mother's bunk, the two women lying together in silence, is nothing less than heartbreaking. When Stella makes her final sacrifice, in a scene flooded with sorrow, it's difficult to imagine being able to take much more. There may be a glimmer of hope, however, in the film's much-discussed closing shot. For perhaps now, untrammelled by the constraints of being a wife and a mother, Stella Dallas can finally find her own place in the world – ruffled dresses, flouncy hats and all.

Heart-rending mother love: Barbara Stanwyck and Anne Shirley

Terms Of Endearment

dir James L. Brooks, 1983, US, 132m
cast Shirley MacLaine, Debra Winger, Jack Nicholson,
Jeff Daniels, John Lithgow *cin* Andrzej Bartkowiak
m Michael Gore

James L. Brooks, the producer/writer/director behind comedy TV smashes *The Mary Tyler Moore Show* and *Taxi* (and, later, *The Simpsons*), made what seemed like a surprising movie debut with the tear-jerking *Terms Of Endearment*. However, the director was not on entirely unfamiliar ground – this acutely observed tragicomedy, adapted from the novel by Texan writer **Larry McMurtry**, is also the kind of ensemble piece that Brooks felt very comfortable with. Actors Shirley MacLaine, Debra Winger, Jack Nicholson, Jeff Daniels and John Lithgow, all at different stages in their careers, were each at the top of their game, and although it's not the most cinematic of films – it's clear that Brooks is still cutting his chops as a movie director – eleven Oscar nominations certainly count for something. The movie went on to win five of them – Best Actress (MacLaine, up against Winger and receiving her first and only Oscar to date) and Best Supporting Actor (Nicholson, up against Lithgow), as well as Best Director, Best Screenplay and Best Picture.

Terms Of Endearment is a family saga that follows the seriously co-dependent relationship between the outrageous Aurora (**Shirley MacLaine**) and her daughter Emma (**Debra Winger**). After Emma marries Flap (a deceptively relaxed performance from **Jeff Daniels**), a charming but selfish academic, all the dramas of the women's lives – money troubles, pregnancies, children, affairs, illness – are raked over in their endless phone calls. When tragedy finally hits this deeply dysfunctional family, they are forced to declare a truce in order to find a new, hopefully healthier, way to survive.

Emma, beautifully played by Winger, forms the moral heart of the story. A long-suffering, lusty woman who loves her mother fiercely and withstands her young son's blind fury, who sticks with her faithless husband while forming a sweet attachment to gentle banker

Deathbed scenes

While male stars get to snuff it in all sorts of creative ways – wrapped like a mummy on their mother's doorstep (Jimmy Cagney, *The Public Enemy*; 1931); during a crazed shoot-out in a hall of shattered mirrors (Orson Welles, *The Lady From Shanghai*; 1947); charging, freeze-frame, into a hail of bullets (Paul Newman and Robert Redford, *Butch Cassidy And The Sundance Kid*; 1969) – women, traditionally, have tended to die nobly, quietly, and very often in bed (unless they're being murdered, of course, which is a very different story).

When it comes to deathbed scenes, *Terms Of Endearment* (1983) has the mother (if you'll excuse the pun) of them all. When the frail and hollow-eyed Emma insists to her moody son Tommy that she knows he loves her, her younger son Teddy crying softly beside her, tests have shown that it is actually physically impossible not to weep. Lifted directly from Larry McMurtry's book, Emma's words touch something that is embedded very deep indeed, and when she finally dies we are in difficult, cathartic territory that's rarely been handled better on screen.

A good deathbed scene is very difficult to pull off. While Ali MacGraw's brave words to Ryan O'Neal in *Love Story* (1970) – "I want you to be merry. You'll be merry, OK?"– might bring a lump to the throat, her final demise can't quite make up for the movie's more famous "Love means never having to say you're sorry", which was lampooned just two years later by O'Neal and Barbra Streisand in the screwball comedy *What's Up, Doc?*, and has been a joke ever since. That's not to say we mind a wee bit of manipulation while we weep. A heart-wrenching musical accompaniment is always welcome – Bette Midler belting out "Wind Beneath My Wings" in *Beaches* (1988; see p.49), for example, as Barbara Hershey finally breathes her last. Director Douglas Sirk, who had impeccable judgement when it came to swelling musical scores, gave us one of the most painful deathbed scenes ever in *Imitation Of Life* (1959; see p.91), as Annie whispers sadly, "I'm just tired Miss Lora, awfully tired…", watched over by a smiling photograph of the angry daughter who has broken her heart.

Any great actress worth their mettle has given a career-defining deathbed performance: from Greta Garbo, exquisitely fading away as *Camille* (1936; see p.66), to the inimitable Bette Davis, nobly expiring in *Dark Victory* (1939), Merle Oberon, collapsing in Heathcliff's arms as they gaze out over their beloved moors in *Wuthering Heights* (1939; see p.141), and Meryl Streep, whose passing in *One True Thing* (1998) captures the ordinary, searing pain of the event. *Terms Of Endearment*'s Debra Winger does it all again as doomed poet Joy Gresham in *Shadowlands* (1993), while Julia Roberts started on her journey to being Hollywood's most bankable actress by falling into a coma and having her life support cut off in *Steel Magnolias* (1989; see p.125).

Some slightly more vigorous chick flick deaths include Mrs Danvers' fiery fate in *Rebecca* (1940; see p.117) and *Thelma & Louise* soaring into the abyss (1991; see p.131).

Sam (**John Lithgow**), she is also remarkable in her unshakeable self-belief. "The men love me just the way I am," she replies breezily in response to yet another of her mother's criticisms. The woman is no saint, however. More than just a wronged wife, she starts her affair with Sam *before* she is certain that Flap is philandering – and her rage when she discovers his unfaithfulness is partly due to her own irrational jealousy. Ultimately, however, of all the flawed human beings in the film, Emma is the sole grown-up, and, ironically, only when she has gone can Aurora, the impossible child-parent, grow up. Aurora's dramatic journey, which includes a painful affair with drunken commitment-phobe Garrett Breedlove (**Jack Nicholson**), leads to some sort of redemption, and a chance to start over as a mother.

Mercifully, *Terms Of Endearment* never strays into sentimentality. Even as it shifts from relationship comedy to cancer movie it doesn't miss a beat. When Aurora tears through the nurses' station bellowing for pain medication for her daughter, the comedy and sorrow are perfectly balanced, mining a dark humour that helps us, far more than schmaltz ever could, to get in touch with the jagged pain of real grief. The sequel, *The Evening Star* (1996), which updates us on how Aurora and the children get on, is not worthy of being mentioned in the same breath.

Thelma & Louise

dir Ridley Scott, 1991, US, 129m
cast Susan Sarandon, Geena Davis, Harvey Keitel, Michael Madsen, Christopher McDonald, Brad Pitt
cin Adrian Biddle *m* Hans Zimmer

No one involved in the making of *Thelma & Louise* expected it to cause such an uproar. American newspapers and conservative commentators, outraged by its feminist message, accused it of being an irresponsible blood-fest, a glorification of anti-male violence. The protestations of the filmmakers, who pointed out, among other things, that only three people die, relatively bloodlessly, in the entire movie – and that two of those are women – fell on deaf ears. Meanwhile, on the other side of the debate, excited fans declared it revolutionary, a film that would change Hollywood forever. A decade and a half later, *Thelma & Louise* is still one of a kind. It didn't start a craze for big-budget female outlaw movies. Buddy films and road movies are still, predominantly, the property of men. The film remains as exhilarating, and devastating, today as it was when it was first released.

The story of two chalk-and-cheese friends who take to the road after one of them shoots a rapist, *Thelma* crackles with a marvellous script by **Callie Khouri**, outlining with no little humour the oppressions that women manage on a daily basis – from domestic neglect through sexist jeering to rape – while creating real, funny characters about whom we come to care passionately. At the centre are two extraordinary performances. Any other combination of actors – Holly Hunter/Frances McDormand, Michelle Pfeiffer/Jodie Foster, and Goldie Hawn/Meryl Streep were all suggested – has become unthinkable. **Susan Sarandon** (see Icons), as the world-weary Louise, a woman with a past, is a pitch-perfect combination of tough and vulnerable, driving not only her beloved car but also the film's action – for the first half at least – in her desperation to ward off unspoken depths of pain. **Geena Davis**, meanwhile, in the lighter role of Thelma, makes

Outlaw girls hit the road

Brad Pitt

Among its many pleasures, *Thelma & Louise* can take credit for bringing the young **Brad Pitt** to the attention of the world. Though he has just fourteen minutes on screen, his impact as J.D., the gentlemanly cowboy bandit, is huge. In a delightful overturning of movie conventions, the film makes no bones about the fact that it is Pitt, rather than either of the women, who is the sex object here. Whether he's lounging like James Dean on a wall, tumbleweed skittering past, or peeling off his white T-shirt to reveal an astonishingly honed torso, the camera can barely drag itself away from him. Apparently, an up-and-coming actor named George Clooney auditioned five times for the part of J.D.; though it may be diverting to imagine, it's practically impossible now to picture the suave George in that rakish cowboy hat – let alone half-dressed and straddling Geena Davis. Pitt had exactly the *Rebel Without A Cause*-style boyishness that was required, an image that continues to haunt him even as he approaches his mid-40s.

Like many sex objects, from Marilyn Monroe to Robert Redford, Brad Pitt has had to work twice as hard as less beautiful stars to achieve recognition. And though in *Thelma & Louise* he gives one of the charismatic, intelligent performances that have since characterized his career – in films like *Se7en*, *Fight Club*, *Snatch*, *Ocean's Eleven* and *Twelve*, among others – for many viewers, female and male, he will always be associated with J.D.'s unforgettably lazy drawl, sexy smile and rippling abs.

the more dramatic journey – her transformation from kook to hero propels the movie's second half and, ultimately, its lump-in-the-throat finale. Gradually stripping themselves of make-up, jewellery and all feminine trappings, these two warmly human women end up dusty, bare-faced and luminously beautiful, throwing convention, expectation and whiskey bottles to the wind in their euphoric quest for a life lived to the full.

A road movie par excellence, *Thelma & Louise* is also a valentine to old-style Americana. Their vehicle is a 1966 Thunderbird convertible, the landscape one of oil derricks, monster trucks and crop-dusters. Leaving behind a string of weird motels and smoky honky-tonks, the two women's internal voyages become more profound as the landscape becomes lonelier and increasingly mythic. Ancient red rock monoliths loom above them as **Hans Zimmer**'s score twangs its moody refrain. The car purrs through the moonlit Southwestern desert as Marianne Faithfull's broken voice mourns lost hope and dreams in "The Ballad Of Lucy Jordan". The stakes grow higher by the minute.

The men in Thelma and Louise's lives are crucial. While Thelma's doltish husband, Darryl (**Christopher McDonald**), is a hilarious comedy creation, the others, though perhaps just as dangerous, are more attractive – Louise's on-off lover Jimmy (**Michael Madsen**), seductive but unreliable; J.D. (**Brad Pitt**), the sexy double-crosser; and good cop Slocumb (**Harvey Keitel**), the father figure who understands their plight but must bring them to justice. In the end, however, Thelma and Louise, swamped by a barrage of masculine hardware – a fleet of screaming cop cars and a monstrous, looming helicopter – have only themselves, their car and their impossible dreams. And with their dreams to propel them, our heroines, while seeming to have no choice, choose the only ending they can possibly imagine.

Titanic

dir James Cameron, 1997, US, 195m
cast Leonardo DiCaprio, Kate Winslet, Billy Zane, Kathy Bates, Frances Fisher, Gloria Stuart, Bill Paxton
cin Russell Carpenter *m* James Horner

It's impossible to approach *Titanic* without falling back on its staggering statistics. Costing more than $200 million to make – far more than the cost of building the real ship –it was, at the time of its release, the most expensive film ever. Predictions were made that this vastly over-budget behemoth would flop; the naysayers were silenced, however, when it earned fourteen Oscar nominations and won eleven, including awards for Best Picture and Best Director. On release for nearly a full year, it became the biggest box office movie in film history – and remains so – grossing nearly $2 billion worldwide.

Mere statistics, however, cannot account for the enduring fascination of this sumptuous romance. The movie starts in the present day, when deep-sea treasure-hunter Brock Lovett (**Bill Paxton**), searching the Titanic wreckage for the famous "Heart of the Ocean" diamond, discovers a safe, which holds a drawing of a young woman wearing the jewel. After a TV interview, Lovett has a visit from a 101-year-old woman, Rose (**Gloria Stuart**), who claims to be the person in the drawing, and who is compelled to tell her story. What follows is an account of the ship's doomed voyage as reflected in the upstairs-downstairs romance between rich American beauty Rose (**Kate Winslet**) and poverty-stricken adventurer/artist Jack (**Leonardo DiCaprio**). As you might predict, however, their story is not all plain sailing – not only do they have Rose's snobbish mother (**Frances Fisher**) and caddish fiancé (**Billy Zane**) to contend with, but after the deadly iceberg hits, together they must fight for their lives.

Despite, or perhaps because of, its colossal popularity, many people have found things to laugh at in *Titanic*. For all its many Oscars, it won none for acting. DiCaprio is here more cup cake than beefcake, displaying little chemistry with his feisty co-star. His famous "King of the World!" moment has been lampooned endlessly, especially after **James Cameron**, bouncing around the stage at the Oscars, shouted the phrase over and over. Nonetheless, this was the film that made Leonardo a sex symbol, catapulting him, along with Winslet, into the A-list. And it's hard, despite all the silliness, not to root for the young lovers in the same way that, despite all the odds, we find ourselves rooting for the doomed ship.

Ultimately, the only way to watch *Titanic* is to give yourself over to the sheer majestic spectacle. Cameron, who had previously combined heightened emotion with delirious action in the *Terminator* movies (1984, 1991 and 2003) and *Aliens* (1986), knows how to entrance an audience; here he combines state-of-the-art computer graphics with haunting real-life footage of the ghost ship to invoke profound emotional responses. With its painstaking reconstruction of something that is forever gone, something that, as Rose puts it, "exists only now in my memory", *Titanic* melds the pain of loss as represented by the "Ship of Dreams" with a melancholy glimpse back at the idealism of youth. And, no matter what you think of Celine Dion, it is testament to the romantic impact of this giant film that by the time "My Heart Will Go On" soars over the soundtrack, resistance is, quite simply, futile.

The Way We Were

dir Sydney Pollack, 1973, US, 118m
cast Barbra Streisand, Robert Redford, Bradford Dillman, Lois Chiles, James Woods *cin* Harry Stradling Jr.
m Marvin Hamlisch

Intelligent, elegiac and deeply romantic, *The Way We Were* is as much about politics as it is about love. Set against the upheavals of pre- and

"Streisand and Redford together!"

post-World War II America, leading up to the anti-Communist witch-hunts in 1940s Hollywood, the movie follows the chalk-and-cheese love story of Katie Morosky (**Barbra Streisand**) and Hubbell (**Robert Redford**). She is Jewish, passionate, politically active; he is the all-American boy, restrained, light-hearted, non-committal. Secretly drawn to each other during their college days, they begin their complex, demanding affair after a chance meeting years later. Through her he finds the drive to fulfil his long-held dream of writing, while she learns to lighten up and to laugh more; years of painful arguments, separations and tender love scenes unfold as they become the great loves of each other's lives.

The film was marketed with the tagline "Streisand and Redford together!", and there is certainly chemistry between the two young actors. Bold, independent-minded and left-wing, Streisand (see Icons) was also the first openly Jewish female movie star, and the part of Katie was practically made for her. Redford, however, had to be persuaded to accept the role of Hubbell. The actor, who had made an impact in movies like *Barefoot In The Park* (1967) and *Butch Cassidy And The Sundance Kid* (1969), worried that Hubbell was little more than a dumb blonde to Katie's gutsy heroine. And it's true that this is Katie's movie – we see most of it from her point of view, and tend to identify and sympathize with her, however impossible she might be. Redford's subtle performance, however, gives Hubbell complexity. Though he is certainly the lust object (we first see him, asleep at a bar, through Katie's yearning eyes, the camera lingering on his soft blonde hair and white naval uniform), he is also a real, conflicted person. The voice of containment versus Katie's excess, the lightheartedness versus her intensity, he believes people are more important than mere principles, whereas Katie believes people *are* their principles.

The movie as first conceived was more explicitly political than the finished product. Responding to audience screenings, **Sydney Pollack** dropped the crucial final scenes in which Katie, informed upon by a fellow ex-Communist, refuses to do the same. Katie and Hubbell's subsequent agreement to split, so that he can continue to work in Hollywood, is a painful decision that prioritizes politics above love – and makes the fact that Hubbell leaves far more understandable than in the movie as it stands.

The Way We Were rewards countless viewings. Every scene is a small work of art in itself, each one telling a honed, self-contained story with huge emotional impact: young Katie winning the jeering college crowd round at a peace rally only to realize, with horror, that they are mocking her; the couple shyly talking as he drinks to celebrate the sale of his first story; the bittersweet night when he makes love to her – too drunk to know who she is; the long, terrible phone call in which Katie begs a silent Hubbell to come back; and, of course, the unforgettable and heartachingly pared-down final scene. Katie's final gentle brush of Hubbell's fringe, echoing the moment at the start of

The Way We Were – the music

The Way We Were's haunting score, written by **Marvin Hamlisch**, is essential to the emotional power of this delicately wrought movie. Reprising and reworking the melody of the title ballad, which **Barbra Streisand** sings over the opening and closing credits, it has a nostalgic charm, like a half-forgotten tune that you find yourself humming out of the blue. Although asked to write a melody in the minor mode, Hamlisch chose to write it in the major, believing that a minor mode would be too mournful. "I wrote a melody that was sad," he said, "but also had a great deal of hope in it."

The song itself Hamlisch wrote with husband-and-wife songwriting team, **Marilyn and Alan Bergman**, with significant contributions from Streisand – she changed the original "Daydreams/Like the corners of my mind" to the more effective "Memories/Like the corners of my mind", for example. Both the song and the score won Oscars for Hamlisch, who made Academy Award history that year by winning in all three music categories (including an award for his adaptation of Scott Joplin's ragtime music for *The Sting*).

Streisand, whose musical career was wobbling, went on to release "The Way We Were" as a single. Slightly faster, poppier and less lush than the film version, in February 1974 it became her first number-one hit. Part torch song, part ballad, the song was the perfect vehicle for Streisand's vocal range and gutsy performing style. It stayed on the Billboard charts for five months, won the Grammy for Song of the Year, and hit number eight in the AFI's 100 best movie songs of all time.

the movie when she discovers him asleep in the bar, is a pinpoint of unadulterated melancholy in a film which, having recalled and mourned the past, recognizes that it can never be regained.

When Harry Met Sally...

dir Rob Reiner, 1989, US, 95m

cast Meg Ryan, Billy Crystal, Carrie Fisher, Bruno Kirby, Steven Ford *cin* Barry Sonnenfeld *m* Marc Shaiman

With a popular body of work already under his belt – a wildly successful mockumentary (*This Is Spinal Tap*, 1984), a quirky teen comedy (*The Sure Thing*, 1985), a nostalgic drama (*Stand By Me*, 1986) and a fairy tale romp (*The Princess Bride*, 1987) – in 1989 director **Rob Reiner** turned his Midas touch to the rom-com with *When Harry Met Sally...*, a sleeper hit that provided the blueprint for at least a decade's worth of smart relationship comedies. It also made a megastar of **Meg Ryan**, and sent **Nora Ephron** (see Icons) straight into the ranks of A-list screenwriters. Ephron's wry, Oscar-nominated screenplay is beautifully observed – and, apparently, heavily based upon real conversations she had with Reiner. So Rob met Nora, and, native New Yorkers both, they managed to produce a very New York movie – talky, Jewish, and with more filmic references than you can shake a popcorn carton at. Along with obvious echoes of Woody Allen, the romantic classic *Casablanca* (1942; see p.69), is frequently invoked, not least in the jazz standards soundtrack.

The story is simple. Harry (**Billy Crystal**) meets Sally (Ryan) for the first time in the summer of 1977 when she gives him a ride to New York from their college in Chicago. She is sunny, optimistic and self-contained; he, with typically gloomy Jewish humour, revels in his dark side and is compelled to express every thought and feeling he has. She can't order from a restaurant without making endless adjustments; he pontificates at length about his outrageously chauvinistic world view. They say goodbye at the end of the trip with little love lost, but, encountering each other by chance over the next couple of years, slowly form a friendship that spans more than a decade. The two central questions running through the movie are: can a man and woman ever be just friends? And, if sex gets in the way, will it ruin the friendship? As Harry and Sally grow older their hairstyles, clothes and attitudes alter; sex does get in the way, it does ruin things, and the friendship, ultimately, has to change.

As befits a film that wears its love of cinema on its sleeve, *When Harry* boasts some classic movie moments – the infamous deli scene, for example, in which Sally yells and whoops her way to convincing Harry that women do indeed fake orgasms. While Crystal gets most of the sharpest gags, as in all the best rom-coms the two main characters' best friends – **Carrie Fisher** as the neurotic Marie and **Bruno Kirby** as Jess – give great comic support. Dotted with straight-to-camera "how we met" stories from elderly couples, the film is expertly paced, structured like a long conversation with a trusted friend that takes unexpected, but always satisfying, turns.

Ephron, who had previously produced dramatic screenplays for *Silkwood* (1983) and *Heartburn* (1986), went on to write and direct the two *When Harry* rom-com clones: *Sleepless In Seattle* (1993) – with its many references to classic weepie *An Affair To Remember* (1957; see p.43) – and *You've Got Mail* (1998), which updates Ernst Lubitsch's sweet *The Shop Around The Corner* (1940). In both films Meg Ryan reprises her Sally formula as the angelic kook, this time playing opposite the somewhat less charismatic Tom Hanks. They are entertaining enough, but neither movie sparkles quite as brightly as *When Harry Met Sally….*

When Rob met Woody

Though often thought of as a classic late-1980s movie, full of therapy-savvy, navel-gazing yuppies, When *Harry Met Sally…* is in many ways a homage to **Woody Allen's** relationship comedy *Annie Hall* (1977). Quite apart from the smart dialogue, you have Harry's gloomy, neurotic Jewish humour and the classic Manhattan locations, the nostalgic credits and the romantic jazz score – including the song "It Had To Be You" (which also features in *Casablanca*). Even the direct-to-camera sequences and split screens recall Allen's masterwork. And, of course, Harry meets Sally in 1977, the year *Annie Hall* was released.

The Wicked Lady

dir Leslie Arliss, 1945, UK, 104m, b/w

cast Margaret Lockwood, James Mason, Patricia Roc, Griffith Jones, Michael Rennie *cin* Jack Cox *m* Hans May

A rip-roaring romp derided by British critics at the time, *The Wicked Lady* was the biggest box office hit of 1945 and still offers heaps to enjoy. The date is 1683, and the lady in question is Lady Barbara Skelton (**Margaret Lockwood**), a woman so utterly without scruples that if she had a moustache she would surely spend most of the movie twirling it. Stealing Ralph (**Griffith Jones**) from the arms of her drippy cousin Caroline (**Patricia Roc**), marrying him and then refusing to play lady of the manor, taking to highway robbery, entering a passionate affair with dashing highwayman "Lucky" Jerry Jackson (**James Mason**, *the* heartthrob of the day and still darkly sexy with his lazy, sadistic drawl), and eventually resorting to (triple) murder, this woman will stop at nothing to get her kicks. Adapted from the popular novel *The Life And Death Of The Wicked Lady Skelton* by **Magdalen King-Hall,** *The Wicked Lady* is a classic Gainsborough melodrama, one in the series of costume dramas produced by that studio (see p.17) that revelled in fancy, flippancy and rumbustious fun. These films were a world apart from many other British movies of the time – from Ealing Studio's quirky realist comedies and Powell and Pressburger's art movies (see p.121), to stiff-upper-lip romances like *Brief Encounter* (1945; see p.64), which extolled the virtues of restraint above all else.

Margaret Lockwood: banned in the USA

Restraint is largely absent here, not least in **Elizabeth Haffenden**'s extraordinarily sexy costumes, all curls, frills and ruffs, revealing acres of creamy cleavage – wartime Britain hadn't seen the like for years, and the film was banned in the US. The dialogue is witty and fast-paced, and filled with enough bawdy double entendres to fill a *Carry On* movie: "I drive a *hard* bargain," Jerry growls in one of his sadomasochistic tussles with the fiery Barbara. Lockwood and Mason look like they're having a blast, whether thundering along on their powerful steeds or taking a tumble in the long grass, and Barbara, be she sashaying up and down grand staircases in flounced skirts or striding manfully in her highwayman gear, is more than a match for the dastardly Jackson, who has a tendency to slap his thighs, boom with laughter and roar, " I like your spirit, my pretty lamb!"

Though she is less interested in their sexual affair than in the thrill of robbery, Barbara warns Jackson not to wrong her, and after discovering him with a buxom doxy at the Leaping Stag Inn, reports him anonymously and sends him to the gallows. That night, as she prepares herself for a night of sin with Kit (**Michael Rennie**), whom she met on her wedding day and has loved ever since, Jackson returns, half-strangles her, begs her to come out on the road again and, when she refuses, proceeds to rape her. After a dramatic shoot-out, and Barbara's heartfelt confession of all her sins (which include poisoning and smothering a particularly tiresome old servant), the story gallops to its inevitable conclusion.

You can't help but root for the dynamic, beautiful Barbara – "I've got brains and looks and personality! I want to use them!" – above goody-goodies like Ralph, Caroline and Kit. And while she may get the comeuppance that the plot demands, she at least gets to have some wicked fun – and wear some truly wicked outfits – along the way.

Wuthering Heights

dir William Wyler, 1939, US, 103m, b/w

cast Merle Oberon, Laurence Olivier, David Niven, Flora Robson, Geraldine Fitzgerald *cin* Gregg Toland *m* Alfred Newman

The best of the many movie adaptations of **Emily Brontë**'s magnum opus, this 1939 version of *Wuthering Heights* is one of Hollywood's all-time great romances. Covering roughly the first half of the novel, it excises the book's later emphasis on Heathcliff's vindictive revenge on the Linton family to focus instead on his all-consuming love for the wild and beautiful Cathy, his soul mate and his obsession.

The film starts as a creepy Gothic horror story, with a lost wanderer, Mr Lockwood (**Miles Mander**), turning up at Wuthering Heights during a dreadful blizzard. Heathcliff (**Laurence Olivier**), the master of the gloomy manor house, barely speaks to him, but eventually agrees to give him a room; his downtrodden wife,

The battle of the firebrands – Cathy vs Scarlett

Vivien Leigh, Laurence Olivier's lover (and soon to be his second wife), originally wanted the part of Cathy in *Wuthering Heights*, and turned down producer Sam Goldwyn's offer of the smaller part of Isabella, deeming it too minor for her first Hollywood role. She had the last laugh, however, by almost immediately going on to win the plum role of Scarlett in *Gone With The Wind* (1939; see p.86). The great Civil War saga swept the boards that year at the Oscars, with Leigh winning the coveted Academy Award for Best Actress. **Merle Oberon**, a ravishing Leigh lookalike, gives an intense performance as Cathy, but it's intriguing to wonder what kind of film *Wuthering Heights* might have been had Leigh and Olivier – who were notoriously passionate lovers – played opposite each other.

Isabella (**Geraldine Fitzgerald**), meanwhile, silently slopes away. Disturbed by the unfriendliness of his hosts, tormented by the howling wind and banging shutters, Lockwood is unable to sleep and thrusts his hand through the window in order to fix them – only to hear a strange ghostly wail, and to feel an icy hand clasp his. When he tells Ellen, the housekeeper (**Flora Robson**), she insists that it was the phantom of Cathy, and settles down to tell him the story of all that has happened in that blighted house. And so the flashback begins, taking us to forty years before when the young, tousle-haired Heathcliff, found wild on the streets of Liverpool, was brought to Wuthering Heights by kindly Mr Earnshaw (**Cecil Kellaway**). Finding himself in a cheerful family home, the boy quickly forms an intense friendship with Cathy, Earnshaw's spirited daughter, while Hindley, her brother, becomes increasingly jealous. After the death of their father, the adult Hindley (**Hugh Williams**) turns to treating Heathcliff like a servant, and Cathy (**Merle Oberon**), now a restless young woman, begins to vacillate. One minute she is proclaiming love for Heathcliff out on the moors, her hair whipping around her face; the next she is violently rejecting him to spend time with the respectable and wealthy Lintons. When he overhears her declaring her intention to marry the sappy Edgar Linton (**David Niven**), craving "dancing and music and a pretty world", Heathcliff flees to America in torment, returning months later to wreak his revenge on both families.

The movie's dialogue, a combination of the source novel and a deft screenplay by master screenwriters **Charles MacArthur** and **Ben Hecht**, is exceptional, each line honed to its raw bones and oozing either passion or pain. Guided with a sure hand by solid director **William Wyler**, the very beautiful Olivier gives a career-defining performance as the gypsyish Heathcliff, managing to tone down his stagey English thesp style and shining from the screen like a matinee idol. His is a tortured soul more sorrowful than the brutal Heathcliff of the book, while Oberon's Cathy swings between great ardour and pure hatred – towards both Heathcliff and Edgar – with schizophrenic abandon. Cathy and Heathcliff's ill-fated love may not be portrayed as earthily as in later movie versions, but it is a relationship as skewed and as sadomasochistic as it's possible to imagine.

Despite *Gone With The Wind*'s 1939 Oscar sweep, *Wuthering Heights* did get a look in, with the great cinematographer **Gregg**

Toland scooping the award for Best Cinematography. Every frame is a work of art, though purists do sniff about the Yorkshire moors landscape – recreated in a suburb of LA – and in particular the heather, which under the California sun grew ridiculously high.

You Can Count On Me

dir Kenneth Lonergan, 2000, US, 111m

cast Laura Linney, Mark Ruffalo, Matthew Broderick, Rory Culkin, Jon Tenney *cin* Stephen Kazmierski *m* Lesley Barber

A small film that made huge waves on the indie circuit, winning numerous major film festival awards, *You Can Count On Me* is an unusual chick flick in that its central relationship is between a woman and her brother. Sammy (**Laura Linney**) and Terry (**Mark Ruffalo**), orphaned at a young age, have gone their separate ways. Sammy, now a capable single mother, lives with her son, Rudy (**Rory Culkin**), in the upstate New York home where she and her brother grew up; Terry, meanwhile, has drifted, staying in touch only intermittently and worrying Sammy to death. When Terry re-enters Sammy and Rudy's lives after an absence of two years, they struggle to make it work, clashing, hurting each other and falling into the same old habits along the way.

As a delicately observed slice of life, this movie is an absolute feast. Director **Kenneth Lonergan** is best known as a playwright, and the film actually began its days as a one-act play. That's not to say it's wordy, or that it doesn't translate beautifully to the screen. The writer's love of words sings out in his pared-down, witty script – which was nominated for an Oscar – while the three adult leads, who all started as theatre actors, put in natural, relaxed performances that are as far from stagey as it's possible to be. Lonergan also has an eye for locations, effectively conveying the ordinary-strange-ness of small-town USA as well as the wild lushness of the Catskill mountains.

Linney, a fine actress who has yet to reach superstar status, received an Oscar nomination for her performance as the bright-as-a-button care-taker who works hard, attends church and bakes cookies in an attempt to manage the world. Her on-off affair with the ineffectual Bob (**Jon Tenney**) is going nowhere, but it gives her something to do. Ruffalo, meanwhile, has a touch of the Marlon Brando about him as the evasive and infuriatingly childish Terry. Together they paint a poignant picture of two people very attached to each other who, without parents, have simply grown up as best they can. No solutions are offered, nobody is redeemed, but as we go through this small journey with them our preconceptions do shift. Sammy, it transpires, has never been quite the goody-two-shoes she might at first appear; her affair with the strange, anal bank manager Brian (a comic tour de force from **Matthew Broderick**) may be somewhat bizarre, but not, we come to realize, entirely out of character. Meanwhile, the gently comic scenes between Terry and Rudy – the illicit late-night pool game, for example, or the conversation where Terry baffles his nephew with his anger about the small town in which they live – give us not only a man who opens up the boy's life to fun and play, but also one who, despite his best intentions, has little clue about how to take care of him.

Ultimately it is left to the nominal adult, Sammy, struggling to both save her brother and keep her son safe, to make a decision. Doing so, however, does not alter her conflicted feelings. Although Sammy finally extricates herself from her self-destructive, if deliciously mischievous, affair with Brian, it's less clear how she's going to resolve her chronic inability to hurt Bob's feelings – and, more importantly, to deal with the loss, once again, of the brother she so deeply loves.

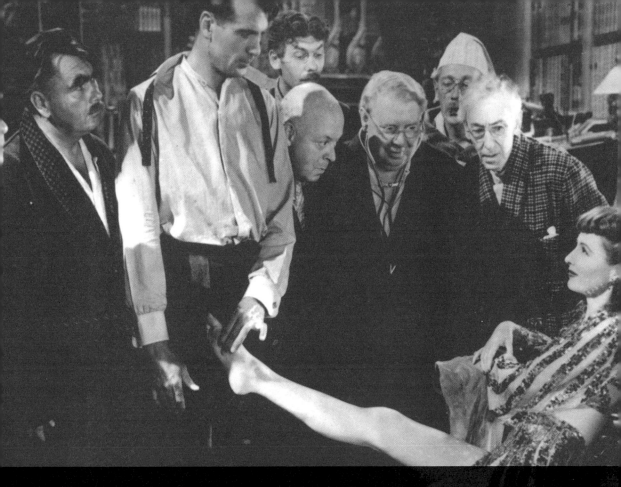

The Icons: chick flick legends

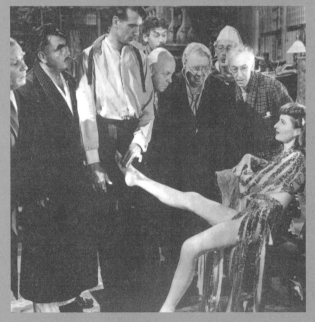

Barbara Stanwyck: as ever the centre of attention in *Ball of Fire* (1941)

The Icons:
chick flick legends

From the tough broads of the 1940s to the post-feminist ironists, from silent heart-throbs to New Men, this chapter pays homage to some of those risk-takers and revolutionaries who – whether working in front of or behind the camera – have inspired us to laugh, cry and lust our way through a lifetime of pleasurable movie viewing.

Dorothy Arzner

Director, 1900–1979

One of the few women to make it as a director in 1930s and 40s Hollywood, Dorothy Arzner was responsible for some of the era's most interesting women's movies. With her short, mannish hair and tweedy trouser suits, she cut a dashing figure behind the camera, while directing her films with a female, proto-feminist sensibility. Showing complex, non-stereotypical women in a sympathetic light and making them particularly appealing to female audiences, she never denied that she was a woman working in a man's world.

Interviewed in the 1930s she remarked: "There should be more of us directing. Try as any man may, he will never be able to get the woman's viewpoint in directing certain stories ... A great percent of our audience is women. That too is something to think about."

In the 1920s Arzner worked her way up from secretary at Famous Players studio to script girl and then film editor, quickly becoming chief editor at Realart, a subsidiary of Paramount Studios. After working on Rudolph Valentino's *Blood And Sand* (1922), for which she devised the idea of saving money by intercutting stock footage of real bullfights with close-ups of the star,

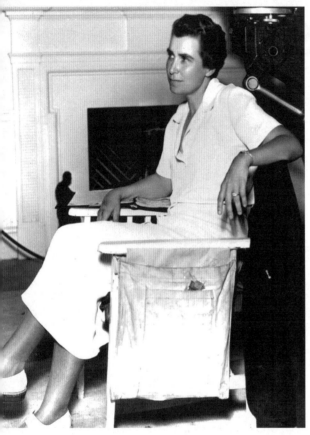

Directing trailblazer Dorothy Arzner

first film to feature movable boom microphones, an innovation that Arzner herself suggested to the cameraman. Though Bow didn't make a successful transition to the talkies, Arzner continued a thriving career, making the quirky *Working Girls* (1931), a double entendre-filled story of modern women's dilemmas, and *Merrily We Go To Hell* (1932), a sophisticated battle-of-the-sexes comedy (and an early outing for young actor **Cary Grant**). In 1933 she directed *Christopher Strong*, the tragic tale of a fiercely independent aviatrix; it wasn't a major hit, but the movie did give **Katharine Hepburn** one of her finest roles, and has since been reappraised by feminist film critics as having intriguing sexually ambiguous undertones. Equally compelling, *Dance, Girl, Dance* (1940), starring an effervescent **Lucille Ball** and **Maureen O'Hara** as dancer friends, features a bold scene in which O'Hara furiously turns on the men who are watching her and berates them for their voyeurism.

During World War II, Arzner put her efforts into a series of patriotic WAC training movies, as well as coaching women in film editing and directing the anti-Nazi *First Comes Courage* (1943), with **Merle Oberon** as a heroic resistance fighter. Becoming ill before the end of shooting, she stopped directing and turned to teaching. In a quirky twist, she also made scores of Pepsi TV commercials, starring the great 1940s icon **Joan Crawford**, before retiring and living out the rest of her years in the California desert.

she moved into movie writing, and eventually threatened to leave Paramount unless they let her direct. The studio didn't want to lose her, and so in 1927 she directed "It girl" **Clara Bow** in the fizzy farce *Get Your Man*. Her cool restraint created an elegant contrast with the actress's famed vivacity, and the two teamed up again for *The Wild Party* (1929), a lively celebration of female friendship. Paramount's first talkie, it was also the

🎬 Merrily We Go To Hell
dir Dorothy Arzner, 1932, US, 78m, b/w

The kind of comedy they loved in the 1930s, this movie has socialites in fabulous clothes, suave scoundrels who drink too much, long-suffering heroines and a dash of decadence with a risqué edge. Elegantly directed, as ever, by Arzner.

Christopher Strong
dir Dorothy Arzner, 1933, US, 77m, b/w

A painful, feminist-tinged romance, with a touching performance from a young Katharine Hepburn as Lady Cynthia Darrington, the androgynous aviatrix who must choose between her career and her one true love.

Craig's Wife
dir Dorothy Arzner, 1936, US, 75m, b/w

Rosalind Russell stars in her first major role, playing a calculating upper-class woman who uses her husband to further her own position. Russell is terrific, and with Arzner's direction the character becomes three-dimensional and, against the odds, not entirely unsympathetic.

The Bride Wore Red
dir Dorothy Arzner, 1937, US, 103min, b/w

A *Pretty Woman*-style rags-to-riches story, in which Joan Crawford camps it up in one of her characteristic roles as an ambitious working-class woman who, searching for love, tastes the high life and likes it. Amazing costumes by Hollywood maestro Adrian.

Sandra Bullock

Actress, 1964–

Sandra Bullock's relaxed intelligence and likeable girl-next-door charm – at high school she was voted "Most Likely To Brighten Your Day" – have contributed to her career as a genuinely popular actress. Though she has starred in as many stinkers as successes, and is generally ignored by the critics, her unaffected star persona has won her a steadfast fan base that remains loyal whatever she may do. Suited equally to action movies and romantic comedies, she also wowed audiences with her psychologically complex performance as an uptight LA yuppie in the intense drama *Crash* (2004).

A child performer, born in a suburb of Washington DC to a German opera singer and an American voice teacher, Bullock went on to make the classic journey from the stage via TV sitcoms to the movies. This was no overnight success story, however: though she showed great comic potential in the screwball-inspired *Love Potion No. 9* (1992), and put in a strong supporting role in **Peter Bogdanovich**'s sensitive *The Thing Called Love* (1993) – a film about aspiring country music stars for which she wrote and performed her own material – she won little attention. It was her turn as Sly Stallone's love interest in the intelligent action movie *Demolition Man* (1993) that caught the eye of cinematographer **Jan De Bont**, who was about to direct his first film, an action adventure called *Speed* (1994). Physically wiry but not a conventional beauty, Bullock made a great foil for her co-star, the handsome, if wooden, **Keanu Reeves**. Female audiences flocked to see the film as much for the feisty, funny heroine as for the heart-throb hero, and what Bullock later called "a bus movie" became both a surprise worldwide hit and her breakthrough vehicle.

She went from strength to strength in rom-coms (*While You Were Sleeping*, 1995) and action movies (*The Net*, 1995), before losing momentum. The dismal *Speed 2: Cruise Control* (1997) suffered from a lack of Keanu, and diminished the heroic Annie of the original into a ditzy drip – word was that Bullock had had her fifteen minutes of fame. Undeterred, the star formed her own production company, Fortis Films, and achieved more success with the schmaltzy but not unlikeable *Hope Floats* (1998). Both the witchy *Practical Magic* (1998), in which she displays considerable on-screen chemistry with **Nicole Kidman**, and the off-the-wall *Forces Of Nature* (1999), with **Ben Affleck**, took chick flicks into almost edgy territory; the drama *28 Days* (2000), in which Bullock flexes her acting muscles as an alcoholic newshound forced to take control of her life, is more conventional. There followed a comic tour de force in *Miss Congeniality* (2000), one of the sharper chick flicks of the post-feminist era; a show-stealing turn opposite **Hugh Grant** in the well-meaning *Two Weeks Notice* (2002); and a nuanced turn as the grumpy daughter in *Divine Secrets Of The Ya-Ya Sisterhood* (2002). *Miss Congeniality 2: Armed And Fabulous* (2005) is a rare sequel that more than lives up to the original, and along with her against-type performance as the miserable, lonely Jean in *Crash*, and, a welcome reunion with Reeves in the time- travel romance *The Lake House* (2006) confirms Sandra Bullock to be an actress well deserving of her fond place in many people's hearts.

Sandra Bullock: not always congenial

While You Were Sleeping
dir Jon Turteltaub, 1995, US, 103m

This one ticks all the boxes. It's a sweet rom-com classic, with Bullock at her appealing, vulnerable best as lonely ticket girl Lucy, who gets caught up in subterfuge after her love object (Peter Gallagher) falls into a coma.

Forces Of Nature
dir Bronwen Hughes, 1999, US, 106m

Though the plot owes everything to screwball – an uptight writer (Ben Affleck), attempting to travel to his wedding, is lumbered by bad weather, transport problems and Sarah, a free spirit with a shady past (Bullock) – this chick flick feels decidedly hip. Affleck and Bullock don't exactly sizzle, but that barely matters: it's kitsch and slightly surreal, with quirky supporting characters and a supercool soundtrack.

Miss Congeniality
dir Donald Petrie, 2000, US/Aus, 110m

With its shamelessly broad comedy and affectionate take on both the beauty pageant industry and post-feminist preconceptions, this makeover movie-cum-action adventure is both funny and smart. Bullock creates a fabulous comic character in Gracie Hart, the clumsy FBI agent who wouldn't know a beauty parlour if she fell over one.

Divine Secrets Of The Ya-Ya Sisterhood
dir Callie Khouri, 2002, US, 116m

A relatively successful attempt by first-time director Khouri, who wrote *Thelma & Louise*, to recreate the quirky Southern sisterhood, secrets and sass that made Rebecca Wells's novel such a smash hit. Bullock puts in a credibly sulky performance as Sidda, who comes to understand her mother, and her own damaged childhood, during an encounter with her mother's oldest friends.

Jane Campion

Director, 1954–

With her profoundly personal, risk-taking movies and her distinctive visual style, Jane Campion is the archetypal auteur. She also has an identifiably Antipodean sensibility, her early films in particular slotting in with quirky Oz gems like Peter Weir's *The Cars That Ate Paris* (1974), Gillian Armstrong's *Starstruck* (1982), Baz Luhrmann's *Strictly Ballroom* (1992) and P.J. Hogan's *Muriel's Wedding* (1994; see Canon). All her films have a whiff of the Gothic about them, shifting from light to dark in a heartbeat, and all of them mine a deep seam of sexual repression. And she has a brilliant eye for place, be it the majestic sweep of a New Zealand beach (*The Piano*), the intense emptiness of the Australian outback (*Holy Smoke*), the claustrophobic interiors of suburban Sydney (*Sweetie*), the elegant decay of nineteenth-century Europe (*The Portrait Of A Lady*), or the rain-soaked underbelly of New York City (*In The Cut*).

Born in Wellington, New Zealand, Campion had an unconventional, not always happy, childhood, during which her parents, who ran a theatre company, left their three children in the care of nannies. Her father was distant, while her mother, frequently depressed, regularly underwent electric shock treatment. After studying anthropology in New Zealand and art in London, Campion attended the famed Australian Film, Television and Radio School in Sydney, and following a number of original, award-winning shorts, made a triumphant feature-length debut with *Sweetie* (1989). A haunting vision of suburban insanity, the movie fearlessly took Australian camp to the dark side and elevated it to the status of art. Campion continued to thrive with *An Angel At My Table* (1990), an emotionally resonant biopic about New Zealand author Janet Frame, followed by the film with which she is most associated, the ravishing *The Piano* (1993; see Canon), which picked up more than thirty international awards. However, just days after the movie won the Palme D'Or for Best Film at Cannes, Campion's newborn son died. Since then, the director, who in her grief barely noticed the accolades for *The Piano*, has talked about her daughter Alice, born in 1994, as being her greatest achievement.

In 1996 she adapted Henry James's novel *The Portrait Of A Lady* for the screen. Despite two Oscar nominations and a raft of fine actors, including **Nicole Kidman**, who had recently caused a stir as the insanely ambitious weather girl in *To Die For* (1995), this elegant movie didn't hit a chord with audiences. Neither did *Holy Smoke* (1999), an uneasy mix of erotic mood piece, broad comedy and philosophical treatise that gave us the bizarre treat of seeing **Harvey Keitel** in drag, but little else. In 2003 Campion took yet another leap with the erotic thriller *In The Cut* (see Canon). Both **Mark Ruffalo** and **Meg Ryan**, playing against type, give phenomenal performances, as does their sexy co-star, Jennifer Jason Leigh.

Actors adore Campion – Harvey Keitel has called her a "goddess" – and without exception she garners marvellous performances from everyone she works with. Her movies depend heavily not only on metaphor and symbolism, but also on the power of the people who inhabit them, and in particular the strong, unconventional, struggling women at their centre.

Not immediately likeable, perhaps, Campion's women are always recognizable and credible – easy to identify with and hard to forget.

Following her segment in *8* (2006), a movie by eight directors about the world issues that bother them, Campion is currently taking a break from filming, concentrating on painting and family life and looking to move into television.

Sweetie
dir Jane Campion, 1989, Aus, 100m

A wickedly bleak take on a dysfunctional sibling relationship in suburban Sydney. Poetic, nightmarish and warmhearted in turn, it leaves you unsure whether to laugh or shiver.

The Portrait Of A Lady
dir Jane Campion, 1996, UK/US, 144m

This devastating version of Henry James's novel is a fine, if unsettling film. Nicole Kidman gives a career-best performance as the doomed American aristocrat Isabel Archer, a rebellious spirit who falls under the power of Barbara Hershey and John Malkovich, two malevolent European aesthes.

Gurinder Chadha

Director, contemporary

Gurinder Chadha is a leading light among the generation of British–Asian directors who emerged onto the movie scene in the 1980s. Unlike many of her contemporaries, however, Chadha's flair for broad comedy and lively storytelling – her skill at saying some pretty subversive things about racism and sexism with a light touch – has given her a populist appeal, and won her huge worldwide success.

Chadha, born in Kenya, lived in India for a spell and moved with her family to Southall, West London, in 1961. She began her career as a journalist before turning to movies in the 1980s, an era when public funding was available to back projects – from documentaries to avant-garde works – that engaged with contemporary political and social issues. British movies had long had a love affair with the exotic pull of the subcontinent; now, for the first time, Asians were vocalizing their own experiences on film. Chadha's feature debut, the lively bhangra-driven *I'm British But...* (1989), gave voice to second-generation British-Asians as they forged a new identity based upon their heritage and their own evolving youth culture; a year later she produced a short fiction film, the gently feminist *A Nice Arrangement* – scripted by and featuring comic writer/actress **Meera Syal** – about an arranged Indian wedding in London.

In 1993 Chadha caught the attention of the mainstream with her first fiction feature, the mischievous *Bhaji On The Beach*, about three generations of Indian women on a day trip to Blackpool. As ever in her work, the push and pull between tradition and modernity, India and Britain, was at the movie's heart, as well as the director's warmth for her subject. *Bhaji* was a runaway success, and started a fashion for feel-good Brit-Asian movies – *East Is East* (1999) and *Anita And Me* (2002) among them – that celebrated the culture, questioned it and gently poked fun. Chadha, however, was distinctive in placing Indian women at the forefront.

Bhaji's triumph allowed the director to head for Hollywood, where she made *What's Cooking* (2000), a cross-cultural comedy drama that follows four fraught LA families (Hispanic, Vietnamese, African-American and Jewish) as they prepare for Thanksgiving. However, it was with the entertaining Brit-flick *Bend It Like Beckham* (2002; see Canon) that Chadha really struck gold; what started as a small story about an Asian London girl's obsession with football touched buttons all over the world. The ebullient *Bride & Prejudice* (2004), a homage to both Bollywood and Jane Austen, was less successful, but has not dented Chadha's career. Having produced and written *Mistress Of Spices* (2005), a magical realist love story directed by her husband and writing partner Paul Mayeda Berges, she currently has her finger in a number of high-profile Hollywood pies, including an action-packed *I Dream Of Jeannie* prequel, and a high-profile movie version of the TV soap *Dallas*. Wherever her career takes her, it seems that ambition and adventure are never going to be in short supply for the genre-mixing, cliché-busting and very British Chadha.

Bhaji On The Beach
dir Gurinder Chadha, 1993, UK, 101m

A deceptively light road movie about a bunch of Asian women who take off from Birmingham to Blackpool, despite the protestations of their menfolk. Though it has lost a little of its shine today, it was hugely influential, and its boldness in tackling taboo subjects, including inter-racial romance, Asian racism and domestic violence, was gently ground-breaking.

What's Cooking
dir Gurinder Chadha, 2000, US/UK, 110m

Chadha takes her knack for domestic drama to LA with this saga of secrets, lies and family feuds played out around the kitchen and the dining room table. Though it ends up feeling a little too pat, there is much to enjoy, and the strong female cast – including Joan Chen, Julianna Margulies as a feisty lesbian daughter, and Alfre Woodard as the career woman battling her traditional mother-in-law – is superb.

Bride & Prejudice
dir Gurinder Chadha, 2004, UK/US, 111m

Chadha remakes Jane Austen's ironic English classic as a colourful Bollywood extravaganza, a masala mix of comedy of manners and big musical numbers. The tale of money, marriage and love globetrots through Amritsar, London

and LA, and the leads – Martin Henderson as an American Darcy and the wildly popular Bollywood star Aishwarya Rai as Lizzie/Lalita – do a great job.

Joan Crawford
Actress, 1904–1977

One of Hollywood's most magnificent faces, all raw cheekbones, beetle brows and anguished eyes, Joan Crawford is all too often remembered these days for her ghoulish cruelty to her children. To pick over the scurrilous rumours surrounding her private life, however, would be to do an injustice to this larger-than-life star, whose roles ran the gamut from vivacious flappers in the silents to tough and often quite terrifying femmes fatales. Men weren't quite sure what to make of Joan Crawford; at the peak of her career in the 1940s, however, this imposing woman was a firm favourite with female audiences, who rushed out in droves to copy her masculine, shoulder-padded style and her full "hunter's bow" lips. Suffering and surviving, tough yet fragile, and never anything less than theatrical, she also won legions of gay fans, and has become a camp icon par excellence.

Born Lucille Fay Le Sueur in San Antonio, Texas, Crawford came from a broken home and a theatre background, and by the age of 16 was working as a chorus girl and nightclub dancer. Signed to MGM, she caught audiences' attention with her vivacious table-top dance in the silent *Our Dancing Daughters* (1928), and unlike many silent stars, her sonorous voice allowed her to make the transition into talking pictures with relative ease. After her first talkie, *Untamed* (1929), proved a winner, she became determined to prove herself as a serious actress, and though destined to play second fiddle to MGM's top stars, Norma Shearer and

Joan Crawford: anguish writ large

sympathetically directed by **George Cukor** – the bitchy *The Women* (1939) and *A Woman's Face* (1941) – by the early 1940s Joan Crawford's appeal was waning. Like Katharine Hepburn before her, she earned the damning label "box office poison", and in 1943 moved to Warner Bros, where she campaigned hard to win the leading role in the moody *film noir* *Mildred Pierce* (1945; see Canon). Picking up an Oscar for her powerful portrayal of the ambitious mother driven to crime by her monstrous daughter, suddenly Crawford was big business again, inhabiting colossal roles in dark melodramas like *Humoresque* (1946), *Possessed* (1947), which won her another Oscar nomination, and *Flamingo Road* (1949).

Later roles built on Joan's camp cult status: she gave imperious performances as the housewife from hell in *Harriet Craig* (1950), the vengeful wife in *Sudden Fear* (1952, another Oscar nomination) and the sexy saloon-keeper in the proto-feminist Western *Johnny Guitar* (1954). In 1962 she hammed it up with arch rival **Bette Davis** in the cult, self-parodying *Whatever Happened To Baby Jane*, starting a run of horror movies that continued up to her final film, *Trog* (1970).

Crawford's personal life was as colourful as her career. She was married five times, and, apparently, each time changed the name of her Hollywood estate and had new toilet seats fitted. Her final marriage, to Pepsi-Cola chairman Alfred Steele, ended with his death in 1959; she remained on the board of directors, however, and made scores of TV commercials for the company. A year after Crawford died of cancer,

Greta Garbo, carved out a niche playing modern working girls looking for love, or glamorous socialites with down-to-earth hearts. In melodramas like *Possessed* (1931), *Grand Hotel* (1932) and *Mannequin* (1938) she put in some striking performances, and wore some fabulous clothes, but despite a couple of top-notch bad-girl roles, in which she was her adopted daughter, Christina, wrote *Mommie Dearest*, which detailed endless cruelty and abuse. Filmed in 1981, with Faye Dunaway playing Joan, the story leaves a nasty aftertaste for anyone who enjoyed the great diva's vigorous work in a long and illustrious career.

Flappers

Though it is not the image for which she is nowadays best remembered, **Joan Crawford** started out as one of the sassiest flapper girls of the Jazz Age. Free-spirited flappers were all the rage in the Roaring Twenties, raising their hemlines, bobbing their hair and, in a peculiarly risqué fashion statement, wearing their stockings rolled down below their (powdered) knees. Flirtier and more playful than vamps, feistier than ingénues, flappers represented all that was modern – wearing make-up, smoking, shimmying their way through saucy dances like the charleston and the black bottom, and cocking a snook to Prohibition while guzzling bootleg gin. If there was something desperate, and doomed, in their drive to forget the past and ignore the future, these jazz babies were determined to go down in style.

Crawford's fizziest flapper moment is her abandoned table-top dance in *Our Dancing Daughters* (1928), but she was great, too, as an effervescent minx in *Our Modern Maidens* (1929) and in *Our Blushing Brides* (1930), one of her early incarnations as a good-hearted shop girl. Other fab flappers include **Louise Brooks**, the eternal fashion icon with the sleek black bob (flapper faves: *Love 'Em And Leave 'Em*, 1926; *Rolled Stockings*, 1927); vivacious redhead **Clara Bow** (*The Plastic Age*, 1925; *Mantrap*, 1926; *It*, 1927; *The Wild Party*, 1929); **Colleen Moore**, who actually originated Brooks' trademark hairstyle (*Flaming Youth*, 1923; *The Perfect Flapper*, 1924; *Orchids And Ermine*, 1927); and titchy toon temptress **Betty Boop** (*Minnie The Moocher*, 1932; *The Old Man Of The Mountain*, 1933).

Chained
dir Clarence Brown, 1934, US, 76m, b/w

Glorious MGM gloss, in which Crawford models a range of stunning gowns, sashaying through art director Cedric Gibbons' decadent white-on-white Deco sets. The plot is typical of the star's 1930s work: working-class girl (Crawford) meets an older, married millionaire (Otto Kruger), but while pondering whether to become his mistress falls for a rakish ladies' man (Clark Gable).

Possessed
dir Curtis Bernhardt, 1947, US, 108m, b/w

Influenced by expressionism and not to be confused with Crawford's 1931 movie of the same name, this feverish women's picture has Joan in fine *film noir* fettle as a disturbed woman who recounts to a psychiatrist her murderous tale of obsessive love.

Sudden Fear
dir David Miller, 1952, US, 110m, b/w

Another intelligent performance in this taut, stylish thriller. Joan plays a wealthy playwright who discovers that her struggling actor husband (Jack Palance) is planning, with his floozy (Gloria Grahame), to murder her for her money. Determined to wreak her revenge, she hatches a scheme of her own…

Johnny Guitar
dir Nicholas Ray, 1954, US, 110m

Crawford steals the show in this intriguing Western as the gunslinging saloon-keeper Vienna, who battles it out with the spiteful Emma Small (Mercedes McCambridge) for control of a town. Sterling Hayden plays the eponymous love interest, a wanderer with a past.

George Cukor

Director, 1899–1983

Famed for his gentle, calming directing style and his sparkling, dynamic movies, George Cukor was called the ultimate "women's director". A firm favourite with most of Hollywood's screen goddesses, he worked particularly well with the independent-minded **Katharine Hepburn** (see p.176), whom he directed in ten films over a period of nearly fifty years. In 1968 he accepted the Best Actress Oscar for the star, who, as was her habit, didn't attend the ceremony.

A Jewish-Hungarian New Yorker, Cukor began his career in the 1920s as a Broadway stage director, before, like so many others in the business, decamping to Hollywood when movies started talking. In 1932 he teamed up with legendary producer **David O. Selznick** to make *A Bill Of Divorcement*, featuring the up-and-coming actress Katharine Hepburn. One of the few to spot movie star potential in this coltish gamine, the director inserted numerous lingering shots of her androgynous beauty into the film, creating an intriguing and effective debut for the New England tomboy. Soon after, Cukor followed Selznick to MGM, where he directed the comedy *Dinner At Eight* (1933), with young sex symbol Jean Harlow; *Romeo And Juliet* (1936), with MGM queen Norma Shearer; *Camille* (1936; see Canon) with Greta Garbo; and *Holiday* (1938), with Hepburn and Cary Grant. In 1939, citing artistic disagreements, Selznick quickly replaced Cukor as director of *Gone With The Wind* (1939; see Canon) with **Victor Fleming** (who, coincidentally, had also taken over from Cukor as director of *The Wizard Of Oz* the previous year). Rumours spread that the decision was inspired by Clark Gable's unease in the face of Cukor's homosexuality, and his resentment at the attention the director paid to the movie's female stars. Whatever the reason, Vivien Leigh and Olivia de Havilland were particularly upset at Cukor's departure, missing his sensitive direction, which was in marked contrast to Fleming's rougher touch.

Fielding snidely homophobic jibes about being Hollywood's "greatest female director",

Cukor proceeded, undeterred, to direct ever more popular women's movies, including the catty all-female *The Women* (1939), featuring Norma Shearer, Rosalind Russell and Joan Crawford, and *The Philadelphia Story* (1940), another sparkling comedy pairing for Hepburn and Grant. After a relatively quiet period in the 1940s, he showcased the dynamic chemistry between Hepburn and her lover, Spencer Tracy, in the witty *Adam's Rib* (1949; see Canon) and *Pat And Mike* (1952), both of which also benefited from sharp scripts by writing team Ruth Gordon and Garson Kanin. With his theatrical background, Cukor always adored working with good writers. After *Adam's Rib*, Cukor, recognizing great quirky potential in the young supporting actress **Judy Holliday**, starred her in *Born Yesterday* (1950), a screwball-style comedy that shot her to fame as one of Hollywood's all-time great comediennes. In 1954's *A Star Is Born*, his first musical and first colour film, he brought **Judy Garland** to the screen after an absence of four years, using her bruised fragility to heartbreaking effect.

The 1960s was something of a lost decade for Cukor, though he did win his only Oscar for *My Fair Lady* (1964), a frothy musical extravaganza starring Audrey Hepburn as Eliza Doolittle. His final film, *Rich And Famous* (1981), a remake of the 1943 Bette Davis movie *Old Acquaintance*, is a not unlikeable curiosity, in which Jacqueline Bisset and Candice Bergen play lifelong friends and rivals.

A Bill Of Divorcement
dir George Cukor, 1932, US, 75m, b/w

Katharine Hepburn, in her first movie, plays the spirited daughter of a mental patient (John Barrymore), who escapes after years to his wife (Billie Burke) on the day she is set to divorce him. Though dated, it's fascinating to see the young actress's raw talent being moulded by her soon-to-be favourite director.

Holiday
dir George Cukor, 1938, US, 95m, b/w

Cukor's sensitive touch is much in evidence in this sophisticated adaptation of Philip Barry's Broadway hit. Cary Grant and Katharine Hepburn, of course, make a wonderful team: he typically charming as freethinking Johnny, whose fiancé Julia (Doris Nolan) wants him to join the family firm; she full of crackling energy as Julia's unconventional sister.

A Woman's Face
dir George Cukor, 1941, US, 105m, b/w

Joan Crawford was never better than when working under Cukor's skillful direction. Here the diva gives a moving performance in a dramatic tale of a bitter, twisted blackmailer with a violent facial disfigurement – and lives up to her reputation as camp icon at the same time.

Gaslight
dir George Cukor, 1944, US, 114m, b/w

A wonderfully overblown thriller set in a spooky Victorian London, where the innocent Paula (Ingrid Bergman) is driven to the point of madness by her evil husband (Charles Boyer), who is desperate to get his hands on her aunt's jewels.

Bette Davis
Actress, 1908–1989

Bette Davis was one of Hollywood's greatest stars – a larger-than-life actress and an uncompromising rebel who cared little what people thought of her. After winning some acclaim on the stage, in 1930 she started making minor movies at Universal Studios, before moving on to become a contract player at Warner Bros. Though initially cast as flirty coquettes, she never really fit that mould, being far too spiky – and not quite the right kind of pretty – to play ingénues with any conviction. Undeterred, however, and sure of her own worth as an actress, she battled on. Loaned

out to RKO, she had a breakthrough hit with *Of Human Bondage* (1934), in which she plays an unredeemable (and Cockney!) bad girl, far outshining her matinee idol co-star Leslie Howard. This was followed by another great performance as the wicked actress in *Dangerous* (1935), for which she became the first Warner Bros player to win the Best Actress Oscar. From here on she carved a niche playing complex, strong and not always sympathetic characters – tough and yet vulnerable – that won her great affection from female audiences.

In addition to her acting talents, the outspoken Davis was also a trailblazer within the industry. In 1936, frustrated with Warners' notoriously low wages and the uninteresting roles they were offering her, she accepted an invitation to work in London. A seminal court case ensued, and though it was judged in favour of Warner Bros, who won the right to keep the actress tied into her seven-year contract, it saw the beginning of a shift of power in Hollywood away from the studios. Davis continued to fight her ground, demanding control over her work, claiming appropriate recompense, and winning herself the not entirely complimentary nickname "the Fourth Warner Brother". The studio took her seriously, giving her meaty roles in films like *Marked Woman* (1937) and *Jezebel* (1938) – which won her another Oscar – and throughout the 1940s she put in consummate performances in a string of fine melodramas. Cornering the market in women who were playing a role or living a lie, she was equally adept at acting bitter and twisted (*The Letter*, 1940; *The Little Foxes*, 1941), noble and self-sacrificing (*Now, Voyager*, 1942; *Old Acquaintance*, 1943), or both (the identical twins in *A Stolen Life*, 1946). In 1941 she became the first female president of the Academy of Motion Picture

Rebel, trailblazer, fighter, trooper: the one and only Bette Davis

Arts and Sciences – resigning two months later, convinced that she was expected to be nothing more than a figurehead – and by 1942 was the highest paid woman in America.

Even when suffering, Bette was never a victim: a fighter and a survivor, she is one of those great Hollywood icons that have won not only generations of female fans but also a faithful male gay following. The gay fan base is particularly hooked into her two final major roles, both of which have become paragons of high camp. In *All About Eve* (1950), Bette sizzles as the bourbon-guzzling 40-year-old actress whose studied cynicism masks a bruised fragility, while in *Whatever Happened To Baby Jane* (1962) she offers a deliciously grotesque self-parody, terrorizing her long-time rival Joan Crawford. Famously declaring, "Old age is no place for sissies," she continued to act right up until the end, often in cheap horror films and on TV, before dying from cancer in Neuilly-sur-Seine, France. Her epitaph reads, "She did it the hard way," a suitable tribute to this unique and charismatic trooper.

Jezebel
dir William Wyler, 1938, US, 106m, b/w

Davis, all flouncing crinolines, is delightfully stroppy as Southern belle Julie Marsden, who scandalizes pre-Civil War New Orleans by daring to wear a scarlet dress to a society ball. Horrified by her wickedness, her fiancé (Henry Fonda) runs off and marries a Yankee (Margaret Lindsay), leaving Julie to learn the error of her ways.

Dark Victory
dir Edmund Goulding, 1939, US, 106m, b/w

A tear-drenched melodrama in which Davis plays a spoiled heiress who suffers a brain tumour before being cured by dashing surgeon George Brent. Love blossoms, but all is still not entirely well with Bette's health…

All This, And Heaven Too
dir Anatole Litvak, 1940, US, 140m, b/w

This historical melodrama has Davis as the innocent governess who, after falling in love with her employer (Charles Boyer), is accused of murdering his glamorous wife and being responsible for his suicide. Perfect Sunday afternoon viewing.

The Little Foxes
dir William Wyler, 1941, US, 116m, b/w

Bette is irresistible as Regina Giddens, another ruthless Southern belle. The screenplay was adapted from Lillian

---

The wry wit and worldly wisdom of Bette Davis

While she had some unforgettable movie lines – "Fasten your seat belts. It's going to be a bumpy night" (*All About Eve*, 1950); "Cute! I'd like to kiss ya, but I just washed my hair" (*The Cabin In The Cotton*, 1932); "Oh Jerry, don't let's ask for the moon. We have the stars"(*Now, Voyager*, 1942) among them – Ms Davis was no slouch when it came to off-screen quips either:

On Joan Crawford: Why am I so good at playing bitches? I think it's because I'm not a bitch. Maybe that's why Miss Crawford always plays ladies.

On Marilyn Monroe: She's the original good time that was had by all.

Until you're known in my profession as a monster you're not a star.

I'm the nicest goddamn dame that ever lived.

I was thought to be "stuck-up". I wasn't. I was just sure of myself. This is and always has been an unforgivable quality to the unsure.

If you have never been hated by your child, you have never been a parent.

If you want a thing well done, get a couple of old broads to do it.

Hellman's play; where Hellman's heroine is relatively sympathetic, however, Bette plays her as a little minx who will stop at nothing, it seems, to secure her ailing husband's riches.

Doris Day
Actress and singer, 1924–

Too often undervalued, dismissed as "the perpetual virgin", the effervescent Doris Day – virtuoso comedienne, brilliant dancer and one of the world's great singers – was also, at the height of her fame in the early 1960s, the most popular movie actress in the world. A strong, hard-working and upbeat woman, whose vexed private life never defeated her, Doris is one of Hollywood's great talents and great survivors.

Born in Cincinnati, Ohio, young Doris von Kappelhoff was a gifted dancer; disconsolate following an accident that damaged her legs, she started singing along with the radio to pass the time. Soon, still only a teenager, she was singing on the radio for real, fronting big bands and winning popularity for her velvety, easy vocal styling. Behind the scenes, however, life was not so easy. At 17 she married band member Al Jordan, an abusive man who, furious when she fell pregnant, threatened to shoot her in the stomach. Doris had the baby and fled home to her mother in Cincinnati; Jordan later shot himself. Returning to the big band circuit, Doris snagged a smash hit in 1944 with the seductive "Sentimental Journey", and two years later, after another brief failed marriage, took a screen test with Warner Bros, who signed her up immediately for a seven-movie deal. A vivacious performer with superb comic timing, Day was perfectly cast in lavish, happy-ever-after musicals like *By The Light Of The Silvery Moon* (1953), in which she played plucky girls-next-door. In other, lesser-known films, including *Storm Warning* (1951), an indictment of the Ku Klux Klan, she proved herself equally able to handle serious drama. Perhaps her finest and best-known role, however, was as the hilarious, buckskin-wearing *Calamity Jane* (1953), whose plaintive "Secret Love" won her a Best Song Oscar – and a keen gay following.

Upon completing her contract with Warner Bros, Day – now managed by and married to the controlling, widely disliked Marty Melcher – was able to spread her wings, putting in a career-best performance as the tough torch singer Ruth Etting in biopic *Love Me Or Leave Me* (1955), and shining in Hitchcock's *The Man Who Knew Too Much* (1955). In the musical comedy *The Pajama Game* (1957), taken from the wildly popular Broadway show, she was at the top of her game as a union leader in love with her boss. At home, however, things were difficult: her marriage was disastrous, relations with her teenage son Terry had broken down, and, at the age of 32, she discovered that she needed a hysterectomy. A triumphant, Oscar-nominated return came with the battle-of-the-sexes comedy *Pillow Talk* (1959; see Canon), in which she plays a career girl with fabulous outfits and a chic bachelor-girl pad. Sophisticated and clever, the film paired Doris with the handsome **Rock Hudson** (see p.179); their chemistry was palpable, and they became firm friends. This winning "sex comedy" formula was repeated twice with Hudson, and later with Cary Grant, Rod Taylor and James Garner. Often described as conservative, these slick movies are anything but: sizzling with tongue-in-cheek innuendo, playing on the plight of the modern single girl, they still feel sprightly, and Day's performances are just superb.

As the 1960s drew on, however, fashions changed. Refusing the part of Mrs Robinson in *The Graduate*, Doris made one more film, the lacklustre *With Six You Get Eggroll* (1968), before discovering, upon Marty's death that same year, that he had left her in catastrophic debt. Television was to prove her saviour, and after three years of the self-produced *The Doris Day Show*, she cleared her debts and devoted herself to animal welfare. Today, while it may take some time before Doris Day is publicly afforded the accolades she deserves, her wonderful body of work stands as testament to this supremely talented woman.

Calamity Jane
dir David Butler, 1953, US, 101m

Doris plays the cussing, brawling, thigh-slapping cowgirl who has to be taught, somewhat unwillingly, to be a lady in this rumbustious classic. Funny and feisty, Day is firing on all cylinders – it was her own personal favourite – and the great Sammy Fain songs make wonderful use of that heart-melting voice.

Love Me Or Leave Me
dir Charles Vidor, 1955, US, 122m

This searing biopic of band singer Ruth Etting and her thuggish manager, "Moe the Gimp" (James Cagney), may have been closer to life than audiences knew. Day shines as the tough, sexy singer, and audiences loved her.

The Man Who Knew Too Much
dir Alfred Hitchcock, 1955, US, 120m

Hitchcock, long keen to work with Day, cast her in this tense thriller as an ex-singer, stifled in her marriage to a doctor (James Stewart), whose child is kidnapped. The actress puts in a nuanced performance, and twice sings "Que Sera, Sera", which won her her second Best Song Oscar and became her biggest hit.

Move Over, Darling
dir Michael Gordon, 1963, US, 103m

A typically smart and frothy sex comedy – a remake of 1940's *My Favorite Wife* – which has Day playing the long-lost (believed to be dead) wife attempting to stop James

Garner's brand-new marriage from developing any further. The movie was a phenomenal success, as was its risqué title song, written by Doris's 21-year-old son, Terry.

Nora Ephron
Writer and director, 1941–

At her best, screenwriter Nora Ephron turns out biting, sharply observed scripts that foreground strong, interesting female characters. She has also, more unusually for a woman in Hollywood, made a commercially successful transition to directing, helming a handful of comedies that includes two of the key rom-coms of the 1990s. Born to Hollywood scriptwriting team Henry and Phoebe Ephron, Nora started out as a journalist, going on to pen the bestselling essay collection *Crazy Salad* (1975) and the roman à clef *Heartburn* (1983), which exposed the breakdown of her marriage to Watergate journalist Carl Bernstein. Her first screenplay, a collaboration with another female screenwriter, **Alice Arlen**, was for the biopic *Silkwood* (1983), which took an uncompromising swipe at the nuclear industry in the US. The movie starred **Meryl Streep** in one of her most powerful performances, featured a show-stealing turn from Cher as the lovelorn best friend, and bagged Ephron her first Oscar nomination. In 1986 she adapted *Heartburn* for the screen, portraying the terrible dreariness of a marriage breakdown with honesty, intelligence and no little wit. Things turned lighter for Ephron's next outing, the screenplay for **Susan Seidelman**'s *Cookie* (1989), which she co-wrote with Arlen. However, despite a sprightly premise – a caper movie centring on a mobster (Peter Falk) and his rebellious daughter (Emily Lloyd) – the script lacked focus, and the movie flopped.

Ephron's comedy smarts were put to better use in **Rob Reiner**'s *When Harry Met Sally…* (1989; see Canon), the classic relationship comedy that spends ninety enjoyable minutes contemplating whether men and women can be friends. Reiner and Ephron, a couple of cynical Jewish New Yorkers who themselves had been friends a long time, claim that the movie is based on banter they shared after the newly divorced Reiner began proclaiming about the differences between the sexes. Ephron admits she used a lot of herself to portray Sally, an essentially optimistic, if controlling, romantic, and scribbled down actual quotes from Reiner to help create the character of Harry, the gloomy neurotic. With its smart urbanity, recognizable characters and romantic heart, *Harry* was a huge smash, and earned Ephron her second Oscar nomination.

After scripting *My Blue Heaven* (1990), a workaday mafia spoof with Steve Martin, Ephron turned to directing with the acerbic *This Is My Life* (1992), which she invited her sister Delia to co-write with her, and *Sleepless In Seattle* (1993), a rom-com in the style of *When Harry Met Sally…* Drawing parallels with the classic weepie *An Affair To Remember* (1957; see Canon), *Sleepless* shared *Harry*'s winning combination of sardonic humour and gentle romance, and was nearly as big a hit; however, in pitching America's sweetheart, **Meg Ryan**, against Tom Hanks, an actor altogether softer and less neurotic than *Harry*'s Billy Crystal, it did lack the earlier film's edge. Ephron's next outings as director, again co-written with her sister, were the best-forgotten *Mixed Nuts* (1994), a corny Christmas comedy featuring Steve Martin, and the quirkier *Michael* (1996), starring John Travolta as an unconventional angel. *You've Got Mail* (1998), which pushed all the same buttons as *Sleepless In Seattle* – Ryan and Hanks, romantic New York setting, mistaken identities, modern relationship crises – was hardly a stretch, but did well at the box office. The misguided *Bewitched* (2005), however, based on the cult 1960s TV series and starring Nicole Kidman and Shirley MacLaine, was a sorry waste of talent; it remains to be seen whether Ephron can regain her magic touch.

Heartburn
dir Mike Nichols, 1986, US, 109m

Written after Ephron split from philandering journalist Carl Bernstein, this does a good job of portraying the ordinary joys of domesticity – and, without histrionics or drama, the aching pain of splitting up. An impressive cast includes a young Kevin Spacey, Meryl Streep and Jack Nicholson

This Is My Life
dir Nora Ephron, 1992, US, 105m

Ephron's directorial debut – a mischievous, if patchy, comedy – sees the welcome return of the wonderful comic actress Julie Kavner as the single mom turned stand-up comedienne who neglects her daughters in her hunger for fame.

You've Got Mail
dir Nora Ephron, 1998, US, 119m

Meg Ryan and Tom Hanks team up again in a classic mistaken-identity love story given a modern twist. Though it still just about works – especially if combined with a tub of ice cream on a rainy afternoon – it does wring the last gasp of life from the formula.

Jane Fonda

Actress, 1937–

One of the most intriguing figures in Hollywood, Jane Fonda has gone through almost as many metamorphoses in her personal life as on screen. Adored, desired and despised in the US, where many have still not forgiven her for her forceful anti-Vietnam War stance in the 1970s, she has been a sex kitten and a revolutionary, an aerobics queen and a feminist – but also, and this is less often mentioned, an accomplished and important actress.

A wealthy New Yorker, daughter of the Hollywood star **Henry Fonda** and sister to Peter, Jane was encouraged to act in the late 1950s by her father. Having studied the Method at Lee Strasberg's legendary Actors Studio, she made her movie debut as a man-hunting cheerleader in *Tall Story* (1960); undeniably dated now, the movie did showcase her mischievous comedy talent. Although she did star in dramas, including the deliciously camp brothel-set *Walk On The Wild Side* (1962) and the intriguing *The Chase* (1966), she excelled in playing kooky dolly birds in romantic comedies like *Barefoot In The Park* (1967). She was pitch-perfect in two seminal Sixties spoofs: the Western *Cat Ballou* (1965) and the trippy sci-fi romp *Barbarella* (1968), directed by her then-husband **Roger Vadim**. Curvaceous and catsuit-clad, Jane Fonda was now a sexual icon. Just a year later, in one of the surprising shifts that characterize her career, she earned a Best Actress nomination for the searing Depression-era tragedy *They Shoot Horses, Don't They?*, which is as far away from the kitsch erotica of *Barbarella* as can be imagined.

Horses heralded a new, "serious" Jane Fonda. Barbarella cut her hair, donned a turtleneck, split from the womanizing Vadim and turned to radical politics, protesting with her new husband, activist Tom Hayden, against America's involvement in the Vietnam War. She won an Oscar for her portrayal of a hard-boiled prostitute in the feminist *film noir Klute* (1971), but, perhaps due to her political activity, received few movie offers over the next few years. The bouncy caper *Fun With Dick And Jane* (1976) provided a comeback of sorts, and she received an Oscar nomination for her role as playwright Lillian

Hanoi Jane

"The image of Jane Fonda, Barbarella, Henry Fonda's daughter, just a woman sitting on an enemy aircraft gun, was a betrayal. It was like I was thumbing my nose at the military and at the country that gave me privilege." – Jane Fonda, 2005

In 1970 **Jane Fonda**, who felt strongly about the lies that Americans were being fed in order to justify their government's involvement in the Vietnam War, joined actor Donald Sutherland in entertaining US troops with a satirical anti-war review. This was deemed shocking enough for the woman who had previously been best known for her role as the sexy space-girl Barbarella, but her biggest mistake was in visiting the Vietcong in 1972 and being photographed atop a North Vietnamese anti-aircraft artillery launcher. This was a woman, the photo suggested, who was not preaching pacifism, but was actually supporting a North Vietnamese victory. As such, "Hanoi Jane" was branded a traitor of the worst kind, and is still today reviled among many American conservatives. She later claimed that the photo was a misunderstanding, and apologized for her thoughtlessness, but not her intentions, in a televised meeting with Vietnam vets in 1988. The hatred still felt for Fonda in some quarters of the US was clearly demonstrated in 2005, when a veteran spat at her during a book signing.

Hellman in *Julia* (1977). Forming her own production company, IPC (Indo-China Peace Campaign), Fonda concentrated on producing issue-based movies, and received a vindication by winning her second Oscar for *Coming Home* (1978), which, in its engagement with the effect of the Vietnam War on ordinary people, had more than a sniff of anti-war sentiment. Other IPC productions in which she starred include the elegiac Western *Comes A Horseman* and *The China Syndrome* (both 1978), about a nuclear power plant cover-up.

The next decade brought huge commercial success with the Women's Lib-inspired comedy *Nine To Five* (1980) and the family drama *On Golden Pond* (1981). The latter was given extra piquancy by the fact that she starred with her notoriously remote father, with whom she had always had a difficult relationship. In 1982 she also kick-started the worldwide aerobics craze by donning a leotard and releasing *Jane Fonda's Workout*, which became the bestselling video ever. Though she has since admitted that her initial exercising mania was linked to her eating disorders and low self-esteem, Fonda's workout videos remain top-sellers to this day.

Following a number of lacklustre movie roles, she married media mogul Ted Turner in 1991 and announced her retirement from acting. The marriage ended ten years later, and in 2005, the year in which she published her autobiography, *My Life So Far*, Fonda returned to the screen with the slapstick chick flick *Monster-In-Law*. The movie, co-starring Jennifer Lopez, received mixed reviews, as did her book, an analytical, no-holds-barred account that illuminates an extraordinary life.

Barefoot In The Park
dir Gene Saks, 1967, US, 105m

Adapted from Neil Simon's play, this is classic Sixties fun, with a free-spirited Fonda and wry Robert Redford playing young newlyweds struggling to make a life together. Fonda's performance, like the film itself, is light and sexy, with a poignant edge.

Klute
dir Alan J. Pakula, 1971, US, 114m

The shaggy-haired Fonda enters a new phase with her nuanced portrayal of the fiercely independent New York hooker Bree in this feminism-tinged psychological thriller. Moody, atmospheric and gripping.

Julia
dir Fred Zinnemann, 1977, US, 117m

An exciting female friendship film, based on the memoirs of American playwright Lillian Hellman (Fonda), who, on the eve of World War II, sets off on a dangerous mission to save her dear friend Julia (Vanessa Redgrave), a Resistance fighter in Europe. Meryl Streep features in an early role.

Monster-In-Law
dir Robert Luketic, 2005, US, 101m

Though it takes time to get going, this uneven comedy is worth watching for Fonda alone, hamming it up as Viola, the mother-in-law from hell in an all-guns-blazing comeback. Jennifer Lopez is outshone as the object of her fury, while Wanda Sykes adds wisecracks as Viola's world-weary sidekick. In a wicked aside, Fonda claimed that she based her character on her ex, Ted Turner.

Jodie Foster

Actress and director, 1962–

It's a rare person that makes a successful transition from precocious child star to respected adult actor; one such, Jodie Foster, who started her career aged 3 in commercials, is remarkable not only for her longevity, but also for the range of work she has produced over the last forty years. Brought up by a single mother and supporting her family with her movie income, Foster showed unique ability right from the start. Early standouts included Audrey, the rebellious tomboy in **Martin Scorsese's** *Alice Doesn't Live Here Any More* (1974; see Canon),

and the wise-beyond-her-years siren Tallulah in kiddy gangster spoof *Bugsy Malone* (1976), but it was her Oscar-nominated performance as Iris, the child prostitute in Scorsese's *Taxi Driver* (1976), that defined her for a generation – snapping gum in satin hotpants, she was more than a match for her co-star, **Robert De Niro**. The girl next door with brains and street smarts, the young Foster was both sexual and empowered, with a tough, knowing persona that kept her firmly in charge. Since then she has never played anything but brave, bold and independent, inhabiting every role with innate intelligence and intuitive ease. Whether bad girl or good, white trash or yuppie, Foster is always a heroine – usually a solitary figure, she fights her own battles, and even when under attack is never, ever, a victim.

In 1980 Foster graduated with flying colours from the private Lycée Français in LA, and went on to study English literature at Yale. A year later she handled with characteristic dignity the attempt by John Hinckley, an obsessive fan, to assassinate President Reagan in order to impress her; after a brief press conference, she lay low and to this day refuses to comment further. Juggling studying and movie acting, she graduated magna cum laude in 1985, and after a few commercial flops (the indie teen flick *Five Corners* and the overwrought thriller *Siesta*, both 1987), won her first Oscar for a gut-punching turn as Sarah Tobias, the working-class rape victim in *The Accused* (1988). Her second Oscar came soon after, for a career-best performance as FBI rookie Clarice Starling in *The Silence Of The Lambs* (1990; see Canon).

By 1991 she had turned to directing, helming *Little Man Tate*, a gentle movie about a child prodigy that also gave Foster her first single mother role. She stole the show opposite

Never a victim: Jodie Foster in *The Accused* (1988)

Richard Gere in *Sommersby* (1993), a patchy remake of Gérard Depardieu's *The Return Of Martin Guerre*, and won another Best Actress Oscar nomination for her portrayal of feral mountain woman *Nell* (1994), which she also produced. With *Home For The Holidays* (1995), her second outing as a director, Foster used a great cast to breathe new life into an old premise (dysfunctional family get together for Thanksgiving); she then turned in an assured performance as the maverick UFO scientist in *Contact* (1997), and went on to corner the market in middle-class mums in peril with *Panic Room* (2002) and *Flightplan* (2005).

Throughout her career the woman who once said, "Being understood is not the most essential thing in life," has fielded curiosity about her private life. Ignoring demands that she come out as a lesbian, or reveal the identity of the father of her two children (born in 1998 and 2001), she instead brings quiet integrity to everything she does, raising her kids while continuing to act in, direct and produce consistently intriguing films.

The Accused
dir Jonathan Kaplan, 1988, US, 111m

Based on a true story, *The Accused* is a movie about rape that is neither exploitative nor voyeuristic. Foster brings her toughness to the role of the gang rape victim who hires a female attorney (Kelly McGillis) to put forward a criminal case against her attackers, only to find her own sexual history coming under the spotlight.

Mothers get some action

First we had **Lieutenant Ripley** (Sigourney Weaver), weighed down with Uzis, scooping up the orphaned Newt in *Aliens* (1986); then ferocious **Sarah Connor** (Linda Hamilton) donned a skimpy vest and heavy weapons in order to save her son – and the world – in *Terminator 2: Judgment Day* (1991). Since then, mothers have had far more to do in the movies than just bake and weep. Whether simply stroppy or downright murderous, these moms aren't interested in noble sacrifice; and though they may be reluctant heroes, their hearts heavy at the violence they have to commit, there's no holding back when their children's lives are on the line. In *The Long Kiss Goodnight* (1996), for example, when **Geena Davis**'s cosy family life is torn apart after her cute daughter is kidnapped, mom's secret past as a bloodthirsty assassin rapidly comes to light. A quick hairstyle change and a lot of gunslinging ensues. **Uma Thurman**, too, despite dreams of putting her violent past behind her, doesn't take long to zip herself up in a yellow catsuit and sword-fight her way to bloody revenge for the death of her baby in *Kill Bill: Vols. 1* and *2* (2003 & 2004). Mother rage gets even hipper in the stylish Korean movie *Lady Vengeance* (2005), when the revenge taken by **Lee Yeong-ae**, an avenging angel fuelled by a fierce maternal instinct, is particularly sadistic.

Jodie Foster has a special place in the ranks of maternal warriors. Though she has played a mother in peril twice to date – fighting to save herself and her daughter from intruders in *Panic Room* (2002), and to find her missing daughter on an airborne plane in *Flightplan* (2005) – she relies more on her wits than heavy weapons to win the day. No ex-assassin or sci-fi soldier, Foster, despite the suspense and violence in her action movies, comes through with her woman-next-door image intact, just an ordinary, intelligent single mother, doing what she has to do for herself and her kids.

Nell
dir Michael Apted, 1994, US, 113m

An affecting movie about an untamed girl (Foster) who, having lived wild in the backwoods, emerges into civilization after her mother's death. Fought over by a kindly doctor (Liam Neeson) and various heartless psychologists, Nell has to find a way to survive on her own terms. Visceral and nuanced, the performance is one of Foster's best.

Panic Room
dir David Fincher, 2002, US, 112m

A woman-in-peril thriller with a modern twist. Claustrophobic single mother Foster and her spirited daughter (Kristen Stewart) hole up in their yuppie mansion's failsafe panic room to protect themselves from violent intruders; daughter, however, is diabetic, and mom has to venture out in order to save her. It's enjoyably manipulative, with a typically polished turn from Foster as the action heroine, ably matched by the young Stewart.

Cary Grant

Actor, 1904–86

The debonair Cary Grant had a devastatingly attractive quality that appeals as much to audiences today as it did during his lifetime. There's something about the twinkle in his eye and the dimple in his chin, the way he teases and challenges his feisty female co-stars and pokes fun at himself, which tells us that this is a man who genuinely liked women. And whatever the truth about his sexuality – though he was married five times, and had a passionate affair with Sophia Loren in the 1950s, rumours abounded that he was bisexual – women most certainly like him.

Born Archibald Leach in Bristol, England, and starting his career as a vaudeville acrobat, young Archie first came to the US on tour in 1920. After a spell on the British stage, he returned to the States, heading for Hollywood – and a name change – in 1932. A generous actor with a relaxed screen presence, he was matched with many of the leading female stars of the day, among them Marlene Dietrich in *Blonde Venus* (1932), Mae West – whom he later claimed taught him more than anyone he'd worked with – in her saucy comedies *She Done Him Wrong* and *I'm No Angel* (both 1933), and Jean Harlow in *Suzy* (1936).

Grant could turn his hand to everything from war movies to costume dramas, but it was in the madcap world of screwball that his suave, knowing comedy style found its niche. The perfect foil for his strong-willed heroines, he was regularly paired with fast-talking dames **Irene Dunne** (*The Awful Truth*, 1937; *My Favorite Wife*, 1940) and **Katharine Hepburn** (*Holiday*, *Bringing Up Baby*, both 1938; *The Philadelphia Story*, 1940) – and also proved a cracking match for rapid-fire Rosalind Russell in *His Girl Friday* (1939; see Canon). Meanwhile, he earned an Oscar nomination as Irene Dunne's husband in the heart-rending women's picture *Penny Serenade* (1941), and became something of a muse to **Alfred Hitchcock** (*Suspicion*, 1941; *Notorious*, 1946). Playing on his handsome looks and sardonic persona, the Hitchcock movies also gave Grant's cool sex appeal a new twist, often keeping audiences guessing as to whether he was hero or villain. Grant won another Oscar nomination for his performance as the Cockney waster who changes his ways when he realizes his mother is dying in *None But The Lonely Heart* (1944), and made a convincing Cole Porter in the otherwise lame biopic *Night And Day* (1946). He kept his comedy star ascendant with *Every Girl Should Be Married* (1948), opposite Betsy Drake – who became his third wife – and the frenzied curiosity *I Was A Male War Bride* (1949), in which he spends much of the time dressed in drag.

Following a turn in Joseph L. Mankiewicz's biting social satire *People Will Talk* (1951), Grant

The debonair Grant teases Irene Dunne in *The Awful Truth* (1937)

returned to his screwball roots with the merry *Monkey Business* (1952) – starring with Ginger Rogers, Marilyn Monroe and a cheeky chimp – and set hearts fluttering in the classic weepie *An Affair To Remember* (1957; see Canon). A brace of Hitchcock classics, *To Catch A Thief* (1955) and *North By Northwest* (1959), had fun with his middle-aged charm; he brought the same qualities to *That Touch Of Mink* (1962), one of **Doris Day**'s sophisticated sex comedies, and the comedy thriller *Charade* (1963), opposite **Audrey Hepburn** – in the latter he insisted on script changes to clarify that it was she, the young woman, who was pursuing him, the older man, and not vice versa. With typical grace Grant chose to retire from movies altogether in the mid-1960s. He died, aged 82, having suffered a stroke before going on stage with his one-man show, *An Evening With Cary Grant*.

Bringing Up Baby
dir Howard Hawks, 1938, US, 102m, b/w

Grant is gently daffy as bespectacled paleontologist David Huxley, whose life is thrown into disarray with the arrival of Katharine Hepburn's fast-talking heiress. Delicious chaos ensues, involving a missing dinosaur bone, an impudent dog, a leopard named Baby, and a short spell in jail.

My Favorite Wife
dir Garson Kanin, 1940, US, 88m, b/w

One of Grant and Irene Dunne's sparkiest screwballs. She, shipwrecked and believed dead for seven years, turns up on the very day her husband (Grant, naturally) is due to remarry. When he discovers she was stranded with a dashing scientist (Randolph Scott), the jealousy goes two ways.

Penny Serenade
dir George Stevens, 1941, US, 125m, b/w

Grant and Irene Dunne act their socks off in this shameless weepie about a woman, on the point of leaving her husband, who takes a melancholy trip down memory lane while listening to a pile of old gramophone records. An honest reflection on childlessness, adoption and family tragedy, it pulls no punches, and Grant is truly heartbreaking.

To Catch A Thief
dir Alfred Hitchcock, 1955, US, 107m

One of Hitchcock's sexiest comedy thrillers, with supercool Grant, an ex-jewel thief, playing a slinky cat-and-mouse game with the glacial Grace Kelly. Delightfully risqué, and notable especially for the moment when Kelly purrs, "Do you want a leg or a breast?", while offering him some chicken.

Hugh Grant
Actor, 1960–

Hugh Grant's famous mug shot, snapped in 1995 after he was discovered by LA police in a compromising position with prostitute Divine Brown, shows him hunched awkwardly, shame-faced and sulky. He's also well-groomed, his rather unhip spectacles carefully hooked over the collar of his rugby shirt. Here, we can surmise, is a well-to-do overgrown public schoolboy with a naughty streak, a little petulant, arrogant maybe, but certainly the acceptable face of kerb crawling. That he managed to come back from that moment to gain kudos as an actor is testament to his intelligence, his staying power and, probably most of all, his wry, rather English humour.

The actor who made a career out of playing foppish and awkward English gents had a very respectable suburban English childhood before winning a scholarship to study at Oxford. After dabbling in drama at university, and playing the comedy club circuit with a sketch group, the Jockeys of Norfolk, he drifted into acting. A touching performance in Merchant Ivory's same-sex love story *Maurice* (1987) brought him attention, though he struggled for years through some dreadful movies – and was woefully miscast as Lord Byron in the Spanish *Remando al viento* (*Rowing In The Wind*, 1988), which also featured the young, beetle-browed actress **Elizabeth Hurley**, who would be his girlfriend for more than a decade. Though his accent and his manner brought him a stream of sundry aristocrats and bumbling Englishmen – including a solid supporting role in Merchant Ivory's tragic *The Remains Of The Day* (1993) – Grant had yet to find himself as an actor.

With the rom-com *Four Weddings And A Funeral* (1993) everything seemed to fall into place. The film was the highest-grossing British movie ever, and Grant won a BAFTA and a Golden Globe – along with a lot of credibility – for his accomplished performance as the quintessential British bachelor. There followed more stammering and blushing as a well-meaning priest in *Sirens* (1994) and a lovelorn suitor in Ang Lee's *Sense And Sensibility* (1995), before, while publicizing the execrable *Nine Months* in the summer of 1995, the now-legendary Divine Brown incident occurred. Bizarrely, the scandal, which could have ruined his career, was the making of him. Arrested for lewd conduct in a public space, Hugh Grant suddenly became interesting, edgy even. His

Hugh Grant, a terribly English hero (or villain)

appearance on TV chat shows, both apologizing and poking fun at himself, made him seem honourable, self-deprecating and sexy at the same time. Suddenly we could pick up a certain note of irony in his performances – though this did little to improve the otherwise dreary *Notting Hill* (1999; see p.63), it did add edge to the daft mafia comedy *Mickey Blue Eyes* (1999). He was a revelation in *Bridget Jones's Diary* (2001; see Canon), and, insisting that the caddish Daniel Cleaver was more like the real Hugh Grant than any other role he had played, carried elements of the character into his superb performance as the commitment-phobic Will in another massive Brit flick, *About A Boy* (2002).

It was something of a disappointment, then, to witness him shuffling around in the shadow of the high-energy **Sandra Bullock** in *Two Weeks Notice* (2002), and coasting through Richard Curtis's *Love Actually* (2003) and the *Bridget* sequel *Bridget Jones: The Edge Of Reason* (2004) – complete with the obligatory comedy fight with Colin Firth. Grant, who has never been very passionate about acting, has stated repeatedly that he would like to direct; it remains to be seen whether his charm and his determination will give him that opportunity.

Four Weddings And A Funeral
dir Mike Newell, 1993, UK, 117m

Scripted by wunderkind Richard Curtis, *Four Weddings* kick-started a new commercial British film industry, one based on contemporary rom-coms rather than prestige costume dramas. Spawning a generation of cookie-cutter copies, this is the original and the best, and Grant plays the eternal bachelor with wit and style.

About A Boy
dir Paul and Chris Weitz, 2002, Ger/US/Fr/UK, 101m

A new look for Grant as the crop-haired Will, a feckless trust fund boy who never grew up. This may be the performance of his career, nuanced, with great support from Toni Collette as well as Nicholas Hoult as the geeky boy who teaches him how to love. Based on Nick Hornby's novel, it's genuinely touching stuff.

Love Actually
dir Richard Curtis, 2003, UK/US/Fr, 135m

Another smash hit Working Title/Richard Curtis/Hugh Grant collaboration. The strand in which Grant plays the PM-with-a-heart, wooing winsome tea girl Martine McCutcheon, is one of the strongest in this multi-narrative Brit-flick.

Edith Head
Costume designer, 1897–1981

"I never look back, dahhling – it distracts from the Now." – Edna Mode, *The Incredibles*, 2004

Edith Head is probably the most famous costumier in the world. A little over 5´ tall, with a chic helmet of black hair, she was invariably photographed wearing plain suits, staring sternly out from behind round sunglasses (these were, in fact, blue lenses that revealed how colours and textures would appear on black-and-white film) – a distinctive image that has become iconic, even so far as being parodied in cartoon form by Edna Mode, the pint-sized powerhouse of Pixar's *The Incredibles* (2004). In a career that spanned nearly sixty years and an extraordinary one thousand films, Head was nominated for 34 Oscars and won eight – a record for any costume designer, and any woman, in Hollywood. One of the reasons for her notoriety, and her influence, was her sheer hard graft: as well as designing for the movies, she edited a fashion magazine, penned numerous newspaper columns, popped up on TV and radio, wrote a couple of books and designed her own range of evening dresses for Vogue patterns.

After earning a Masters in languages at Stanford, Head taught French and Spanish in Hollywood before applying for a job as sketch artist at Paramount Studios in 1923. Lacking confidence in her ability to draw the human body, she borrowed sketches from fellow students at an art class she was taking and presented them as her own. The ruse worked, and though she initially took the job to supplement her teaching income, she ended up staying 44 years. Working under Paramount's chief designers Howard Greer and then **Travis Banton**, Head learned fast, starting out designing for dogs and children before moving, via a stint on B-movies, up to stars like "It girl" **Clara Bow** and the formidable **Mae West**. Known for her diplomacy, able to handle the most highly-strung stars and demanding directors – even taking their advice on designs – she understood above all that a costume should highlight a character rather than compete with it. She was also a tireless collaborator, working with sound technicians, cinematographers and scriptwriters in her attempt to tie in a movie's costumes with its overall vision. Head took over as Paramount's chief designer after Banton left in 1938 – becoming the first woman in Hollywood to take on such a post – and for the next thirty years worked with all the greats, from **Carole Lombard** to **Barbara Stanwyck**.

Though she claimed to prefer designing for men, it is for her work with female stars that Head is best remembered, whether emphasizing Elizabeth Taylor's animal sensuality in *A Place In The Sun* (1951) or spotlighting Grace Kelly's glacial sexiness in Hitchcock's *To Catch A Thief* (1955). After dressing **Audrey Hepburn** (see p.000) in *Roman Holiday* (1953), the film that made the gamine actress both a star and a fashion icon, Head had to concede most of the clothes in Hepburn's next film, *Sabrina* (1954) – a classic Audrey makeover movie, in which tomboy

What to wear: Edith Head dresses Shirley Maclaine for *Sweet Charity*

urchin transforms into sophisticated swan – to couture designer **Hubert de Givenchy**, whom she scandalously failed to mention when accepting the film's Best Costume Oscar.

When Head left Paramount for Universal in 1967, the golden era of Hollywood was over; realism, rather than glamour, was the new trend. The ever adaptable designer was in her element, however, creating particularly memorable costumes for **Shirley MacLaine**'s tart with a heart in *Sweet Charity* (1968), and having fun with hats in *Butch Cassidy And The Sundance Kid* (1969) and *The Sting* (1973). She continued designing right up to her death, working on her final movie, the *film noir* spoof *Dead Men Don't Wear Plaid* (1982) – for which she

recreated costumes she and her contemporaries had designed in the 1930s and 40s – at the grand age of 81.

All About Eve
dir Joseph L. Mankiewicz, 1950, US, 138m, b/w

Edith Head won her third Oscar for dressing Bette Davis and Anne Baxter in this sharp-as-a-whip tale of Broadway bitching and betrayal. Ironically, Davis's famous off-the-shoulder cocktail dress – in which she utters the immortal line "Fasten your seatbelts, it's going to be a bumpy night" – was the result of a mistake: discovering at the last minute that the neckline and bodice were too big for her, the actress simply tugged them down, and Head made a few hurried stitches to create the striking finished result.

The two Irenes

While Edith Head was ruling the roost at Paramount, fashion designer and freelance film costumier **Irene** (full name Irene Lentz, 1901–62) was also making waves on the Hollywood scene, designing fabulous frocks for movie stars such as Carole Lombard, Ginger Rogers and Marlene Dietrich. Like costume maestro Adrian, whom she replaced as MGM's head designer in 1942, Irene's work embodied the grown-up glamour for which the studio was renowned, and she designed only for its top stars – Rosalind Russell, Claudette Colbert, Barbara Stanwyck and Joan Crawford among them. Specializing in contemporary wear, she was known for her frothy "soufflé" dresses, modelled to perfection by Rita Hayworth *You Were Never Lovelier* (1942), and caused a stir with her white-on-white wardrobe for femme fatale Lana Turner in *The Postman Always Rings Twice* (1946). In 1949 Irene left MGM to open her own fashion house, returning as a freelancer to work with Doris Day on *Midnight Lace* (1960) and *Lover Come Back* (1961), before, in 1962, slashing her wrists and jumping to her death from a fourteenth-floor motel room.

Irene is not to be confused with **Irene Sharaff** (1910–93), who also worked at MGM for a few years during the 1940s. Starting out as a theatre designer, this Irene put her witty stamp on many of the studio's famously opulent musicals – notably the jaunty stripes, ruffles and flounces sported by Judy Garland & Co. in the period-piece *Meet Me In St Louis* (1944) – and after going freelance in 1945 helped create some of the defining musicals of a generation. Sharaff was behind the astonishing "French painters" ballet sequence in *An American In Paris* (1951), and also perfected the sharp fashions of a cruel Hollywood for an older, more bruised Judy Garland in *A Star Is Born* (1954). She created colourful, cartoonish hoods and molls in *Guys And Dolls* (1955), overblown exotica for *The King And I* (1956) and a hip street style for *West Side Story* (1961), returning to *Meet Me*-type nostalgia in Barbra Streisand's *Funny Girl* (1968) and *Hello, Dolly!* (1969). She also designed for Elizabeth Taylor, notably in the monumental epic *Cleopatra* (1963), *Who's Afraid Of Virginia Woolf?* (1966) and *The Taming Of The Shrew* (1967), and created Faye Dunaway's retro outfits for her role as a crazy Joan Crawford in *Mommie Dearest* (1981).

Roman Holiday
dir William Wyler, 1953, US, 119m, b/w

That Audrey Hepburn looks quite so ravishing in her breakthrough picture is in no small part due to Head's clever costumes. Uncomfortable and a little dwarfed at first in her princess's brocade ball gown, she transforms into a free spirit during her escapade in Rome, where her simple wide skirt, casual white shirt and espadrilles create a classic 1950s look that has remained timeless.

To Catch A Thief
dir Alfred Hitchcock, 1955, US, 107m

Head once said that Hitchcock was her favourite director, and that this sophisticated caper, starring Cary Grant and Grace Kelly, was her favourite assignment. The eighteenth-century gold lamé ball gown worn by Kelly during the suspenseful costume party scene renders the icy star extraordinarily sexy – apparently, upon seeing her in it, the ever-subtle Hitchcock leered, "There's hills in them thar gold!"

Sweet Charity
dir Bob Fosse, 1968, US, 149m

A Hollywood remake of the Broadway show based on Federico Fellini's Italian art movie *Nights Of Cabiria,* this is a lush production, very much of its time. Head's kooky costumes sum up the crazy 1960s spirit of the piece, best demonstrated in the virtuoso numbers from "Hey, Big Spender" to "If My Friends Could See Me Now".

Audrey Hepburn
Actress, 1929–93

An iconoclast in ballet pumps, Audrey Hepburn is the epitome of gamine chic. In an age when sex appeal was defined by pneumatic curves and bee-stung lips, her explosion onto the scene in *Roman Holiday* (1953) was nothing short of revolutionary. With her big dark brows, wide grin and choppy short hair, this faun of a girl was not a conventional beauty, but she changed notions of feminine beauty forever. And the elegant Hepburn "look" – Capri pants, little black dresses, boat necks and big shades – is still copied and sought after, both in couture and on the high street. As an actress she was a breath of fresh air, bringing at first a mischievous energy, and later a dignified wisdom, to her performances. And as a person she was, and still is, almost universally adored. To call something or someone "very Audrey Hepburn" is the highest form of flattery.

Hepburn's true-life story adds to her enduring appeal. The vulnerability that lurks behind the pixie charm hints at the trauma of her early years, especially: an evocative tale of riches-to-rags-and-back-again. Born in Belgium to a British banker and a Dutch baroness, Hepburn had to adjust quickly during the war from privilege and private schools to eking out a meagre existence in Occupied Holland. It's claimed that malnutrition during these years – the often-invoked image of the doe-eyed teen having to survive on tulip bulbs is striking – was responsible for her famously skinny frame. That the duckling-turned-swan spent her later years as a determinedly non-starry humanitarian, campaigning as a UNICEF ambassador against child hunger, neatly brought her story full circle.

Having trained as a ballerina, Hepburn started her career as a model in London, did some well-received stage work and went on to win small parts in British movies. In 1953 she stormed Hollywood with the delightful *Roman Holiday*, winning an Oscar for her guileless performance as the princess who longs to be ordinary. She was Oscar-nominated again for her second Cinderella-style fairy tale, *Sabrina* (1954), which set in place the elegant "Audrey" image, as fashioned by couturier **Hubert de Givenchy**, before

TIFFANY

Givenchy-fabulous: the divine Audrey with George Peppard in *Breakfast At Tiffany's* (1961)

co-starring with Mel Ferrer, who was to become her husband, as Natasha in *War And Peace* (1956). After dancing with Fred Astaire in the exquisite satire on the fashion business, *Funny Face* (1957), and sparring with an ageing Gary Cooper in

Love In The Afternoon (1957), she was Oscar-nominated again for the affecting *The Nun's Story* (1959), her most challenging role to date, which saw her grow from gamine into woman as the conflicted Sister Luke. It ended up being her most profitable film ever.

Hepburn claimed that she was miscast as kooky Holly Golightly in *Breakfast At Tiffany's* (1961; see Canon), but managed to make **Truman Capote**'s hard-nosed hooker into a woman of charm and class, and received another Oscar nomination. She and the suave **Cary Grant** carried off the feather-light caper *Charade* (1963) with aplomb, and she even got away with an excruciating Cockney accent as Eliza Doolittle in *My Fair Lady* (1964), another Cinderella tale writ large. Things got edgier with *Two For The Road* (1967), about the breakdown of a marriage, and riskier with *Wait Until Dark* (1967), a bleak thriller produced by Ferrer, in which she portrays, with startling power, a blind woman in peril.

The 1970s marked a new stage in Hepburn's life. Devoted both to her children and to humanitarian causes, she was more often photographed cradling babies than wearing couture gowns, and seemed to have left her past behind. However, in 1976 she made a well-judged comeback as a middle-aged Maid Marian opposite **Sean Connery**'s greying Robin Hood in the wistful *Robin And Marian* (1976), one of her finest films. She worked intermittently over the next few years, and gave her last movie performance in 1989 as an angel in Steven Spielberg's weepie *Always*, a fittingly serene swan song.

Roman Holiday
dir William Wyler, 1953, US, 119m, b/w

The young star gives a wonderfully natural, vivacious performance as princess-cum-free spirit in this lump-in-the-throat romance. The scene in which Gregory Peck's

Hubert and Audrey: a love story

"I'm as dependent on Givenchy as some Americans are on their psychiatrists."

– Audrey Hepburn on Hubert de Givenchy

"She was capable of enhancing all my creations. And often ideas would come to me when I had her on my mind."

– Hubert de Givenchy on Audrey Hepburn

Audrey Hepburn, a trained dancer, had a tall, slender frame ideal for couture. She always adored clothes, and from a young age affected her own quirky style. Although she had worked successfully with Edith Head (see p.170) on *Roman Holiday*, and was set to work with her again on her next film, *Sabrina*, fashion-mad Hepburn asked director Billy Wilder if she could have a fitting with the new young prince of couture, **Hubert de Givenchy**. The debonair Parisian, expecting to meet Katharine Hepburn, was amazed to be confronted by a slip of a girl wearing narrow trousers, T-shirt and pumps, sporting a straw gondolier's hat. Instantly the two clicked, and Givenchy allowed her to try on a few samples from an old collection. Suddenly the waif was transformed into a glamorous beauty; and the very clothes she pulled on during that first meeting were those she eventually wore in *Sabrina*.

While Head designed the clothes Sabrina wears before her transformation in Paris, post-Paris Sabrina is pure Givenchy – a fitted suit with narrow waist that she wears at the railway station upon her return; the ravishing white embroidered sheath ball gown with the shooshy organdie train; the black cocktail dress with wide skirt, deep-cut armholes and witty bows at the shoulders. Just as in *Roman Holiday*, the clothes in *Sabrina* tell the story, and from here on, Hepburn was closely identified with the designer's simple, elegant style, both on-screen and off. With her own self-assured take on fashion, she was his Muse, modelling his designs everywhere from press shows to her wedding day. She claimed that his clothes allowed her not only to fully inhabit her roles, but also to feel most herself. Givenchy dressed Hepburn in *Funny Face* (1957), *Love In The Afternoon* (1957), *Breakfast At Tiffany's* (1961), *Charade* (1963), *Paris When It Sizzles* (1964), *How To Steal A Million* (1966) and *Love Among Thieves* (1987). They were beloved, lifelong friends.

eyes brim with tears is emblematic of the Audrey appeal – here is a woman so exquisite, so classy, she can make grown men cry with love.

Sabrina
dir Billy Wilder, 1954, US, 114m, b/w

"Once upon a time," begins this unabashed latter-day fairy tale. Hepburn is radiant as a chauffeur's ragamuffin daughter who, following a Cinderella-like transformation in Paris, gets to choose between the two wealthy brothers for which her father works: roguish William Holden (with whom the actress had an affair while filming) and stuffy Humphrey Bogart (in an odd piece of casting).

My Fair Lady
dir George Cukor, 1964, US, 175m

A sumptuous musical version of George Bernard Shaw's *Pygmalion,* with wildly opulent Cecil Beaton costumes, great songs and a quite preposterous, but much beloved, performance from Hepburn as Eliza Doolittle, the Cockernee flower girl who gets made over into a lady. Rex Harrison is spot on as her tyrannical Svengali.

Two For The Road
dir Stanley Donen, 1966, UK, 111m

This half-poignant, half-cynical comedy-drama charts a marriage breakdown through flashbacks, flash forwards and flash fashions. Hepburn looks groovy in Mary Quant and Paco Rabanne, and there's considerable chemistry with the typically brusque Albert Finney. Very 1960s, with a catchy soundtrack from Henry Mancini.

🎬 Robin And Marian
dir Richard Lester, 1976, US, 107m

A mellow Audrey Hepburn shines as Maid Marian in her later years, whose encounter with her old love, Robin Hood (Sean Connery), home from the Crusades, makes for an elegiac, wonderfully wrought two-hander.

Katharine Hepburn

Actress, 1907–2003

With her haughty cheekbones and androgynous frame, her arch vocal style and no-nonsense New England demeanour, Katharine Hepburn was never going to be your typical movie star. In her first film, *A Bill Of Divorcement* (1932), the great "women's director" **George Cukor** (see p.155) – who was to become one of her favourite collaborators – wove in a number of shots of the young actress's face simply to inveigle her quirky beauty into the audience's consciousness. The gambit succeeded, and Hepburn, until then a theatre actress, was set for movie fame. It wasn't always an easy ride, however; a headstrong woman who refused to play by the rules, she actually grew more popular with age.

Raised in a progressive Connecticut family, Hepburn had a rebellious streak and a fierce intelligence that was often taken for arrogance in Hollywood. Unafraid to make her feelings about her scripts and her directors known, she also chose her roles with care. Sometimes she got it wrong – hillbilly faith healer Trigger Hicks in the bizarre melodrama *Spitfire* (1934) comes to mind – but mostly her choices were spot on. Spanning genres from frothy comedy to high drama, she cornered the market in resilient women and made every role her own, from the spirited aviatrix in Dorothy Arzner's *Christopher Strong* (1933) right up to Henry Fonda's pragmatic septuagenarian wife in *On Golden Pond* (1981).

Though it means little to talk of a "heyday" when referring to an actor whose career spanned five decades, twelve Oscar nominations and a (so far) record-breaking four Oscars (none of which she turned up to accept), Hepburn's 1930s screwball heroines are among her most memorable roles. These women were a modern breed: active and irreverent, and more than a match for their leading men. Unsurprisingly, perhaps, contemporary audiences didn't know what to make of them, and the actress's career faltered during this period, only to have been reassessed and celebrated since. Hepburn's spiritedness, comic timing and wiry physicality made her an ideal screwball heroine, as did her generosity as an actress. At her best when pitted against other gifted actors, she shone especially bright with the debonair **Cary Grant** (see p.166), with whom she was first teamed in the curious *Sylvia Scarlett* (1935). Sharing a genuine affection based on a mutual sense of mischief and wry intelligence, the two went on to raise the bar for comedy partnerships in *Holiday* and the classic screwball *Bringing Up Baby* (both 1938). Neither film was successful at the time, however, and Hepburn was soon tarred with the damning label "box office poison". Her career was saved when, after a stint on Broadway playing headstrong heiress Tracy Lord in *The Philadelphia Story*, she bought the play's movie rights. The film of the same name (1940) – directed by Cukor and co-starring Grant – earned her her third Best Actress Oscar nomination.

By far Hepburn's most important sparring partner was **Spencer Tracy**, with whom she had a discreet affair – he remained married – for more than twenty years until his death in 1967. Tracy's gruff manliness was the perfect foil for Hepburn's mercurial femininity, playing to great effect in sprightly battle-of-the-sexes comedies like *Woman Of The Year* (1942), *Adam's Rib* (1949; see Canon) and *Pat And Mike* (1952).

The actress continued working into her 70s, cornering the market in eccentric spinsters. *The African Queen* (1951) pits her buttoned-up missionary against Humphrey Bogart's boozy river trader, while as lonely Jane Hudson in the bitter-sweet romance *Summertime* (1955) she reprises her screwball days by tumbling into a Venice canal – a comedy moment both knowing and knockabout that perfectly captures the spirit of this unique actress.

Morning Glory
dir Lowell Sherman, 1933, US, 74m, b/w

Mirroring Hepburn's own story, this sprightly tale of a plucky small-town girl who longs to make it on Broadway won the promising young movie star her first Best Actress Oscar.

Bringing Up Baby
dir Howard Hawks, 1938, US, 102m, b/w

The screwball to beat them all. Hepburn is phenomenal as the fast-talking heiress who sets her sights on daffy paleontologist David Huxley (Cary Grant). Chaos ensues,

Kate and Spence – America's favourite couple

Kate and Spence

When **Katharine Hepburn** and **Spencer Tracy** first met in 1941, Hepburn exclaimed to the esteemed actor, "Mr Tracy, you're not as tall as I expected!" His friend, director Joseph L. Mankiewicz, responded, "Don't worry Kate – he'll cut you down to size." That short exchange not only set off one of Hollywood's greatest love stories, but also defined the unique chemistry between Kate and Spence, the la-di-da thoroughbred and the salt-of-the-earth man's man who fell in love while filming their first movie, *Woman Of The Year* (1942), and stayed together for 25 years. Their relationship was an open secret – Tracy, a Catholic, felt unable to divorce his wife – accepted both by their peers and the public. Renowned rogue Tracy drank heavily and sulked when Kate left him for too long, and despite his devotion to her, he indulged in affairs. Ever pragmatic, Hepburn looked after him and contained the worst of his self-destructive excesses, but refused to sacrifice her career to his neediness.

A private couple, Hepburn and Tracy lived out a public version of their romance in their movies. In each of the nine films they made together they play sparring, independent-minded characters who adore one another, despite their dramatic differences; this, it seemed, was a true partnership of equals. Growing old together on screen, they came to embody an ideal American couple, and their comedies, especially *Adam's Rib* (1949; see Canon) and *Pat And Mike* (1952), made with director George Cukor, proved to be among their very best work.

In 1967, soon after filming *Guess Who's Coming To Dinner*, in which the two are as comfortable together as a pair of old slippers, Hepburn discovered Tracy slumped on the floor in the cottage they shared. He had died suddenly of a heart attack. Ever discreet, she stayed away from the funeral so as not to embarrass his family. The film went on to be the most commercially successful movie either of them made, together or apart.

involving a missing dinosaur bone, a cheeky dog, a leopard named Baby and a short spell in jail.

The Philadelphia Story
dir George Cukor, 1940, US, 112m, b/w

A sparkling romantic comedy, with the stars and director at the top of their game. Hepburn plays spoiled heiress Tracy Lord, about to marry dull George (John Howard) in the society wedding of the year. Complications ensue when her roguish ex-husband (Cary Grant) turns up along with a gossip reporter (James Stewart).

Woman Of The Year
dir George Stevens, 1942, US, 112m, b/w

Kate and Spence's first movie is one of their finest, with the sparky twosome squabbling exquisitely both as newshounds and newlyweds.

The African Queen
dir John Huston, 1951, UK/US, 103m

Boys' own adventure plays second fiddle to the charming chalk-and-cheese romance between a missionary (Hepburn) and a hard-drinking river-boat captain (Humphrey Bogart), battling Nazis from his boat in the Congo. Bogart, who won an Oscar, was ably matched by Hepburn, who, as ever, was at her best when sharing the screen with an actor of equal calibre.

Summertime (aka Summer Madness)
dir David Lean, 1955, US, 99m

Hepburn is wonderful as the American spinster holidaying solo in Venice, the most romantic city in the world, and embodies the emotional yearning of a lonely, hopeful woman with humanism and grace. Venice has never looked lovelier, only made more atmospheric by the haunting score; Latin lover charm comes in the shape of Rossano Brazzi.

Rock Hudson

Actor, 1925–85

With his matinee idol looks – athletic 6′ 4′′ frame, soulful eyes, sensuous mouth and dark, sleek hair – the young Rock Hudson was the epitome of the glossy Tinseltown hunks that were being churned out by the Hollywood studios in the 1950s. Though belittled, especially in his early career, as being nothing more than a beefcake, he actually emerged to stand head and shoulders above other chiselfaced wannabes, with a suave charisma and dry humour that informed many great acting performances. By the late Fifties Hudson had become Hollywood's hottest property, an oldstyle movie star steeped in old-style glamour. He has also, since then, come to signify a great deal more, revealing Hollywood's double standards – notoriously gay, he was forced to cover up his sexuality with a sham marriage – and eventually, upon his death, changing the way the world thought about AIDS.

Roy Scherer, a shy blue-collar boy from Winnetka, Illinois, dreamed of being an actor even while scraping together a living as a cinema usher, mechanic, door-to-door salesman and truck driver. After moving to California in 1946, taking acting lessons, mixing with the right people, working out and capping his teeth, he eventually changed his name to Rock Hudson in 1948. Though demonstrating no great acting talent at first, he looked undeniably good on screen, starting out in B-movies while fan magazines abounded in stories about the handsome young star's "bachelor lifestyle". In 1954 **Douglas Sirk** cast him as a bewigged Indian in *Taza, Son Of Cochise*, a laughably camp 3D Western that was followed, swiftly and fortuitously, by a role in one

of the director's finest melodramas, *Magnificent Obsession* (1954). *Obsession* was a smash, and Hudson – playing a wealthy playboy whose irresponsible behaviour has tragic consequences – received great reviews. Over the next years, his powerful work in Sirk's melodramas – *All That Heaven Allows* (1955), *Written On The Wind* (1956) and *The Tarnished Angels* (1957) – proved him to be far more than a slab of meat, and he finally achieved the recognition he craved when his strong performance as the patriarch in *Giant* (1956) earned him an Oscar nomination. This was also the movie where he met **Elizabeth Taylor**, who was to become a lifelong ally.

Rock was able to show his funny side, making sly digs at his on- and off-screen images, in the delightful bedroom comedy *Pillow Talk* (1959; see Canon); he proved a brilliant comic foil for his co-star, **Doris Day** (see p.159), another actress with whom he became firm friends. The two were paired again in *Lover Come Back* (1961) and *Send Me No Flowers* (1964), and though Hudson's comic output over the next decade was prodigious, he is probably most associated with these three sparkling movies he made with Day.

The 1970s didn't see many great Hudson films, though he did make a successful move into TV with the witty detective show *McMillan And Wife* (1971–77). A heavy smoker, he had quintuple heart bypass surgery in 1982, and although he put in a debonair turn as horse-breeder Daniel Reece on the glossy Eighties US soap *Dynasty*, it was clear that his health was deteriorating. Rumours that he was suffering from AIDS, a then little-understood virus, were only compounded by his shockingly frail appearance on a Doris Day TV special in 1985. Shortly afterwards he announced that the rumours were true, and months later Rock Hudson, the last of the great movie idols, was dead.

Rock Hudson and AIDS

Though Rock Hudson's homosexuality was an open secret in Hollywood, he hid the fact that he had AIDS from all but a select few. In his final years, many of his friends believed him to be suffering from anorexia. The world's press, however, had been stoking up rumours for months, printing photos of the big, strong star looking frighteningly fragile alongside snide, salacious stories about his "bizarre lifestyle". Following a definitive statement by his press agent, confirming that Rock Hudson did indeed have AIDS, uproar ensued. Coming as it did at the height of Reaganism, anti-gay pundits in the US had a field day – some journalists accused him of intentionally trying to give *Dynasty* star Linda Evans the virus by kissing her on the show – but the actor also received huge support from gay groups, despite having spent a lifetime in the closet. By now bedridden, he received thirty thousand cards and letters from fans after the news broke. Stars including Elizabeth Taylor, Doris Day and writer Armistead Maupin offered voluble support for their dear friend. Eventually Hudson himself made a formal statement, hoping that his decision to go public might encourage scientists to work harder to find a cure, and, most radically, daring to suggest that it may not have been sexual activity that gave him the virus.

The death of Hudson on October 2, 1985 would change public perceptions about AIDS forever. The virus could no longer be relegated as the scourge of junkies and prostitutes. If it could afflict Rock Hudson, the very definition of robust American virility, it could afflict anyone. While this was devastating, instigating an era of terror, it also marked the beginning of a better understanding of the virus.

In an unpleasant footnote, Rock's long-time lover Marc Christian announced in November 1985 his intention to sue the Hudson estate, claiming that the star had duped him into having unsafe sex without revealing he had AIDS. The ensuing trial, which raked over the finer details of Hudson's private life, definitively destroyed his carefully nurtured image, and eventually, after an appeal, won Christian $5.5 million.

All That Heaven Allows
dir Douglas Sirk, 1955, US, 89m

Hudson plays the devilishly handsome young gardener that lonely widow Jane Wyman falls for in Sirk's painful tale of forbidden love. An indictment of small-town America and the 1950s American dream, it also dares to touch on issues of ageing and motherhood, with some deliciously suggestive moments provided by the very game Rock ("Would you like to come to my house and see my silver-tipped spruce?").

Giant
dir George Stevens, 1956, US, 197m

Rock was Oscar-nominated for his performance as stubborn cattle baron Bick Benedict in this sweeping Texas-based family saga, which had a big influence on the US TV soap *Dallas*. Some camp fun – he and Elizabeth Taylor age preposterously as the story progresses – and a typically charismatic turn from James Dean in his final film.

Lover Come Back
dir Delbert Mann, 1961, US, 107m

A very funny rerun of the *Pillow Talk* formula, with Rock and Doris as competing New York ad execs. Hudson is a rakish playboy, Day a hard-working career girl. Cue droll sparring, mistaken identities and lots of innuendo at the expense of Rock's masculinity. Tony Randall provides typically neurotic support.

Man's Favorite Sport?
dir Howard Hawks, 1963, US, 120m

Though the premise sounds doubtful – a romantic comedy revolving around a fishing contest? – this is a brilliantly paced gem from one of Hollywood's great screwball directors. As usual in these frothy comedies, Hudson plays a puffed-up chauvinist, sparring this time with Paula Prentiss. And, as ever, there's plenty of good-natured mockery of Rock's beefcake image.

Diane Keaton

Actress and director, 1946–

While her ditzy image can irritate or appeal – **Woody Allen**, with whom she made nine films, once said, "In real life, Keaton believes in God. But she also believes that the radio works because there are tiny people inside it" – it would be a mistake to underestimate Diane Keaton. Closely associated with the films she and Allen made in the 1970s, she was a great partner for the comic actor/director at the height of his powers – matching him neurosis for neurosis – and her skilfully mannered performances in his best work played a major part in his success. Since then, her career has sustained rather better than his, and, unusually for a woman in Hollywood, she's continued to thrive after hitting the age of 50.

Though she has come to typify a certain type of nervy New Yorker, Keaton was actually born, Diane Hall, in LA. She started on the stage, moving via TV commercials into movies. After debuting in the unjustly forgotten comedy *Lovers And Other Strangers* (1970), she became part of the hip New Hollywood, doing her best with an under-written role as Al Pacino's lonely WASP wife in **Francis Ford Coppola**'s *The Godfather* (1972) and *The Godfather II* (1974). She met Allen, who was to become her on-off lover, in 1969, while performing in his Broadway comedy *Play It Again, Sam*. They starred together in his 1972 movie version of the show, and again in his sci-fi parody *Sleeper* (1973) and Dostoevsky spoof *Love And Death* (1975). Then came *Annie Hall* (1977), a bittersweet relationship comedy set among a bunch of neurotic New Yorkers. Catapulting Allen into the mainstream, the film won four Oscars, including Best Actress for Keaton, whose performance as the individualistic

Annie was the defining point of her career. It's common knowledge that the character was based upon Keaton's own, but this is not to detract from her skill as an actress, and, in her insistence on wearing her own clothes – mannish suit, tie and fedora – as a style leader.

Now at the top of her game, Keaton carried the dark erotic drama *Looking For Mr Goodbar* (1977) practically single-handed, but after Allen's dreary drama *Interiors* (1978), and his monochrome valentine to New York, *Manhattan* (1979), the early 1980s proved patchy. She was Oscar-nominated for her vigorous turn as the Socialist writer Louise Bryant in the ambitious *Reds* (1981), directed by and co-starring her then-lover Warren Beatty, but her restrained performance in *Mrs Soffel* (1984), a period drama directed by **Gillian Armstrong**, was underrated. The neurotic tics descended into hysteria in the appalling *Crimes Of The Heart* (1986), about three Southern sisters, while she sailed through the delightful *Baby Boom* (1987) – which, with its yuppie preoccupations, became one of the decade's seminal movies. Having enjoyed a healthy career as a photographer, she took up directing, though her tricksy documentary *Heaven* (1987), about the afterlife, was too arch for some, and she has yet to achieve good reviews for her feature films.

As an actress, Keaton's career picked up again in the mid-1990s with the outrageous comedy *The First Wives Club* (1996), based on Olivia Goldsmith's zeitgeisty novel, and a sensitive, Oscar-nominated turn in the terminal illness weepie *Marvin's Room* (1996). The 2000s have been kind to Keaton, too, with an Oscar nomination for her brilliant take on middle-aged romance in *Something's Gotta Give* (2003), and well-disposed reviews for *The Family Stone* (2005), a slick chick flick with Sarah Jessica Parker.

Annie Hall
dir Woody Allen, 1977, US, 93m

Coining the catchphrase "la-di-da", sporting waistcoat and tie, Keaton is in her element as the eccentric Annie, object of the endlessly neurotic Woody's desire. It's an iconic performance in an iconic movie and remains fresh some thirty years later.

Baby Boom
dir Charles Shyer, 1987, US, 111m

Keaton puts her nervy mannerisms and comic skills to brilliant use as J.C., the hard-nosed yuppie career woman who, suddenly inheriting a baby, comes to want more out of life. Smart, slightly screwball and just the right side of slushy (who could resist Sam Shepard as a strong, silent country doctor?), with a sweetly utopian ending.

Something's Gotta Give
dir Nancy Meyers, 2003, US, 128m

A delicious fantasy that proves romance has no age limits. Jack Nicholson does his thing as the ageing lothario who, despite himself, falls for the uptight Erica (Keaton, on top form), mother of his latest conquest (Amanda Peet). However, he has to compete with handsome young doctor Julian Mercer (Keanu Reeves) for her attentions.

Carole Lombard

Actress, 1908–42

Carole Lombard practically defined the screwball genre. Smart, beautiful, a fast-talking fashion plate, she also had an agile tomboy physicality; more intelligent than kooky, she was as adept at wry verbal sparring as she was at slapstick, as keen on telling dirty stories as she was on playing practical jokes.

Though she was born a country girl in Indiana, Lombard (née Jane Alice Peters) was living in California by 1916, where she was spotted, playing baseball in the street, by director Allan Dwan and was selected for a minor role in *A Perfect Crime* (1921). Following an unaccomplished spell in amateur theatre, in the mid-1920s she signed a contract with Fox, changing her name and featuring in the studio's quickie comedies and Westerns. Fox cancelled her contract, however, after a car crash in 1926 left her with facial scarring; after plastic surgery, she returned to the movies by working with the legendary slapstick director **Mack Sennett**, gaining a reputation, while still a teenager, as one of his top comedy stars. Though her standing as a comedienne allowed her to sign a contract with Paramount Studios, Lombard had yet to achieve star status. Her speaking voice, spirited and clear, proved a blessing. She was ideal for talkies, and even more so for the emerging genre of screwball, which combined the exuberant slapstick of the silents with a wordier, urbane humour. In 1931 she starred with the debonair **William Powell** in *Man Of The World*, and despite a sixteen-year age gap, the two soon married, divorcing amicably in 1933. She was matched in the light comedy *No Man Of Her Own* (1932) with the dashing **Clark Gable**; his dark masculinity proved an appealing contrast with her mercurial mischievousness, and the two got along famously.

Lombard soon became one of the studio's biggest draws, shining in zany screwballs like *Twentieth Century* (1934) and, with ex-husband Powell, the Depression-era satire *My Man Godfrey* (1936) – for which she earned her only Oscar nomination as a madcap heiress who takes a homeless tramp under her wing – and by 1936 was earning $35,000 a week. In 1939 moviegoers were thrilled to discover she had eloped with Gable, who was busy filming *Gone With The Wind*. Though they had made only one film together, their marriage was widely celebrated as a lively meeting of kindred spirits.

She was brilliantly matched with the handsome Robert Montgomery in **Alfred Hitchcock**'s quirky *Mr & Mrs Smith* (1941) – in which, ever-stylish, she also wore some particularly stunning gowns – while in 1942 came the role for which she is perhaps best remembered: the neurotic Polish actress Maria Tura in **Ernst Lubitsch**'s outrageous anti-Nazi satire *To Be Or Not To Be*. America was just entering World War II, and, soon after filming, the patriotic Lombard went home to Indiana to perform at a war bond rally. When it came to returning to LA, the story goes that her mother, who had joined her in Indiana, had a bad feeling about flying. Lombard, however, was keen to return home quickly. They tossed a coin, Carole won, and they boarded the aircraft. On January 16, 1942, the plane went down, just outside Las Vegas; all the passengers were killed.

Twentieth Century
dir Howard Hawks, 1934, US, 91m, b/w

A crazy-paced screwball, with Lombard having fun as the barmy diva Lily Garland. She's beautifully paired with the hammy thesp John Barrymore, camping it up here for all it's worth as her megalomaniac director.

Nothing Sacred
dir William Wellman, 1937, US, 75m

Lombard is effervescent as the small-town girl who, diagnosed with radium poisoning, becomes a local star, and after discovering that she is in fact well, decides to keep up the subterfuge. Scripted by Ben Hecht, this is screwball at its knockabout noisiest, and a clever satire on the press to boot.

Mr & Mrs Smith
dir Alfred Hitchcock, 1941, US, 95m, b/w

The screwball queen brings her effortless grace to this increasingly frantic, very witty comedy about a husband (Robert Montgomery) and wife (Lombard) who, in the process of theatrically splitting up, discover they were

Ma and Pa: a screwball romance

Though they had worked together on *No Man Of Her Own* in 1932, **Carole Lombard** and **Clark Gable** were first drawn to each other at a Hollywood party held in January 1936. They quarrelled, she sent them a batch of live white doves as an apology, and when they encountered each other again a few weeks later they got on rather better. Aware of his penchant for sleek cars, Carole delivered Clark a clapped-out old banger painted white and decorated with red hearts for Valentine's Day, and the pair – even though he was married – soon became an item. In 1939, when the sexy "King of Hollywood" (as voted in a 1938 newspaper poll) finally eloped with the dirty-mouthed screwball goddess, Hollywood was delighted. He had been married twice before, she once, but it was clear that these two fun-loving, charismatic figures had at last met their match. Hunkering down in a country farmhouse, calling themselves "Ma" and "Pa" while hunting, fishing and raising chickens, they each continued to make some of the most popular movies of the era, fulfilling everyone's fantasy of the perfect Hollywood couple. Meanwhile, they ribbed each other mercilessly, Lombard once famously declaring, "If his pee-pee was one inch shorter, they'd be calling him the Queen of Hollywood!"

Though Lombard told gossip columnist Louella Parsons that she was keen to start a family – "I'll let Pa be the star and I'll stay home, darn socks and look after the kids" – that was never to be. After the plane crash that took her life, Gable was inconsolable. He began to drink heavily, and remarried twice, both times to women bearing a resemblance to his beloved Carole. He died in 1960, after filming *The Misfits* with Marilyn Monroe, and was buried, with the blessing of his new wife, next to the woman with whom his name will forever be associated.

never married at all. Cue much crockery flinging, risqué humour and intricate plot meandering. Delightful.

To Be Or Not To Be
dir Ernst Lubitsch, 1942, US, 99m, b/w

With its rapid-fire dialogue, witty visual jokes, splendid performances and heartfelt patriotic message, this anti-Nazi satire – about a Polish theatre troupe that gets embroiled in Resistance espionage – remains as audacious today as it did upon release. Lombard does her narcissistic diva shtick as only she can, while Jack Benny hams it up as her husband.

Frances Marion
Screenwriter, 1887–1973

Hollywood's early years offered great opportunities for female writers, among them screenwriter Lenore Coffee, playwrights Zoe Akins and Lillian Hellman, satirist Anita Loos, and the journalist and novelist Adela Rogers St Johns. Head and shoulders above them all, however, in terms of influence, recognition and salary, was Frances Marion. In a career that spanned thirty years, Marion wrote some two hundred scripts, successfully crossing over from the silents to the talkies to become the highest-paid screenwriter of her generation and one of the most famous screenwriters ever. As skilled at adaptations as at original screenplays, penning hard-boiled dramas and melodramas, Marion wrote unsentimental scripts populated with credible, richly textured characters, whose very real dilemmas were expressed simply and with emotional depth. Spending as much time on set, in the editing suite, or in casting sessions as on writing, she had a canny understanding of the medium; she also understood the value of the pause, of leaving things unspoken in order to tell a story. In the hands of great actors – Mary Pickford, Lillian Gish or Greta Garbo, say,

all of whom had a lot to thank Marion's scripts for – her screenplays expressed volumes.

After working as a journalist, model and artist in San Francisco, Marion moved to Hollywood in 1913. Her friend, Adela Rogers St Johns, introduced her to the female film director Lois Weber, who hired Marion as an actress, stunt-woman, writer and editor. She penned her first movie, *The Foundling* (1915), for **Mary Pickford**, and the two became great friends. Marion went on to write most of "Little Mary's" major scripts, including *The Poor Little Rich Girl* (1917) and *Pollyanna* (1920), and helped to create the enduring image of Pickford as "America's Sweetheart". Her scripts were also instrumental in developing the career of **Marion Davies**, the wife of millionaire newspaper magnate William Randolph Hearst; sensing that Davies was not being used to her best advantage in sappy dramas, Marion pushed the actress's comedic talents to the fore in movies like the spoof Western *Zander The Great* (1925).

Following a stint as a war correspondent, Marion returned to Hollywood in 1920, and spent much of the rest of her career under contract to MGM. Among her countless achievements she directed the wartime melodrama *The Love Light* (1921), featuring Pickford; produced a heartbreaking adaptation of Olive Higgins Prouty's novel *Stella Dallas* (1925); adapted Nathaniel Hawthorne's "unadaptable" book *The Scarlet Letter* (1926), starring **Lillian Gish** (another great friend); and penned *The Son Of The Sheik* (1926) for sex god **Rudolph Valentino**. She wrote for Gish again with the seminal melodrama *The Wind* (1928), and for **Greta Garbo** with the star's first talkie, *Anna Christie* (1930), which also resuscitated the career of the character actress Marie Dressler, yet another of Marion's many actor friends.

In 1930 she became the first woman to win the Best Writing Oscar for her gritty prison drama *The Big House,* and in 1931 picked up another Academy Award for the father-and-son boxing melodrama *The Champ.* She also created, along with Zoe Akins and James Hilton, the definitive screen *Camille* (1936; see Canon), adapted from Alexandre Dumas's novel and starring an incandescent Garbo. By 1946, in a studio climate where creative control for scriptwriters was diminishing, Marion left Hollywood to write novels and teach her craft.

The Poor Little Rich Girl
dir Maurice Tourneur, 1917, US, 65m, b/w

This deftly composed family melodrama was one of Marion's most successful collaborations with Mary Pickford. "Little Mary", by now in her mid-20s, was uncannily convincing as a lonely 11-year-old moppet neglected by her wealthy family; audiences loved the film, and the actress continued to play little girls for another decade.

The Scarlet Letter
dir Victor Sjöström, 1926, US, 98m, b/w

Adapted from Nathaniel Hawthorne's multilayered story of repression and witchcraft in Puritan seventeenth-century America, this is one of silent cinema's greatest melodramas. Marion's screenplay foregrounds the story of Hester Prynne (Lillian Gish), the seduced woman who is branded with a red "A" as punishment for her sins.

Anna Christie
dir Clarence Brown, 1930, US, 90m, b/w

MGM head Irving Thalberg trusted Marion implicitly with the onerous task of writing Greta Garbo's first talkie. He wasn't wrong: from her first utterance, the world-weary

Pioneering Frances Marion, the "Dean of Hollywood scriptwriters"

"Gimme a visky!", the Swedish sphinx's status as screen goddess was secure. Marion used her influence to cast the fading comedienne Marie Dressler as Anna's father's drunken companion – a brilliant move.

Julia Roberts
Actress, 1967–

With an offbeat beauty that the camera adores, and a comic ability that is often underrated, Julia Roberts is one of the highest-paid Hollywood actresses in history, regularly earning $20million per movie. Though she's worked in a range of genres, from thrillers to arthouse indies, she's most associated with chick flicks, and especially with romantic comedies; smart enough to play against her angelic looks – the unruly mane, doe eyes, heart-melting grin – she regularly portrays complex, funny women who can be tetchy, selfish, angry or confused. Faced with a press obsessed by her relationship breakdowns, Roberts is sometimes described as "difficult" (it's notable how many of the female Icons in this book have been tarred with that brush). When filming a scene in *Sleeping With The Enemy* (1991) that entailed being repeatedly soaked in water while wearing only her underwear, she is rumoured to have demanded the entire crew strip off with her. And in April 1999, at the British premiere of *Notting Hill*, she had the audacity to reveal unshaved armpits while waving to the crowd. That combination of wilfulness and rebelliousness imbues her performances, convincing us that Julia Roberts, despite her supersonic smile and old-style screen glamour, could be just an ordinary girl – waitress, prostitute, working mother – struggling to make good.

Roberts, born in Georgia, abandoned early dreams to become a vet and in the 1980s took acting classes in New York. After a few minor roles came *Mystic Pizza* (1988), in which Roberts gave an assured performance as the fiery Daisy Arujo, all gum-snapping and miniskirts. The following year she played the diabetic Shelby in *Steel Magnolias* (see Canon), and received an Oscar nomination for Best Supporting Actress – quite a feat, given the calibre of her co-stars Sally Field, Shirley MacLaine, Olympia Dukakis and Dolly Parton. The role she is most identified with, however, is Vivian, the ingénue prostitute in *Pretty Woman* (1990; see Canon), for which she received another Oscar nomination. The same year she branched out into sci-fi with

Flatliners, and began a much-publicized relationship with co-star Kiefer Sutherland. Gossip spread that Roberts broke Sutherland's heart, practically leaving him at the altar; she, however, maintained that their split was mutual, before shocking the world in 1993 with her marriage to quirky Country singer Lyle Lovett. Few could get beyond the apparently extraordinary fact that she was just so much *prettier* than him, and fewer were surprised when they divorced two years later.

Meanwhile, Roberts' career was faltering. The failure of the abysmal *I Love Trouble* (1994) was partly due to her relationship with co-star Nick Nolte – they hated each other and it showed – while even the Roberts charisma failed to ignite the woefully drab chick flick *Something To Talk About* (1995). A couple of intriguing roles in the IRA biopic *Michael Collins* and Woody Allen's musical *Everyone Says I Love You* (both 1996) followed, before she returned to fine comedy form in the screwball-influenced *My Best Friend's Wedding* (1997; see Canon) and *Runaway Bride* (1999), both of which, concerned as they were with commitment-phobes, had a playful whiff of self-parody. While her powerhouse performance in the stylish biopic *Erin Brockovich* (2000; see Canon) won her the Best Actress Oscar (she was lambasted for forgetting to include the real-life Brockovich in her acceptance speech), the papers were still gossiping about her love life – this time her on-off relationship with TV actor Benjamin Bratt. When filming the underrated comedy thriller *The Mexican* (2001) with **Brad Pitt**, Roberts met cameraman Danny Moder – who was married – and finally, amid much tabloid scepticism, settled down, married him, and in November 2004 gave birth to twins. As her movies got darker – Mike Nichols' bleak four-hander *Closer* (2004), for example – Roberts turned to theatre, making her Broadway debut in 2006. The play, however, closed early, and, she remains tight-lipped about the rumours – she's going to retire, she's going to concentrate on live performance – that continue to dog her.

🎬 Mystic Pizza
dir Donald Petrie, 1988, US, 104m

Roberts is the best thing about this feather-light tale of female friendship and man trouble. Her confident, charismatic performance belies her experience (this was her first major movie role), and goes way beyond the limitations of the part. She has superstar written all over her.

🎬 Runaway Bride
dir Garry Marshall, 1999, US, 116m

Capitalizing on *Pretty Woman's* enormous success, Roberts, Richard Gere and the wry Hector Elizondo are teamed up again nearly a decade later in this likeable romance. Roberts, at the peak of her powers, proves her comic credentials as the madcap Maggie, Gere is as relaxed as ever and Joan Cusack offers fine kooky backup.

Mark Ruffalo

Actor, 1967–

Mark Ruffalo is an anomaly. Though a star, he doesn't quite fit the Hollywood mould – and despite a broad and credible body of work, he still isn't quite counted as A-list. This may be due in part to his muted style, a kind of lazy sexiness that makes him a subtle actor, one who doesn't push to the forefront. This generosity, and an almost-feminine gentleness that underpins his masculine looks, has made him a brilliant male lead opposite some of Hollywood's biggest female stars, though he has yet to carry a film alone. His roots, and continuing involvement, in the theatre, along with his long-standing background in indie movies, might also have something to do with the fact

that mainstream audiences are only just waking up to him.

Raised in a middle-class Italian-American family in Wisconsin, Ruffalo was more interested in athletics at school than drama. However, after moving to LA at the age of 18, he studied acting at the Stella Adler Conservatory, co-founded a theatre company, and got busy acting, writing and directing. A rash of film roles cropped up throughout the 1990s, mostly in small indie comedies, while he also continued his work on the stage. After rave reviews in 1998 for his performance in **Kenneth Lonergan**'s off-Broadway play *This Is Our Youth*, he was a natural to play **Laura Linney**'s drifter brother in Lonergan's low-key indie film *You Can Count On Me* (2000; see Canon); the movie won numerous awards – and an Oscar nomination – with Ruffalo's edgy, almost Brando-esque, performance earning high praise.

He continued to balance theatre work with a growing movie career, until, in 2000, he was diagnosed with a brain tumour. The tumour was benign, but surgery led to temporary facial paralysis and a long convalescence – a brush with mortality that gave Ruffalo a new zest for acting. He brought a certain vulnerability to his roles in the love triangle movie *XX/XY* (2001) and *My Life Without Me* (2002), in which he provides a last stab at romance for a dying woman. The execrable *View From The Top* (2003) – in which Gwyneth Paltrow dreams of being an air hostess – was followed by a staggering performance as Detective Malloy in **Jane Campion**'s erotic thriller *In The Cut* (2003; see Canon). The part of the ambiguous Detective Malloy – threatening, sensitive, macho, feminine – could have been made for the soft-spoken Ruffalo, and seemed set to transform him into an all-out sex symbol.

Ruffalo: a sex-symbol for our times? (*Just Like Heaven*, 2005 with Reese Witherspoon)

He carried that low-hum sexiness into the hard-going *We Don't Live Here Anymore* (2004), an overwrought story of infidelity, before taking a supporting role in the surreal *Eternal Sunshine Of The Spotless Mind* (2004), and entering chick flick territory with the bubblegum rom-com *13 Going On 30* (2004). And – excluding a sympathetic police detective in *Collateral* (2004) – chick flick territory is where he has stayed, giving us devilishly attractive male leads in *Just Like Heaven* (2005) with **Reese Witherspoon**, and *Rumor Has It…* (2005) with Jennifer Aniston, before shifting gear to take part in Sean Penn's *All The King's Men* and *Margaret*, another collaboration with Lonergan (both 2006).

XX/XY
dir Austin Chick, 2001, US, 91m

An unsuccessful ménage à trois has a lasting impact on Coles (Ruffalo), Sam (Maya Stange) and Thea (Kathleen Robertson) in this indie meditation on modern sex and love. Ruffalo is typically nuanced – neither entirely despicable nor lovable – as the guy who can't grow up.

13 Going On 30
dir Gary Winick, 2004, US, 98m

The rom-com that made a megastar of Jennifer Garner – who is fresh and likeable as the teen who gets transported, *Big*-style, into her own future – also shows Ruffalo to be an excellent chick flick hero: rumpled, sensitive and a tiny bit tortured. Teenage girls the world over sat up and took notice.

Meg Ryan
Actress, 1961–

Rarely has an actress faced such a backlash as Meg Ryan. The lovable cherub who breezed her way through some of the key chick flicks of the 1980s and 90s is, in the mid-2000s, the target of endless criticism about anything from her collagen-puffed "trout pout" to her choice to adopt a Chinese baby. Trapped, like some latter-day Marilyn Monroe, by her looks, Meg Ryan is a woman who refuses to play the game and won't, it seems, be forgiven for it.

Ryan, a Connecticut girl, started acting to fund her journalism studies in New York. She played Candice Bergen's daughter in George Cukor's *Rich And Famous* (1981) and took a small part in *Top Gun* (1986), before starring in the daft comedy sci-fi *Innerspace* (1987) with the handsome cad with a rakish grin **Dennis Quaid**. The actors' on-screen chemistry was mirrored in real life, and after working together again in the *noir*ish *D.O.A.* (1988), they married on Valentine's Day 1991. Sunny, funny and gorgeous, Ryan and Quaid, it seemed, were the ideal Hollywood couple.

Following her turn as bubbly Sally Albright in *When Harry Met Sally…* (1989; see Canon) – the part with which she will always be identified – Ryan played three decidedly un-cutesy characters opposite **Tom Hanks** in *Joe Versus The Volcano* (1990). (The movie bombed, but the stars looked good together, and they teamed up again for *Sleepless In Seattle* and *You've Got Mail*.) The role of Jim Morrison's druggy girlfriend in Oliver Stone's *The Doors* (1991) was a thankless one; Ryan seemed more comfortable with husband Quaid in the atmospheric thriller *Flesh And Bone* (1993). Her career continued to seesaw: following *Sleepless In Seattle* (1993) with the daft *I.Q.* (1994), she impressed audiences as a recovering alcoholic in *When A Man Loves A Woman* (1994), and embarrassed them as Robert Downey Jr.'s loony lover in *Restoration* (1996). She played a fighter pilot in the Gulf War drama *Courage Under Fire* (1996), an ex-from-Hell in *Addicted To Love* (1997), and a stripper in the sour Hollywood satire *Hurlyburly*

(1998). None of these won her as much attention, however, as the lovelorn book shop owner in *You've Got Mail* (1998), or the vulnerable surgeon in the poignant *City Of Angels* (1998).

In 2000 rumours leaked out that Ryan was having an affair with her *Proof Of Life* co-star Russell Crowe. While the film, a kidnap drama, was forgettable, the affair proved to be catastrophic: after a clumsy attempt at reconciliation, her golden marriage to Quaid ended messily, and Meg, who appeared bitter and angry, lost her fairy tale crown. It's hardly surprising that she seemed so uneasy in the dreadful time travel rom-com *Kate & Leopold* (2001); more interesting is her appearance in Rosanna Arquette's *Searching For Debra Winger* (2002), a feminist documentary about female stars in Hollywood. Her turn as the serious, brown-haired Frannie in **Jane Campion**'s erotic thriller *In The Cut* (2003; see Canon) spawned acres of column space about a "change in direction", and despite her splendid performance, seemed to win her more disdain than admiration. Matters weren't improved by a teeth-clenchingly tense interview with British chat show host Michael Parkinson, when, irritated by his questions about the movie's nudity and that old "change in direction" chestnut, she simply clammed up. In 2004 she starred in the boxing biopic *Against The Ropes*, and in 2006 in the black comedy *In The Land Of Women*, but her performances were overshadowed by endless discussions about her ill-judged plastic surgery. Meg Ryan, it seems, has a long way to go before she will find peace.

Sleepless In Seattle
dir Nora Ephron, 1993, US, 105m

A sassy relationship comedy that easily stands up to comparisons with *When Harry Met Sally…*, having the same gooey centre and knowing, movie-savvy sheen. Ryan does her wrinkle-nosed cutie to perfection, Tom Hanks wrings hearts with his wistful widower shtick, and Rosie O'Donnell adds a welcome dash of cynicism.

When A Man Loves A Woman
dir Luis Mandoki, 1994, US, 125m

Ryan pulls out all the stops as Alice, the troubled alcoholic mom with the seemingly perfect life. She is ably supported by Andy Garcia as her long-suffering husband, whose good-guy image crumbles as he becomes increasingly threatened by her recovery.

City Of Angels
dir Brad Silberling, 1998, US/Ger, 114m

Based on Wim Wenders' major arthouse hit *Wings Of Desire* (1987), this is a bittersweet and well-handled LA fairy tale about a lonely angel (Nicolas Cage, perfectly cast) who falls for a guilt-ridden surgeon (Ryan). Suspend your disbelief and wallow.

Susan Sarandon

Actress, 1946–

Thoughtful, articulate and unafraid, Susan Sarandon brings an integrity to her performances that elevates anything she appears in. She is a rare creature in Hollywood: a politically active, left-wing actress, who is celebrated for her intelligence and strength as well as her warm sexuality – and, unusually, is increasingly respected the older she gets.

A good Catholic girl, born in New York, Sarandon started her career as a model. Her first experience of the movies was in 1969, when she accompanied her then-husband – actor Chris Sarandon – to an audition and ended up being cast as a junkie in the violent *Joe* (1970). She next made a splash as the semi-clad Janet in the cult classic *The Rocky Horror Picture Show* (1975), which was far more successful than *The*

Great Waldo Pepper (1975), despite the presence of golden boy Robert Redford in the latter. Though most of the attention was given to Brooke Shields as the New Orleans child prostitute in **Louis Malle**'s *Pretty Baby* (1978), Sarandon gave an assured performance as her mother, and did splendid work with Malle again in his elegiac *Atlantic City* (1980), earning her first Oscar nomination for her nuanced performance as the hopeful would-be croupier Sally.

Sarandon's sexy image redoubled after she got naked with lesbian vampire Catherine Deneuve in the arty *The Hunger* (1983), another cult movie, while she let her comic talents shine with Jack Nicholson, Michelle Pfeiffer and Cher in the pseudo-feminist *The Witches Of Eastwick* (1987). There was more comedy with the baseball rom-com *Bull Durham* (1988); as well as hooking her up with her soon-to-be husband **Tim Robbins**, the movie practically belonged to her, and set her on her way to a lucrative career playing older, independent, earthy women. Both *White Palace* (1990) and *Thelma & Louise* (1991; see Canon) allowed her to riff upon that theme, adding a tough-yet-fragile edge: in the former she brought a bruised feistiness to her role as the blue-collar waitress who falls, despite herself, for a younger yuppie, while in the latter, as Louise, she became a chick flick icon. Smart, brave and adventurous, a woman's woman who has been around the block, Louise provides the heart and soul of **Ridley Scott**'s feminist outlaw movie, and Sarandon more than deserved her second Oscar nomination.

She changed direction with the laborious family drama *Lorenzo's Oil* (1992), as a lawyer in John Grisham's *The Client* (1994) – both of which earned her Oscar nominations – and as saintly "Marmee" in Gillian Armstrong's *Little Women* (1994), before finally winning an Academy Award for her pared-down performance as Sister Prejean in Tim Robbins's worthy death row movie, *Dead Man Walking* (1995). She swerved again with *Stepmom* (1998), a three-hankie weepie that works, despite its tired formula, by pitting her against superstar Julia Roberts to create an effective two-hander.

The Banger Sisters (2002), co-starring Goldie Hawn, was an affectionate piece of froth that allowed Sarandon to poke fun at ageing, and she brought quiet candour to the role of Richard Gere's wife in the dancing-as-redemption chick flick *Shall We Dance* (2004). She was by far the best thing about Cameron Crowe's abysmal *Elizabethtown* (2005), tap-dancing her way through bereavement, and fabulous in John Turturro's crazy musical *Romance & Cigarettes* (2005). As this charismatic actress hits her 60s, we can only expect greater things to come.

Bull Durham
dir Ron Shelton, 1988, US, 108m

Sarandon sealed her sexy older woman persona with her performance as baseball groupie Annie in this enjoyable rom-com. While Kevin Costner is the nominal love interest, it's the inspired comedy turn from Tim Robbins as the dim-witted pitcher Nuke LaLoosh that really appeals – he and Sarandon got together soon after.

White Palace
dir Luis Mandoki, 1990, US, 103m

Though the premise of this elegantly composed movie is old as the hills – boy (rich, repressed) meets girl (poor, free-spirited), and a passionate, yet surely impossible, love affair ensues – Sarandon brings guts and pathos to her blue-collar waitress, while James Spader is perfect as the yuppie she falls for. The age gap (she's around 15 years older) adds a poignant twist.

The Banger Sisters
dir Bob Dolman, 2002, US, 98m

The Sisters of the title are two estranged old friends – Sarandon and Goldie Hawn – who were once wild rock

groupies. Thirty years on, Sarandon has put all that behind her, while rock chick Hawn refuses to grow up. Though there's little that's surprising here, this is a warm and funny movie, with the two leads playing off each other to great effect.

Susan Seidelman
Director, 1952–

After majoring in art and fashion design and making two award-winning shorts at NYU film school, Susan Seidelman emerged onto the 1980s New York indie arts scene with a bang. Her first feature, the low-budget *Smithereens* (1982), was the first-ever US independent selected for competition at Cannes. The story of an itinerant girl drifting through New Wave New York, the movie is kitsch and drily funny, and it firmly established Seidelman as a voice to be reckoned with. While she attained cult status alongside other indie directors like Jonathan Demme and Jim Jarmusch, her films always had a distinctly female voice. With their poppy scores, strong screwball-inspired heroines, and their recurring play with fashion, dressing up and disguise, Seidelman's movies invariably push women and women's experiences centre stage.

Smithereens was followed by the ground-breaking *Desperately Seeking Susan* (1985; see Canon), in which a young, super-hip pop star called **Madonna** made her acting debut. The presence of the singer, who had just had a major hit with her album *Like A Virgin*, pulled in a huge youth audience, and the film was an unexpected box office smash. *Susan* is far more than a Madonna vehicle, however: a sumptuous gal buddy/caper movie, it was sheer delight for female audiences hungry for fantasy and fun. Seidelman's next, eagerly awaited, feature *Making*

Mr Right (1987), set in Miami, was a black sci-fi comedy that no one knew quite how to take – widely underrated, it was nowhere near as commercially successful as *Susan*. 1989's *Cookie*, a mafia caper with fine performances from its strong cast (Emily Lloyd, Peter Falk, Dianne Wiest, Brenda Vaccaro), looked great, but the script, though co-written by chick flick stalwart **Nora Ephron** (see p.161), just didn't make the grade. Her bankability rapidly diminishing, Seidelman still had enough kudos to make *She-Devil* (1989). The credentials were immaculate: based on Fay Weldon's feminist novel, the twisted comedy pitched the outrageous **Roseanne Barr** (in her first movie role) against **Meryl Streep** (in her first comedy role). However, the verve that had illuminated and inspired Seidelman's first few films was faltering.

In the 1990s Seidelman turned to TV, directing a string of movies and shows that included 1998's *Sex And The City* pilot. She returned to the big screen in 2001 with the bizarre and little-seen *Gaudi Afternoon*, based on the novel by Barbara Wilson and starring a raft of fine actresses, including Judy Davis, Marcia Gay Harden and Juliette Lewis. While it remains to be seen how her latest movie, *Boynton Beach Club* (2006), a gentle rom-com set in a community of retirees, will fare, Seidelman's legacy remains a valuable and exciting one, her early work in particular capturing the spirit of a decade when girls just wanted to, and often did, have a lot of fun.

Smithereens
dir Susan Seidelman, 1982, US, 93m

An energetic, warmhearted and grungily hip little movie, concerning the exploits of feisty punk Wren (Susan Berman) – forerunner to Madonna's Susan – on the mean streets of New York's Lower East Side. Very much of its time.

Making Mr Right
dir Susan Seidelman, 1987, US, 98m

Frankie (Ann Magnuson), a successful career woman, discovers she can only find true love with a robot (John Malkovich). This is no conventional boy-meets-girl story, and as her dream guy literally falls apart each time they make love, the "romantic" happy ending does raise some doubts.

She-Devil
dir Susan Seidelman, 1989, US, 99m

Mouthy TV comedienne Roseanne Barr plays Ruth, the frumpy, wronged wife determined to ruin everything for her cheating husband and his new – sickeningly perfect – lover, romantic novelist Mary Fisher (Meryl Streep). Barr relishes the delicious nastiness of her role, while Streep is a revelation as a comedienne.

Gaudi Afternoon
dir Susan Seidelman, 2001, Sp, 97m

Despite its strong cast and intriguing premise, this is something of an oddity. Cassandra (Judy Davis), a neurotic expat writer living in Barcelona, gets caught up with the stylish and mercurial Frankie (Marcia Gay Harden), who pays Cassandra to find her "husband" so he can sign some papers. All, however, is not as it seems in this farce of shifting identities.

Douglas Sirk
Director, 1900–1987

Douglas Sirk, who brought us some of the most passionate Hollywood tearjerkers of the 1950s, was the maestro of the melodrama. A German emigré, his recurring themes – isolation, repression, despair and loss – surely stem, at least in part, from his experiences in Nazi Germany, years that he later referred to as miserable, paranoid and above all lonely. The man who once said, "If you try to grasp happiness, your fingers only meet a surface of glass, because happiness has no existence of its own," brought a dark sensibility to his gloriously colourful movies that lingers long after their putative happy endings have faded to black.

In the late 1960s Sirk was lauded by French and British film academics as an auteur – a filmmaker whose vision transcends the conventions of Hollywood, and who uses particularly cinematic aesthetics to create spectacular works of art. So while we might allow ourselves a few ironic smirks at the overwrought plots, the dialogue or even the acting styles of these melodramas, at the same time something in the disorientating camera angles, the swelling music, the overblown mise-en-scène (decor), the moody, saturated and totally non-naturalistic lighting, and even the performances of the stars, inspires strong emotions that can't be contained. Sirk loved to leave things open and ambiguous – especially those so-called "happy" endings, which more often than not leave us sobbing inconsolably. As he himself put it, in typical melancholy mode, his films' endings "express the weak and sly promise that the world is not rotten and out of joint, but meaningful and ultimately in excellent condition" – a weak and sly promise that most of us would give our right arm to believe.

Sirk, born Detlef Sierck, began his career as a left-leaning theatre director in Weimar Germany. As the Nazis gathered force, he turned to moviemaking, intending to use those skills to find work outside Germany. By 1942 he was a Hollywood screenwriter, going on to direct a series of B-movies for Universal Studios, including the camp 3D Western *Taza, Son Of Cochise* (1954). *Taza* starred a young **Rock Hudson** (see p.179), the handsome actor in whom Sirk saw something more than the beefcake status he'd been afforded until then. He went on to cast him alongside big star **Jane Wyman** in *Magnificent Obsession* (1954), a fabulous tearjerker that established Sirk's reputation

as a melodrama director and Hudson as a movie idol. The successful Hudson/Wyman/Sirk formula was replayed in *All That Heaven Allows* (1955), the archetypal Sirkian melodrama, which influenced all manner of (mostly gay) directors, from **Rainer Werner Fassbinder**, working in Germany in the 1970s, to **Todd Haynes**, whose *Far From Heaven* (2002; see Canon) pays elegant homage to Sirk's masterpiece. A year later came *Written On The Wind*, a Freudian feast of sexual obsession, alcoholism and neurosis, in which Sirk pulled out all the stops to create, as he put it, a "drama of psychic violence". Starring Hudson and Lauren Bacall, the movie is also notable for its supporting players, **Dorothy Malone** (who won an Oscar for her portrayal of the frustrated nymphomaniac with the hots for Rock) and **Robert Stack**, her tortured alcoholic brother. The director gathered Hudson, Stack and Malone together again to make *The Tarnished Angels* (1958), an elegiac black-and-white drama set in the world of carnival stunt pilots that is often quoted to be his best work.

Sirk's final Hollywood movie, *Imitation Of Life* (1959; see Canon), is perhaps the weepiest weepie of them all. Both a heart-rending mother-daughter story and a searing view of race relations in postwar America, *Imitation* still stands up as an agonizing examination of powerlessness, repression and loss. It was a brilliant swan song for this complex director, who in 1959, tired, ill and weary of Hollywood, moved to Switzerland, where he lived, quietly enjoying his newfound status as a genius and an original, for the rest of his life.

Magnificent Obsession
dir Douglas Sirk, 1954, US, 108m

Sirk, as ever, transcends a preposterous plot to create a sumptuous emotional feast, the very apogee of overwrought 1950s melodramas. Rock Hudson is a wealthy playboy who, struck with remorse after a tragic accident, becomes a surgeon to assuage his guilt. Jane Wyman co-stars as the widow he falls in love with.

Written On The Wind
dir Douglas Sirk, 1956, US, 99m

Fast cars, wild jazz, madness, lust and murder – arguably the most camp and rumbustiously enjoyable of Sirk's melodramas, following the fortunes of the spoilt and damaged children (Robert Stack and Dorothy Malone, both fabulous) of a Texas oil millionaire. Rock Hudson and Lauren Bacall play the saintly outsiders, far less interesting than those crazy siblings.

Barbara Stanwyck

Actress, 1907–1990

Barbara Stanwyck was, along with Bette Davis and Joan Crawford, one of the three grandes dames of 1930s and 40s Hollywood. An assured actress whose career spanned nearly 100 films, ranging from screwballs through *film noirs* and melodramas to Westerns, she was also the one of the three that *everyone* liked. Strong, sexy and resourceful, she brought a warmth and an earthy wit to her performances that had universal appeal.

In many ways Stanwyck's beginnings and early career echo those of Joan Crawford (see p.153). Born Ruby Stevens, she escaped a difficult and disrupted childhood by becoming a chorus girl in the 1920s, and gained some success on Broadway. In 1930 the comedy movie director **Frank Capra** starred her as a spirited good-time girl in *Ladies Of Leisure*, and went on to work with her again on a couple of dramas, including the lush melodrama *The Bitter Tea Of General Yen* (1933). Like Crawford, she perfected a line in ambitious working girls; she lacked, however, the whisper of victimized vulnerability that surrounded the iconic Joan, and in her comedies always convinced us that under the tough exterior there beat a heart of

gold. She could also turn her hand to steely vamps in gritty movies like *Baby Face* (1933), in which she plays an amoral minx who boldly sleeps her way to the top. Just a few years after reaching the peak of her career as the self-sacrificing mother in the tear-jerking melodrama *Stella Dallas* (1937; see Canon), she gave characteristically humane comedy performances as the shoplifter in *Remember The Night* (1940), the crafty con woman in *The Lady Eve* (1941), an unscrupulous reporter in Capra's idealistic *Meet John Doe* (1941) and sassy Sugarpuss O'Shea in the screwball *Ball Of Fire* (1941). Meanwhile, again like Crawford, her shopworn working-girl roles turned darker and more twisted under the shadow of *film noir*. In the classic *Double Indemnity* (1944) she stormed the screen as Phyllis Dietrichson, the peroxide-blonde devil in a dress (the same year becoming the highest-paid woman in the US), and was icily, if poignantly, hardhearted in the intriguing *noir*/melodrama *The Strange Love Of Martha Ivers* (1946).

In the 1950s, when Joan and Bette had begun to resort to self-parody, Stanwyck kept her dignity. She continued with the *film noirs*, putting in a brace of hard-boiled performances in *The File On Thelma Jordan* (1950) and *Clash By Night* (1952), before moving into Westerns (where she had already ventured with *Annie Oakley*, 1935, and *Union Pacific*, 1939), playing a sequence of gritty pioneer women who would sling a gun as soon as look at you. From Sierra Nevada Jones in *Cattle Queen Of Montana* (1954) and saloon owner Kit Banion in *The Maverick Queen* (1956) to Jessica Drummond, the tyrannical rancher in Sam Fuller's *Forty Guns* (1957), Stanwyck gave us gutsy Western heroines that were unusual in the genre. It was an easy transition to matriarch Victoria Barkley in the popular US TV series *The Big Valley* (1965–69), and in the 1980s she remained a powerful small-screen

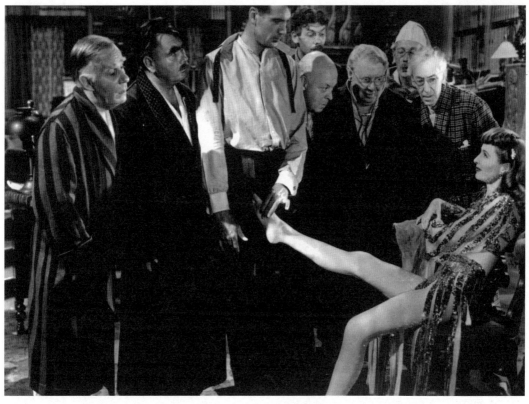

Barbara Stanwyck: as ever the centre of attention in *Ball Of Fire* (1941)

presence as the lustful Mary Carson in the hit *The Thorn Birds* (1983) and as Constance Colby in *The Colbys* (1985–86). Having been nominated four times for an Oscar, she finally won an honorary Academy Award in 1982 for "superlative creativity and unique contribution to the art of screen acting" – an accolade long overdue for this, in her own words, "tough old dame from Brooklyn".

The Bitter Tea Of General Yen
dir Frank Capra, 1933, US, 88m, b/w

An unusual inter-racial love story, with Stanwyck playing a missionary trapped in civil war-torn China, rescued by a seductive Chinese warlord (Nils Asther). Fabulously atmospheric, with a strangely erotic dream sequence and wonderful sets.

Baby Face
dir Alfred E. Green, 1933, US, 68m, b/w

Hard-bitten and spare, this is the film that showed Barbara could be very, very bad. Even so, her Lily Powers is not entirely unsympathetic – raised in an abusive home and forced by her father into prostitution, this resourceful gal has few other options but to work her way to the top of the ladder "wrong by wrong".

Annie Oakley
dir George Stevens, 1935, US, 83m, b/w

A rip-roaring Western romp, with Stanwyck playing real-life sharpshooter Annie, star of Buffalo Bill's Wild West Show. The movie crackles with gunslinging action, and we have romantic interest, too, as Annie's increasing success in the show threatens her love life.

Ball Of Fire
dir Howard Hawks, 1941, US, 112m, b/w

Stanwyck is hilarious as the wisecracking Sugarpuss O'Shea, a nightclub singer who rocks the academic world in this uproarious screwball. Absentminded Professor Potts (a handsome Gary Cooper) attempts to analyse American slang by making a study of the fast-talking broad; Sugarpuss, however, who happens to be on the run from both the police and the mob, has her own agenda.

Meryl Streep

Actress, 1949–

The name Meryl Streep is met with both adulation and irritation. Her propensity for accents has become a joke in some quarters, and is seen as the apogee of the actors' craft in others. Her ethereal looks – including a distinctively wonky nose – which change, chameleon-like, with each role she plays, are described variously as beautiful or plain. Some revere her as a goddess; others, including the formidable Katharine Hepburn, have dismissed her as stagey and affected. What is indubitable is her astonishingly wide repertoire, her longevity, her integrity, and the respect she has been afforded by the Hollywood Academy. With her Oscar nomination for 2002's *Adaptation*, Streep overtook Hepburn as the most

nominated actress ever, her tally currently standing at thirteen, though she has only won two. A vocal activist, supporting a number of civil rights, human rights and environmental causes, Streep is also a woman who refuses to play coy. As she said upon accepting her Emmy for *Angels In America* (2003), the TV mini-series in which she played four parts, including that of a male rabbi, "There are some days when even I think I'm overrated … but not today."

Born in suburban New Jersey, Streep studied drama at the prestigious Vassar, Dartmouth and Yale colleges, starring in the big student shows and making a rapid transition to Broadway. Her Hollywood ascent was meteoric; after debuting as the snooty Anne Marie in the Jane Fonda-Vanessa Redgrave friendship movie *Julia* (1977), she promptly snagged a Best Supporting Actress Oscar nomination for *The Deer Hunter* (1978), in which she improvised many of her lines. The next year saw her play Woody Allen's lesbian ex in *Manhattan*, and win an Oscar as the mother in the feminist backlash movie *Kramer Vs. Kramer*.

In the 1980s Streep reigned supreme over Hollywood's prestige movies. After a dual role in *The French Lieutenant's Woman* (1981), she won the Best Actress Oscar for her emotionally bruised performance as a Holocaust survivor in *Sophie's Choice* (1982). Both movies were intense, on the edge of arty; she ventured into more commercial territory with the gritty biopic *Silkwood* (1983) and low-key *Falling In Love* (1984), in which she plays a married woman who falls for the (also married) Robert De Niro. She went in all guns blazing as the frustrated wife and ex-Resistance fighter in *Plenty* (1985); the Danish author Karen Blixen in the epic romance *Out Of Africa* (1985); Jack Nicholson's betrayed wife in *Heartburn* (1986) and his boozy cohort in *Ironweed* (1987); and an Australian mother accused of murdering her baby in *A Cry In The Dark* (1988). In 1989 Susan Seidelman's black comedy *She-Devil* showed a different side to Meryl Streep – though the film bombed, her comedic turn opposite Roseanne Barr was a refreshing new direction.

Streep continued her foray into comedy – and showed off her singing voice – by teaming up with Shirley MacLaine to play battling mother and daughter in *Postcards From The Edge* (1990; see Canon); the grotesque black comedy *Death Becomes Her* (1992), with Goldie Hawn, was less successful. After the little-seen *The House Of The Spirits* (1993), based on Isabel Allende's magical realist novel, she broke hearts again in the bittersweet *The Bridges Of Madison County* (1995; see Canon), putting in a nuanced performance (complete with Italian accent) as a middle-aged housewife who falls in love with a handsome stranger (Clint Eastwood). Two well-handled terminal illness weepies followed: *Marvin's Room* (1996) and *One True Thing* (1998).

While gliding gracefully through her 50s, Streep has returned to the theatre while also continuing a prodigious movie output. She starred in the most compelling segment of the otherwise dreary *The Hours* (2002), shone as the writer in Spike Jonze's surreal comedy *Adaptation.*, and relished her roles as the evil mother in *The Manchurian Candidate* (2004),

Uma Thurman's analyst in the drily funny *Prime* (2005), a c'n'w temptress in Robert Altman's all-star *A Prairie Home Companion* (2006) and an evil magazine editor in *The Devil Wears Prada* (2006). Where next for Meryl Streep? Fittingly, among many upcoming parts, she is set to play the President of the United States – with, deliciously, Robert De Niro as her husband!

Sophie's Choice
dir Alan J. Pakula, 1982, US, 158m

The actress sealed her reputation as the accent queen of her generation with her portrayal of the haunted mother who tells her harrowing Holocaust story in flashback.

Meryl Streep haunts the seashore as *The French Lieutenant's Woman* (1981)

Intense, accomplished and profoundly painful, this is classic early Streep, with strong support from Kevin Kline.

Silkwood
dir Mike Nichols, 1983, US, 131m

Though the film could lose twenty minutes or so, this true story still has the power to shock. Streep is superb, replacing accents and noble suffering with chain smoking and attitude as the whistle-blowing nuclear-facility worker Karen Silkwood. Cher, who plays her tough lesbian friend Dolly, is a revelation, while a young Kurt Russell offers low-key love interest. Scripted by Nora Ephron.

A Cry In The Dark
dir Fred Schepisi, 1988, Aus, 121m

Another astonishing performance from Streep, who turns her hand this time to an unprepossessing, self-contained Seventh Day Adventist who is accused of murdering her baby while camping in the Australian outback. Based on a true story, it's a fascinating account of what becomes of a woman who refuses to play by the rules – less seriously, it also gave rise to the oft-lampooned catchphrase "A dingo took moy baybay!"

Marvin's Room
dir Jerry Zaks, 1996, US, 98m

This blackly comic examination of a seriously dysfunctional extended family is one of Hollywood's less harrowing terminal illness movies, with a stellar cast – including Diane Keaton, Robert De Niro and Leonardo DiCaprio – that allows Streep to demonstrate her generosity as an ensemble player.

Barbra Streisand

Actress, singer, director and producer, 1942–

Barbra Streisand is a powerful woman: powerful voice, powerful presence, powerful in Hollywood, powerful in politics. She has also been called the first Jewish superstar – true or not, she was certainly the first Jewish superstar to make no attempt to hide her Jewishness, one who celebrates her Brooklyn background and insists to the world that she is beautiful, no matter what the dominant image of beauty might be. A lifelong Democrat, she speaks out boldly against the Bush administration, and devotes much of her time and money to campaigning for the many issues – human rights, civil rights, AIDS and environmental awareness – she supports. She is also the bestselling female singer of the twentieth century, second only to Elvis in the all-time charts, and, after more than thirty years, is still churning out number one albums. In addition, Streisand – and this sometimes gets forgotten – is a splendid, vivacious actress, and (more unusually) a movie director and producer, who, as in all areas of her life, fights for projects she believes in, takes risks and damns the consequences.

At the age of 22, starring in the stage show *Funny Girl* and making the role of Jewish comedienne Fanny Brice her own, Babs was the toast of Broadway. A barnstorming, Oscar-winning performance in the film version (1968) followed, and suddenly she was equally in demand in Hollywood. Charismatic turns in the overblown *Hello, Dolly!* (1969), another costume musical, and the intriguing *On A Clear Day You Can See Forever* (1970) came next. The musical genre was waning, but Streisand, a natural comedienne, was also able to breeze through non-singing roles in the screwball-inspired *The Owl And The Pussycat* (1970) and *What's Up, Doc?* (1972).

The star set up her own production company, Barwood Films, in 1972; its first movie, *Up The Sandbox*, was a peculiar creature, influenced by the emerging Women's Lib movement. She was terrific in the bittersweet romance *The Way We Were* (1973; see Canon), but although the movie's theme song rejuvenated her flagging recording career, her film work went downhill with the drab comedy *For Pete's Sake* (1974) and the flat *Funny Girl* sequel *Funny Lady* (1975). In 1976 Streisand produced and starred in *A Star Is Born*, the third version of the classic story about the vagaries of celebrity; she won a Best Song Oscar for "Evergreen", but the film was dreadful, and the accusations of egotism and hubris that still hound her began. These increased in 1983, when with *Yentl* she became the first woman ever to produce, direct, co-write, star and sing in a Hollywood movie. An earnest, ambitious feminist musical about a Jewish girl who refuses to play by the rules, it has more than a hint of autobiography about it, and though nominated for five Oscars, it was dismissed within the business as "Barbra's folly".

Streisand continued undeterred, starring in and writing the music for *Nuts* (1987), in which she plays an abrasive prostitute accused of murder, before her next two outings as director/star, *The Prince Of Tides* (1991), a melodramatic romance dealing with childhood damage, and the lame comedy *The Mirror Has Two Faces* (1996). Her movie work has dwindled since then, though she did turn in a hilarious performance as Ben Stiller's hippy mother in *Meet The Fockers* (2004).

A woman of many talents: Streisand plays the kook in *What's Up Doc?* (1972)

her smoking, discovers her past lives and falls for one of them. Fab outfits – including period costumes from Cecil Beaton – great performances, a small role for Jack Nicholson, and a poignant sense that this is the musical genre's last gasp.

🎬 The Owl And The Pussycat
dir Herbert Ross, 1970, US, 96m

Barbra at her snappy comedic best, nicely teamed with George Segal in a risqué opposites-attract comedy about an exasperating hooker and uptight would-be novelist. It's notable, too, for being the first movie in which a female star (Babs, naturally) shouts "fuck off!" – a line that has since been cut from some versions.

🎬 On A Clear Day You Can See Forever
dir Vincente Minnelli, 1970, US, 130m

An unusual, haunting musical. Streisand plays Daisy Gamble, whose hypnotist (Yves Montand), aiming to stop

Up The Sandbox
dir Irvin Kershner, 1972, US, 98m

A curious slice of film history, with Streisand playing – brilliantly – against type as a harassed, put-upon housewife who increasingly loses herself in fantasies. Slightly trippy and occasionally earnest, with a pre-*Ally McBeal* vibe.

Yentl
dir Barbra Streisand, 1983, UK, 133m

Aged 40, Barbra was mocked for playing an 18-year-old girl from a Polish *shtetl* (the age gap would have been less of a problem had she been able to get the movie made when she wanted, in 1968). Yentl longs to study the Talmud; because only boys can be scholars, she straps herself up, cuts her hair and transforms herself into Anshel. With its gentle questioning of gender and sexual attraction, this is a mischievous delight. Even the much-derided songs, which act as a running commentary on Yentl's state of mind, have a quirky charm.

Rudolph Valentino

Actor, 1895–1926

Rudolph Valentino, Hollywood's first, and greatest, male sex symbol, was born Rodolfo Pietro Filiberto Raffaele Guglielmi in Castellaneta, Italy. Rejected by the Navy after failing his medical (which, apparently, initiated his lifelong obsession with keeping fit), he moved to Paris, hung out with a Bohemian crowd and learned to dance, before upping sticks to New York in 1913. Life was tough for a young Italian boy in Brooklyn, but "Signor Rodolfo" managed to eke out a living as a tango dancer (and, some say, gigolo). Eventually, he moved to California, working as a dance instructor and chorus boy; he also danced, and played small parts, in a handful of silent movies. In 1919 he met the bisexual starlet **Jean Acker**, married her a few weeks later, and then, after a blazing row, separated from her within hours. It was this kind

The pink powder puff

With his exotic looks, slinky figure and dapper outfits – gaucho garb, bullfighter's boleros, Arab robes, loincloths and pearls – **Rudolph Valentino** was hardly a macho man, and rumours persisted throughout his life that he and his two wives were, in fact, gay. The lost early years in Paris; the shady period when he danced at New York's *Maxim's* nightclub and allegedly sold himself to both men and women; his close friendship with fellow actor Ramon Novarro, a young man as handsome as he; his unconsummated quickie marriage with the bisexual Jean Acker – many things seemed to suggest that the androgynous Rudy was not as much of a ladies' man as his thousands of fans might have wished. A die-hard romantic interested in spiritualism, he wrote in *Movie Weekly*: "I have tastes in literature and art, ideal perhaps, that are peculiar to my origin, and ancestry. I am certain that I have a strong leaning toward the beautiful, even the arabesque."

Many men felt threatened by the feminized sex symbol and his devastating effect on women, and in 1926 an article in the *Chicago Tribune* lambasted him as a "pink powder puff". The outraged and humiliated Valentino challenged the anonymous author to a fight, but was never taken up on it. He did, however, have a boxing match on the roof of his New York hotel with the sportswriter Frank O'Neill, who pronounced him to be quite a fighter. Even at the end, as he lay dying of septicaemia, stoically coping with his agony, it is said that Valentino whispered to his doctor, "And now, do I act like a pink powder puff?"

of drama, combined with his Latin looks, sexual charisma and erotic dance moves, that contributed to the potent mythology surrounding Valentino.

In 1920 Metro's head screenwriter, **June Mathis**, persuaded the production company to cast Valentino as the hero in *The Four Horsemen*

Of The Apocalypse (1921). Giving a performance both restrained and smouldering – and dancing an extraordinarily sexy tango – suddenly Rudolph Valentino was a star, and the film became the highest-grossing silent movie ever. While playing the idealistic young lover Armand opposite Alla Nazimova in *Camille* (1921), he met the talented movie designer and former ballerina **Natacha Rambova** (an Irish girl who had changed her name from the rather less exotic Winifred Hudnut), who was soon taking over most facets of his career. Later that year, the lust-in-the-dust romp *The Sheik* showed Valentino at his sexiest, devilish best – and introduced the term "sheik", to denote the height of male cool, into the American vernacular. In 1922's *Blood And Sand*, adapted by his mentor Mathis, he gave a characteristically sensual per-formance as Gallardo, the beautifully attired toreador. He eloped with Natacha to Mexico the same year, and was almost immediately jailed (briefly) for bigamy – under California law his divorce from Jean was not yet final. The lovers married again as soon as was legally possible, and lived a flamboyant lifestyle, joined by a lion cub, two Great Danes, a large snake and a green monkey.

Frustrated with the limited nature of his film roles, Valentino, encouraged by Natacha, split from his produc-tion company, Paramount. The couple then undertook a dancing tour of the US, while he wrote a book of wistful poetry, *Day Dreams* (1923); both enter-prises were extremely successful, and a year later he returned to Paramount. The star had high hopes for his next movie, the elaborate *Monsieur Beaucaire*

(1924), which Rambova designed; it flopped, however, and he signed up with United Artists – who made it a proviso that the forthright Natacha should not be allowed on any of his sets. She, understandably, was furious. The two soon divorced and were never reconciled.

While publicizing *The Son Of The Sheik* (1926), Valentino was stricken with peritonitis. His illness

The screen's greatest lover and his smouldering stare

and sudden death in August of that year was surrounded by as much publicity, and as much passion, as the rest of his short career, and his two funerals (see p.7) were as theatrical as any of his movies. His untimely death saw the loss of a unique character, a fine and beautiful actor who pushed at the bounds of masculinity, and without whom Hollywood would have been a poorer place.

The Sheik

dir George Melford, 1921, US, 80m, b/w

A deliciously perverse fantasy in which Valentino plays Ahmed, the cruel Arab sheik who abducts the spirited Lady Diana Mayo (Agnes Ayres), tries to rape her – "When an Arab sees a woman he wants, he takes her!" – falls in love, and pounds through the sands to rescue her from a dastardly desert rival.

Blood And Sand
dir Fred Niblo, 1922, US, 80m, b/w

Valentino's personal favourite; a romantic tragedy in which his sensitive performance as a passionate, doomed toreador shows him to be far more than just a sex symbol. Nita Naldi sizzles as the wicked vamp, and the costumes, as in all Valentino's movies, are simply divine.

Monsieur Beaucaire
dir Sidney Olcott, 1924, US, 106m, b/w

Designed by Rambova, this historical romp sees the great lover don a wig and white powder to play a simple barber disguised as an aristocrat in eighteenth-century France. One of his camper outings, with lots of dancing and dueling, it was a rare flop, though Valentino still shines.

The Son Of The Sheik
dir George Fitzmaurice, 1926, US, 68m, b/w

One of the first movie sequels, Valentino's final film was an enormous success. He plays not only the original sheik, but also his son, who falls for a beautiful, unavailable dancing girl (Vilma Bánky, handpicked for the role by Valentino). The inevitable ravishment ensues, with lots of father-son conflict played out through clever split screen effects.

Reese Witherspoon
Actress, 1976–

Reese Witherspoon seemed to sneak up on Hollywood. A chick flick stalwart and talented comedienne, excelling at playing perky, often fiercely ambitious women, she had always been likeable – a down-to-earth star who was friendly in interviews and enjoyed a happy family life with movie actor Ryan Phillippe and their two children. Then, in 2006, following her Oscar-winning performance as country singer June Carter in the Johnny Cash biopic *Walk The Line* (2005), she surpassed **Julia Roberts** (see p.186) to become the highest-paid actress of all time. Suddenly the slip of a girl previously best known for breezing through the two *Legally Blonde* movies was being taken very seriously indeed. Ironically, however, Witherspoon had always been far more than a pretty face, and even before her white-hot turn in *Walk The Line* had a strong body of intriguing work behind her. Whether in rom-coms or horror movies, she embodies her roles – invariably courageous and independent-minded women – with such intensity that it's difficult to tear your eyes from the screen.

Like Julia Roberts, Witherspoon is a Southern girl. Born in Louisiana and raised in Nashville, Tennessee, the daughter of a surgeon and a medical academic, she had a privileged, high-achieving childhood. After working as a child model and in TV commercials, she made an impressive movie debut in the well-regarded rites of passage movie *The Man In The Moon* (1991), and eventually dropped out of Stanford University to continue her movie career. After giving striking performances as a wealthy hostage in the nihilistic indie movie *S.F.W.* (1994) and a tough teen in *Freeway* (1996) – a skewed take on the Little Red Riding Hood story – she turned down leads in *Scream* and *I Know What You Did Last Summer*, and chose instead to put her pixie features to clever use both as an American-as-apple-pie sweetheart in the 1950s fantasy *Pleasantville* (1998), and as an insanely high-achieving high-school girl in *Election* (1999). She had less to do in the stylish thriller *Best Laid Plans* (1999), but was credibly steely as the virginal Annette in *Cruel Intentions* (1999), which updated *Dangerous Liaisons* (1988), tacked on a hip soundtrack and transported it to preppy New York.

Brilliantly brittle as Christian Bale's spoiled fiancé in *American Psycho* (2000), she had her first major starring role as the not-so-ditzy wannabe lawyer in *Legally Blonde* (2001) – and then sleepwalked through the hugely popular chick flick *Sweet Home Alabama* (2002). *Legally Blonde 2: Red White & Blonde* (2003) ticked all the boxes, but far more intriguing is Mira Nair's adaptation of the nineteenth-century classic *Vanity Fair* (2004); Witherspoon's Becky Sharp is an alluring combination of brainy and bawdy, displaying a beady-eyed cunning and a clearly pregnant belly (the actress was about to have her first baby). It was back to chick flick territory with *Just Like Heaven* (2005), which, though overshadowed somewhat by *Walk The Line*, cleverly played her blonde buzzy energy against **Mark Ruffalo**'s lo-fi charisma. With her usual discrimination, she chose something entirely different for her next project – a supporting role in *Penelope* (2006), a fairy tale in which Christina Ricci plays a woman with the face of a pig. If she continues to select her roles with the same intelligence, Reese Witherspoon looks set to maintain her steely grip on both her chick flick supremacy and her cool arthouse cred.

Election
dir Alexander Payne, 1999, US, 103m

Witherspoon's performance is at the heart of this bleak satire on democracy and political correctness. She's both funny and frightening as the ambitious high-school girl determined to get on the school council, her all-American smile locked into a prim rictus of barely controlled rage.

Legally Blonde
dir Robert Luketic, 2001, US, 97m

Though it pales in comparison to its inspiration, *Clueless*, this likeable piece about a vacuous Valley girl (Witherspoon is just perfect) who manages to train as a lawyer *and* wear fluffy pink outfits at the same time, keeps the flame flying for post-feminist bottle blondes everywhere.

Vanity Fair
dir Mira Nair, 2004, UK/US, 141m

It's hard to imagine any Hollywood actress making a better Becky Sharp – wicked but sympathetic – and this opulent movie, based on Thackeray's mighty novel, is an ambitious adaptation. Intriguingly, Nair brings a Bollywood edge to the very British story, which enriches both the look of the film and its bite.

Just Like Heaven
dir Mark Waters, 2005, US, 95m

A bittersweet rom-com with a big heart, in which workaholic Witherspoon learns, perhaps too late, what it means to fall in love. Mark Ruffalo is appealing as ever as her depressed love interest, and the surprising chemistry between the two chalk-and-cheese actors is a delight.

Renée Zellweger
Actress, 1969–

Though she may forever be associated with the British singleton that became a worldwide phenomenon, there is far more to Renée Zellweger than Bridget Jones. That's not to say her achievement in the two *Bridget* movies isn't extraordinary – despite initial doubts, in particular from British fans, it's hard to think of anyone else who could have brought to life the chubby comic creation so entirely. It's the fallout that has surrounded the Renée/Bridget transformation that has proved hard to shift – and, ultimately, Bridget Jones may turn out to be Renée Zellweger's nemesis. With her distinctive features, handed down from her Laplandish mother, the actress has never been a conventional Hollywood beauty. However, since *Bridget* her appearance has sparked off a deluge of speculation that would prove suffocating for even the strongest of personalities. The fact that after fattening up to play Bridget she rapidly shed the weight to become a stick-thin red-carpet superstar has led to concern about her self-image and her health; and, as is the case with many super-skinny stars, the concern frequently takes the form of accusation and vitriol. Add to this an up-and-down love life – which in 2005 included a quickie marriage (and quickie divorce) to country and western singer Kenny Chesney – and it looks like it will be some time before the tabloids leave Zellweger alone.

The press may be ambivalent, but Zellweger has a legion of devoted fans – "Zellots" – who are drawn to her down-to-earth, girl-next-door qualities. Something of a style icon, she also exudes a clownish, tomboyish presence that has a whiff of Doris Day about it, and though she is a fine dramatic actress, it is as a comedienne that she truly shines. A small-town Texas girl, Zellweger first came to attention in 1996 as the devoted single mum Dorothy opposite **Tom Cruise**'s commitment-phobic *Jerry Maguire*. Though with the line "You had me at hello" a Hollywood star was born, the actress had started out as an indie chick, following her media studies degree at Austin's University

of Texas with roles in Ben Stiller's *Reality Bites* (1994), the lovers-on-the-run movie *Love And A .45* (1994) and the little-seen but powerful love story *The Whole Wide World* (1996).

After the success of *Jerry Maguire*, Zellweger wisely moved away from cutesy to play Meryl Streep's angry daughter in the tear-jerking *One True Thing* (1998) and a crazed soap-opera fan in the bizarre *Nurse Betty* (2000). Following her Oscar-nominated tour de force in *Bridget Jones's Diary* (2001; see Canon), she received rave reviews, and another Oscar nomination, for her all-singing, all-dancing Roxie Hart in *Chicago* (2002) – though widespread shock about her skeletal post-Bridget frame consumed as many column inches as her performance – and finally won the Oscar for her show-stealing turn as rumbustious Ruby, the rough-and-ready frontierswoman in Anthony Minghella's epic Civil War romance *Cold Mountain* (2003). That same year, *Down With Love*, a candy-coloured spoof of the sophisticated sex comedies of the 1960s, unjustly fell below the radar, and ultimately got lost in all the hoo-ha surrounding the long-awaited *Bridget Jones: The Edge Of Reason* (2004). Though Zellweger is terrific in the *Bridget* sequel, the film was widely reckoned to be inferior to the original, and once more it was the actress's weight gain that hit the headlines. She took a thankless supporting role in the worthy *Cinderella Man* (2005), a Depression-era biopic starring Russell Crowe as a washed up boxer; fans have far more to look forward to in her upcoming projects, which include, bizarrely, biopics of both Beatrix Potter and Janis Joplin.

One True Thing
dir Carl Franklin, 1998, US, 127m

This unashamed weepie is one of Hollywood's finer cancer movies, elevated beyond schmaltz by its fantastic performances. Zellweger more than holds her own in a stellar cast as the resistant career girl who returns home to care for her ill mother (beautifully played by Meryl Streep) and reappraises her relationship with her father (William Hurt) along the way.

Nurse Betty
dir Neil LaBute, 1999, US, 110m

Zellweger reveals her dark side in this blacker-than-black – and occasionally violent – comedy. She plays a soap-opera-obsessed waitress who, after witnessing the grisly murder of her husband, heads for Hollywood to find her favourite TV doctor (Greg Kinnear), whom she now

believes is not only a real doctor, but also her ex. Morgan Freeman provides quirky love interest.

Down With Love
dir Peyton Reed, 2003, US/Ger, 101m

A delightful pastiche of all those sophisticated 1960s battle-of-the-sexes comedies, with Zellweger and Ewan McGregor relishing the opportunity to channel the spirits of Doris Day and Rock Hudson (with a dash of James Bond). Fresh and frothy, with fizzy dialogue and fab frocks, it's totally daft, and hard to dislike.

Women's Books And Women's Movies:
the lit/flick crossover

The best Austen adaptation?: *Clueless*
(1995)

Women's books and women's movies:

the lit/flick crossover

It is a truth universally acknowledged that women love to watch movies based on books. And that they love reading the books that inspire the films. And, almost invariably, the women who pen the books upon which some of the greatest chick flicks are based have life stories as rich and interesting as anything they write about. There follows a selective account of some of those great women writers who produced great books that were turned into great films.

Louisa May Alcott

American novelist **Louisa May Alcott** (1832–88) turned to writing to help support her impoverished parents: philosophers and social activists, they surrounded their children with high ideas, great literature and stimulating company, but offered little financial stability. In her most popular book, *Little Women* (1868), Alcott created the kind of family – poor but happy, and full of love – for which she, and then generations of children, secretly longed. Seen through the eyes of aspiring writer Jo March, a vivacious tomboy, it's a classic coming-of-age story, set against the background of a distant civil war, with sisters Jo, Meg, Beth and Amy, and their beloved mother, "Marmee", valiantly coping while Pa is away serving as a minister to the Union troops. Romance, friendship, illness, marriage, rivalry, ambition – Alcott wrote about them all with a crisp, cheerful style that, while sometimes dismissed as sentimental, still holds a cherished place in many young women's affections. The novel, a smash hit, was followed by a string of successes including *An Old-Fashioned Girl* (1870); *Little Men* (1871), in which Jo, now married, starts an experimental school for boys; *Work* (1873), about a young woman's struggle as a governess; and *Jo's Boys* (1886), which picks up where *Little Men* left off. An active suffragette, Alcott certainly knew how to write meaty roles for women; it's less well known that she also penned money-spinning thrillers, such as *Pauline's Passion And Punishment* (1862), under the pseudonym A.M. Barnard.

Though *Little Women* has been filmed five times in all, including silent versions in 1917 and 1918, the sprightly 1933 adaptation, with a lively Oscar-winning script and a coltish performance from the young Katharine Hepburn (see Icons) as Jo, counts as the definitive version. However, Mervyn LeRoy's 1949 adaptation also has its charms – all Technicolor MGM opulence, it certainly looks fabulous, with art direction by the great Cedric Gibbons and costumes by Walter Plunkett. The most recent treatment of *Little Women* (1994), from Australian director Gillian Armstrong – whose other literary adaptations include *My Brilliant Career* (1979), *Mrs Soffel* (1984), *Oscar And Lucinda* (1997) and *Charlotte Gray* (2001) – is a tad disappointing, the uncharacteristically twee performances from Susan Sarandon (see Icons) as Marmee and Winona Ryder as Jo undermining the film's putative modern-day feminist message. *Little Men* has been filmed, to little effect, three times – in 1934, 1940 and 1997.

Little Women
dir George Cukor, 1933, US, 115m, b/w

Katharine Hepburn might have been born to play Jo, the feisty New England tomboy. Supported by a strong cast and in the sure hands of director Cukor, she simply shines. The movie itself is a genuinely enchanting slice of old-style Americana, just perfect for a Sunday afternoon's viewing.

Little Women
dir Mervyn LeRoy, 1949, US, 121m

As a lush costume drama, this is up there with MGM's best. The vibrant cast includes June Allyson as Jo, Margaret O'Brien as Beth (who here becomes the youngest sister), a bizarrely blonde Elizabeth Taylor putting in a good comedy turn as selfish Amy, Janet Leigh as Meg, and an early English-language role for Italian singer Rossano Brazzi as the dashing love interest, Professor Bhaer.

Jane Austen

Though the novels of **Jane Austen** (1775–1817), a clergyman's daughter from Hampshire, did well enough in her lifetime, it was not until the late nineteenth century that she became the cult favourite she remains today. Suffused with a knowing irony and populated with beautifully drawn characters, Austen's acerbic books expose the hypocrisy that underpinned respectable Georgian society, when money, status and land were all. And with their spirited heroines, brooding heroes and elegantly paced love stories, they also translate beautifully to the screen: all

six of Austen's major novels have been adapted for either the cinema or TV, many of them more than once. There's been a particular flurry since the mid-1990s – the Jane Austen brand, it seems, guarantees big bucks for filmmakers.

The novel that has struck the most resonant chord at the movies is *Pride And Prejudice* (1813). The Bennet family, refined but poverty-stricken and with no male heirs, need to marry off their five daughters in order to keep their home. The

Austen Power: *Pride & Prejudice* (2005)

Emma comes to Beverly Hills: Alicia Silverstone in *Clueless* (1995)

daughters, however, and in particular Elizabeth – one of literature's most appealing heroines – have their own ideas. Centring on the volatile relationship between Elizabeth and the misunderstood Mr Darcy, this is one of Austen's greatest romances. Its first screen outing (1940) is a star-studded affair, co-adapted by Aldous Huxley and starring the phenomenally popular Greer Garson as Elizabeth. Laurence Olivier, fresh from his star turn in *Rebecca* (see Canon), is suitably sulky as Mr Darcy, but comes across as more grumpy than complex, while Lady Catherine, who in the novel is evil incarnate, is disappointingly bland.

In 1995 a BBC TV adaptation of the novel was seen, and adored, around the world: Jennifer Ehle had just the right amount of pluck as Elizabeth, while, unlike the beautiful Olivier, the rather ordinary Colin Firth made a delightfully vulnerable Mr Darcy. As in the book, he became increasingly attractive as the series continued, and the image of him emerging, drenched, from a pond has become nothing less than iconic. The script, too, adapted by TV darling Andrew Davies, had a crisp edge that Austen herself would have admired. In many ways Joe Wright's *Pride & Prejudice* (2005) has similar strengths: Keira Knightley is suitably stubborn, if a bit too pretty, as Elizabeth, while Matthew Macfadyen nails it as the uptight, inarticulate Darcy, all pent up emotion and wounded pride.

We mustn't overlook *Bridget Jones's Diary* (2001; see Canon) either, an adaptation of Helen Fielding's novel of the same name (see p.217), which not only makes several sneaky references to *Pride And Prejudice* but also echoes Austen's drily ironic voice. In Fielding's book Mark Darcy was based on Colin Firth's Mr Darcy in the TV series; to cast Firth as Darcy in the *Bridget* movie was nothing short of genius. Austen buffs will find further parallels, from the long-standing feud between Cleaver and Darcy, which mirrors Mr Darcy's relationship with Wickham, to Bridget's job at Pemberley Press (Austen's Mr Darcy lives at Pemberley estate). There is also *Bride & Prejudice* (2004), directed by Gurinder Chadha (see Icons), which gives a zingy Bollywood twist to the proceedings.

The earliest of Austen's major novels, *Sense And Sensibility* (1811) is a comedy of manners about the two Dashwood sisters, who, impoverished after their father's death, must make good marriages in order for their family to survive. The 1995 movie version, scripted by Emma Thompson, keeps the novel's knowing edge – helped by Ang Lee's cool-headed direction – while also going down the sunshine-and-picnics route. With a raft of polished turns from stalwart British character actors, it's hard to fault.

Probably Austen's most sophisticated work, *Emma* (1815), about a matchmaking minx whose arrogance gets her into all sorts of tangles, is not only packed with quirky minor characters – the vulgar Mrs Elton and chatty Mrs Bates stand out – but is also her most slyly ironic book. The movie *Emma* (1996), like 2005's *Pride & Prejudice*, is at pains to present itself as modern, almost edgy, with its sweeping camerawork and kinetic energy. Gwyneth Paltrow's gutsy Emma is all girl power, driving her own carriage and the like – we even see her competing with Mr Knightley (Jeremy Northam) in an archery tournament. Such obvious metaphors would surely have Austen turning in her grave. Far truer to the spirit of the original is Amy Heckerling's film *Clueless* (1995; see Canon), which transports early-nineteenth-century English snobbery to a status-obsessed Beverly Hills high school. The story of matchmaking babe Cher (a career-best role for Alicia Silverstone) – a blonde teen who

is at once arrogant, lovable and, naturally, clueless – it breezes deceptively through the dark ironies and pain of the novel, with a relish for spoken language that Austen herself would have envied.

Mansfield Park (1814), the story of impecunious Fanny Price, sent to live with her snooty relatives, is long, dense and – in its engagement with the issue of colonial slavery – explicitly political. Canadian director Patricia Rozema loosely used the novel, along with Austen's own letters and journals, to make the compelling movie *Mansfield Park* (1999), which benefits from a light touch and an interesting injection of Austen's own character to make Fanny a little feistier.

Austen completists will want to check out *Persuasion* (1995), based on her final book (1818), which is less satirical and a little less complex than the writer's earlier works. Anne Elliot is an older heroine, nursing dreams of a lost love and about to be left on the shelf – rumour has it that the book is semi-autobiographical, though Austen herself dismissed the mild-mannered Anne as being "almost too good". Originally made for British TV, the movie translated well to the big screen, with a touching performance by Amanda Root, a familiar face from a number of BBC period dramas.

Sense And Sensibility
dir Ang Lee, 1995, US, 136m

With its happy combination of crisp direction and smart screenplay, this confident adaptation also boasts some classic best-of-British performances. Emma Thompson and Kate Winslet as the Dashwood sisters are, as they should be, more handsome than pretty, with plenty of brains between them, while their love interests – Hugh Grant (mumbling, clumsy), Alan Rickman (still waters run deep) and Greg Wise (handsome but feckless) – are spot on.

Mansfield Park
dir Patricia Rozema, 1999, US/UK, 112m

This bold adaptation benefits from a darker tone than many, and approaches the original novel with brio, using aspects of Austen's own life to blur fiction with memoir. The Australian actress Frances O'Connor is superb as Fanny, with strong support from Jonny Lee Miller and Alessandro Nivola as the two, very different, men in her life.

Pride & Prejudice
dir Joe Wright, 2005, Fr/UK, 127m

The much-vaunted "realism" of this most recent adaptation of Austen's beloved novel – squawking chickens running around the Bennets' shabby house, for example, and greasy, straggly hair for Lizzie – does add atmosphere, but glamorous star appeal (in particular, the lingering shots of Keira Knightley's luminous face) and endless lush sweeps through the glorious English countryside are also crucial to its considerable charm.

Charlotte Brontë

Charlotte Brontë (1816–55) was brought up by her aunt and father, a strict curate, in a draughty old house in Haworth, Yorkshire. By all accounts hers was a dour upbringing, and after being sent to a strict school for girls (the inspiration for *Jane Eyre*'s gloomy Lowood), she and her siblings began to create their own intricate fantasy worlds, peopled with generations of richly drawn characters. Much like one of the heroines in her books, Charlotte worked for a while as a governess before travelling, with her sister Emily, to Brussels, where she studied languages and fell in unrequited love with a dashing Belgian professor. Returning home with a broken heart, she threw herself into her writing, and in 1847 published *Jane Eyre* under the pseudonym Currer Bell. The novel, a beautifully told story of a rebellious,

abused girl who becomes a reserved governess, was regarded as a little risqué at the time with its strong, silent seam of sexual passion. Following the tragic deaths in 1848 of her sisters Anne and Emily, and her alcoholic brother Branwell, Charlotte continued to write, publishing *Shirley* (1849), a socially conscious novel that called for active roles for women, and *Villette* (1853), based on her sad experience as a teacher in Brussels. Charlotte married an aged curate in 1854, and died months later from complications due to pregnancy. Criticized by her contemporaries for their emotionalism – the poet and essayist Matthew Arnold spat that she was full of "nothing but hunger, rebellion and rage" – her novels are infused with passion and frustration, abounding in subtle abuse and dysfunctional families.

Jane Eyre saw five silent movie adaptations between 1910 and 1921, plus another, truly abominable, version in 1934. The 1944 film, however, is just right: a skewed, deliciously Gothic love story, all low angles, swirling fog and looming shadows. The scowling, ugly-handsome Orson Welles, cape billowing in the howling wind, throws himself with gusto into the role of the tormented Mr Rochester, evolving from threatening to blustering, and finally to vulnerable; Joan Fontaine, meanwhile, plain and querulous as the browbeaten Jane, comes across as at once masochistic, otherworldly and tough. Franco Zeffirelli's 1996 version, starring – in surely the most bizarre casting decision ever – William Hurt (Mr Rochester, blonde?) and Charlotte Gainsbourg, can't hold a flickering candle to it.

Jane Eyre
dir Robert Stevenson, 1944, US, 96m, b/w

With its magnificent performances and sparky dialogue, Bernard Herrmann's emotional soundtrack and George

Barnes's brooding cinematography, this is one of the best screen adaptations of any novel ever, translating Charlotte Brontë's passionate, psychologically complex prose into an expressionistic masterpiece.

Emily Brontë

Emily Brontë (1818–48) was the most mysterious of all the Brontë sisters, an isolated and intense woman who wrote brilliant poetry and was deeply attached to the wild Yorkshire moors where she lived. *Wuthering Heights* (1847), a strange, dark novel about forbidden love, was slated as morbid by contemporary critics; after Emily's death from consumption, however, it was reappraised, and by the end of the century was being lauded as a work of Gothic genius. With some of the most ardent dialogue ever put to paper – take, for example, Heathcliff's, "Haunt me, then! Haunt your murderer! I know that ghosts have wandered on the Earth. Be with me always! Take any form, drive me mad, only do not leave me in this dark alone where I cannot find you. I cannot live without my life! I cannot die without my soul!" – *Wuthering Heights* is ideal material for the big screen. The secret, however, lies in preventing all that passion from descending into histrionics. The book has been adapted at least eight times, including a Spanish-language version, *Abismos de pasión* (1953), directed by surrealist Luis Buñuel; a Turkish version, *Ölmeyen ask* (*Immortal Love*, 1966); *Arashi ga oka* (1988), which transports the story to medieval Japan; and a Filipino melodrama *Hihintayin kita sa langit* (*I'll Wait For You In Heaven*, 1991).

The definitive *Wuthering Heights* movie, however, was made in 1939 (see Canon). Romantic beyond belief, it covers the first half of the novel only, boiling the story down to the doomed love between the foundling Heathcliff (Laurence Olivier) and his sister by adoption, the wild-hearted Cathy (Merle Oberon). If you're after something a little more naturalistic, take a look at the 1970 version, which features a young, feral Timothy Dalton, along with Anna Calder-Marshall, who brings a wind-ravaged, bruised quality to the role of Cathy. For perversity, however, 1992's *Wuthering Heights* – in which Ralph Fiennes's seriously damaged Heathcliff makes mincemeat of Juliette Binoche's Cathy – has the edge.

Daphne du Maurier

Born into a privileged family – her grandfather was the artist and writer George du Maurier, her father a famous actor/manager – **Daphne du Maurier** (1907–89) wrote bestselling romances, often historical pieces, for female audiences on both sides of the Atlantic. Usually set in the author's beloved Cornwall, they are strongly evocative of place, Gothic masterpieces with a rich vein of psychological realism. *Jamaica Inn* (1936) and *Frenchman's Creek* (1941) are favourites, but by far the most popular is *Rebecca* (1938), a suspenseful story of jealousy, obsession and insanity that boasts one of the most compelling opening lines in literature – "Last night I dreamed I went to Manderley again" – and, famously, an unnamed heroine. At once a Gothic thriller and a Cinderella story, it has strong echoes of *Jane Eyre* (the gloomy house with an insane female presence, the brooding hero, the mysterious ex-wife, the meek heroine), and, interestingly, Joan Fontaine played the female lead in both the movies of the books. Though dismissed by some as fluff, the novel generally

A quiet word: the second Mrs de Winter with Mrs Danvers, the housekeeper from Hell, in *Rebecca* (1940)

received rave reviews. Rumours abounded that the nameless second Mrs de Winter was based on du Maurier herself, haunted by the memory of her domineering father, and, perhaps, her husband's glamorous ex-fiancé. Alfred Hitchcock directed the movie version in 1940 (see Canon), an unnerving psychological chiller that made du Maurier one of the most famous writers in the world. It's a story that gets under your skin, and leaves many questions unanswered; in 1993 Susan Hill wrote *Mrs De Winter*, which takes up where *Rebecca* left off, while Sally Beauman's *Rebecca's Tale* (2001), a prequel, tells the story from the first Mrs de Winter's point of view.

My Cousin Rachel, which appeared in 1951, is a suspense novel set in nineteenth-century Cornwall. There are echoes of *Rebecca* – a huge country manor, an unreliable narrator, a seductive heroine and an uneasy swirl of suspicion and paranoia – but this time there is no resolution, and the doubts that surround the mysterious Rachel remain. The movie version (1952) is less compelling than *Rebecca*, but well worth a look.

My Cousin Rachel
dir Henry Koster, 1952, US, 98m, b/w

An atmospheric piece of psychological intrigue, featuring a young Richard Burton, Oscar-nominated for this, his first Hollywood role, and Joan Fontaine's sister, Olivia de Havilland (who was more often seen in good-girl roles like Melanie in *Gone With The Wind*), playing against type as the mysterious Rachel.

Helen Fielding

After publishing *Cause Celeb* (1994), a patchy comedy about celebrity fund-raising, British journalist **Helen Fielding** (1958–) agreed to pen a column in *The Independent* in order to finance her next novel. The result, *Bridget Jones's Diary*, was a deceptively light, sly satire on urban relationship and work dilemmas, given extra kudos by appearing in a respectable, vaguely left-wing newspaper. Dinner parties and wine bars all around Britain rang with thirty-something women recounting the hapless Bridget's latest scrapes, and it became self-evident that Fielding should adapt the column into a book. The novel was published in 1996; rave reviews and record-breaking paperback sales followed, and a phenomenon was born. The column's closely observed details, recognizable characters and distinctive comic voice – the pithy,

truncated sentences necessitated by newspaper word counts – translated beautifully to a full-length book, which Fielding, a talented ironist, loosely based on Jane Austen's *Pride And Prejudice* (see p.211). Drawn from events and conversations in the author's own life as a single professional Londoner, *Bridget Jones's Diary* created a new vocabulary – singleton, smug marrieds, fuckwittage – and though it was criticized in some quarters as being "anti-feminist", representing all that was supposedly despicable about chick lit, in fact Bridget's breezy intelligence undercuts any putative paranoia or low self-esteem. There were doubts at first as to whether its particularly self-deprecating British humour would strike a chord in the rest of the world, but massive international sales – including in the notoriously tricky US – soon put paid to the naysayers. The eagerly awaited film, directed by Fielding's friend Sharon Maguire, happily lived up to all expectations. *Bridget Jones's Diary* (2001) broadens the comedy of the book, adeptly mingling its sly irony with British sitcom humour. Renée Zellweger (see Icons), a gifted comic actress, makes an endearing Bridget, while casting Colin Firth – who had audiences swooning with his portrayal of Mr Darcy in the 1995 BBC TV adaptation of *Pride And Prejudice* – as Mark Darcy, and Hugh Grant (see Icons) – who had cornered the market in playing a certain type of bumbling English male – as the sleazy love-god Daniel Cleaver, was nothing short of inspired.

Fielding's third novel, *Bridget Jones: The Edge Of Reason* (1999), chronicles what happens after Bridget and Darcy get together. Naturally, all does not run smoothly – there's even a spell in a dodgy Thai jail – and Fielding also included a cheeky in-joke about Bridget's obsession with the BBC's *Pride And Prejudice*, and in particular with actor Colin Firth. Though it lacked the freshness of the first novel, fans remained loyal, and *Bridget* mark two sold well. It was the same with the film version (2004), which, despite some sharp comic moments, didn't quite deliver – and was forgiven anyway.

Fielding returned to top form with her fourth novel, *Olivia Joules And The Overactive Imagination* (2004), a contemporary spy spoof with another lovable heroine; and in August 2005 Bridget returned to *The Independent*, older but little wiser, and obsessing about pregnancy.

Olivia Goldsmith

Larger-than-life American businesswoman **Olivia Goldsmith** (1949–2004) faced rejection after rejection while sending out her manuscript *The First Wives Club* (1992) to publishers. When it was finally sold, after a huge bidding war resulting from interest from the major Hollywood film studios, she threw a "so there" party, invited all the publishing bigwigs, and with characteristic chutzpah decorated the room with her rejection letters. For the book jacket, and all publicity, she donned a blonde wig and shades, taking a swipe at the industry's standards of glamour and beauty. A wickedly funny revenge fantasy that spoke to any woman tossed aside for a younger model, *The First Wives Club* caught the zeitgeist and shot to the top of the bestseller lists. The film version (1996) was also a smash, its immortal catchphrase, "Don't get mad, get everything," becoming a battle cry for scorned middle-aged women everywhere.

Goldsmith has been credited with creating her own chick lit sub-genre: "get even" fiction. Her other novels – among them *Flavor Of The Month* (1993), in which an ageing star remodels herself into a glamorous starlet, and *Switcheroo* (1998), about a woman who tries to win back her husband by recreating herself in the image of his girlfriend – return again and again to the themes of divorce, self esteem and getting older. In a cruel twist, Goldsmith – who even while satirizing plastic surgery in her novels was no stranger to the scalpel – died after suffering a heart attack during a chin tuck.

🎬 The First Wives Club
dir Hugh Wilson, 1996, US, 103m

Veteran stars Diane Keaton, Bette Midler and Goldie Hawn relish the broad comedy in this high-octane revenge movie, approaching "Operation Hell's Fury" with relish. The film combines heartfelt pathos with savage one-liners – and a rousing chorus of Leslie Gore's classic 1960s pop song "You Don't Own Me".

Joanne Harris

The half-French Yorkshire woman **Joanne Harris** (1964–) was still teaching at a grammar school in Leeds when her third novel, *Chocolat* (1999), became an international bestseller. A gentle fable about a woman who shakes up a puritanical French village by arriving with her young daughter and opening a chocolate shop, it particularly appealed to women who understood that most ills can be cured by a nice box of Dairy Milk. The film version (2000) looks scrumptious, and is worth watching for Juliette Binoche (who wears some darling 1950s outfits) and a short but sweet turn from Johnny Depp. Without the dark undertow of the book, however, it can verge into the territory of twee, and might leave a slightly sickly aftertaste.

Adaptations in The Canon

If you need further proof of the intimate relationship between great books and great movies, turn to the Canon chapter; almost half the fifty classic chick flicks included there started life as novels.

Fannie Hurst

Of all the writers featured in this chapter, popular American novelist **Fannie Hurst** (1889–1968) can boast the highest number of works that have been adapted into films – 29 in all. With a career spanning more than fifty years, Hurst started writing short stories for the *Saturday Evening Post* in 1912 and published her first novel in 1914. Her books dealt with the day-to-day trials of poor urban workers, frequently women – shop girls from New York and rag trade workers from the slums, for example – and, unusually, often featured Jewish and black characters in leading roles. Derided by other authors and critics, who liked to dismiss them as "trash", they were nonetheless hugely popular, and by 1925 Fannie Hurst, along with novelist Booth Tarkington, was the highest earning writer in the US.

Born to first-generation Jewish parents in Hamilton, Ohio, Hurst suffered a disrupted, difficult childhood; she went on to graduate from university before taking a number of menial jobs where she could observe people going about their daily business. From a young age she was interested in social issues, including equal pay for women and civil rights. Radically, in 1920, after it was revealed that she had secretly married five years earlier, and that she and her husband lived in separate houses, she insisted that a married woman had the right to keep her own name and her own freedom. In the 1930s she was closely associated with both Eleanor Roosevelt and the African-American writer Zora Neale Hurston, and continued to work for liberal and left-wing causes throughout her life.

Humoresque (1920), a film based on Hurst's 1919 story about a poor Jewish violin prodigy, was perceived as controversial in its portrayal of the hardships faced by Jews in America; when it was remade in 1946, however, audiences were more preoccupied by the spectacular performances from John Garfield as the tormented musician and Joan Crawford (see Icons) as the society woman who adores him. Hurst's novel *Five And Ten* (1929) tells a gripping story of a nouveau riche family that falls apart after moving to New York City; the 1931 movie, however, despite the presence of soon-to-be matinée idol Leslie Howard and popular comic actress Marion Davies – long-time lover of millionaire newspaper tycoon William Randolph Hearst – doesn't really deliver.

With its account of two single mothers – one white and one black – struggling to get by, *Imitation Of Life*, published in 1933, pushes all the melodrama buttons while also foregrounding tricky social issues. The 1934 movie, with Claudette Colbert, was lauded by the *New York Times* as "a gripping and powerful, if slightly diffuse drama, which discussed the mother love question, the race question, the business woman question, the mother and daughter question and the love renunciation question". Above all, however, the film works as a beautifully drawn character study. And the 1959 remake by Douglas Sirk (see Canon), a heart-rending melodrama that didn't flinch from portraying the trauma of racism in the US, remains as freshly painful today as it was then.

Sister Act (1937), a novel about the lives and loves of four musical sisters, was adapted four times for the screen (but never with Whoopi Goldberg): *Four Daughters* (1938) was so successful that it was quickly followed by the sequels *Four Wives* (1939), which deals with the sisters' problems with marriage and child-rearing, and the less successful *Four Mothers* (1941). *Young At Heart* (1954), starring Doris Day (see Icons) and Frank Sinatra, is a breezy musical replay of *Four Daughters*; its classic singalong title track became one of Sinatra's standards.

Hurst's bestselling weepie *Back Street* (1931), about a woman who, having missed her chance to marry her true love, lives out her life in shabby backstreet apartments as his mistress, was adapted for the screen three times. The first version (1932) is by far the best – a women's picture in the classic mould. In the 1941 adaptation Margaret Sullavan and Charles Boyer never quite convince, while in 1961 Susan Hayward is far too feisty, her clothes too gorgeous and her lodgings too fabulous (in Italy and France, no less!) to really pluck our heartstrings.

Back Street
dir John M. Stahl, 1932, US, 92m, b/w

This little-seen and highly recommended melodrama boasts a quietly heartbreaking turn from the wonderful

Irene Dunne as the woman who sacrifices her own happiness for an impossible love affair. With understated direction from Stahl, it's nonetheless a searing commentary on society's double standards; stock up on the tissues.

Humoresque
dir Jean Negulesco, 1946, US, 125m, b/w

A fabulous role for Joan Crawford as the needy, lustful socialite who becomes dangerously obsessed with a handsome young violinist (John Garfield). Bette Davis said that the final close-up of Crawford's face was one of the greatest in film history – high praise indeed from the star's great rival.

Grace Metalious

You may not know the name **Grace Metalious** (1924–64), but you will probably have heard of her one successful novel: she's the woman behind the sensational blockbuster *Peyton Place* (1956), a notoriously savage exposé of the rot at the core of American suburbia. *Valley Of The Dolls*, *The Stepford Wives*, *Dallas*, *Twin Peaks*, *Desperate Housewives* – all owe a debt to Grace and her tawdry tale.

Born Grace de Repentigny, the Franco-American writer spent most of her life poor, catapulting straight from a broken home into a marriage with her penniless childhood sweetheart. Life changed drastically, however, with the publication of her steamy book, which became the biggest seller of the decade and soon overtook Margaret Mitchell's *Gone With The Wind* as the bestselling novel of all time. *Peyton Place* reveals the dirty secrets and sexual scandal beneath the surface of a respectable small New England town: illegitimacy, abortion, rape, teenage sex, incest, suicide, murder – nothing was out of bounds. Dismissed as "literary sewage" by leading critics,

the book was banned in many places throughout the US, including the author's home town, Gilmanton in New Hampshire, upon which it was thought to be based. Metalious, however, who earned the nickname "Pandora in Blue Jeans" – she was often photographed, decidedly ordinary-looking, wearing denim – remained unapologetic.

The overblown 1957 movie, starring Lana Turner, was as big a hit as the novel. Days after the Oscar ceremony, from which the film came away with none of the nine awards for which it had been nominated, Turner's 14-year-old daughter Cheryl killed her mother's mobster boyfriend with a butcher's knife, an incident that read like something straight from the pages of the book. A less successful sequel, *Return To Peyton Place,* followed in 1961, along with a five-year-long American prime time soap that made stars of Ryan O'Neal and Mia Farrow.

Metalious's follow-up novels, *Return To Peyton Place* (1959), *The Tight White Collar* (1961) and *No Adam In Eden* (1963), didn't do much amid rumours that they, and perhaps even the original novel, were ghostwritten. A heavy drinker, Metalious divorced her husband and remarried, partying wildly and throwing her considerable earnings around. She remarried her first husband in 1960; the union lasted just three years before she finally descended into full-blown alcoholism and depression, dying of cirrhosis of the liver aged 39.

Peyton Place
dir Mark Robson, 1957, US, 162m

Although it was nominated for nine Oscars, this histrionic melodrama has dated terribly; Lana Turner, however, puts in a typically charismatic performance as Connie, the single mother with a past, and the movie is without doubt a camp curiosity, a gruesomely compelling cavalcade of simmering sexual secrets.

Margaret Mitchell

Margaret Mitchell (1900–49) may have just one book to her name, but what a book it is. A sweeping epic romance, set during and after the American Civil War, *Gone With The Wind* (1936) is probably the most popular novel ever written, and gives us one of the greatest heroines of our time, the strong-willed Scarlett O'Hara. At once profoundly romantic, darkly elegiac and hard-nosed – Scarlett is driven less by love than by a fierce determination to keep her land – this 1000-page tour de force also shaped a popular image of the Deep South that endures to this day.

Mitchell, born in Atlanta to a suffragette mother and lawyer father, led a comfortable, cultured childhood. A spirited girl and a history buff, at the age of 15 she wrote: "If I were a boy, I would try for West Point, if I could make it, or I'd be a prize fighter – anything for the thrills." Having spent a year on the east coast studying medicine at prestigious Smith College, Mitchell moved back home after her mother's death in 1919. A debutante who, somewhat like Scarlett, shocked polite society with her rebellious behaviour – she once performed the outrageous "Apache" dance at a swanky ball – she spent the early 1920s writing pithy Jazz Age articles for local publications, and suffered a brief, abusive marriage. After remarrying, she gave up journalism, burrowed herself away in her small, shabby apartment ("the Dump") and, in 1926, began working on a novel. Fiercely protective about her manuscript, Mitchell worked on it for a full ten years before presenting a dog-eared, stained version to a publishing bigwig who, sniffing gold, immediately snapped it up. *Gone With The Wind* received mixed critical attention, both for its writing style and for its nostalgic portrayal of the Old South,

Margaret Mitchell

but within weeks it had broken sales records. In 1937 the book was awarded the Pulitzer prize – highly unusual for a popular 1000-page blockbuster written by a woman. Publishing a historical novel about the American South is not without its pitfalls, however, and the controversy surrounding the book's race politics – the inclusion of Klan characters, for example – raged for decades. Mitchell herself, who always denied accusations of racism, anonymously established fifty scholarships for African-American medical students at a local college.

In 1939, after years of feverish speculation, gossip and publicity, the opulent three-hour movie *Gone With The Wind* (see Canon) finally premiered in a star-studded three-day extravaganza in Atlanta. Despite sniffy reviews from some quarters, the film was a glorious success, going on to win ten Oscars including Best Picture. The book's references to the Ku Klux Klan, along with any use of the word "nigger", were excised from the movie, but its portrayal of black stereotypes remained controversial. That said, the black characters, far from being mere ciphers, are unusually pivotal for a mainstream film of the period. Hattie McDaniel is particularly memorable as Scarlett's plain-speaking Mammy, a performance for which she became the first African-American ever to win an Oscar. With its pitch-perfect performances and visual opulence – not to mention that iconic musical refrain – *Gone With The Wind* still stands up as one of the best melodramas ever seen on screen.

Mitchell, who never finished another novel, died after being knocked down by a car near her home. *Gone With The Wind* fans, however – of whom there continue to be millions worldwide – were desperate to see Scarlett and Rhett get back together, and so in 1991 Alexandra Ripley produced an authorized sequel, *Scarlett*. Lacking the verve of the original, it received universally bad reviews; nonetheless, that didn't deter the fans, and it topped the bestseller lists in the wink of an eye. There is no sign yet, however, of a movie.

Toni Morrison

Following her working-class childhood in Ohio, where she grew up reading Tolstoy and listening to her father's retelling of African-American folk tales, **Toni Morrison** (1931–) – real name Chloe Anthony Wofford – graduated in English literature and went on to work as a teacher and book editor. Her first novel, *The Bluest Eye*, about a black girl who prays every night that she will wake up with blue eyes, was published in 1970 after a dozen rejections by publishers; it was followed by *Sula* (1973), a story of female friendship, the acclaimed family saga *Song Of Solomon* (1977), and *Tar Baby* (1981), a gripping romance. With *Beloved* (1987), Morrison, who combines her fierce political sensibility with a delicate, melancholy beauty in her storytelling, reached the peak of her powers. A haunting novel – ghost story, maternal melodrama, murder mystery and romance – it is above all about the unspeakable evil of slavery. Rarely had a novel mined such forbidden, dreadful emotion with such humanity, and in 1988 it won the Pulitzer prize. To translate such a book to the screen was going to be a tough challenge, and credit has to go to director Jonathan Demme for his dreamy, disturbing 1998 movie, *Beloved*. Oprah Winfrey, who had snapped up the book's film rights soon after publication, is superb as Sethe, the mother tormented by the past, while Danny Glover, Thandie Newton and Kimberly Elise all put in finely honed performances.

Morrison's later novels – *Jazz* (1992), *Paradise* (1998) and *Love* (2003) – are increasingly abstract. They warrant the effort it takes to read them, but it's difficult to imagine any of them being adapted for the screen. Toni Morrison became the first black woman to win the Nobel prize for literature in 1993.

Beloved
dir Jonathan Demme, 1998, US, 172m

With its otherworldly translation of Morrison's astonishing prose, Demme's ambitious film does a brilliant job. It received rave reviews from the critics, but was a little too strange – and, with its savage indictment of America's history, too challenging – to make much of a dent at the box office.

Olive Higgins Prouty

American novelist **Olive Higgins Prouty** (1882–1974), prolific throughout the 1930s and 40s, is best known for her books *Stella Dallas* (1923) and *Now, Voyager* (1941), both of which were adapted into screenplays. Her novels count as both popular women's fiction and respected "literature", often dealing with the struggle of a rebellious, frustrated woman to define herself, and never afraid to confront thorny issues surrounding class, age and motherhood. Most importantly, they're gripping tales.

Born into a wealthy Boston family, Prouty found it hard to balance her writing, which she loved but worried made her selfish, with the demands of being a "good" wife and mother. Following the death of one of her children in 1919, she vowed to devote herself to her family – only to suffer a nervous breakdown four years later when another child, her beloved daughter Olivia, died of encephalitis. A spell in a sanitarium followed, where her psychiatrist advised her to take up writing again; a year later she produced *Stella Dallas*, a heart-rending tale of maternal sacrifice that focuses on two very different, but very good, mothers. Adapted into a play, it was filmed in 1925, and then again in 1937, and also inspired a long-running radio soap (which Prouty hated). A classic women's movie, starring the incomparable Barbara Stanwyck, the 1937 *Stella Dallas* (see Canon) packed a devastating emotional punch and was adored by female audiences. Stanwyck is perfect as Stella, bringing to the part just the right combination of wrong-side-of-the-tracks street smarts and loving big-heartedness. Bette Midler, however, who played the role in the 1990 version, *Stella*, is too much larger-than-life, and at the same time too fragile, to be really convincing. Updated to the present day, the story loses its focus, its historical context, and its credibility.

Prouty's *Now, Voyager* offers another fascinating take on motherhood. In the 1942 movie (see Canon), Bette Davis brings her usual tough-but-fragile brittleness to the role of Charlotte Vale, a middle-aged spinster so bullied by her mother that she has a nervous breakdown. Prouty's own spell in a sanitarium led to a long period of creative fulfillment; in this story Charlotte, following treatment from a kindly psychiatrist (Claude Rains), emerges like a faltering butterfly to take on the world anew. A classic weepie, the film is brimful of iconic moments, not least when Paul Henreid, as Charlotte's forbidden love, lights two cigarettes in his mouth before meaningfully handing one to her.

Prouty was a philanthropist and a graduate of the private Smith College, and in later years established a scholarship there for a promising writer – it was awarded to the young poet Sylvia Plath, whom the older woman continued to support throughout her life. Prouty's reward? To appear, thinly disguised, as the trashy and unfeasibly rich writer Philomena Guinea in Plath's semi-autobiographical novel *The Bell Jar.*

Jacqueline Susann

The ebullient **Jacqueline Susann** (1918–74) was an acerbic celebrity-hound who turned her hand to acting, singing, modelling, TV presenting and playwriting, before becoming the bestselling author of the 1960s – and one of the bestselling female authors ever. Her personal life was as juicy as anything she wrote about: starting out in the 1930s as a minor starlet, she married the public relations maestro Irving Mansfield in 1939, before having numerous affairs with partners as varied as Eddie Cantor, Ethel Merman and Coco Chanel.

In 1963 Susann published *Every Night, Josephine!*, a whimsical tale told from the point of view of a pampered poodle. *Josephine* did well enough, but it was with *Valley Of The Dolls* (1966), a racy exposé of Hollywood's sleazy underbelly, that she really hit pay dirt. A brash, vulgar doorstopper of a book, telling the interweaving stories of a top model, a Broadway star and a Hollywood starlet, it was an instant success. Reviewers hated it, audiences loved it (gossiping and speculating about which real-life figures the characters were based on), and the indefatigable Susann pounded the talk show and book tour circuit to sell it. Glamorous and larger-than-life, all Pucci trouser suits and bouffant hair, she summed up a certain decadent spirit of the 1960s – and above all she knew how to milk it. Her 1969 novel, *The Love Machine*, did for TV what *Dolls* had done for the movies, while *Once Is*

Not Enough (1973) was another scathing look at Hollywood, written while Susann was suffering from the cancer that finally killed her.

Valley Of The Dolls the movie (1967) was as popular as the book, and equally slammed by the critics. Susann, meanwhile, hated the tacked-on happy ending, claiming that the real world didn't work like that; the cynical re-release of the movie in 1969, after one of its stars, Sharon Tate – by now eight months pregnant – was stabbed to death in her home by members of Charles Manson's "family", would seem to back up her point. The movie version of *The Love Machine* (1971) is pretty dire, while *Once Is Not Enough* (1975), though not as irresistibly tacky as *Dolls*, is another delicious slice of kitsch.

In 1999 Bette Midler played Susann in the lacklustre biopic *Isn't She Great?* – an opportunity wasted if ever there was one.

🎬 Valley Of The Dolls
dir Mark Robson, 1967, US, 123m

From the director of *Peyton Place,* this is, if anything, even more overblown than the earlier film, with drugs added to the sordid mix. Starring Barbara Parkins as Anne (who, it was rumoured, was based on Susann), Patty Duke as Neely (Judy Garland? Betty Hutton?), Susan Hayward as Helen (Ethel Merman?) and Sharon Tate as Jennifer (Marilyn Monroe? Or perhaps Carole Landis, another doomed starlet who was said to have been Susann's lover?), it's a camper-than-camp bitch fest, and has become an enduring gay favourite.

Amy Tan

In her youth, California-born **Amy Tan** (1952), the daughter of first-generation Chinese immigrants, had a vexed relationship with her mother. They battled over everything from her boyfriends to where, and what, she should study. The differences between the two women – one who, having lost custody of her children, was forced to leave them behind when she escaped Communist China for the West, the other a young woman struggling to define herself as an American – seemed insurmountable. A trip to China together in 1987 shifted something, however, and Tan, with a new perspective on her mother's experience, vowed to fashion the small collection of short stories she was working on into a novel. The result, *The Joy Luck Club* (1989), a multifaceted maternal melodrama about four sets of Chinese-American women, received rave reviews for its heartfelt storytelling, and was an immediate bestseller.

Tan worked on the screenplay for the film version (1993), directed by Wayne Wang – who had covered similar territory with the lovely *Dim Sum* in 1985, and was still, long before his execrable *Maid In Manhattan* (2002) and so-so *Last Holiday* (2006), an interesting moviemaker. The collaboration was successful, and although the book's multi-story structure didn't translate brilliantly to the screen, the film did well at the box office.

Tan's later novels, *The Kitchen God's Wife* (1991), more explicitly inspired by her mother's traumatic life, and *The Bonesetter's Daughter* (2001), an accomplished account of a Chinese-American woman's search for her past, continue the mother-daughter theme; in *The Hundred Secret Senses* (1995), meanwhile, the central relationship is between two half sisters.

🎬 The Joy Luck Club
dir Wayne Wang, 1993, US, 139m

A satisfying maternal melodrama that grapples with age gaps and cultural clashes among three close-knit generations of Chinese-American women. Keeping the book's rich characterizations intact, it's compelling viewing, but relies a little too heavily on voice-overs, and by packing in so many fascinating stories never quite gives each strand the time it deserves.

Alice Walker

The extraordinary life story of African-American novelist/poet **Alice Walker** (1944–) reads just like something from one of her books. Born the youngest of eight to a family of sharecroppers in Georgia, she was blinded in one eye at the age of 8 after her brother accidentally shot her during a game of cowboys and Indians. Bullied because of her ugly scar, the once outgoing and tomboyish Alice turned to poetry and the Classics as a refuge. 1958, however, saw a cataract operation and a restoration of her confidence; in an all-American happy ending she was even made Prom Queen. An academic high-achiever, she went on to attend a couple of prestigious women's colleges, and, already a vocal civil rights activist, travelled to Africa on an exchange visit. After a traumatic abortion, and her subsequent depression, Walker was inspired to write her first poetry anthology, *Once*, which was eventually published in 1968. In 1967 she married a white lawyer and moved to Mississippi, where they lived as the state's first ever legally married inter-racial couple and worked tirelessly for the civil rights movement.

While pregnant with her daughter Rebecca, Walker wrote her first novel, *The Third Life Of Grange Copeland* (1970), about the effects of poverty and marginalization on black people; although admired for its literary merit, the book was criticized for its negative portrayal of African-American men. She remained politically active, however, writing *Meridian* (1976), about women in the civil rights struggle, and publishing her most famous book, *The Color Purple*, in 1982. A rich, epic epistolary novel about a black woman's eventual triumph over a lifetime of abuse, *The Color Purple* boasts vibrant characterizations and a gripping story, told in a distinctive African-American voice. It won the Pulitzer prize in 1983 – a first for an African-American female author. The eagerly awaited movie (1985), which starred Oprah Winfrey, Danny Glover and a young comedienne called Whoopi Goldberg, received a mixed reception in the US. Again, some criticized the depiction of the black men, and others were furious that white male blockbuster director Steven Spielberg had got his hands on this black woman's story. Spielberg, however – who if nothing else certainly knows how to reach a mass audience – handles the material with grace, creating an unabashedly sentimental melodrama with a big heart and uplifting message.

In *The Same River Twice: Honoring The Difficult* (1996), Walker writes about her time as consultant on the movie – during which she was incapacitated with Lyme disease – and her feelings about the reception of both the novel and the film; it also includes her original, eventually unused, script. Though she continues to be one of America's most important black writers, producing poetry, essays and children's books, so far none of Walker's later novels – *The Temple Of My Familiar* (1989), *Possessing The Secret Of Joy* (1992), which is about female genital mutilation, and *By The Light Of My Father's Smile* (1998) – have achieved the broad success of *The Color Purple*.

The Color Purple
dir Steven Spielberg, 1985, US, 154m

It may be a different creature from the book, but as a women's picture *The Color Purple* pushes all the right buttons: a big, visually lush experience, it boasts beautiful performances all round and a delicious dose of shameless heart-tugging. Newcomer Whoopi Goldberg is splendid as the poor Southern girl Celie, whose painful life is enriched by her relationships with Sofia (Oprah Winfrey) and her violent husband's glamorous mistress, Shug (Margaret Avery).

Edith Wharton

Born Edith Jones, **Edith Wharton** (1862–1937) came from a wealthy New York family, and was schooled from an early age in the etiquette and expectations of the east coast elite. In 1885 she married Teddy Wharton – a relationship that broke down soon after it was revealed he kept a mistress – and began to write stories and articles. By 1908 Edith, living alone in Paris, had begun a brief but torrid affair with a journalist from the *London Times*; after her divorce from Teddy in 1912, she spent the rest of her life hosting glittering literary salons on the Left Bank. One of the finest writers of her era, imbuing crisp, sardonic prose with an overriding sense of melancholy, Wharton penned dark, precise reflections on the American aristocracy of the early twentieth century, in which women were invariably trapped, excluded or gripping on for dear life.

Her first big seller, *The House Of Mirth* (1905), a painful account of a scarlet woman's attempts to find security in polite society, was transferred to the stage the next year, and filmed – with a new, happy ending – in 1918. In 2000 Terence Davies directed a superb adaptation: starring the luminous Gillian Anderson as tragic social climber Lily Bart, and with accomplished performances from Laura Linney and Dan Aykroyd in a rare dramatic role, it's a sombre yet exquisite film, all elegance and claustrophobia. In a similar vein, Wharton's *The Age Of Innocence* (1920), which recounts the impossible love affair between a New York lawyer and bohemian divorcee Countess Olenska, was the first novel written by a woman to win the Pulitzer prize; it was filmed just four years after its release, and then again in 1934, with Irene Dunne as the countess. Martin Scorsese's chillingly brilliant adaptation (1993) evinced career-best performances from Michelle Pfeiffer and Daniel Day-Lewis as the doomed couple, with a splendidly frosty turn from Winona Ryder.

In 1921 Wharton wrote *The Old Maid*, about a girl who grows up unaware that her maiden aunt is her true mother, and that because of this she may never be accepted in polite society. It was adapted into a deft three-hander by leading playwright Zoe Akins, and then filmed in 1939 as a classic women's weepie, where the focus shifted firmly to the formidable Bette Davis as the self-sacrificing aunt.

The Old Maid
dir Edmund Goulding, 1939, US, 95m, b/w

Bette Davis suffers terribly in this Civil War-set maternal melodrama. She's simply splendid as the lively young woman who has to give up her illegitimate daughter to be raised by her nasty cousin (Miriam Hopkins), and is destined to live her life being despised as the dowdy spinster aunt.

The Age Of Innocence
dir Martin Scorsese, 1993, US, 138m

A visually stunning, profoundly sad film. Scorsese's genius lies in revealing not only the suffocating trappings of fashionable society in early nineteenth-century New York, from its fine furniture to its excruciating etiquette, but also the hollowness beneath that decorative surface. The Oscar-winning costumes, from Italian designer Gabriella Pescucci, are wondrous.

The House Of Mirth
dir Terence Davies, 2000, UK, 140m

Davies foregrounds the dark psychological aspect of Wharton's tragic novel, lingering on the unhappiness of its characters and reputedly getting the actresses to wear real dresses – and corsets – from the era in order to feel their pain. With a muted, shadowy patina, its visual impact is as strong as its pared-down script, adapted by the director himself.

Virginia Woolf

Virginia Woolf (1882–1941), who famously wrote, "A woman must have money and a room of her own if she is to write fiction," was born Virginia Stephen into a wealthy, intellectual family. Moving to London's Bloomsbury in 1904, she started writing for the *Times Literary Supplement*, and very soon, along with her brothers and sister Vanessa (later Vanessa Bell), became a key player in the influential Bloomsbury set of artists and writers. In 1915 she produced her first novel, *The Voyage Out*; two years later, she and her husband, Leonard Woolf, a political theorist, founded the Hogarth Press, publishing authors like T.S. Eliot, Katherine Mansfield and Maxim Gorky. After her second novel, *Night And Day* (1919), about the relationship between two women, and *Jacob's Room* (1922), based upon the life of her deceased brother, came *Mrs Dalloway* (1925), in which Woolf experimented with the poetic, impressionistic "stream of consciousness" style for which she became famous; she later took it to the realms of abstraction with her more difficult modernist novels *To The Lighthouse* (1927) and *The Waves* (1931).

Mrs Dalloway is perhaps her most accessible work, recounting a day in the life of a society hostess preparing for her party and using a mixture of interior monologues from various interrelated characters. A brilliant evocation of time, place and class, it also offers deft psychological insights with its kaleidoscope of richly drawn characters. The 1997 film, directed by Marleen Gorris, with a first-time screenplay by veteran actress and Woolf expert Eileen Atkins, feels a little like a vehicle for Vanessa Redgrave, who gives an unnervingly mannered performance as the hostess. It's beautifully acted, nonetheless, and gives a strong visual sense of 1920s London.

Woolf dedicated *Orlando* (1928), a fanciful biography of a beautiful male/female aristocrat, to her lover, the poet Vita Sackville-West. In 1992 avant-garde director Sally Potter translated the magical story into a moving work of art, starring the androgynous Tilda Swinton (best known for the films she made with Derek Jarman) as the hero/heroine. Swinton's to-camera asides echo Woolf's direct address to the reader, but the film is more linear than the book, focusing on Orlando's centuries-long struggle to keep her inheritance. With intelligence and no little wit (Quentin Crisp's turn as Queen Elizabeth I, for example) it's an ambitious, popular British art movie, the like of which they just don't seem to make any more.

In 2002 director Stephen Daldry, of *Billy Elliot* fame, tackled Michael Cunningham's tripartite novel *The Hours* (1998), which was loosely based on both *Mrs Dalloway* and Woolf's own life. Nicole Kidman, amid much muttering about her false nose, won an Oscar for her portrayal of the suicidal writer, Meryl Streep gives

Tilda Swinton as Orlando: fabulous costumes and a fairy tale ride

a magnificent performance as a latter-day Mrs Dalloway, and Julianne Moore shines – as ever – as a frustrated 1950s housewife, but overall the film feels dull and pretentious.

In 1941 Virginia Woolf, plagued by depression throughout her life, weighed down her pockets with rocks and drowned herself in the River Ouse.

Orlando
dir Sally Potter, 1992, UK/Rus/Fr/It/Neth, 93m

Tilda Swinton, is radiant as Orlando, an immortal man who becomes a woman in Potter's elegant – and easily digestible – screen version of Woolf's modernist novel. Original and audacious, with the most fabulous costumes by Sandy Powell, it's a satisfying, visually delicious romp through English history.

Women Of The World: chick flicks
go global

An unlikely candidate for chief of the tribe:
Keisha Castle-Hughes in *Whale Rider* (2002)

Women of the world:

chick flicks go global

When we venture into the realms of world cinema, the chick flick genre as we know it, that most Hollywood of creatures, can be evasive. That said, there are, of course, armfuls of exciting films out there that have a particularly strong appeal for women, whether through their subject matter, their historical context or their stars. What follows is a rundown of key countries and regions, cherry-picking from each the most interesting films for, about and by women throughout the history of that country's cinema. The aim is to point readers towards a range of enjoyable movies, so there are plenty of reviews of the landmark titles – with some little-known gems thrown in for good measure.

Australia

Silent cinema was popular entertainment in Australia, audiences favouring folksy yarns about pioneers, convicts and gold rushes. With the coming of sound, and then World War II, production dwindled, until, in the 1970s, a distinctive new Australian cinema, the so-called "Australian new wave", emerged. Suddenly, screens down under were dominated by mythic outback landscapes and arty historical dramas – Peter Weir's dreamy chiller *Picnic At Hanging Rock* (1975), for example – which, despite often expressing anti-colonial sentiments, also went down very well in Europe and the US. While Bruce Beresford directed *The Getting Of Wisdom* (1977), a lush, heart-warming tale set in a Melbourne girls' school in 1910, and Fred Schepisi concerned himself with Aussie Westerns, **Gillian Armstrong** made a splash with *My Brilliant Career* (1979), an outback-girl-makes-good costume drama based on Miles Franklin's autobiographical novel. The new wave wasn't all nostalgia and wistful soft focus, however – there was a distinctly trashy element to George Miller's *Mad Max* series (1979–85) and Weir's schlocky *The Cars That Ate Paris* (1974) – and Armstrong followed *My Brilliant Career* with the surreal *Starstruck* (1982), a musical comedy that in its loving celebration of kitsch anticipated later Aussie hits *Strictly Ballroom* (1992), *Muriel's Wedding* (1994; see Canon) and *The Adventures Of Priscilla, Queen Of The Desert* (1994). Although she has gone on to achieve mainstream success, Armstrong's best work, including the bittersweet *High Tide* (1987) and *The Last Days Of Chez Nous* (1990), has always been in her native Australia.

Jane Campion (see Icons), although born in New Zealand, has made most of her major films in Australia, and is jealously claimed by each country. In 1989 she slotted straight into Oz's offbeat moviemaking tradition with *Sweetie*, a particularly dark take on Antipodean suburbia, before going on to triumph with *The Piano* (1993; see Canon), a work of heartbreaking beauty set in nineteenth-century New Zealand. With her credible, conflicted and not always likeable female characters, Campion has produced a consistently watchable body of women's movies, all the way up to the erotic thriller *In The Cut* (2003; see Canon).

In 1992 theatre director **Baz Luhrmann**, along with **Catherine Martin**, his production/costume designer wife, blazed onto the scene with the sweet-hearted *Strictly Ballroom*, the first in their carnivalesque "red curtain trilogy", dealing with different aspects of theatre and performance. *Romeo & Juliet* (1996), starring Leonardo DiCaprio and Claire Danes, was a high-octane, dazzlingly cinematic rendition of Shakespeare's play, while the bohemian burlesque of *Moulin Rouge!* (2001; see Canon) was unlike anything before seen on the big screen.

Few **Aboriginal** filmmakers, or movies that have grappled with the more shameful periods in white Australia's history, have crossed into the mainstream. In 2002, however, the award-winning *Rabbit-Proof Fence* managed just that. A delicately wrought true story about three young half-caste girls who refuse to submit to forced assimilation during the 1930s, it tells a devastating tale while sure-footedly remaining this side of sentimental.

My Brilliant Career
dir Gillian Armstrong, 1979, Aus, 100m

Armstrong brings Miles Franklin's autobiographical 1901 novel to the screen with dash. The young Judy Davis is superb as the independent-minded outback girl Sybylla, who longs to be a writer and comes to learn that she can't have it all; her on-screen chemistry with suitor Sam Neill is palpable.

Starstruck
dir Gillian Armstrong, 1982, Aus, 102m

A zany new wave musical about two working-class wannabes who enter a talent contest. With its whacky songs, over-the-top costumes, sly suburban humour and brash intelligence, it clearly influenced a generation of Australian filmmakers from P.J. Hogan to Baz Luhrmann.

High Tide
dir Gillian Armstrong, 1987, Aus, 104m

Stranded in the middle of nowhere when her car breaks down, Elvis-impersonator backup singer Lilli (a typically assured performance from Judy Davis) meets the feisty Bet (Jan Adele) and her granddaughter Ally (Claudia Karvan), a passionate surfer. A shocking secret is revealed and a superb three-hander unfolds in this delightful, poignant film.

Strictly Ballroom
dir Baz Luhrmann, 1992, Aus, 94m

Luhrmann's first movie feels as fresh today as when first released, offering both a gentle satire on, and warm tribute to, the competitive ballroom dancing scene that the director had experienced as a younger man. The story – underdog refuses to conform and eventually makes good – has been told countless times, but Luhrmann and Catherine Martin bring to it an originality that leaves you exhilarated – and, probably, a little dewy-eyed. Fabulous soundtrack, too.

Holy Smoke
dir Jane Campion, 1999, US, 115m

With its dramatic vision of the outback, skewed take on suburbia, existential musing and off-beat eroticism, this bizarre movie, perhaps unsurprisingly, bombed upon release. Its curiosity value, however, is undeniable, as is the power of the performances – Kate Winslet feisty and cruel as the girl who finds a guru in India; Harvey Keitel vulnerable as the sleazy cult exit programmer hired by her concerned family.

Rabbit-Proof Fence
dir Phillip Noyce, 2002, Aus/UK, 93m

It's 1931, and half-caste Aboriginal children are being snatched from their families by the authorities in order to assimilate them into white society and keep the nation's bloodlines pure. Three such girls set out to walk the 1500 miles back to their mothers from their detention camp, following the fence that they know will lead them home. The film's simple emotion lingers, wrought both in Christopher Doyle's dream-like visuals and in the pitch-perfect performances from the three (non-professional) leads.

Japanese Story
dir Sue Brooks, 2003, Aus, 107m

Australia's vast open spaces, which stretch for thousands of miles, offer untold scope for movie drama. In this unsettling film Toni Collette stars as a grumpy geologist heading into the void with a Japanese businessman (Otaro Tsunashima). Collette is fabulous as ever in this unlikely buddy movie that turns bad, her ever-shifting emotions played out against the endless red desert.

China

If you hanker for delicately wrought films that make a profound emotional impact, Chinese cinema can't be bettered. The country's earliest movies had a strong emphasis on **melodrama,** along with distinctive cultural traditions like the Chinese opera and warrior stories; by the 1920s these had combined with Hollywood influences to create a canon of sentimental romances, tragedies and gangster pictures, set in contemporary China and usually featuring suffering, oppressed heroines. **Swordplay movies** (*wuxia*) remained popular; the nation's first movie serial, *Burning Of The Red Lotus Temple* (1928–31), featured

Gong Li (sitting) illuminates *Raise The Red Lantern*

fearsome female sword-fighters, who made a striking contrast with the contemporary melo-drama heroines.

The 1930s, in the wake of Japanese inva-sion, brought a surge in nationalist feeling and a crop of left-wing films – *Crossroads* and *Street Angel* (both 1937), for example – many of which used the popular forms of the 1920s to get their political message across. Following the outbreak of the Sino-Japanese War in 1937, filmmaking in China was severely disrupted, but in 1945 many of the veteran leftist directors of the 1930s resur-faced, producing politically tinged melodramas like the two-part *The Spring River Flows East* (1947 & 1948) – China's *Gone With The Wind* – and *Crows And Sparrows* (1949), a slice-of-life tale set in a Shanghai tenement in the dying days of Nationalist rule. By contrast, Fei Mu's *Springtime In A Small Town* (1948), considered by many to be the best Chinese film of any era, was a sensitive, melancholy melodrama about forbidden love.

After the Communist revolution in 1949, and the establishment of the People's Republic of China, movies became more concerned with what Chairman Mao called "revolutionary realism"; their rousing stories of heroic peasants and politicized workers included many strong and central female characters. Though censorship restrictions were introduced almost immediately, this didn't stop interesting movies being made, and some directors continued to use the melodrama form to tell political stories – Xie Jin's *Red Detachment Of Women* (1960) and *Two Stage Sisters* (1964), for example. The Cultural Revolution (1966–76), when any artist seen to be taking an anti-Party line could be sentenced to time in work camps, prison or worse, all but put paid to a creative film industry.

When the Party officially retracted its hard cultural line in the 1980s, a handful of films, including Xie Jin's *Hibiscus Town* (1986), were able to engage with the traumas wrought by the Cultural Revolution. Xie Jin's lyrical work in many ways presaged the so-called **Fifth Generation**, directors like **Chen Kaige** and **Zhang Yimou**, who were the first filmmakers to graduate from the Beijing Film Academy after it was reopened in 1978. These new directors, though all very different, produced haunting films that, while frequently censored or banned in China itself, became major arthouse hits overseas. Zhang Yimou's *Red Sorghum* (1987) is an ebullient celebration of life, imbued with exceptional visual power; his later films, made after the horrors of Tiananmen Square – *Ju Dou* (1990) and *Raise The Red Lantern* (1991), which was produced in Hong Kong, for example – are just as gorgeous, if more tragic in spirit, each telling the story of a young woman (played by the compelling **Gong Li**) trapped in a repressive feudal system. Gong Li also appears in Chen Kaige's *Farewell, My Concubine* (1993), another sumptuous, devastatingly sad melodrama, about a love triangle between two male Peking Opera actors and the prostitute who marries one of them.

The biggest crossover success, however, has been *Crouching Tiger, Hidden Dragon* (2000), whose Taiwanese director **Ang Lee** had already caused a stir with *The Wedding Banquet* (1993) and *Eat Drink Man Woman* (1994) before directing Hollywood hits *Sense And Sensibility* (1995) and *The Ice Storm* (1997). With *Crouching Tiger* he turned to the martial arts movie, wrapping established Eastern conventions in a visually exhilarating package that delighted Western audiences unfamiliar with the joys of watching sword-wielding warrior women soar through the treetops. The highest-grossing subtitled film ever released in the US, it won the Oscar for Best Foreign Language Film, and created something of a new Chinese-language genre, which used stars from Hong Kong, Taiwan and mainland China, and funding from overseas, to gain worldwide appeal. Zhang attempted something similar with *Hero* (2002), which was a huge success in the East and topped the US box office for two weeks, and *House Of Flying Daggers* (2004), but both lacked the passion of their forerunner. All three films featured the ethereal beauty **Zhang Ziyi**, who, much like Gong Li before her, was "discovered" by Zhang and, in the same way, has become a major crossover star. Following a part in Wong Kar-Wai's *2046* (2004), she had her first English-speaking starring role in the Hollywood movie *Memoirs Of A Geisha* (2005), which was controversial for choosing Chinese actresses over Japanese (Gong Li and Michelle Yeoh, of *Crouching Tiger*, also star) for the lead parts.

Hong Kong

Hong Kong, as a British colony, had its own enormous film industry, churning out popular movies for the Chinese market around the world. Cantonese cinema is particularly identified with its slapstick comedies and frenetic action movies – kung fu ("kick flicks"), urban Triad thrillers and *wuxia*, all of which have had a cult following and wielded influence overseas – but it also has a strong seam of romantic melodrama. Since its return to Chinese sovereignty in 1997, Hong Kong has maintained a distinctive film industry, with a wave of arthouse movies that have made a massive impact on the film festival circuit overseas. Director **Wong Kar-Wai**, in particular, has given us some infinitely rich and melancholy love stories, including *In The Mood For Love* (2000; see Canon) and its ravishing sequel, *2046* (2004).

The Goddess (Shennü)
dir Wu Yonggang, 1934, China, 78m, b/w

The great silent star Ruan Lingyu gives an intriguing performance – combining melodrama and naturalism – in this poignant movie about a Shanghai prostitute who struggles against the odds to provide her young son with a good education.

Street Angel (Malu tianshi)
dir Yuan Muzhi, 1937, China, 100m, b/w

A touching left-wing melodrama, clearly influenced by Hollywood, telling the story of four different characters – a musician, a prostitute, a singer and a news-seller – in the slums of Shanghai during the Japanese occupation.

Two Stage Sisters (Wutai jiemei)
dir Xie Jin, 1964, China, 114m

Two young women (Xie Fang and Cao Yindi), both of whom work for a musical troupe, find their intense friendship comes under strain as they take different paths in life. Made before the Cultural Revolution, the film was later derided by Chairman Mao for its "bourgeois

humanism", but its angle on Chinese Communism is sympathetic, and the overlap between politics and personal life is delicately portrayed.

Sacrificed Youth (Qingchun ji)
dir Zhang Nuanxin, 1985, China, 96m

The Cultural Revolution is in full swing, and teenage Beijing student Li Chun (Li Fengxu), like many others, is sent off to work with the peasants in a remote agricultural backwater. Resistant at first, the girl finally succumbs to the sensual way of life she finds down there. A standout film from one of China's female directors of the 1980s.

Hibiscus Town (Furong zhen)
dir Xie Jin, 1986, China, 136m

Charting the effect of the Cultural Revolution on one family in a small Chinese village, this harrowing movie – banned for a short while in China – refrains from histrionics, telling its painful story carefully and with consummate style.

Ju Dou
dir Zhang Yimou, 1990, China/Jap, 94m

A strong pulse of post-Tiananmen Square pain throbs through this exquisite tragedy, banned in China upon its release. Gong Li is spectacular as the rebellious young woman in 1920s China, forced to live a lie in an abusive marriage, and the film's visual motifs – richly coloured swathes of silk tumbling like water over a flagstoned courtyard, for example – are hard to forget.

Raise The Red Lantern (Dahong denglong gaogao gua)
dir Zhang Yimou, 1991, HK, 125m

Another heartbreaking film made post-Tiananmen, and one of Zhang's finest. Gong Li plays a spirited young woman in the 1920s, who marries an elderly, despotic clan-leader (the faceless "Master") and must contend with his three other wives. Simply ravishing.

Crouching Tiger, Hidden Dragon (Wo hu zang long)
dir Ang Lee, 2000, China/Thai/US, 120m

It's hard to resist this sumptuous love story and exhilarating *wuxia*, which has fabulous roles for Michelle Yeoh and the young Zhang Ziyi as warrior women both in search of the "Green Destiny", a mythical sword. The dazzling fighting sequences were choreographed by Yuen Wo Ping, of *The Matrix* fame.

Springtime In A Small Town (Xiao cheng zhi chun)
dir Tian Zhuangzhuang, 2002, China/HK/Fr, 116m

A remake of Fei Mu's classic 1948 Chinese melodrama, in which a miserable married couple (Hu Jingfan and Wu Jun) are shaken up by the arrival of his old friend (Xin Baiqing), who turns out to have also been her childhood sweetheart. Mesmeric, a little cold-hearted, but intriguing nonetheless.

2046
dir Wong Kar-Wai, 2004, HK/Fr, 123m

With an intricate structure loosely based around a science fiction novel being written by Mo-wan, the lovelorn hero of *In The Mood For Love*, *2046* revisits the earlier film's themes of nostalgia, loss and obsession in an equally dazzling way. It looks stupendous, the performances break your heart and the soundtrack is to die for.

France

On December 28, 1895, in a café in Paris, the Lumière brothers demonstrated their revolutionary Cinématographe to a paying audience for the first time, projecting various short documentary scenes onto a large screen. Suddenly, a train appeared, pulling into a station. The audience – so the story goes – screamed, thinking it was real, and thus cinema was born. France went on to have one of the world's great film industries, boasting the first woman director, **Alice Guy Blaché**, who made both the first fiction film, *La fée aux choux* (*The Cabbage Fairy*), in 1896 and one of the world's first colour films, *La fée*

printemps (*The Spring Fairy*), in 1906. In 1922 another woman director, **Germaine Dulac**, made *La souriante Madame Beudet* (*The Smiling Madame Beudet*), a dreamy and sometimes bizarre account of a woman trapped in an unhappy marriage; and in the 1940s, when American movies were banned in occupied France, there emerged a slew of melodramas targeted towards a female audience. After World War II, director **Jacqueline Audry** made a string of costume melodramas centred on female characters, among them the evocative period piece *Gigi* (1949), based on Colette's novel about a young girl being schooled as a courtesan (and which was remade as a Hollywood musical in 1958); *Olivia* (1950), a boarding school story of repressed lesbian love; and *Huis clos* (*No Exit*, 1954), an existential drama about the afterlife based on the play by Jean-Paul Sartre. All bustles and clinking china teapots, these were the kind of lush, theatrical dramas against which the so-called French *nouvelle vague* (new wave) of the 1960s rebelled. The new wave brought us some wonderful cinematic films, but little that caught the imagination of female audiences in particular. However, *nouvelle vague* muses like Anna Karina and Jeanne Moreau undeniably had their own alluring cool (and later went on to direct movies themselves), while the young **Brigitte Bardot**, with her unashamed sexuality, shook up bourgeois France as radically as any student revolutionary. Indeed, throughout its history France has produced a raft of fascinating female **film stars**, from the androgynous Musidora – the slinky vamp Irma Vep in the spooky silent series *Les Vampires* (1915–18) – to the earthy and radical Simone Signoret and arthouse favourite Juliette Binoche. Each brings a quality to her performance that elevates whatever she appears in – and unlike in Hollywood, French female stars don't fade into the background after hitting middle age. François Ozon's irreverent spelt whodunnit *8 femmes* (*8 Women*, 2002), which comes complete with gorgeous outfits and kitsch musical numbers, gives a rare opportunity to see a cross-generational bunch of the greats together, including 1950s icon Danielle Darrieux, Catherine Deneuve, Fanny Ardant, Isabelle Huppert, Emmanuelle Béart, Virginie Ledoyen and Ludivine Sagnier, all of whom poke gentle, knowing fun at their own, and each other's, star images.

Post-1968 France saw a wave of films directed by women like **Agnès Varda** and the actress/writer/director **Nelly Kaplan**, all of them influenced, however obliquely, by radical new feminist ideas – both in their subjects and

Isabelle Huppert and Miou-Miou, best of friends in *Coup de foudre* (1983)

in how they were filmed. Movies like Varda's *One Sings, The Other Doesn't* (1976), about two friends whose lives are changed by Women's Lib, offer an intriguing insight into a particular moment in French history, while Kaplan's surreal bawdiness remains timeless. In 1985 **Coline Serreau**'s *3 hommes et un couffin* (*3 Men And A Cradle*), a jokey dig at French bachelorhood, was a huge success, as was its more sentimental US remake, *Three Men And A Baby* (1987); Serreau went on to direct the brave inter-racial romance *Romuald et Juliette* (*Romeo And Juliet*) in 1989. Cabaret actress **Josiane Balasko** also proved to be a comedy hit, directing and starring in the quirky farces *Ma vie est un enfer* (*My Life Is Hell*, 1991), about a woman who sells her soul to the devil, and 1995's likeable *Gazon maudit* (*French Twist*), a mischievous take on an old ménage-à-trois story.

France has produced a particularly high number of films about **adolescence**. While sometimes one suspects that these are mere excuses to present nubile young girls to a self-satisfied audience of grown men, some genuinely moving examples of the genre, often semi-autobiographical, have been directed by women. Diane Kurys's *Diabolo menthe* (*Peppermint Soda*, 1977), *Cocktail Molotov* (1980) and *La baule-les-pins* (*C'est la vie*, 1990); Véra Belmont's *Rouge baiser* (1985), about growing up on the Left Bank in the 1950s; Agnès Varda's desolate *Vagabonde* (1985); and Claire Denis's accomplished *Chocolat* (1988), set in colonial West Africa, are all fine examples. The controversial director **Catherine Breillat** – who has been wrongly accused of being a pornographer for the way in which she challenges assumptions about sex and female sexuality in explicit movies like *Parfait amour!* (*Perfect Love!*, 1996) and *Romance* (1998) – gave us a range of all-too-real teenage girls in *Virgin* (1988) and the devastating *A ma soeur!* (*Fat Girl*, 2001).

La fiancée du pirate (Dirty Mary)
dir Nelly Kaplan, 1969, Fr, 106m

A wickedly subversive tale – Picasso called it "insolence raised to the status of fine art"– in which an outcast (Bernadette Lafont), sexually exploited by the men of her local village, wreaks her revenge by seducing them and then, through blackmail, forcing them to pay. The utopian ending is a mischievous delight.

Diabolo menthe (Peppermint Soda)
dir Diane Kurys, 1977, Fr, 101m

Flash back to the agonies of adolescence and the early 1960s in this unsentimental account of a year in the life of two teenage sisters living with their mother. Kurys shows her usual panache, and there are great performances from Odile Michel and Eléonore Klarwein as the siblings.

Coup de foudre (At First Sight)
dir Diane Kurys, 1983, Fr, 111m

Starting in 1942 and ending up in the 1950s, this female friendship film has housewives Miou-Miou and Isabelle Huppert (both excellent) attempting to deal with their intense mutual attraction. The costumes and period detail add a certain nostalgic melancholy.

An Impudent Girl (L'effrontée)
dir Claude Miller, 1985, Fr, 97m

One of those classic tales of adolescent angst that the French do so well, with a teenage Charlotte Gainsbourg putting in a terrific performance as the frustrated young girl whose life is rocked by the appearance of the accomplished Clara (Clothilde Baudon).

Vagabonde (Sans toit ni loi)
dir Agnès Varda, 1985, Fr, 106m

Sandrine Bonnaire is remarkable as Mona, the young drifter who affects everyone she encounters. Powerful and harrowing, the movie never judges, simply presenting us with a girl who refuses to conform.

Manon des sources
dir Claude Berri, 1986, Fr/It/Switz, 120m

This sequel to the phenomenally popular *Jean de Florette* (1986), which starred Gérard Depardieu, picks up the story ten years later. Emmanuelle Béart plays Manon, Jean's 18-year-old daughter, who determines to wreak revenge on Soubeyran (Yves Montand) and his nephew (Daniel Auteuil) for what they did to her father. Elegant direction, glorious Provencal countryside and a gorgeous leading lady – international audiences adored it.

Romuald et Juliette (Romeo And Juliet)
dir Coline Serreau, 1989, Fr, 112m

Bearing little resemblance to the Shakespeare play, this is a sweet rom-com about a company director (Daniel Auteuil) who forms an odd-couple friendship with a warmhearted, super-smart black cleaning woman (Firmine Richard) and her five kids. Really quite subversive, in its own charming way.

Amélie (Le fabuleux destin d'Amélie Poulain)
dir Jean-Pierre Jeunet, 2001, Fr/Ger, 123m

Wearing its chic Parisian whimsy on its sleeve, this love story about a lonely girl who does good deeds was an enormous international success. Though a little too fey for some tastes, it has undeniable verve, and Audrey Tautou will charm anyone with a soft spot for doe-eyed gamines.

A ma soeur! (Fat Girl)
dir Catherine Breillat, 2001, Fr/It/Sp, 86m

Like all of Breillat's work, *A ma soeur!* makes fascinating and sometimes uncomfortable viewing, and raises some brave questions. The setting here is a seemingly innocent family holiday, in which sibling rivalry, sexual awakening, romance, fantasy and brutality are all played out with devastating results.

Germany

The early years of German cinema produced some of the most distinctive movies ever made. Art cinema thrived throughout the 1920s, inspiring filmmakers around the world, and the long shadows and stylized stage sets of expressionist films like *The Cabinet Of Dr Caligari* (1919), among many others, have become iconic. In 1928 the exquisite American star **Louise Brooks**, dissatisfied with the roles she was given in Hollywood, agreed on a whim to move to Germany to work with the director **G.W. Pabst**: their two collaborations, the stunning *Pandora's Box* and *Diary Of A Lost Girl* (both 1929), were not hits at the time, but have since been recognized, particularly in terms of Brooks's charismatic performances, as two of the major movies of the era. By the 1930s, however, with Hitler and his National Socialist party on the horizon, many key figures in Germany's movie industry were fleeing, some of them to Hollywood, and the nation's cinema was losing energy. The early all-female talkie *Mädchen in Uniform* (*Girls In Uniform*, 1931), made on the threshold of Nazi victory, held out hopes for a kinder and more tolerant society; with its attack on the school system, and its lesbian element, it was soon banned, however, and **Leontine Sagan**, its Jewish female director, fled to the UK and to her original love, the theatre.

During the Third Reich, cinema was put to work as a propaganda machine. After a fallow period following World War II and Germany's "denazification", in the 1960s a new generation of West German filmmakers began to make the experimental, non-commercial movies that became known as **New German Cinema**. In an anti-American, anti-authoritarian fervour, directors like Wim Wenders, Werner Herzog and Volker Schlöndorff grappled with their country's history, its politics and its deep psychological scarring in a variety of different ways. The gay filmmaker **Rainer Werner Fassbinder**, a passionate fan of the great Hollywood director **Douglas Sirk** (see Icons), reworked and updated Sirk's classic melodrama *All That Heaven Allows* in *Fear Eats The Soul* (1973), and created a string of unique, highly emotional movies including the historical melodrama *Effi Briest* (1974) and *The Marriage Of Maria Braun* (1978), a savage attack on love, marriage and postwar Germany. **Margarethe von Trotta**, who co-wrote and co-directed with Schlöndorff the seminal *The Lost Honour Of Katharina Blum* (1975), about the fallout that descends upon a woman who unknowingly beds a terrorist, went on to direct some of the key films of her generation. A feminist, she makes movies that vary from the heavily political – *The German Sisters* (1981) – to romantically bittersweet – *The Promise* (1994); all of them revolve around women, their relationships, and their personal and social histories. Her most recent film, *Rosenstrasse* (2003), tells the true story of a 1943 Berlin uprising of German women against the Nazis.

Melodrama gets gritty in Fassbinder's *Fear Eats The Soul*

Other female directors include **Helke Sander**, whose *The All-Round Reduced Personality* (1977) is a seminal feminist film about a Berlin photographer struggling to make sense of both her divided city and her fractured self, and **Helma Sanders-Brahms**, who made *Shirin's Wedding* (1976), a blistering attack on the conditions for immigrants in Germany, as well as *Germany, Pale Mother* (1979), a personal and political exploration of her relationship with her mother. **Doris Dörrie**, meanwhile, has had the most crossover appeal: *Men* (1985), her satirical take on men's dependence on women, was particularly popular in the US. Many German films continue to address the nation's vexed history, and the country has also produced a crop of quirky thrillers, comedies and rom-coms, among them *Vaya con Dios* (2002), a sweet road movie featuring three monks and a free-spirited girl. With some exceptions, few of these have travelled well.

 ### Mädchen in Uniform (Girls In Uniform)
dir Leontine Sagan, 1931, Ger, 98m, b/w

Motherless Manuela (Hertha Thiele) falls in love with her kindly teacher (the lovely Dorothea Wieck), a passion that her strict Prussian boarding school cannot permit. A cult classic largely thanks to its lesbian element, the movie is also beautiful to look at, with hints of expressionism, and brings compassion and a topical edge to its school story.

Fear Eats The Soul (Angst essen Seele auf)
dir Rainer Werner Fassbinder, 1973, WGer, 92m

Fassbinder takes overblown Sirkian melodrama to the German working class with this poignant tale of a love affair between a middle-aged cleaning woman (Brigitte Mira) and a young Moroccan immigrant (El Hedi Ben Salem, a lover of Fassbinder's, who later committed suicide in prison). Made in four weeks, it's evocative, rough around the edges and ultimately rather wonderful.

The Marriage Of Maria Braun (Die Ehe der Maria Braun)
dir Rainer Werner Fassbinder, 1978, WGer, 119m

The audacious director's most commercially successful movie is as emotionally blistering as all his others. Set in postwar Germany, it charts the life of a frustrated woman (Hanna Schygulla) who thrives in the absence of her husband (Klaus Löwitsch).

Sisters, Or The Balance Of Happiness (Schwestern oder die Balance des Glücks)
dir Margarethe von Trotta, 1979, WGer, 95m

This unsettling meditation on the attachment between two sisters (Jutta Lampe and Gudrun Gabriel), one a student

and the other a successful career woman, unfolds with slow intensity, creeping under the skin like a nasty fairy tale.

The German Sisters (Die bleierne Zeit)
dir Margarethe von Trotta, 1981, WGer, 107m

The film that brought von Trotta to the attention of the world replays many of the concerns of her earlier *Sisters*. Here the relationship between the two sisters (Jutta Lampe and Barbara Sukowa) tells a personal and political story that unflinchingly faces Nazism, terrorism and sibling relationships.

 ### Men (Männer)
dir Doris Dörrie, 1985, WGer, 99m

A sly and sweetly witty odd-couple comedy about a man (Heiner Lauterbach) who moves in with his wife's lover (Uwe Ochsenknecht) to work out what she sees in him, and then determines to ruin their affair. A rare German comedy that translates well into English.

 ### Run Lola Run (Lola rennt)
dir Tom Tykwer, 1998, Ger, 80m

Crimson-haired Berliner Lola (Franka Potente) has just twenty minutes to turn into a turbocharged action heroine and literally run for her boyfriend's life in this frenetic high-concept movie. Bold, breathless and just a bit barmy.

Mostly Martha (Drei Sterne)
dir Sandra Nettelbeck, 2001, Aus/Ger/It/Switz, 107m

The rom-com gets given a German makeover in this likeable film, in which the uptight chef of a swanky restaurant (Martina Gedeck, terrific) finds her ordered life turned upside down by the arrival of her young motherless niece and an unruly Italian sous chef.

India

India has always had a thriving film industry, creating movies not only for the vast domestic market but also for Indian audiences throughout the world. The main centre of production is Mumbai (Bombay), or **Bollywood**, which specializes in colourful, spectacular Hindi romantic musicals, born from vibrant Parsi theatre, classic folk tales and traditional north Indian opera. Excised of any overtly sexual content, Bollywood films can nonetheless be highly suggestive, bursting with saucy dance moves, wet saris, tantalizing tribal costumes and romantic interludes behind conveniently placed shrubbery.

Bollywood movies have traditionally abounded in devoted daughters, loving wives and, in particular, saintly mothers; there are also a fair few tragic courtesans, along with evil vamps dressed up in killer Western outfits. Fascinating exceptions include the hugely

Rain fails to stop festivities in Mira Nair's *Monsoon Wedding* (2001)

popular 1930s stunt queen **Fearless Nadia** (real name Mary Evans Wadia), a half-Greek circus artiste born in Australia, who fought tyrants and saved oppressed people in movies like *Hunterwali* (*The Princess And The Hunter*, 1935). During the 1930s some melodramas attempted to engage with the real experiences of Indian women: **Rajaram Shantaram**'s *Duniya na mane* (*Marriage Of Children/The Unexpected*, 1937), for example, tells the story of a man who comes to understand, through the actions of his rebellious wife, the injustices that many women face. And the filmmakers that emerged following Independence in 1947 – directors like Guru Dutt, **Mehboob Khan** and Bimal Roy – continued to use the conventions and form of classic melodrama even while grappling with issues surrounding Independence, modernization and history. Megastars of this era include **Nargis**, who came to prominence in the lavish costume dramas of Mehboob Khan and went on to corner the market in innocent women doomed to cause havoc with their beauty. She could, however, turn her hand to anything from giggling dancing girls to modern career women, and later, in a move not uncommon for Indian stars, went into politics, becoming a member of parliament for India's Congress party.

The 1960s saw the emergence of India's "alternative" or "parallel" cinema, headed by filmmakers like **Satyajit Ray**, Mrinal Sen and Ritwik Ghatak, who adopted a more naturalistic style – preferring black-and-white film over the spectacular colour of the Bollywood extravaganzas – to explore contemporary political issues. In these movies women often represented the pull the country felt between the old ways and modernity; usually, however, they faced tragic outcomes, and some Indians, including Nargis, attacked Ray in particular for cynically

making their country's poverty look beautiful for an overseas market. One of the major stars of the new cinema was the independent and lively **Smita Patil**, who had an intense screen presence; after crossing over into the mainstream, she was hounded by a prurient press, and died at the age of 31 due to complications from childbirth. In the 1970s **Shyam Benegal** combined the colour and elevated emotion of the Bollywood musicals with Ray's subtle characterizations to make something new, often foregrounding female characters. His *The Role* (1977), for example, is a fabulous melodrama to rival any of the Hollywood women's movies of the 1930s and 40s.

The 1980s brought a crop of intriguing melodramas made by women directors, including **Aparna Sen**'s *Paroma* (1984), about a middle-aged woman who has an affair with a younger man. Today there are many female filmmakers in Bollywood, among them exmovie star Revathi (*Mitr, My Friend*, 2002), Meghna Gulzar (*Filhaal…*, 2002) and Honey Irani (*Armaan*, 2003), all of whom give women central roles in contemporary stories. India-born **Deepa Mehta**, who is based in Toronto, specializes in melodramas that take an unflinching look at the cultural and social pressures faced by Indian women. Her trilogy *Fire* (1996) – which was banned in Pakistan for its frank portrayal of lesbian love – *Earth* (1998) and *Water* (2005) approaches serious subjects with sensitivity and verve. **Mira Nair**, another expat Indian filmmaker, now based in the US, came to the world's attention in 1988 with *Salaam Bombay!*, a beautifully composed movie about street kids, and had her first Hollywood hit with *Mississippi Masala* (1991), an inter-racial love story between an expat Indian woman (Sarita Choudhury) and an African-American man (Denzel Washington) in the American South. Nair's *Kama Sutra: A Tale Of Love* (1996) is best passed over, but in 2001 her big-hearted *Monsoon Wedding*, an exuberant family drama set against the backdrop of an arranged Punjabi wedding, won huge international audiences and a raft of awards. In a mischievous twist she managed to include another spectacular Indian wedding in her next movie, *Vanity Fair* (2004), a sprightly adaptation of Thackeray's novel that starred Reese Witherspoon.

Mother India (Bharat Mata)
dir Mehboob Khan, 1957, Ind, 172m

Nargis is phenomenal in this heart-rending epic melodrama, one of the most famous Bollywood movies ever made, about a low-caste, long-suffering mother forced to commit infanticide. A great success upon its release, it was the first Indian film to be nominated for a Best Foreign Language Film Oscar.

Devi (The Goddess)
dir Satyajit Ray, 1960, Ind, 93m, b/w

Director Ray explores the struggle between religious superstition and modern secularism in this intriguing tale of a young woman (Sharmila Tagore), who, when her father-in-law becomes convinced she is the reincarnation of the goddess Kali, begins to believe it herself.

The Role (Bhumika)
dir Shyam Benegal, 1977, Ind, 142m

A tragic biopic about a 1940s Bollywood film star (Smita Patil), whose struggle both to be a good family woman and maintain her career eventually destroys her. It's a fantastic melodrama and a savage indictment of the movie industry.

Bandit Queen
dir Shekhar Kapur, 1994, Ind/UK, 121m

Causing a huge stir upon its release, this harrowing rape revenge movie tells the true story of Phoolan Devi (Seema Biswas), a low-caste woman who, after a succession of brutal (explicitly portrayed) attacks from high-caste men, leads a band of outlaws in violent raids against them.

Biswas, in her first movie role, gives a visceral rendition of Devi as a ball of fury.

Zubeidaa
dir Shyam Benegal, 2001, Ind, 153m

Benegal's lively biopic of Zubeidaa (Karisma Kapoor), the real-life movie star who fell in love with a Rajasthani maharajah, is a sumptuous feast, and the director does a good job of combining India's art cinema tradition with a populist appeal.

Water
dir Deepa Mehta, 2005, Can/Ind, 114m

Set in 1938, at the height of India's Independence struggle, the third film in Mehta's elemental trilogy follows a group of oppressed widows forced by poverty to live in a temple in the holy city of Varanasi. Controversial for its view of India's subjugation of women, it is also visually glorious, with a hopeful, humanistic message.

Iran

Iranian cinema is currently the talk of the art cinema world, raking in the prizes at international festivals. This is a relatively new development: the earliest films in Iran, far from being forms of mass entertainment or works of artistic experiment, were short documentary features enjoyed only by the royal family. Public cinemas were barely heard of until the 1930s, when the industry began to produce its own musical comedies and melodramas in the vein of Bollywood. Highlights over the next two decades included Esmail Kushan's *Sharmsar* (*Ashamed*, 1950), a romantic musical about a peasant girl (played by popular singer Delkash) who, seduced by a cad from the city, becomes a star and returns home triumphant. In the 1960s came a rash of

Young Iranian director Samira Makhmalbaf

films contrasting the decadence of the upper classes with the simple nobility of the poor, including *Ganje-qarun* (*Croesus' Treasure*, 1965) and *Qeysar* (1969) which started a nationwide craze for tragic action movies.

Meanwhile, poetess **Forugh Farrokhzad**'s *Khaneh siah ast* (*The House Is Black*, 1963), a lyrical documentary about a leper colony, sparked off a flurry of movies that drew upon Iran's long-held poetic tradition to make expressive works of art. One such picture, Daryush Mehrjui's *The Cow* (1968), about a man's love for his animal, was smuggled to the Venice film festival in 1970, won a major prize, and brought Iranian art cinema to the attention of the West. After the revolution of 1979, when the Islamic Republic toppled the Shah, the Ayatollah Khomeini announced that cinema was to focus on educational and elevated themes. Facing new restrictions on what could be shown on screen – no romance, sexual desire, physical touching or violence – moviemakers turned increasingly to allegory, using untrained actors and digital cameras, and often placing children at the centre of visually striking fables about courage, stoicism and innocence. Directors like **Abbas Kiarostami**, Majid Majidi and former revolutionary **Mohsen Makhmalbaf** achieved worldwide acclaim, along with a fine crop of female directors, including Makhmalbaf's astonishingly precocious and prolific daughters. **Samira Makhmalbaf** made the transfixing docudrama *The Apple* (1998) when she was 18, while her sister Hana, having started a career behind the camera at the age of 9, directed *Joy Of Madness* (2003), a digital documentary following her sister casting *At Five In The Afternoon* (2003), just five years later. Other Iranian female directors worth watching out for are Marziyeh Meshkini (Samira and Hana's mother), Rakhshan Bani Etemad and Mania Akbari, all of whom use a refreshing and dynamic cinematic language to engage with what it means to be a woman in contemporary Iran.

Khake sar beh morh (The Sealed Soil)
dir Marva Nabili, 1977, Iran, 90m

An intriguing pre-revolutionary film from a woman director, about a rebellious young woman (Flora Shabaviz) who, refusing all marriage proposals and daring to remove her veil, is thought to be possessed by evil spirits. Smuggled out of the country and completed in the US, the movie has never been shown in Iran.

The Apple (Sib)
dir Samira Makhmalbaf, 1998, Iran, 85m

The eldest Makhmalbaf sister's beautifully even-handed docudrama follows what happens when two young girls, who have been locked up by their parents for eleven years, are freed and allowed to roam the streets of Tehran. All the family play themselves in scenes that are sometimes reconstructed and sometimes improvised, giving the film an immediate, urgent quality. An unsettling, deeply affecting work of art.

The Day I Became A Woman (Roozi keh zan shodam)
dir Marziyeh Meshkini, 2000, Iran, 78m

Three separate episodes – a young girl must don the veil and stop playing with boys; a rebellious wife enters a cycle race against her husband's wishes; an old lady goes shopping – combine whimsy, poetry and poignancy to paint a vivid picture of Iranian women's lives.

Baran
dir Majid Majidi, 2001, Iran, 94m

Not quite as heart-wrenching – nor as sentimental – as Majidi's earlier films *Children Of Heaven* (1997) and *The Color Of Paradise* (1999), this is the story of a young girl (Zahra Bahrami, who never speaks) who disguises herself as a boy in order to work on a Tehran building site and support her Afghani family. Beautifully shot and elegantly composed, this works as an art movie, a bittersweet love story and a searing commentary on life in contemporary Iran.

Ten
dir Abbas Kiarostami, 2002, Iran/Fr, 94m

A visually spare but emotionally stirring experience, filmed with a digital camera placed on the dashboard of a car. Mania Akbari plays a female taxi driver in Tehran, who in the course of ten journeys has ten intense conversations with seven passengers, including her resentful young son, a jilted bride, a prostitute and a religious woman on her way to prayer.

At Five In The Afternoon (Panj é asr)
dir Samira Makhmalbaf, 2003, Fr/Iran, 106m

Samira collaborated with her father on this bleakly lyrical film about the realities for women (and men) in the devastation of post-Taliban Afghanistan. Languorously paced, it looks stunning, and Agheleh Rezaie puts in a staggering performance as the young Noqreh, who dreams of becoming her country's first woman president.

20 Fingers
dir Mania Akbari, 2004, Iran, 72m

An accomplished writing and directorial debut for Mania Akbari, the taxi driver in Kiarostami's *Ten*. There are similarities between the two movies: here, Akbari and her producer Bijan Daneshmand play a set of seven different couples talking about their lives, confronting a range of taboos including sex, abortion and lesbianism.

Italy

Early Italian cinema is generally identified as being all about spectacle, with glamorous stars, opulent costumes and a penchant for huge historical dramas. The country had its own breed of female star, the **diva** – the likes of Pina Menichelli, Lyda Borelli and Hesperia were flamboyant, tormented figures, far better known than the directors who made the fervent melodramas in which they starred. Beyond spectacle, however, Italian audiences could also see surreal futurist experiments, slapstick comedies, and searing documentaries in a strong tradition spearheaded by filmmaker **Elvira Notari**. The 1930s saw the arrival of the escapist "white telephone" films, sentimental comedies or romances so called because they were invariably set in glamorous Art Deco surroundings dripping with glossy trappings. After World War II, and the fall of fascism, Italy went to the other extreme and developed its distinctive **neorealist** cinema, a short-lived movement that used non-stars in real locations, working with natural light and black-and-white film to tell contemporary stories and express emotional complexity with integrity. Directors like **Roberto Rossellini** brought neorealism to worldwide attention with his emotionally devastating *Roma, città aperta* (*Rome, Open City*, 1945), which starred **Anna Magnani**, a powerhouse of a performer whose striking looks and earthy presence were a world away from Hollywood. Rossellini later fell in love with the Swedish-born star **Ingrid Bergman**, who lent her ethereal charisma to a number of his neorealist masterpieces, including *Stromboli* (1949) and the exquisite *Viaggio in Italia* (*Journey To Italy*, 1953).

The Marxist bisexual **Luchino Visconti** made a number of neorealist films, but was also an opera director with a flair for melodrama. The tormented *Ossessione* (*Obsession*, 1942) has a seedy noirish element, complete with lush femme fatale Clara Calamai, while his later sumptuous Technicolor costume dramas, *Senso* (*The Wanton Countess*, 1954) and the elegiac *The Leopard* (1963), gave full rein to his ambitious, emotionally charged vision.

He often collaborated with the female scriptwriter **Suso Cecchi D'Amico**, whose elegant scripts worked just as well with gritty realism as with psychological melodramas; she also worked with **Michelangelo Antonioni** on bleak women's movies like *La signora senza camelie* (*Camille Without Camellias*, 1953) and *Le amiche* (*The Girlfriends*, 1955). Antonioni went on to achieve success on the European arthouse scene with his coolly existential trilogy *L'avventura* (*The Adventure*, 1960), *La notte* (*The Night*, 1961) and *L'eclisse* (*The Eclipse*, 1962), none of which have dated well, despite the transfixing presence of **Monica Vitti**. With a cool, intelligent beauty that epitomized existential angst, Vitti also starred in Antonioni's *Deserto rosso* (*The Red Desert*, 1964), a harrowing account of insanity, and, quirkily, made a great mod spy in the whacky British James Bond spoof *Modesty Blaise* (1966).

Federico Fellini, the comic strip fan who as a young boy ran away to join the circus, is famed for his flamboyant, surreal movies peopled with crazy characters. His early work, however, has a strong neorealist influence; he wrote for and assisted Rossellini before making *La strada* (*The Road*, 1954) and *Le notti di Cabiria* (*Nights Of Cabiria*, 1956) with his wife, **Giulietta Masina**, whose waifish clown face expressed untold depths of emotion. Fellini's ground-breaking *La dolce vita* (*The Sweet Life*, 1960), gave us the unforgettable image of a decadent Anita Ekberg dancing in the Trevi fountain, but was hardly a chick flick; it's difficult, too, to identify with the gaudy hysterics of *Juliet Of The Spirits* (1965), a journey into the psyche of a miserable housewife (Masina again).

Italy continued to produce big-budget commercial movies throughout the 1960s, and in particular a crop of distinctive comedies that cheerfully satirized modern mores. Among the voluptuous divas of the day – others included Claudia Cardinale and Gina Lollobrigida – **Sophia Loren** reigned supreme. While her earthy Latin glamour translated well to a

Anita Ekberg, a decadent diva in *La Dolce Vita* (1960)

Hollywood fixated on pneumatic bombshells, Loren was an even bigger force in her home country. Comedies like the Oscar-winning *Ieri, oggi, domani* (*Yesterday, Today And Tomorrow*, 1963) and *Matrimonio all'italiana* (*Marriage Italian-Style*, 1964) saw the tough, sexy Sophia battling, screwball-style, with the somewhat weaker, though charming, **Marcello Mastroianni**. The sizzling chemistry between the two stars led to the movies being smash hits both at home and in the US, where audiences loved their refreshingly frank, and very European, attitudes to sex.

As in the rest of mainland Europe, 1970s Italy saw a flowering of movies made by women and influenced by feminism but few of these did well abroad. In 1975 **Lina Wertmüller** became the first woman ever to be nominated for a Best Director Oscar for *Seven Beauties*, a broad and now very old-fashioned comedy about a macho cad; none of her other films have translated or lasted well.

Stromboli
dir Roberto Rossellini, 1949, It, 107m, b/w

A classic neorealist movie made particularly intriguing by the presence of Hollywood star Ingrid Bergman, who fell pregnant with Rossellini's baby soon after filming. Stripped of all glamour, she has a luminous, visceral presence as the restless Karin, a Lithuanian refugee who marries a Sicilian soldier to escape a detention camp. Life on her husband's home territory proves as oppressive as any prison, however, and her attempts to rebel become increasingly dangerous.

Viaggio in Italia (The Lonely Woman)
dir Roberto Rossellini, 1953, It, 100m, b/w

Though audiences didn't take to it upon its release, critics adored this poetic neorealist masterpiece. Ingrid Bergman and George Sanders give perfectly judged performances as the jaded, increasingly hostile English couple who reappraise their lonely marriage in the light of a trip to Italy. Repressed emotion is expressed through the sensuality of the landscape and the lure of the country's ancient past.

Senso (The Wanton Countess)
dir Luchino Visconti, 1954, It, 115m, b/w

This visually lush melodrama, set in Austrian-occupied Venice in the 1860s, is also a work of psychological depth, with a pared-down script (by Suso Cecchi D'Amico, Paul Bowles and Tennessee Williams) and a characteristically sharp take on history from Visconti. The elegant Alida Valli is stunning as the countess of the title, driven by a passion operatic in scale.

Le amiche/The Girlfriends
dir Michelangelo Antonioni, 1955, It, 104m, b/w

Following the tangle of relationships between ten overwrought women in Rome, Le amiche is an entertaining and intriguing melodrama, more accessible than Antonioni's later works, even while presaging their concern with the impossibility of human connection.

Le notti di Cabiria (Nights Of Cabiria)
dir Federico Fellini, 1956, It/Fr, 117m, b/w

Fellini fabulous – all Fiats, floor shows and frowsy fur coats – this loving portrayal of Rome's seamy underbelly has a gritty neorealist tinge and a humanistic message. Giulietta Masina, with her expressive physical presence, is extraordinary as the tough-vulnerable prostitute Cabiria

– her unique performance, and the sheer beauty of this Oscar-winning movie, elevate it well above exploitation. The Hollywood remake Sweet Charity (1968) has Shirley MacLaine playing the lead.

Ieri, oggi, domani (Yesterday, Today And Tomorrow)
dir Vittorio De Sica, 1963, It, 119m

Sophia Loren exudes formidable presence in this risqué tripartite comedy, playing the spoilt and headstrong Anna, who divorces her husband over a car; kindhearted prostitute Mara; and, most powerfully of all, Adelina, a woman who needs to get pregnant to stay out of jail. Mastroianni provides a delightfully wry comic foil.

New Zealand

The film industry in New Zealand, which had always enjoyed a healthy independent scene, saw something of a creative upsurge in the 1970s with the formation of the New Zealand Film Commission. Movies like *Sleeping Dogs* (1977), an action thriller, *Goodbye Pork Pie* (1980), about two lads on a road trip, and the unremittingly bleak urban Maori drama *Once Were Warriors* (1993) all crossed over internationally. There was not so much as a sniff of a chick flick, however, until Kiwi director **Jane Campion** (see Icons), who had already made *Sweetie* (1989) in Australia, returned home with the highly inventive *An Angel At My Table* (1990), based on the autobiography of New Zealand writer Janet Frame. Although Campion's 1993 triumph *The Piano* (see Canon) is often claimed as a New Zealand film, and is frequently quoted as being the first New Zealand film ever to win an Oscar (or rather three Oscars), it's actually, strictly speaking, a French-financed Australian movie – but given that it was filmed in New Zealand, written and directed by a New Zealander and starred a New Zealander (Sam Neill), it would be churlish to argue the point.

In 1994 *Lord Of The Rings* genius **Peter Jackson** indulged his love of movie monsters and gave us an unlikely chick flick with *Heavenly Creatures*, which features some very creepy fantasy sequences populated by faceless clay figures. As a brutal look at the twisted side of female friendship, the movie has yet to be bettered.

 ### An Angel At My Table
dir Jane Campion, 1990, NZ, 158m

Campion's highly original biopic of the troubled New Zealand novelist Janet Frame is funny, sad and brimful of imagery that, in capturing the absurdity of ordinary things, feels profoundly poetic. Frame, who was wrongly diagnosed with schizophrenia, is played by three carrot-topped actresses – including Kerry Fox – all of whom put in brilliant performances.

Heavenly Creatures
dir Peter Jackson, 1994, NZ, 98m

Based on the true story of two girls in the 1950s whose intense friendship spiralled into bloody violence, this is a gripping study of the kind of obsession and hysteria that only adolescent best friends can create. The young Kate Winslet is a revelation as the crazed Juliet, beautifully matched with the plumper, frumpier Melanie Lynskey as her introverted pal.

Whale Rider
dir Niki Caro, 2002, NZ/Ger 101m

A heart-warming girls' story that appeals hugely to grown-ups too with its uplifting account of a spunky Maori girl who insists she should be allowed to become chief of her tribe. Based on the book by Witi Ihimaera.

A girl's own story, Maori-style: *Whale Rider* (2002)

The Information:

chick flick follow-ups

Finding out the hard way: Pearl White takes
the direct route in *Plunder* (1923)

The Information: chick flick follow-ups

You've seen the movie, rented the DVD, and maybe even watched the director's commentary. Now you want to know more. The following is a selective rundown of some of the best books and websites relating to women's movies, whether you're chasing up your favourite film, star, director or costume designer.

Books

General

BFI Classics, Modern Classics and World
Directors series

The British Film Institute publishes a stylish set of monographs on the world's great films and directors, offering thought-provoking overviews that place their subject in the broadest possible context. The following are well worth a look for fans of women's movies.

BFI Classics

Fear Eats The Soul Laura Cottingham (BFI, 2005)

I Know Where I'm Going! Pam Cook (BFI, 2002)
Mother India Gayatri Chatterjee (BFI, 2002) *Sunrise: A Song of Two Humans* Lucy Fischer (BFI, 1998)
To Be Or Not To Be Peter Barnes (BFI, 2002)

BFI Modern Classics

The Silence Of The Lambs Yvonne Tasker (BFI, 2002)
10 Geoff Andrew (BFI, 2005)
Thelma & Louise Marita Sturken (BFI, 2000)
Women On The Verge Of A Nervous Breakdown Peter William Evans (BFI, 1996)

BFI World Directors

Jane Campion Dana Polan (BFI, 2002)
Wong Kar-Wai Stephen Teo (BFI, 2005)

Emotion Pictures: The Women's Picture, 1930–1955
Hilton Tims (Columbus Books, 1987)

Relishing its subject matter, this lavishly illustrated and highly enjoyable account covers the genre in vivid, rollicking detail.

Fast-Talking Dames
Maria DiBattista (Yale University Press, 2001)

DiBattista's enthusiastically argued celebration of screwball movies and their brainy, vocal heroines – from Carole Lombard and Katharine Hepburn to Irene Dunne and Rosalind Russell – provides a bittersweet reminder that they just don't make movie comediennes like they used to.

The Oxford History Of World Cinema
Geoffrey Nowell-Smith, ed. (Oxford University Press, 1996)

A cornucopia of scholarly essays on nearly every aspect of world cinema imaginable, this mammoth labour of love was just made for dipping into.

Reel Women: Pioneers Of The Cinema, 1896 To The Present
Ally Acker (Batsford, 1991)

In its tribute to the many unsung women who have worked behind the camera, from Alice Guy Blaché to Barbra Streisand – via Frances Marion, Dorothy Arzner, and over 100 more – this is an ambitious endeavour of feminist scholarship. Though the filmographies aren't always entirely accurate, and many of them are now out-of-date, there's a wealth of good information here that gets left out of the mainstream histories.

Women And Film: A Sight And Sound Reader
Pam Cook & Philip Dodd, eds (Scarlet Press, 1993)

This dynamic collection of essays, taken from the BFI's monthly *Sight & Sound* magazine, covers key stars, directors, movies and themes. Subjects include Lillian Gish, Gong Li, Audrey Hepburn, Jodie Foster, Jane Campion, *Thelma & Louise*, *The Silence Of The Lambs* and baby boom movies of the 1980s, with an excellent introductory overview of women's cinema up until the 1990s.

The Women's Companion To International Film
Annette Kuhn & Susannah Radstone, eds (Virago, 1990)

A wide-ranging feminist encyclopedia, somewhat dated now, but with interesting snippets on female filmmakers and stars, genres, themes and world cinema, and some (difficult!) quiz questions.

Costume Design

Costume Design In The Movies: An Illustrated Guide To The Work Of 157 Great Designers
Elizabeth Leese (Dover Books, 1991)

Leese has prepared a sumptuous feast of hard information and gorgeous illustrations. Its scope, from 1909 to 1988, is gratifyingly broad, covering not only the work of the major designers and their iconic stars, but also some of the less famous names.

Fashioning Film Stars: Dress, Culture, Identity
Rachel Moseley, ed. (BFI, 2005)

There's plenty to delight in this thought-provoking collection of articles relating to movie costume, style and star image, with a lot of interesting material on world cinema. Subjects include Doris Day, Audrey Hepburn and Brigitte Bardot.

Fashioning The Nation: Costume And Identity In British Cinema
Pam Cook (BFI, 1996)

A valentine to the flamboyant Gainsborough melodramas of the 1940s – including *The Wicked Lady* – and in particular Elizabeth Haffenden's outrageously sexy costume designs. Lovingly researched and wittily written, its examination

of fashion reveals surprising insights into not only the popular movies of postwar Britain, but also the broader concerns of a nation in transition.

Gowns By Adrian: The MGM Years 1928–1941
Howard Gutner (Harry N. Abrams, 2001)

While its illustrations – production stills, sketches and private photos – are undoubtedly beautiful, highlighting the ruffles, peplums and copious sleeves for which Hollywood costume maestro Adrian was famed, this handsome volume also offers an illuminating account of the studio system during Hollywood's golden age.

Hollywood Dressed & Undressed: A Century Of Cinema Style
Sandy Schreier (Rizzoli, 1998)

American costume expert Schreier examines the influence that movie style icons from Rudolph Valentino and Louise Brooks onwards have had on fashion, focusing on everything from couture to cigarettes, and including interviews with designers and stars.

Icons

Audrey Hepburn
Barry Paris (Putnam, 1996)

Arguably the best among many biographies of the beloved gamine – from an author who has also written books about Greta Garbo and Louise Brooks – with just the right mix of anecdote, adulation and hard research, and some lovely pictures.

Bette Davis – Life & Times
Laura Moser (Haus, 2004)

A full and fascinating biography of the formidable "Fourth Warner Brother"; read it in tandem with Charlotte Chandler's *The Girl Who Walked Home Alone* (Simon & Schuster, 2006), which is based upon personal interviews with the star herself.

Dark Lover: The Life And Death Of Rudolph Valentino
Emily W. Leider (Faber, 2003)

The life of Valentino has been the source of so much spurious gossip that it's a joy to find such a well-researched and written biography, which devotes almost as much space to the characters around him as it does to Valentino himself. Fantastic photos, too.

Doris Day, Her Own Story
A.E. Hotchner (W.H. Allen, 1976)

Doris Day's unputdownable autobiography, which recounts in lively, warm and positive style her dramatic and often difficult life, dispels her squeaky-clean image once and for all.

Edith Head's Hollywood
Edith Head & Paddy Calistro (E.P. Dutton, 1983)

Costume designer Head wrote a number of books advising readers on how to dress for success; this one, delivered with her distinctive style, ventures into more autobiographical territory.

Evenings With Cary Grant: Recollections In His Own Words And By Those Who Knew Him Best
Nancy Nelson (Citadel, 2002)

Steering clear of the rumours about his sexuality, Nelson's collection of personal ruminations – named after the one-man show Grant delivered in his later years – reveals the star to be as witty and charming as his on-screen persona. An engaging, if perhaps not entirely complete, account of an unusual life.

Hollywood Divas: The Good, The Bad, And The Fabulous
James Robert Parish (Contemporary Books, 2003)

Sometimes only salacious gossip will do. This

compendium celebrates female stars from Jean Arthur to Loretta Young – including Joan Crawford, Bette Davis, Jane Fonda, Katharine Hepburn, Julia Roberts, Meg Ryan and Barbra Streisand – who have refused to play nice.

Kate Remembered – Katharine Hepburn: A Personal Biography
A. Scott Berg (Simon & Schuster, 2003)

A heartfelt, fluidly written account composed from the author's conversations with the star and following the flowering of their friendship. It makes a good companion piece to Hepburn's bestselling autobiography, *Me: Stories Of My Life* (Random House, 1991).

My Life So Far
Jane Fonda (Random House, 2005)

Though the earnest tone can grate, Fonda's analytical, weighty and very honest autobiography offers a fascinating insight into the troubled, talented woman who has helped define each decade she has lived in.

My Way Of Life
Joan Crawford (Pocket, 1972)

Why bother trawling through the many biographies devoted to Joan Crawford when this deliciously camp volume, brimful of Joan's tips for a fulfilling life, exists? The author comes across just as outrageous, controlling, smart and

funny as you could wish for, eager to divulge her worldly wisdom on hairstyles, etiquette and household tips.

On Cukor
Gavin Lambert & Robert Trachtenberg (Rizzoli, 2000)

An updated and revised version of Lambert's classic profile, first published in 1972. Compiled from interviews with the great "women's director", it's a pleasure to read, shedding as much light on Old Hollywood as it does on Cukor's films.

Starring Miss Barbara Stanwyck
Ella Smith (Random House, 1985)

You won't find anything here about Stanwyck's private life, but if you're eager to learn about her splendid body of work, and to feast upon hundreds of great photographs, this is the definitive volume.

Without Lying Down: Frances Marion And The Powerful Women Of Early Hollywood
Cari Beauchamp (University of California, 1997)

In her warm portrayal of not only Marion, one of the most important screenwriters in history, but also Mary Pickford and their many other extraordinary female contemporaries, Beauchamp provides an inspiring and sometimes surprising account of Hollywood's formative years.

Websites

General

You're not going to find many good websites devoted to chick flicks or women's movies per se; it's a subject better served by books. The following, however, provide a very good starting point.

The Internet Movie Database
www.imdb.com

IMDb is the ultimate movie reference site. Simple to use, it covers more than 200,000 films, with full credits, trivia, biographies, user reviews and message boards. Whether you want the skinny on the upcoming Sarah Jessica Parker movie, a list of every film that features gowns by Adrian, or a feast of anecdotes about *Titanic*, this should be your first stop.

All Movie Guide
www.allmovie.com

Your second stop after IMDb, especially if you like detailed plot outlines and star biographies.

Greatest Films
www.filmsite.org

A highly browsable treasure trove of "best of" lists from the American Film Institute and other sources, with extensive reviews and background information. Well-written features cover film history, genres and all the great Hollywood classics, including insightful essays on melodramas and weepies.

Images Journal
www.imagesjournal.com

With an enthusiasm for movies that covers anything from the allure of Cary Grant and Joan Crawford to the *nouvelle vague* and *Gone With The Wind*, this online movie journal is worth a look for lively, learned and accessible features.

Reel Classics
www.reelclassics.com

Reel Classics is devoted to the golden age of Hollywood, with useful pages on hundreds of actors, actresses, directors and classic movies, featuring quotations, sound files and good Web links.

Roger Ebert
rogerebert.suntimes.com

America's leading popular movie critic hosts an enthusiastic, accessible and far-reaching site, with reviews of films old and new, intelligent articles on the greats, Q and A sessions and movie news.

Screen Online
www.screenonline.org.uk

The BFI's constantly evolving website holds a feast of information on Britain's great movies, stars and studios – including Gainsborough and Powell and Pressburger's *The Archers* – with sprightly articles and intriguing links.

Sight & Sound
www.bfi.org.uk/sightandsound

This online version of Britain's leading film journal includes the major feature articles and a selection of current movie reviews.

The Canon

Though a scan of the general sites detailed above will yield rewards if you want to read more about your favourite film, the following deserve special attention for making the online experience almost as thrilling as watching the movie itself.

Camille
www.emanuellevy.com/article.php?articleID=197

A fascinating article about *Camille*, George Cukor, Greta Garbo's extraordinary performance, and that famed deathbed scene.

Casablanca
www.vincasa.com

A loving and quirky compilation of all things *Casablanca*, from the story behind "When Time Goes By" to a downloadable Casablanca Maze Chase game. And if you really want to evoke the ambience of Rick's Bar, you can even play roulette online.

Gone With The Wind
www.hrc.utexas.edu/exhibitions/online/gwtw

Nearly everything the (notoriously rapacious) *Gone With The Wind* fan could ask for, with lots of background detail on Walter Plunkett's costumes and the search for Scarlett, and revealing transcripts of producer David O. Selznick's famed memos.

In The Mood For Love
www.wkw-inthemoodforlove.com

Wong Kar-Wai's über-stylish and evocative site offers few extras, but the images and the haunting music alone provide reason enough to visit.

Moulin Rouge!
www.clubmoulinrouge.com

An online spectacular, as visually opulent as you'd expect, including virtual set tours, wonderful content on Bohemian fin-de-siècle Paris and some stunning downloads.

Icons: general

Google the name of a Hollywood star or director and you'll be pointed first to IMDb, next to the subject's official site, if it exists, and then on to a vast morass of options generated by fans. Finding interesting content on lesser-known figures can be trickier. The following represent some of the better one-stop gateways for sustained stargazing (or indeed director-, screenwriter- or costume designer-gazing).

Divas – The Site
www.divasthesite.com

Not exclusively devoted to the movies (singers and historical figures also feature), this is a delightful homage to those female stars who combine glamour, mystery, endurance and a dash of tragedy. Categories include "Sirens" and "Give Good Face", with brief biographies, quotes and juicy trivia.

Screwball Comedy
www.moderntimes.com/screwball

A celebration of the screwball genre and its stars

– including Carole Lombard, Barbara Stanwyck, Cary Grant and Irene Dunne – with links to a number of related articles.

Senses Of Cinema

www.sensesofcinema.com

Though it might take a bit of rooting around to find content relating to women or women's movies in this smart, Australia-based movie journal, the results are always good. The emphasis is on auteurs and on world cinema, with excellent articles on female directors covered less well elsewhere – Gillian Armstrong, Dorothy Arzner, Catherine Breillat, Jane Campion, Margarethe von Trotta and Agnès Varda, for example – including bibliographies and links.

Icons: the legends

Official websites for movie stars are easy to find with even the briefest of Google searches, but they're of variable quality. Better examples include **www.merylstreeponline.net** and **www .barbarastreisand.com**. You can also dig out some gems among the fan sites, many of which display far more pizzazz than the official versions. The following are good enough to bookmark.

Audrey Hepburn

www.audrey1.com

This definitive and very beautiful fan site is a fantastic resource, with a full filmography (plus contemporaneous reviews), articles from the likes of Hubert de Givenchy and Cecil Beaton, lots of sound files, wallpapers and screensavers, wonderful e-cards and more.

Joan Crawford: The Best Of Everything

www.joancrawfordbest.com

Only the best for La Crawford: lavish illustrations, an extensive biography and bibliography, reviews of all her movies, news on DVD releases, transcripts of her copious correspondences, fan memories, a memorabilia marketplace, and much more.

The Ultimate Cary Grant Pages

www.carygrant.net

A comprehensive site covering all things related to the suavest movie actor ever to have graced our screens.

Picture Credits

The Publishers have made every effort to identify correctly the rights holders and/or production companies in respect of images featured in this book. If despite these efforts any attribution is incorrect the Publishers will correct this error once it has been brought to their attention on a subsequent reprint.

COVER CREDITS

Tara Morice In *Strictly Ballroom* (1992), reproduced in Courtesy of ITV PLC (Granada Int'l)/LFI

ILLUSTRATIONS

Corbis: (171) © Bettmann/Corbis (222) © Bettmann/Corbis (248) © Reuters/Corbis (255) © Bettmann/Corbis; Kobal: (58) Jurow-Shepherd/Paramount Pictures (84) 20th Century Fox (136) Columbia Pictures Corporation © Rastar Productions Inc (201) Famous Players-Laskey Corporation/Paramount Pictures (4) Fox Film Corporation (10) Kobal/MGM (21) Columbia Pictures Corporation (22) Incom/Iéna Productions/ Union Cinématographique Lyonnaise (UCIL) (27) Gus Productions/Warner Bros Pictures (158) Samuel Goldwyn Company (185) The Kobal Collection; Movie Store Collection: (9) Paramount Pictures (13) Loew's, Inc/Metro-Goldwyn-Mayer (16) The Archers/ The Rank Organisation Film Productions Ltd/General Film Distributors Ltd (19) Gainsborough Pictures/Eagle Lion Distributors Ltd (25) Metro-Goldwyn-Mayer/Sostar S.A. (30) Meyers/Shyer, MGM/United Artists (31) Warner Brothers (33) Paramount Pictures/ 20th Century Fox/Lightstorm Entertainment (36) IFC Productions/InDigEnt (Independent Digital Entertainment)/Kalkaska Productions © 2003 United Artists Films Inc (37) Sony Pictures/ Asia Union Film & Entertainment Ltd /China Film Co-Production /Corporation Columbia Pictures Film Production Asia EDKO Film Ltd. (as EDKO Films)/ Good Machine / United China Vision/Zoom Hunt International Productions Company Ltd. (44) 20th Century Fox (46) Warner Bros Pictures (52) Warner Bros. Pictures/Lakeshore Entertainment/Malpaso Productions/Albert S. Ruddy Productions/ Epsilon Motion Pictures © 2004 Warner Bros. Entertainment Inc (56) Lightning Pictures/

PICTURE CREDITS

Mack-Taylor Productions/Precision Films/ Metro-Goldwyn-Mayer (62) Little Bird Ltd./Studio Canal/Working Title Films (65) Cineguild/Carlton International Media Ltd (67) Metro-Goldwyn-Mayer (70) Warner Bros Pictures (74) Orion Pictures Corporation (76) Vestron Pictures Ltd./ Great American Films Limited Partnership (79) Jersey Pictures © Universal Studios and Columbia Pictures Industries Inc. (82) Clear Blue Sky Productions /John Wells Productions/Killer Films/Section Eight Ltd./TF1 International/USA Films © Focus Features LLC and Vulcan Productions Inc. (88) Selznick International Pictures/ MGM (90) Columbia Pictures Corporation (94) Pathé Pictures International/Red Turtle © Pathé Productions Limited (103) Paramount Pictures/Interscope Communications/ Lakeshore Entertainment/Touchstone Pictures (106) Warner Bros Pictures (111) Arwin Productions/Universal International Pictures (115) © Touchstone Pictures, Silver Screen Partners IV/Buena Vista (120) Independent Producers/J Arthur Rank Films/The Archers/ Eagle Lion Distributors Ltd (128) Samuel Goldwyn Company MGM (132) © Pathé Entertainment Inc., Metro-Goldwyn-Mayer (MGM)/Percy Main (140) Gainsborough Pictures/Eagle Lion Distributors Ltd (148) Movie Store (150) Warner Bros Pictures, Castle Rock Entertainment/Fortis Films/NPV Entertainment/Village Roadshow Pictures (154) Aldrich/Seven Arts Pictures/Warner Bros Pictures (165) Paramount Pictures (167) Columbia Pictures Corporation (169) Columbia Pictures Corporation/Mirage (174) Jurow-Shepherd/Paramount Pictures (177) Metro-Goldwyn-Mayer (186) DreamWorks SKG/ McDonald Parkes Productions (195) Samuel Goldwyn Company (197) Juniper Films/United Artists (199) Saticoy Productions/Warner Brothers (211) Focus Features/Studio Canal/ Working Title Films © Universal Studios/Scion Films (P&P) Production Partnership (212) Paramount Pictures (216) Selznick International Pictures/United Artists (251) Gray-Film/Pathé Consortium Cinema/Riama Film/Societe Nationale Pathé Cinema/Cineriz (253) Apollo Media/New Zealand Film Commission/New Zealand Film Production Fund/New Zealand on Air/Pandora Filmproduktion GmBH/ South Pacific Pictures © South Pacific Pictures Productions Ltd./ApolloMedia GmbH & Co. 5. Filmproduktion KG; Ronald Grant Archive: (229) Adventure Pictures/British Screen Productions/European Script Fund/Lenfilm Studio/Mikado Films/Rio/Sigma (236) Century Communications/China Film Co-Production Corporation/ERA International/Salon Films/ MGM (240) Alexandre Films/Films A2/ Hachette Premiere/Partner's Productions/Societe Francaise de Production (243) Filmverlag der Autoren/Tango Film (245) Mirabai Films/IFC Productions/Key Films/Pandora Filmproduktion GmbH/Paradis Films

Index

Page references to films discussed in the Canon chapter, people described in the Icons chapter, and specific box features are indicated in bold.

INDEX

INDEX

INDEX

INDEX

INDEX

N

O

INDEX

INDEX

T

INDEX

X

Y

Z

Rough Guides presents...

Other Rough Guide Film & TV titles include:

American Independent Film • British Cult Comedy • Chick Flicks • Comedy Movies
Cult Movies • Gangster Movies • Horror Movies • Kids' Movies • Sci-Fi Movies • Westerns

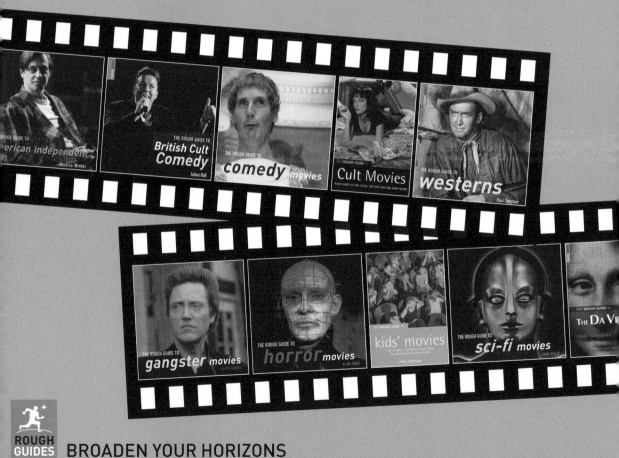

ROUGH GUIDES

BROADEN YOUR HORIZONS

Listen Up!

"You may be used to the Rough Guide series being comprehensive, but nothing will prepare you for the exhaustive Rough Guide to World Music . . . one of our books of the year."
Sunday Times, London

ROUGH GUIDE MUSIC TITLES

Bob Dylan • The Beatles • Classical Music • Elvis • Frank Sinatra • Heavy Metal • Hip-Hop
iPods, iTunes & music online • Jazz • Book of Playlists • Opera • Pink Floyd • Punk • Reggae
Rock • The Rolling Stones • Soul and R&B • World Music

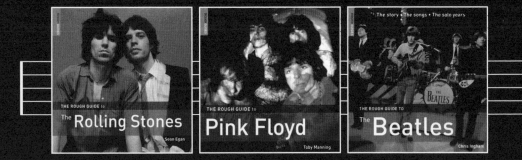

BROADEN YOUR HORIZONS

ROUGH GUIDES

UK & Ireland
Britain
Devon & Cornwall
Dublin **D**
Edinburgh **D**
England
Ireland
The Lake District
London
London **D**
London Mini Guide
Scotland
Scottish Highlands & Islands
Wales

Europe
Algarve **D**
Amsterdam
Amsterdam **D**
Andalucía
Athens **D**
Austria
The Baltic States
Barcelona
Barcelona **D**
Belgium & Luxembourg
Berlin
Brittany & Normandy
Bruges **D**
Brussels
Budapest
Bulgaria
Copenhagen
Corfu
Corsica
Costa Brava **D**
Crete
Croatia
Cyprus
Czech & Slovak Republics
Dodecanese & East Aegean
Dordogne & The Lot
Europe
Florence & Siena
Florence **D**
France
Germany
Gran Canaria **D**
Greece
Greek Islands

Hungary
Ibiza & Formentera **D**
Iceland
Ionian Islands
Italy
The Italian Lakes
Languedoc & Roussillon
Lanzarote **D**
Lisbon **D**
The Loire
Madeira **D**
Madrid **D**
Mallorca **D**
Mallorca & Menorca
Malta & Gozo **D**
Menorca
Moscow
The Netherlands
Norway
Paris
Paris **D**
Paris Mini Guide
Poland
Portugal
Prague
Prague **D**
Provence & the Côte D'Azur
Pyrenees
Romania
Rome
Rome **D**
Sardinia
Scandinavia
Sicily
Slovenia
Spain
St Petersburg
Sweden
Switzerland
Tenerife &
   La Gomera **D**
Turkey
Tuscany & Umbria
Venice & The Veneto
Venice **D**
Vienna

Asia
Bali & Lombok
Bangkok

Beijing
Cambodia
China
Goa
Hong Kong & Macau
India
Indonesia
Japan
Laos
Malaysia, Singapore & Brunei
Nepal
The Philippines
Singapore
South India
Southeast Asia
Sri Lanka
Thailand
Thailand's Beaches & Islands
Tokyo
Vietnam

Australasia
Australia
Melbourne
New Zealand
Sydney

North America
Alaska
Baja California
Boston
California
Canada
Chicago
Colorado
Florida
The Grand Canyon
Hawaii
Las Vegas **D**
Los Angeles
Maui **D**
Miami & South Florida
Montréal
New England
New Orleans **D**
New York City
New York City **D**
New York City Mini Guide
Orlando &
   Walt Disney World® **D**

Pacific Northwest
San Francisco
San Francisco **D**
Seattle
Southwest USA
Toronto
USA
Vancouver
Washington DC
Washington DC **D**
Yosemite

**Caribbean
& Latin America**
Antigua & Barbuda **D**
Argentina
Bahamas
Barbados **D**
Belize
Bolivia
Brazil
Cancùn & Cozumel **D**
Caribbean
Central America
Chile
Costa Rica
Cuba
Dominican Republic
Dominican Republic **D**
Ecuador
Guatemala
Jamaica
Mexico
Peru
St Lucia **D**
South America
Trinidad & Tobago
Yúcatan

Africa & Middle East
Cape Town & the Garden Route
Egypt
The Gambia
Jordan
Kenya
Marrakesh **D**
Morocco
South Africa, Lesotho
   & Swaziland
Syria

Available from all good bookstores